NEITHER CAPITALISM

Theories of Bureaucratic Collectivism

Copyright ©2008
Center for Socialist History

All Rights reserved

Center for Socialist History

PO Box 626
Alameda CA 94501
Tel: 510 601-6460
www.socialisthistory.org
mlipow@pacbell.net

CENTER
FOR
SOCIALIST
HISTORY

ISBN   1456310623
EAN-13   9781456310622

Second Edition
Editors: E Haberkern & Arthur Lipow

NEITHER CAPITALISM NOR SOCIALISM

Theories of Bureaucratic Collectivism

Edited
by
E. Haberkern and Arthur Lipow

A NOTE ON THE COVER ILLUSTRATION:

Most of the articles in this anthology are concerned with the appearance in the 20th century of statified economies which appeared to offer an alternative to traditional capitalism.

The brutality of the Stalinist and Fascist "models" of this new order tended to distract attention from the more important questions raised by these phenomena. To have chosen a cover featuring, for example, Hugarian revolutionaries decapitating Stalin's statue in 1956 would have emphasized this aspect of the new society.

We have chosen instead Max Beerbohm's caricature of Sidney Webb drawn before 1921. As Eric Hobsbawm pointed out in his thesis on the Webbs, they developed their thoroughly bureaucratic concept of the new society well before Stalin or Hitler. In this caricature Webb, guide by THE STATE and *HUMAN NATURE*, arranges the toy soldiers who are the subjects of his new society in a carefully laid out plan. No muss, no fuss, no blood, just the all-knowing bureaucrat doing what is best for everybody.

The only thing we don't understand about this portrait is that Max Beerbohm was supposed to be Sidney Webb's friend.

NEITHER CAPITALISM NOR SOCIALISM
Theories of Bureaucratic Collectivism

TABLE OF CONTENTS

Introduction	i
Chapter I – The Revolution Betrayed	1
From Formula to Reality - James Burnham	3
The Fourth International and the Russian Counterrevolution - Yvan Craipeau	25
Chapter II – The Hitler-Stalin Pact	41
The Managerial Revolution - James Burnham	42
The End of Capitalism in Germany - Dwight MacDonald	60
Is Russia a Workers' State - Max Shachtman	87
Chapter III - The Defense of Collectivized Property	121
The Basis for Defensism in Russia - Ernest Erber	122
Bureaucratic Collectivism - Joseph Carter	135
The Russian Question - Max Shachtman	155
Chapter IV - The Third Camp	171
Triangle of Forces - Hal Draper	172
The Economic Drive Behind Tito - Hal Draper	187
The Nature of The Chinese State - Jack Brad	207
The Strange Case of Anna Louise Strong - Jack Brad	221
Chapter V – Beyond the Third Camp	233
Aspects of the Labor Government – Max Shachtman	235
Neo-Corporatists and Neo-Reformists – Hal Draper	241
The New Social-Democratic Reformism – Hal Draper	270
The Permanent War Economy – Seymour Melman	295
Appendix A - The Myth of Bruno Rizzi	313
Appendix B - The Myth of Max Shachtman	325
Index	331

INTRODUCTION

As this collection was being prepared, the death of socialism and the end of history were once more being announced to the world. For the last several years, the collapse of the international Communist movement and the Soviet Union, so long a thorn in the side of capitalism and its defenders, has been offered as proof that it is no use tampering with the natural order of things.

This is not the first time that such an argument has been made, nor is it likely to be the last. Every previous defeat of a revolution, every previous revelation that a state built by a revolutionary movement has become nothing more than a new bastion of privilege, has produced prophetic warnings against vain, "millenarian", hopes for a better society. Each time the prophets have predicted that this would be the last such attempt. And yet, each time the prophecies have proved false.

A given revolutionary movement, party or government may betray the hope and trust of the people but the hope born of necessity for a better future itself remains. What the defenders of "really existing capitalism" do not understand is that this hope is not based on the attractiveness of the various revolutionary alternatives that have appeared so far and failed; it is based on the impossibility, for billions of people, to continue living under the existing social order.

The Russian Revolution may have failed, like the American and French revolutions before it. But the *idea* of revolution, of remaking society from below, is stronger than ever. The revolutionary upheavals in Eastern Europe of the last couple of decades, while repudiating the discredited formulas of Stalinism, have reinforced in the popular mind the power of the revolutionary democratic ideals which gave birth to the Russian Revolution and its predecessors.

In 1815, the end of the revolutionary period that began in 1789 was marked by the triumph of the military force of the old order over Napoleon. The victors established a new world order—which lasted for nearly fifteen years—from above. Stalinism, however, was overthrown in Eastern Europe, not by external military force, but by the pressure of popular opposition. Our would-be Metternichs—Thatcher, Reagan and, in his own way, Gorbachev—exploited this popular movement as best they could. Their successors have yet to reestablish order of any kind, old or new.

Neither Capitalism nor Socialism

Unfortunately, the response of the left, broadly or narrowly defined, has been demoralization and defeatism. For many, the collapse of totalitarian state planning has proved the impossibility of socialism and the permanence of capitalism. That says very little about socialism itself and a great deal about what many who have called themselves socialists meant by "socialism". Their conclusion is to embrace "the market" unreservedly while arguing for some state aid to help clean up the human mess that is the inevitable byproduct of unregulated capitalism. The triumphant defenders of "market economics" pure and simple see no need for their services. They have nothing to fear and no reason to make concessions.

Others on the left, unwilling to think through the significance of the collapse of "really existing socialism", and quietly nostalgic for the old order, content themselves with pointing out what a disaster "the free market economy" has proved in Eastern Europe economically as well as in human terms. The solution hinted at, though not very boldly, is that a reformed version of the old regime might not be a bad idea. There is even a certain nostalgia for "the good old days." The electoral revival of the parties representing the chastened apparatchiks in Poland and East Germany is seen as a hopeful sign even though the programs offered by these parties differ little from those of the professional anticommunists who have been discredited over the years since the collapse of the USSR.

What is missing is any serious attempt to think about what happened. Were these regimes socialist? Is there something worth preserving in the Stalinist past? What about China? Are the defenders there of the state sector — heavily dependent on slave labor — fighting a progressive battle against the encroaching capitalist "enterprise zones"? There is little discussion of such questions.

Yet, there is a political and intellectual tradition on the left which did begin to deal with these problems long before the Soviet Union collapsed. In the late 1930s, Leon Trotsky opened up a political discussion on the Soviet Union and what was happening to it that raised all the questions being discussed today from a revolutionary point of view. This

Introduction

at a time when *conservative* politicians, for their own reasons, began to look to the new power in the east as a possible ally.

Trotsky's savage attack on the parvenu class that was liquidating the revolutionary tradition ideologically and the revolutionary generation physically provoked a vigorous debate among his followers and the broader left, especially in France and the United States where Trotsky and his ideas had significant influence among intellectuals and trade unionists.

As Isaac Deutscher pointed out in volume three of his biography of Trotsky, the latter's 1936 *The Revolution Betrayed* represented a "new Trotskyism." Originally, Trotsky, along with most other observers, had thought that by restoring normalcy and rejecting the revolutionary ideology of the period from 1917 through the early 1920s Stalin and the new bureaucracy were moving, consciously or not, in the direction of restoring capitalism. From this it followed that the main task of the left was to mobilize whatever forces could be mobilized in defense of nationalized industry.

The belief that the new class of bureaucrats were planning to "privatize" industry predated the passage of Trotsky and Lenin into the ranks of the opposition. The opposition groups of the early 1920s, the adherents of the Democratic Centralist and Workers' Opposition factions, also saw this as the main threat. Trotsky's first attempt at a general synthesis was a "three factions" theory according to which the overwhelmingly peasant population of Russia provided an enormous reservoir of support for an amorphous "right wing" of the Communist Party whose reputed leader was Nikolai Bukharin. On the left was the opposition which remained faithful to the ideals of socialism and revolution.*

---

*. Trotsky sometimes referred to his supporters and the left opposition in general as the "proletarian" wing of the party. But he knew all too well that the massive de-industrialization of the country consequent on years of war, civil war and economic blockade had devastated the Russian working class and destroyed it as an organized political force. "Bolshevik-Leninist" was the more common designation Trotsky chose to describe his position and it more accurately describes the opposition: an ideological current *within* the

(continued...)

Neither Capitalism nor Socialism

Stalin, in this schema, represented the inertia of the bureaucracy. These "centrists" defended the new state created by the revolution against both the restorationist right and the revolutionary left. Of course, they would have been happy with a capitalist restoration that left them in possession of their privileges if that were possible. Meanwhile, however, they were forced to confront the openly restorationist politics of the right.

It should be admitted that there was some validity to this analysis. The bureaucracy whose spokesman Stalin and Bukharin had become did pander to the acquisitive instincts of the Russian peasantry. If the capitalist class of the western countries had been in an expansionist mood in the late 20s an alliance with the Russian new class might have been possible. But international capital was having difficulties of its own at the time and was not in an expansionist mood. Left to its own devices, the new bureaucracy in Russia was forced into a confrontation with the peasant mass of the country. Despite the heated rhetoric of most present day historians and journalists, the horrors of collectivization were not the result of blind adherence to a socialist ideology. Stalin in particular didn't care about ideology — or even about ideas. Without western capital internal accumulation had to come out of the hide of the peasantry. The alternative was the collapse of the economy and the dismemberment of the country.

And this development presented Trotsky with a problem. If the main danger was one of capitalist restoration then the bureaucracy's half-hearted defense of state property had to be encouraged. But Trotsky had already acknowledged by 1930 that the internal threat of capitalist restoration was illusory. "Further talk of Nepmen [entrepreneur elements] and Kulaks [wealthy farmers]" was "unworthy of Marxists." What is more, inside Russia, the opposition, led by the

---

(...continued)
Communist Party and its apparatus that remained faithful, or tried to remain faithful, to the socialist tradition of the party. This sociological fact explains the political weakness of the left their personal courage and integrity notwithstanding.

Introduction

veteran Bolshevik Christian Rakovsky, was, by 1930, unequivocally for the abolition of the collective farms.*

Clearly, Trotsky's analysis and his call for a new revolution in Russia made sense only if the bureaucracy was a new ruling class acting independently of both international capital and the Russian small property owning peasantry. It was just a question of dotting an "i" here and crossing a "t" there. Trotsky did not want to go that far. But he didn't rule out the idea either. As Deutscher, who remained an apologist for Stalinism, complained, this left Trotsky in an awkward position and encouraged his followers to develop his ideas in new directions.

For a while, during the period of the popular front when Stalin and western statesmen, even conservative statesmen, continued their flirtation, the debate on the "Russian Question" remained low key. Stalin's alliance with Hitler and the dismemberment of Poland made it impossible to temporize further. Trotsky tried to postpone a decision on the grounds that the Soviet Union was bound to collapse shortly and it was foolish to baptize the bureaucracy a new ruling class just as it was about to disappear. It was no use.

Now, the notion that capitalism was being replaced by a new system in which the state bureaucracy or "the managers" ruled in place of the capitalist and economic planning took over from the

---

*. See the resolution of April 1930 proposed to the Party Congress. The resolution was, of course, illegal and circulated underground. It was printed abroad in the *Biulletin Oppozitsii* edited by Trotsky's son Leon Sedov. Standard histories of this period ignore this development. Deutscher, Alec Nove and most recently Stephen Cohen adhere to a rigid schema in which Trotsky representing "the left" is for rapid industrialization, Bukharin on "the right" defends the peasant and private property while Stalin allies himself first with "the right" and then leaps over Trotsky's head to take an "ultra left" position on rapid industrialization and confiscation of private property. But, in fact, Bukharin never openly opposed collectivization, the Trotskyist left never advocated it before 1929 and Rakovsky, as leader of the opposition inside Russia, advocated the abolition of the collective farms.

v

Neither Capitalism nor Socialism

market was not invented in the course of this debate. James Burnham, in one of the major studies produced during this discussion, was able to point to a number of predecessors. What was new was that Trotsky's dissident followers were pushed into this debate because they had to decide whether to continue, with Trotsky, to defend this new collectivist society. Was collectivized property, even under Stalin's regime, "progressive" or not?

The word 'progressive was itself somewhat vague. It was part of traditional left jargon and was never defined precisely. In the context of this debate, however, its meaning was clear. Was this Russian state, for all its monstrous features, a step towards the socialist future? There were, and are, essentially three answers to this question.

One was that stated most clearly by Isaac Deutscher. It was the one most widely held on the left throughout the 50s, 60s and 70s. And it is the one most discredited by recent events. For all practical purposes, a plurality if not a majority of people who considered themselves on the left *tacitly accepted* the idea that the Russian bureaucracy was a new ruling class even if, for diplomatic reasons, it was not something one could say openly. The bureaucracy was carrying out the progressive mission of collectivizing the world economy which the working class had proved unable to do. If necessary, the bureaucracy would have to do this *in opposition to* the working class. Deutscher's response to the suppression of the uprisings of the East German and Hungarian workers in 1953 and 1956 made it all very clear. It was regrettable that the working-class had to be suppressed by military means but it was also unavoidable.

In a period in which ignorance of Marx is the stock-in-trade of every academic philistine and social democratic politician it is important to assert that this conception of socialism ran completely counter to everything Marx ever wrote about socialism and the historical role of the working class. Of course, this does not stop many commentators even today from referring to this position which turned Marxism on its head as "Marxist" and to those held it as "Marxists." But this is obscurantism even though apologists for the Stalinist

Introduction

system used the label of Marxism and the terminology of socialism as a means to legitimate that system.

Most leftists, however, tried to avoid confronting the issue so openly. It was simply too embarrassing for *soi-disant* leftists to say openly that Marx was wrong and that the pre- and anti-Marxists socialists like Lassalle were right.

Given this view of "socialism" even Bismarck could be embraced as a "socialist" and Scott Nearing could wonder, as late as 1939, whether Hitler was not introducing some kind of socialism to Nazi Germany.

The current intellectual debacle of the left is directly attributable to the long-lasting hegemony of the idea that socialism equals state ownership and central planning and that this combination is inherently more efficient and productive than capitalism.

What has been revealed in the last few decades, even before the fall of Gorbachev and the Berlin Wall, is that totalitarian state planning is economically regressive as compared to capitalism. So much so that it has discredited even the mildest forms of political intervention in economic life. It has made the equally fantastic and economically reactionary program of Friedmanite free marketism temporarily respectable.

The second answer to the question which is often used as a fallback is the one Trotsky himself most often had recourse to. Stalinism is *nothing but* the result of external pressures. Trotsky at least was consistent. He predicted, wrongly, that Stalinism could not expand beyond Russia's borders because it had no internal dynamism. It could only feed parasitically off, and weaken, the working class movement. The events that followed World War II made this position untenable. Clearly, this new social class was capable of acting on its own. In a period where a native capitalist class was discredited or hardly existed and where the working class was disorganized and demoralized it could impose its own new economic order on a disintegrating society.

And it was this new historic fact that led Trotsky's dissident supporters to a different answer to our question. Stalin's new order

Neither Capitalism nor Socialism

was not 'progressive' and it had nothing in common with socialism. It was a product of, not a way out of, the decay of modern civilization.

Still, in war-ravaged Europe where the prewar ruling class was discredited or in the newly liberated colonial countries threatened with humiliating economic dependence on their late masters, Stalinism could provide some stability and order and some degree of national pride in the midst of chaos. But, after the first flush of excitement, these regimes quickly devolved into rigid and economically backward states. The resentment of the population and in particular of the industrial working class could only be contained by vicious repression.

The articles in this collection were almost alone in predicting, in the late 40s, the dramatic internal convulsions of the 50s and 60s that led to the collapse of these new states. The majority of the left, broadly defined, saw the popular resentment and the police and military measures taken to suppress it as temporary, the result of economic backwardness and outside pressure from the capitalist states which would soon be overcome by the dynamic new economic order. The right sought recourse in military containment. Defenders of the old order had no confidence, right up until the end, that the collapse of Stalinism would lead to a peaceful transition to capitalist normalcy and prosperity. Events have proved them right on this point.

In the 70s and 80s the countries of the Eastern bloc fell further and further behind the developed west. Russia itself was eventually bankrupted by its attempt to compete with the United States as a military and economic superpower. China in the same period went through a series of wild oscillations that have still not ceased.

Not unexpectedly, the collapse of this alternative to capitalism has given rise to an orgy of self-congratulation on the part of right wing ideologues who, right up to the fall of Gorbachev, continued to argue that, unlike merely authoritarian regimes, these totalitarian ones could only be overthrown from the outside. But the tone of the celebration betrays a slightly queasy reaction to this sudden demise of parties and governments which were at least known quantities and did, after all, maintain order. The hollowness of official anticommunism was demonstrated most

Introduction

dramatically by the picture of dedicated cold warriors like Margaret Thatcher, Helmut Kohl and George Bush clinging desperately to Gorbachev long after it became clear that he had lost all popular support in Russia.

The same political point was made when the liberal wing of the Democratic Party in the U.S. Congress, for purely demagogic reasons, tried to embarrass the Republicans by moving a bill that would deny "favored nation" status to the People's Republic of China. How could the "leader of the Free World" continue to grant favored nation status and, by implication, membership in same "Free World", to a government that still employed slave labor on a large scale?— The Democrats' maneuver succeeded. Republicans and their corporate backers fell all over themselves defending their Chinese business partners.

What both these incidents revealed is that the ideological hostility to "big government" and state socialism, however sincere, does not correspond to reality. Long before Gorbachev international capital, especially German and American capital, had been investing in these state run economies. One perceptive author even referred to "Vodka Cola" to describe the volatile mix of capitalist finance and Communist state industry.

In the 1970s and 1980s, the economies of the Eastern Bloc had fallen heavily in debt to international financial institutions and the governments which underwrote this investment. Even in Russia itself the bureaucracy had been turned into something akin to a collective tax farmer for Western banks. They guaranteed that at least some of the interest would be paid and in return were allowed to skim off some for themselves.

In this same period, as we now know, key members of ruling group, particularly those associated with the KGB, were able to export billions and billions of dollars to Swiss Banks or to begin to invest in Hungarian state enterprises which were the first attempts at "market." The new Russian "capitalism" owes not a little to the far-sightedness of these bureaucratic entrepreneurs who realized the ship was sinking and prepared to privatize state property into their own pockets.

Neither Capitalism nor Socialism

And that is why, despite the propagandistic drumrolls on both sides, the nomenklatura has been the prime beneficiary of the new economic order and the military and the security forces hardly touched. The kind of popular explosion that has everywhere produced revolutionary change has not occurred. The *threat* of such an explosion clearly played a role in the collapse of the Soviet Union. Polish Solidarity in 1980-81 was a grim warning of what could have happened. But even in Poland the reform of the economic and political system carried out by the Solidarity government required the destruction of Solidarity as a revolutionary movement and preserved as much as could be preserved of the nomenklatura's privileges and power. No one was more concerned that "stability" and "order" be maintained than the international financial community.

All of this would have been impossible were it not for the internal transformation of capitalism itself. One of the things that the present crisis in the Eastern Bloc reveals is the extent to which contemporary capitalism is dependent on the infusion of enormous sums of money into the private sector by the state. Without such funds the free market produces the devastating result seen in Eastern Europe. In *The Economist* for 19 January 1991, Jeffrey Sachs, one of the principal advisors to the Polish and Russian governments in the heyday of the Eastern European fascination for free markets, pleaded, in considerable distress, for a "Marshall Plan" for Poland lest failure there discredit the whole project. The article is a testimonial to the impossibility of free market capitalism without massive government support.

Nor is this simply a question of "jump starting" a new capitalist economy. On closer inspection, it is clear that the developed capitalist economies also require such aid. In Britain, for example, the Thatcher experiment depended on massive transfers of state funds into private hands. This took the form most notoriously of "privatization. In the case of the public utilities privatization meant the establishment of chartered monopolies created by billions in "seed money" and supported by a continuing tax collected in the form of fees charged for these monopolized services. But it also took the form of direct subsidy

Introduction

as in the case of the arms industry which is now one of the leading branches of manufacturing in Britain.

In the United States, it is the Republican proponents of "free enterprise" who are now the main political beneficiaries and promoters of the defense industry. Unlike Dwight Eisenhower they are not concerned by the growth of the "military industrial complex." This patronage serves for them nationally the same political purpose that city jobs used to provide for the Democratic machines.

And it is not just a question of patronage and corruption. Without massive government planning and regulation, without massive infusions of money transferred from the pockets of the tax payer, the whole system would collapse into a 30s style depression. What we are looking at is not individual greed by a few high-placed and arrogant people. What we are looking at is a new system of economic exploitation in which the lines between corporate and state planning are becoming blurred.

But it is not just on the national scale that this "bureaucratic collectivization" of the capitalist system is taking place. Institutions like the World Bank and the IMF and treaties like GATT and NAFTA are not provided for in classical political economy. Not the political economy of Adam Smith nor that of Karl Marx. That is the institutional reality behind glib phrases like "global economy." In reality, the world economy appears instead to be breaking up into large protectionist trading blocs. But regardless of the way this issue is resolved one thing is clear. The nation state, so far, is not being replaced. Instead, in each country the effect of these international institutions and agreements is to free the executive from democratic legislative control. The admirable goal of international economic cooperation has been subordinated to this bureaucratization of capitalism in the form of corporations which are themselves large bureaucratic entities not accountable to anyone except those who effectively control them.

This is the rational ground for the popular suspicion of the process despite the provincial and even reactionary and xenophobic forms this suspicion has taken. What else can be expected when well-grounded

Neither Capitalism nor Socialism

popular fears can find no democratic political outlet? As long as "modernization" on the left is equated with subservience to this growing corporate state opposition will take the form of sentimental nostalgia for a past that never was. And if the economic consequences of this kind of "modernism" continue to be as grim as they have been this nostalgia will continue to manifest itself in increasingly poisonous guises.

What then is the alternative to this new class society?

Let us phrase the question in the abstract manner so popular today. The current attack on socialism takes the form of a diagram more or less like the following:

```
FE                        ME                        EE
+-------------------------+-------------------------+
```

In this schema, the scale reading from left to right measures the degree of freedom from state interference.

On the left we have FE, or Free Enterprise, which stands for the complete absence of state interference in man's free exercise of initiative. In some libertarian versions of this extreme no traffic lights are allowed.

At the extreme right is, of course, the Evil Empire. Here we have complete state control over every aspect of the individual's life. (Unfortunately, this extreme is not just a figment of libertarian imaginations. In the late 40s in Russia and in China during the Cultural Revolution an approximation of this nightmare was achieved.)

In the middle, somewhere, is the Mixed Economy. Here there is some state regulation. It can vary from well-intentioned liberal restrictions on child labor, to taxation of unearned incomes, to extremes such as free medical care and efficient public transportation.

But there is an alternative schema. One which is based on a scale measuring the degree of democratic control over the economic order. This schema can be represented as follows:

Introduction

```
SE            ME            FE            EE
|─────────────|─────────────|─────────────|
```

Here there is an extreme not found in most orthodox economic paradigms. At the left, we find SE, the socialist economy sketched in Marx's writings on the Commune and Lenin's *State and Revolution*. In this model, democratic control is exercised at every level of the economy, with all officials public or private elected and subject to recall by the appropriate bodies. (This is *not* a model in which an all powerful state lords it over society after the Jacobin, Stalinist or absolute monarchy patterns.) What is even more important is that official service in this model is not a source of economic privilege. Public officials are treated like, and remunerated like, other public employees. It is not relevant to this discussion here to determine whether or not this model is feasible. Any more than it is relevant here to determine whether or not the Free Market model is feasible or has ever existed in the real world. We are describing abstract tendencies and models.

At the extreme right in this spectrum we still have our old friend the Evil Empire. Judged by the criterion of democratic control it is as far to the right as it is from the point of view of the state-control/free-enterprise spectrum. What is interesting in our new diagram is the position of Free Enterprise. It is close to that of the Evil Empire!

Surprising as this may be, there is no way of avoiding the scientific facts. If we keep in mind the question of democratic control, it is undeniable that the Free Enterprise system results in a regime of uncontrolled authority which approximates that of the Evil Empire. True, the existence of democratic freedoms—a free (actually, expensive) press, freedom of assembly, the right to organize trade unions (for those who want to risk it) and free, if again expensive, elections—provides some protection against the unelected masters of the economy. But these constraints are allowed only to the extent that they are ineffective. Their advantage to those who really control the

Neither Capitalism nor Socialism

economy and the state is that they conceal the fact that these parties exist. As the Wizard of Oz said, "pay no attention to the man behind the curtain."

The Mixed Economy, in this schema is, of course, further to the left than Free Enterprise and quite far removed from the Evil Empire. Socialists, quite rightly, have raised questions about the democratic content of nationalization and state planning. The nationalizations of British industries under the first Labor government, to take one example, have been criticized for leaving in place the old executives and the old chain of command. Nevertheless, there was a qualitative change when these old fossils were for the first time made subject, at least potentially, to public scrutiny.

And democratic public control is the key issue. In a world where the dividing line between state and corporation, between politics and economics, is becoming more and more blurred, democratic control and accountability are more crucial than the juridical detail of who owns what. If the experience of Stalinism has shown that nationalization *by itself* is not the same thing as public control, the experience of post war capitalism has shown that democracy cannot be confined to the "political" sphere alone without atrophying.

In the past, socialists and conservatives alike tended to see the political and economic spheres as separable. As long as private property was not threatened, the state could be in the hands of any political party. In fact, such a "night watchman state" has never existed. But today it is clear to all parties that the great multinational corporations require a proactive state that is their agent and partner. In most situations they do not require the kind of one party state that characterizes Stalinism or fascism. Instead, they have tried, with considerable success, to turn democratic politics into a plebiscitarian show which does not challenge their authority but ratifies it.

The crucial front in this new class struggle is found within the left wing parties and movements. It is essential that these movements drop even their anticapitalist rhetoric if the system is to remain stable. They must become "modern" parties which accept multinational corporations and

Introduction

international financial planning institutions as a fact of life, reject their working class roots and confine their role to debating the degree of welfare "the economy" can afford. In effect, rather than being crushed in a one party state, they must be forced to join the no party state.

In this context, it is well worth reconsidering the first attempts to analyze and understand this new bureaucratic society in the 30s and 40s. The particular forms it then took, fascism and Stalinism, are unlikely to be repeated. For one thing, these particular movements are no longer new and untried as they were when they first appeared. For another, the economic tendencies which produced them have continued to operate and have created a different world. Mussolini's corporatism and Stalin's Five-Year-Plans appear today as quaintly old-fashioned as the automobiles the dictators drove. What was impressive then is slightly ridiculous today.

Nevertheless, these early political movements, just because they were new and untried, expressed themselves with greater clarity than we can expect today. No member of the Communist Party today would say openly what even relatively timid fellow travelers would have said sixty years ago. Even Mussolini's granddaughter is today a "post-fascist." And the corporatist economic projects and plebiscitarian politics of the new social-democratic right are likewise phrased so as reveal as little as possible of their anti-democratic content.

The articles in this collection represent the first attempt to face the fact that there could be something new coming into being and to try and analyze it. Familiarity with this debate about the nature of this new state which was neither capitalist nor socialist is not just a matter of historical interest. Understanding it is a necessary prerequisite to understanding what happened to "socialism" in the twentieth century. It is also provides a starting point for understanding the "transitional economies" in Central and Eastern Europe and the former Soviet Union, as well as in China. Only by understanding that the formula "either capitalism or socialism" is too simple (or simple-minded), moreover, can the evolutionary changes in capitalism itself at the beginning of the 21st century be understood. Following Marx's own perceptive insights over a century ago into the contradictory nature of the joint stock company, we are now in a position

Neither Capitalism nor Socialism

to see that what Michael Harrington termed the "unsocial socialization" of capitalism is laying the foundation for a profound transformation of modern society.

Berle and Means' classic study, *The Modern Corporation and Private Property*, provides a useful starting point for understanding the contradictory nature of modern capitalist property, at one and the same time "private" and "collective." In the 1920s, Walter Rathenau, the brilliant German capitalist and writer, wrote insightfully about the modern corporation:

> No one is a permanent owner. The composition of the thousandfold complex which functions as lord of the undertaking is in a state of flux. ...This condition of things signifies that ownership has been depersonalized ... . The depersonalization of ownership simultaneously implies the objectification of the thing owned. The claims to ownership are subdivied in such a fashion, and are so mobile, that the enterprise assumes an independent life, as if it belonged t no one; it takes on an objective existence, such as in earlier days was embodied only in state and church, in a municipal corporation, in the life of a guild or a religious order. . . . The depersonalization of ownership, the objectification of enterprise, the detachment of property from the posssesor, leads to a point wehre the enterprise becomes transformed into an institution which resembles the state in character.[1]

At the end of the 21st century, in the age of the transnational corporations, many of whom dispose of financial resources and exercise power far greater than several individual states put together, Rathenau's words have a great deal of resonance.

In the case of the former Communist states and of China, still under the control the Communist Party, we are told that we are witnessing a transition from "socialism to capitalism". If this is so, however, the question must be raised: what is the nature of modern capitalism, particularly its dominant form, the corporation, to which this "transi-

Introduction

tion" is being made? Could there not be a survival of the old bureaucratic collectivist structures with an admixture of Western capitalist corporate investment under the aegis of the now reconstructed former Communist parties, which would at very least be compatible with what one must call "really existing capitalism", to borrow an earlier locution.

The then director of the Soviet "Institute for the Economics of the World Socialist System", Oleg Bogomolov, told *Guardian* correspondent Jonathan Steele in 1990 that "societies develop from what already exists. As for the West, I don't want to use the word capitalism, which Western sociologists themselves rarely use, preferring terms like the post-industrial society, the information society or post-capitalism. What is the nature of property in the West nowadays? The days of one man ownership are over. There is property which we would call collective rather than private, whether it is owned by shareholders, pension funds, or co-operatives."[2]

Critical insights along these lines are to be found, perhaps not surprisingly, among those who are the most fervent believers in the the free market and the virtues of capitalism. Commenting on an important study by the Adam Smith Institute in London, *The Amnesia of Reform*, one right-wing columnist for the London *Financial Times*, writes that "the quality of much privatisation in post-communist societies is very poor". Indeed, "unless there are substantial reforms in the approach to be taken, *what will emerge will not be real market economies, but inefficient, partially collectivized, hybrid economies in which a bureaucratic elite still succeeds in exploiting the bulk of the population.*"[3]

"Partially collectivized, hybrid economies". Bureaucratic collectivism shorn of a single party state but one which is far, far from democratic -- not too different in this respect from the British or the French state.

The example of China provides yet another example of how the corporatization of state enterprises -- albeit still under the umbrella of the Communist Party -- is creating a "hybrid" economic form. "The legal position of so much private business in China is . . . obscure -- neither fully state owned nor privately owned in the western sense" comments the

Neither Capitalism nor Socialism

doyen of capitalist financial writers, Samuel Brittan. If one sticks to the wooden formula of "either . . . or", what is one to make of Brittan's entirely accurate observation? Or how can one begin to understand Chinese state corporations which are listed on Western stock exchanges, take on capitalist corporations as partners, set up in business in the United States, hire workers, and act for all intents and purposes like General Motors?

"Privatization of companies" in Eastern Europe, complain the authors of the Adam Smith Institute report in words that echo those of socialists who denied that Morrisonian-style state corporations were in any sense socialist, "represent little more than changing the nameplate on the door, with the same management remaining in charge, continuing the same command-economy practices and with the same umbilical relationship with their sponsoring ministry."[4]

What of socialism then? We began this essay with the idea that socialism is a necessity for the great and overwhelming majority of humankind. The twentieth century, to be sure, has been a massive setback for socialism and for democracy. But the failure of socialism has also been a setback for all of humanity. The millions upon millions killed in two world wars; murdered in the gas ovens of Hitler's regime; starved to death in Stalin's drive for collectivization or murdered in the purges; left to die anonymous, unfulfilled, poverty-stricken lives in the the third world; all are ample evidence of this. If socialism has not triumphed in the twentieth century because it was submerged by the twin totalitarian evils of fascism and Stalinism it is also true that the failure of socialism has meant that civilization has lost as well. The outcome is not the utopia of free marketeers like Hayek or Friedman, but an ever deepening and faster running current leading capitalism into a new kind of barbarism of which fascism and, in its own fashion, Stalinism, will be seen to have been the forerunners. Hebert Spencer's prediction of the "coming slavery" and Hillaire Belloc's "servile state" will turn out to be not the outcome of socialism but of its failure, of capitalism's triumph over the democratic and human-centered reordering of society which is the cerntral meaning of socialism.

Introduction

If, that is, if socialism fails and the on-going bureaucratic collectivization of society is unimpeded by a new and reborn democratic socialist movement. Yet, as one of the main contributors to the debate in these pages wrote many years ago, "If we can speak of the inevitability of socialism ... it is only in a conditional sense. First in the sense that capitalism creates all the conditions which make the advance to socialism possible; and second, in the sense that the advance to socialism is a necessity for the further progress of society itself -- even more, the only way in which to preserve society. . . . Marxism ends with a program of human activity: fail to carry out the program, and mankind sees doomed capitalism followed by a general decline whose vileness and gloominess we can see much more clearly today than did Marx and Engels; carry out the program, and mankind takes the step necessary for that 'association in which the free development of each is the condition for the free develpment of all.' The choice is not one between capitalism and socialism. The choice must be made between socialism and barbarism."

"Barbarism": an evocative word as the new world order falls into disorder and we observe the genocidal passions unleashed by the collapse of the cold war system. With the advantage of another forty years experience and the availability of evidence about the growth and functioning of the modern transnational corporation and its intertwined relationship with the contemporary authoritarian and bureaucratic capitalist state, it is possible to to analyze with a greater precision the shape of the new order which will emerge in the absence of an effective socialist movement. Not inevitably, not the "wave of the future": it becomes a reality only to the degree that the forces of democracy fail to meet the enormous challenge posed to them. The ease with which the "corporate property form", slips from one apparently different social order to another, between China and the capitalist west, for example, demonstrates that we are dealing with a qualitative change in the nature of capitalism.

The "unsocial socialization" of capitalism has the potential within it to give way, in the absence of a democratic socialist transformation of society, to a new form of class society -- a possibility the reality of which we have

Neither Capitalism nor Socialism

seen in Communist or Soviet-type states. The prospects for the recreation of a socialist movement in a world of transnational capitalism in which the major actors are powerful authoritarian corporations and bureaucratically organized states in which democracy becomes more and more of a facade are daunting, to say the least. The impoverishment of the third world and the growing crisis of unemployment in the advanced capitalist countries, however, make it a necessity if we are not to drift into barbarism. The ideologies of private property free markets mask the reality of highly organized corporate capitalism and a centralized state.

What is required is a re-creation of the democratic socialist project to make both state and economic institutions accountable to the democratic control of the people whose lives they affect. It is only in the "Realpolitik of Utopia", of the socialist vision of democracy and human freedom, that an alternative to barbarism can be found.

The articles presented in the pages which follow are, we believe, an essential starting point for those who would understand the real choices which confront humanity.

Some articles have been edited for reasons of space. We have also used the real names rather than the pseudonyms of authors and others they refer to. In addition, references to political groups and organizations — mostly defunct — have been eliminated in some places. This has not been done systematically but only where we felt such references would needlessly distract the reader. The alternative would have been to burden the text with footnotes explaining who all these groups and individuals were and it was not our intention to write an account of the organizational history of the anti-stalinist left in the 30s, 40s and 50s.

We have felt free to edit the texts for readability since the unedited texts are available to serious researchers in the Greenwood Press editions of *Labor Action* and *The New International* from which most of this material is taken. Many of the internal documents are also available at research libraries in the collection of *Independent Socialist Mimeogrphia* published by *The Independent Socialist Press* and edited by Hal Draper.

Introduction

NOTES

1. Quoted in Adolph Berle and Gardiner Means, *The Modern Corporation and Private Property* (New York: The Macmillan Company, 1933) p. 352.

2. *The Guardian* (London and Manchester) January 10, 1990.

3. Martin Wolf, "UK Study Criticizes Post-Communist State Sales", *The Financial Times*, December 28, 1994.

4. "Half-hearted Privatization Plagues Eastern Europe", *The Wall Street Journal Europe*, January 16, 1995. Peter Young and Paul Reynolds, *The Amnesia of Reform: A Review of Post-Communist Privatization* (London: Adam Smith Institute, 1994.) See also Roman Frydman and Andrzej Rapaczynski, *Privatization in Eastern Europe: Is the State Withering Away?* (Prague: Central European University Press, 1994). Frydman and Rapaczynski were architects of the privatization programme in Czechoslovakia and Poland: their powerful analysis and their doubts, indicated by the question mark in the subtitle, make the book essential reading.

Chapter I
THE REVOLUTION BETRAYED — 1936

In 1936, Leon Trotsky wrote a book whose English title was The Revolution Betrayed.[1] *His thesis was that the counterrevolution organized by Stalin had succeeded in destroying the last remnants of the socialist movement in Russia. All means of organization and self-expression on the part of the working class, and the population as a whole, had been destroyed by the new totalitarian state bureaucracy. The state which was now the exclusive property of this new bureaucracy was, through its program of collectivization, on the way to becoming the sole proprietor of the national economy. This state and this bureaucracy were not the successors to the workers state created by the revolution but its grave-diggers. It was the enemy of the socialist movement, of the working class and of progress.*

As we pointed out in the introduction this was a "new Trotskyism." Previously, Trotsky, like most other observers, had believed that the bureaucracy was feeling its way to an accommodation with capitalism. He had held a "three factions" theory. According to this theory, one faction, whose spokesman was Bukharin, was pandering to the acquisitive instincts of the small property holding peasant and directly preparing the way for capitalist restoration; a second faction, led by Trotsky's supporters in Russia, was defending the egalitarian and socialist traditions of the revolution; and the third faction, epitomized by Stalin was defending the bureaucracy's new privileged position in an opportunistic and pragmatic fashion. Since its privileges depended on collectivized property, the bureaucracy had to defend that property against attempts at restoration. On the other hand, as a privileged grouping, it also had to fight the egalitarian tendencies of its opponents on the left. Trotsky had initially believed that this bureaucratic faction would be ground between its two opponents and collapse. But he was proved wrong.

Already by 1930, Trotsky was forced to admit that events were not proceeding according to his script. The bureaucracy was destroying what organized opposition existed on the left and simultaneously expropriating the peasantry and rapidly moving to centralize all economic power in the hands of the state.

This picture left Trotsky without a theoretical explanation of what was happening. Logically he should have concluded that the bureaucracy was a

Neither Capitalism nor Socialism

new class in the making. But this was not a conclusion he could accept. The contradiction between his ever more bitter political hostility towards the regime and his belief that in defending a collectivist form of property it was somehow advancing the cause of socialism created confusion and dissension in his movement.

Particularly unsettling was Trotsky's obvious confusion over the new 1936 constitution of the USSR. In it, Stalin announced sweeping reforms, guaranteeing freedom of speech, religion and assembly and rejecting class warfare and "the dictatorship of the proletariat." But behind this facade aimed at Western public opinion, a mass campaign of terror and purges destroyed all opposition. In Trotsky's theory this dismantling of the "workers' state" ideologically and physically should have signaled a turn towards capitalism. Despite the illusions of moderate socialists, liberals and businessmen anxious to open up this new market, inside Russia what little remained of a free market or private property was wiped out.

Eventually, the Trotskyist movement was destroyed by its inability to devise a theoretical basis for its increasingly bitter anti-Stalinism.

In 1937, Trotsky began to prepare his followers for the founding of a new international organization that would be capable of leading the working-class in the revolutionary crisis he believed imminent. In the discussions of the platform to be adopted by this new organization the theoretical confusion of the movement became apparent.

In both the American and French movements, opposition voices demanded a clear break with the old "three factions" theory. Two of the most cogent of these first polemics against Trotsky's position are reprinted here.

The second of the two, by Yvan Craipeau, is reprinted from the report in the French Trotskyist journal. The editorial comments in this article are those of the editors of the journal.

The Revolution Betrayed

FROM FORMULA TO REALITY - James Burnham

> ... Doctrinaire will doubtless not be satisfied with this hypothetical definition. They would like categorical formulae: yes-yes, and no-no. Sociological problems would certainly be simpler, if social phenomena had always a finished character. There is nothing more dangerous, however, than to throw out of reality, for the sake of logical completeness, elements which today violate your scheme and tomorrow may wholly overturn it. In our analysis, we have above all avoided doing violence to dynamic social formations which have had no precedent and have no analogies. The scientific task, as well as the political, is not to give a finished definition to an unfinished process, but to follow all its stages, separate its progressive from its reactionary tendencies, expose their mutual relations, foresee possible variants of development, and find in this foresight a basis for action. (Leon Trotsky, *The Revolution Betrayed*.)

Some Puzzling Omissions ...

It is instructive to notice how much is *omitted* from the resolution of the Committee majority (Cannon-Abern) on the Russian Question. For example:

Nowhere does the resolution state flatly and unambiguously: "In the Soviet Union, the proletariat is the ruling class." Nowhere does the resolution declare itself on the problem of the "dual" or "single" character of the bureaucracy. This problem cannot be dismissed as a trifle. All historical institutions, of course, have in a certain formal sense a "dual" role: even the bourgeois state, even employers, act occasionally, "by accident," in the interests of the proletariat. But for the purposes of action, in order to establish our policies and perspectives, we sum up the character of each institution *taken as a whole*, defining it as on the whole "progressive" or "reactionary", or in certain unusual cases as "dual". Thus we say that the bourgeoisie is in the present epoch reactionary, and we do not support it. We say that

Neither Capitalism nor Socialism

the struggle of the loyalists against Franco, in spite of numerous reactionary features (if we were abstracting out separate elements), is on the whole or rather taken as a whole progressive, and we have supported it. In the first years of the Russian Revolution, we said that the regime was unambiguously progressive. Then, for many years, we have said that it had a dual character: and we advocated defense of the Soviet Union and the revolution, but political struggle against the bureaucracy. Does the bureaucratic regime, does Stalinism that is to say, today preserve that dual character, *taken as a whole*, or has it lost that dual character and become, taken as a whole, reactionary? The Resolution gives no answer.

Nowhere does the Resolution characterize unequivocally, or even mention seriously, *the foreign policy* of Stalinism, the social role of Stalinism and its institutions outside of the boundaries of the Soviet Union.

Nowhere does the Resolution declare itself with reference to the possibility of the completion of the counterrevolution within the Soviet Union without a wide-scale, mass Civil War.

We have observed before this that slogans and formulas, divorced from specific content, are meaningless. Merely repeating "Peace, Bread and Land" did not make the French Stalinists Bolsheviks a few years ago. The Committee majority is concerned for the formula, "Workers' State". But the omissions reveal strikingly the lack of specific content which this formula possesses for them. Why these omissions?

In the first place, behind the back of the formula there is concealed a complete lack of agreement among the supporters of the Resolution. This came rapidly to the surface in the membership discussion. Comrades Cannon and Abern declared that Stalinism has still a dual role; Comrades Weber and Shachtman that it has now a single -i.e., reactionary, counterrevolutionary role. Shachtman, Abern, Cannon declare that Stalinism outside of foreign boundaries has exactly the same social role as internally; Weber (and now comrade Trotsky), that externally (as in Spain) Stalinism has now a purely counterrevolutionary role, and acts solely in the interests of the bourgeoisie; comrade

The Revolution Betrayed

Trotsky making an explicit distinction between its role in Spain and its role internally. Abern ruled out the possibility of a completion of the internal counterrevolution without a mass civil war; Weber admits that possibility; Shachtman, and so far as I can gather Trotsky, do not declare themselves explicitly. Certain supporters of the majority - i.e., Morrow - say that the conception of a "ruling class" has nothing to do with the conception of a "state"; others say that a "workers' state" *means* one in which the proletariat is the ruling class.

In the second place, these omissions serve to give the Resolution a false character in the eyes of the membership. The Resolution professes to declare that something "new" has occurred within the Soviet Union during the past two or three years, and that we must therefore make a new analysis, or rather extend our previous analysis to cover the new phenomena. This profession is even more urgently made in Shachtman's article in the *New International* [2]. But, in reality, the retention of the formula, "workers' state", prevents any extension to cover the undoubtedly new phenomena, and results, if consistently carried through, in simply a restatement of our old analysis [the "three factions" analysis EH] with no change whatever. This is recognized by comrade Victor Fox. His statement in bulletin #2 is a careful and exact formulation of what follows from the retention of the formula "workers' state". The Committee majority insists that it does *not* accept Fox's statement. But in the discussion they have not pointed out a single reason for not accepting it; and they have made absolutely no criticism of it, save for one passing literary criticism of a single phrase made by Cannon. Thus the resolution is *demagogic*: it pretends to be what it is not, and recommends itself to the membership under false colors. Let Fox demand from the Committee majority an explanation of their rejection of his statement. So far they have given none. If they cannot give a political motivation, their rejection must be understood as merely bureaucratic, or at the best stylistic. And they cannot give a political motivation.

Thirdly, the omissions must be understood as hiding the contradictions within the position of the Committee majority, and the inade-

Neither Capitalism nor Socialism

quacy of its formulas for handling the present reality. These contradictions I shall develop more at length in what follows.

And Disturbing Contradictions

I have already cited certain of the contradictions among supporters of the Resolution on key specific problems. There are, however, other contradictions not only among various interpretations, but inherent to the position itself. For example, it is contended by Abern and Sterling that we give unconditional support to the Soviet Union and to the Red Army under any and all circumstances; and Cannon has also expressed agreement with this view. So long as we believe that the Soviet Union is a workers' state, this view is altogether plausible. If it is a workers' state, the possibility of its engaging in a reactionary war is not realistic and does not have to be taken into account. But the past year and a half have made clear that there is a very real possibility that the Soviet Union and the Red Army may engage in a reactionary war: for example, as part of a "League Army" to liquidate the Spanish Civil War, or in China - indeed, this possibility was nearly realized and may yet be. In such a war, do we defend and support the Red Army? Cannon, Abern, and Sterling have said yes. But I do not believe they have thought the problem out. Of course we do *not* support them under such circumstances: to do so would be to support the counter-revolution. Shachtman understands this and recognizes such a possibility, though rightly pointing out that it is less probable than an imperialist attack on the Soviet Union. However, his understanding and recognition are incompatible with his alleged view that the Soviet Union remains a workers' state. Shachtman's inconsistency in this instance enables him to draw a correct political conclusion; Cannon, Abern and Sterling are consistent, and wrong.

If the Soviet Union is still a workers' state, the possibility of the restoration of private property without a mass civil war is excluded, at least if we still retain our traditional view on the nature of revolutions. During the last several years, however, our movement has widely recognized that the restoration might be accomplished without

The Revolution Betrayed

mass civil war (though not without a certain amount of violence - indeed, there has been plenty of violence during this period); and it is clear on the surface of events that it might be. But this recognition is in reality a recognition that the Soviet Union is no longer a workers' state. The *state* - that is, the organs and institutions of coercion in society, the army, police, GPU, courts, prisons, bureaucracy; and even the juridical basis of the state as provided in the New Constitution (the *de jure* locus of sovereignty in the new Parliaments) - *does not have to be overthrown* in order to accomplish the full social and economic counterrevolution. (It does not have to be, though in point of fact it might be, dependent upon the specific developments.) On the other hand, it is by now clear that getting rid of Stalinism, what we call "the political revolution," (what is in truth the re-establishment of the class rule of the proletariat) does in all probability require not the mere "reform" of the bureaucracy, not simply a "change of government", but the *overthrow* of the present state and its organs and institutions, the *abolition* of the bureaucracy, the creation of a *new* "army of the people," the *destruction* of the GPU, the abolition of the New Constitution and its juridical provisions. The "political revolution" will create a *dual power* counter to the present state power, perhaps under the slogan of "All Power back to the Soviets," and will achieve victory through the transfer of power. What does all this mean, what *can* it mean, of the political revolution which we advocate, except that this political revolution involves a change in *class rule*, not merely a change in the *form* of rule by the same class (which is what we advocated up to a few years ago)? If the Soviet Union is still a workers' state, if, that is to say, the working class is still the ruling class within the Soviet Union, then our policies, the program we advocate for the Soviet Union, is *entirely* unjustifiable; and we must return to our policies and programs of four or five years ago. Here again, comrade Fox's statement is enlightening, for Fox is consistent. It is altogether clear from a careful reading of his statement that he cannot really accept our present policy of "political revolution."

Neither Capitalism nor Socialism

The contradictions are even more glaring in connection with the question of the social role of Stalinism outside of the Soviet Union. It is, I have always understood, an elementary tenet of Marxism that the social role of a class or a state is basically the same nationally and internationally, There may be, of course, accidental or temporary deviations from this rule; but in crises and over any considerable period of time it emerges clearly. For many years we have criticized the Lovestonites[7] on exactly this point: we have said that their distinction between the internal role of the Stalinist bureaucracy (beneficial and praiseworthy) and its external role (reactionary and disruptive) is not only a direct violation of Marxism, but makes it altogether impossible to explain either Stalinism or the Soviet Union, or to hold a correct policy with reference to them.

I found rather startling the casual and as if incidental manner in which comrade Trotsky brushed aside this doctrine and this method of analysis. After explaining the internal role of the bureaucracy as dual and as in one aspect genuinely defending the interests of the proletariat; and after insisting that within the Soviet Union the proletariat is still the ruling class and the state a workers' state; he suddenly writes: "The same Stalin in Spain, i.e., on the soil of a bourgeois regime, executes the function of Hitler" (which function he has just defined as defending the bourgeois forms of property). If the thesis itself is startling (involving the conception that Stalinism in Spain has a completely different social role, expresses completely different class interests, form Stalinism within the Soviet union), the suggested explanation - nowhere any further developed - is even more so: "i.e., on the soil of a bourgeois regime..." But Stalinism, even Stalinism in Spain, is surely not a "Spanish phenomenon." Stalinism in Spain as in the Soviet Union and in every other country, springs, we have always taught, from the soil of the Soviet Union, where among other features, nationalized property relations and the monopoly of foreign trade still obtain. It is because these property relations do *not* any longer constitute the Soviet Union a workers' state, because they accompany a state which is *not* a workers' state, because the proletar-

The Revolution Betrayed

iat is *not* any longer the ruling class within the Soviet Union, that Stalinism is able to and does play its current role in Spain. No other consistent explanation can be given for Stalinism in Spain. To say that the bureaucracy within the Soviet Union expresses - even if in distorted manner - the interests of the proletariat , but in Spain only and unequivocally the interests of the bourgeoisie, is if carried to a conclusion, to deny the class analysis of social phenomena. You cannot have it both ways. The fundamental class role of Stalinism must be understood as identical in Spain and in the Soviet Union, whatever modifications we may have to make in the form it takes as conditioned by the particular and local conditions.

Again: Shachtman, in his *New International* article, states and repeats, always in italics: "the victory of the Stalinist bureaucracy marks the victory of a *political counterrevolution.*" The majority spokesmen, including comrade Trotsky, grant us that the state is a "political category." What then can the definitive victory of a political counterrevolution (and we entirely agree that this has taken place) signify? Is Shachtman just playing with words? It can only mean - is it not sufficiently obvious - that the class which once held the state power, the *political* power (it is not a question here of the "forms of government" which is quite a different matter: political power need not shift with a change in the form of government) no longer holds it; as applied to the Soviet Union, that the working class, which once ruled, even if in a distorted manner, no longer rules. Shachtman directly refutes himself.

Light is thrown upon Shachtman's contention (not at all shared by all supporters of the resolution) by recalling a discussion in the National Committee during the time of the formulation of the Resolution. In a long and in fact impassioned speech, Shachtman defended the thesis that what was new in the present situation in the Soviet Union was that "the dictatorship of the proletariat has been overthrown, liquidated, one hundred percent destroyed; but that the workers' state, *in the sense* of the nationalized production, remained." He explained that by "workers' state" he *meant* merely nationalized

Neither Capitalism nor Socialism

production. However awkward this formulation, it was a commendable attempt to expand and dissociate old formulas in such a manner as to make them more suitable for handling present realities. But chastening remarks from Cannon, Abern and others - who in point of fact do not really agree, not simply with Shachtman's formulations, but with Shachtman's views - persuaded Shachtman to withdraw into his present self-contradictory position.

The Argument of the Majority and the Copernican Circles

What is the argument of the Committee majority, reduced to its simplest and essential form? We ask them, what kind of state is the Soviet Union? They answer, it is a workers' state. We ask, why is it a workers' state? They answer *because* there is nationalized property. We ask, why does nationalized property make it a workers' state? And they answer, *because* a workers' state is one where there is nationalized property.

This is, in form, exactly the same argument used by those who tell us that the Bible is the Word of God. We ask them, how do you know it is the Word of God? They answer, *because* the Bible itself says that it is the Word of God. We ask, but how does that prove it to be true? And they answer, *because* nothing that God said could be a lie.

In both instances, the conclusion has been taken for granted in the premisses; the argument is entirely circular, and can prove nothing whatever. At best, it is a definition that the Majority offers us; but it gives no proof that this definition is of the slightest use as a tool in solving our theoretical or practical problems.

The point in dispute is just that point which the Majority *takes for granted* without proof or argument or evidence. The point is: is it a fact that nationalized production *of and by itself* makes a state a workers' state, guarantees the class rule of the workers, assures the transition to socialism. (The point in dispute is not at all whether nationalized production is a *necessary* aspect of a workers' state, which, except for temporary exceptions, no one in the least argues; merely whether it is also a *sufficient* aspect).

The Revolution Betrayed

Now what the last twenty years, in particular the last two or three years, have taught us, if we wish to be taught, is exactly that nationalized production of and by itself does *not* make a workers' state, does *not* guarantee the class rule of the workers, does *not* assure the transition to socialism. For these things there is a *political* as well as a socio-economic precondition. If this conclusion disturbs us, if it seems to disagree with our earlier expectations and predictions, then we must revise, re-adapt or extend these expectations and predictions, and not try to escape facts by explaining them away. Naturalists once proved that all swans are white; but black swans were nevertheless discovered in New Zealand.

When Copernicus revolutionized Ptolemaic astronomy by postulating the sun instead of the earth as the fixed reference point for astronomical calculation, he still retained the older theory that the planets had circular orbits. This was thought to follow from the perfection of God, who would never have been the cause of any motion but perfect motion which was held to be motion in a circle. On this theory, Copernicus was able to explain all of the observed phenomena, but he did so only at the cost of a most cumbersome and awkward mathematical process. Kepler showed that postulated elliptical motions for the planetary orbits made the mathematics enormously simpler, and besides suggested new and fruitful hypotheses for explaining additional phenomena and making additional predictions. (Of course, Kepler also explained that God's perfection could quite consistently express itself in an ellipse.)

The Majority clings to its circle, its definition. And any definition can, if stretched willfully enough, serve. But when it goes beyond a certain point, it becomes so cumbersome, so out of accord with what men ordinarily understand by language, that, instead of being an instrument for the communication of truths and the illumination of events, it acts to obscure and confuse us and others. And this is just what has happened in the *definition* of the Soviet Union as a "workers' state" (for by now it is little more any longer than a question of definition); this definition is now an instrument for hiding reality, for confusing meanings, for obscuring events; and it is time to drop it.

"Proletarian Economy" the Majority Discovers a Theoretical Topsy

In attempting to defend their view by argument (an altogether fruitless attempt, since it, the only argument, is the purely circular one just discussed), the spokesmen of the Majority have discovered that there is a "proletarian economy," comparable to feudal, bourgeois, and socialist economy. Like Topsy, this concept must have "just grown," for there is no slightest indication of its parentage in events, Marxism, or in science generally.

In the Soviet Union, they tell us, there is a "proletarian economy"; and since the state "expresses" the economy, it is therefore a proletarian or workers' state.

If this doctrine becomes publicly known, it will certainly be an unusual surprise for the Stalinist theoreticians. For many years we told them that they couldn't build socialism in a single country, or even maintain a workers' regime indefinitely in a single country, for the precise reason that there is no proletarian economy or society or culture. There is simply an intermediary transitional economy, society and culture, but administered in the direction of socialism by the dictatorship of the proletariat, which is the *political* rule of the working class (as Marx himself explained it.)

It would be no less surprising to Marx, who devoted his entire life, and almost all of his major theoretical work (*Capital* itself) to proving that there *could not* be a proletarian economy; but that bourgeois economy would be and would have to be replaced by a socialist economy.

It is true that all workers' states will take certain similar economic measures - e.g., the expropriation of the bourgeoisie in one after another of the realms of the economy (or of all realms at once), and the nationalization of these realms - in order to assure the continuance of proletarian domination and the transition to socialism. But it is absolutely false that this constitutes a distinctive economy, which involves distinctive property rights held by the members of a distinctive class. This is just what distinguishes the rule of the proletariat from the rule of all other classes in history. The proletariat takes power not to establish a new economic regime, a new system of property rights, for itself as a class, but, by progressive steps, starting with the expropriation and nationalization of the key productive industries, to do away with property rights altogether. There is no distinctive "proletarian" property right. If there is, Marxism in its entirety, in its theory and its politics, is completely wrong.

This has an enormous importance in our understanding of the nature of the state. The state is not *identical* with the economy; to think so, as do some of the spokesmen of the Majority, is the most vulgar sort of monism. If it were there would be no need for a *theory* of the state, since the theory of the economy would in advance have covered the theory of the state. But the theory of the state is probably the key theory of Marxism; and reformism has almost always developed by keeping hold of Marxian economics (sometimes in very orthodox form) but denying the related but not identical theory of the state.

Within any social system the "state" refers to organs and institutions of social and political coercion, the army, police, courts, prisons, bureaucracy. The *theory* of the state asserts that these organs and institutions will on the whole and in general be used as instruments to aid the interests of those who occupy the dominating social position in terms of the economy, of property rights. The *proof* of this theory is not a matter of definition, but of *evidence*; namely, to show how this actually happens in various social systems (Guerin's brilliant book on Fascism,[4] for example, abounds with concrete evidence showing how Fascist states in Germany and Italy do in point of fact uphold the interests of those who occupy the dominating social position in terms of the economy - namely, the bourgeoisie; showing, among other things, the superficiality of the view that fascism involves the "political expropriation" of the bourgeoisie).

In a feudal society, the property relations serve the interests of those who have the chief property rights, namely the feudal lords. The

Neither Capitalism nor Socialism

organs of the state (in considerable part manned by the feudal lords themselves), so long as they defend those property relations, whatever form the state organs take, thus do actually serve as the instrument of the feudal lords as a class, do defend their interests and their domination.

The interests and domination of the bourgeoisie in society is assured whenever the members of the bourgeoisie hold in their persons, directly or indirectly, the decisive property rights in the instruments of production. The state can take many forms (monarchy, parliamentary democracy, personal dictatorship, fascism) and be peopled governmentally by various strata of society; but while it defends and protects bourgeois property rights it is by that act defending and protecting those who hold the rights, since those rights are what serve the interests of the ones who hold them, are what assure their general social rule and domination as a class. This follows not because of any mystical identification of the state with the economy. Nor is the state defending a mere abstraction, a "system of property relations." It defends the interests of a given group of persons, a given class rule and domination; and the concrete property rights are merely the method by which those interests and that class rule are assured. We prove this not by definition, but by examining the facts. And up to the present the facts, even in the case of fascism, bear out our predictions and analyses. There is no direct analogy in the proletarian dictatorship. Under capitalism the proletariat has no property rights (in the instruments of production). Neither does it have such rights under the dictatorship of the proletariat. Under the dictatorship of the proletariat, it is the *state*, not the workers, which has the property rights. Therefore, the supreme question becomes, whose state is it? Whose interests does it express? For whom and against whom does it function?

The bourgeoisie, so long as its property rights are intact, is guaranteed class domination. Not so the proletariat; for it has no property rights. It can assert its class domination only *through* the state; and therefore if it loses the state, if the state no longer expresses

The Revolution Betrayed

its interests, if the state functions primarily against it and not against the class enemy, this means that its class domination has been destroyed.

And this is just what has happened in the Soviet Union. Under Stalin, for many years, the state was undermining the class domination of the workers; it was, as we said, a degenerate workers' state. Within the last two or three years, it has completed that divorce from the proletariat; and, consequently, the state is no longer a workers' state. Twenty years ago, perhaps, we would have thought this impossible without the prior destruction of the nationalized economy. History teaches us. It shows us that the class rule of the proletariat can indeed take a number of forms - free soviets, many parties, one party, bureaucratic distortion, bureaucratic dictatorship, and perhaps others we do not yet know. But it shows us also that the nationalized economy can remain and the rule of the workers be destroyed. How else, possibly, can we describe and explain what has happened?

The doctrine of a "proletarian economy" leads, if carried out to its conclusion, to many most ludicrous conclusions. Comrade Trotsky nowhere states this doctrine. But Trotsky also in the present article (though not at all in previous years, when he defined the significance of the term "workers' state " in quite a different manner) treats the nationalized economy as the *sole* and *sufficient* criterion of a workers' state. He makes nationalized economy equal to and identical in meaning with "workers' state"; and this is in substance the doctrine of a "proletarian economy."

But Trotsky must at once modify his own doctrine. The workers' state existed from November 1917 on, though the economy was not nationalized until later. How, then, did you know *at the time* (not looking backward *after* the economy had been nationalized) that it *was* a workers' state? (obviously, you knew *not* by an economic criterion, which you here advance as the only and sufficient criterion, but by a social and more particularly a *political* criterion - the workers had the power.) But let us grant the brief "exceptional" period, and charge it to the lags of history.

Neither Capitalism nor Socialism

But we suddenly find: "Should a bourgeois counterrevolution succeed in Russia, the new government for a *lengthy period* would have to base itself upon nationalized economy." (My emphasis.) What has become of our sole and sufficient criterion for judging the nature of a state? Why would not this new government be a workers' state? It conforms absolutely to the definition of a workers' state given by Trotsky himself. How is this to be reconciled with the statement a few pages later: "However, so long as that contradiction has not passed from the sphere of distribution into the sphere of production and has not blasted nationalized property and planned economy, the state remains a workers' state." In truth they cannot be reconciled.

Trotsky, however, violating his logic, attempts a reconciliation, to explain how a bourgeois counterrevolution could rule on the basis of nationalized economy. "But what does such a type of temporary conflict between economy and state mean? It means a *revolution* or a *counterrevolution*..." But, how, during the time, during the "*lengthy period*" when the nationalized economy still endures, do you know that a revolution or a counterrevolution has taken place? Only by a change in the economy, (which has *not* taken place), according to your own criterion. But here we are once again in a circle. Do you know not by what has already happened, but by what the new state prepares to do, intends to do, what its direction and perspective is? But the *present* bureaucracy prepares the economic change, very clearly "intends" to consolidate a new class position, to destroy the nationalized economy; that is its direction and perspective; how then does it differ from the bourgeois counterrevolution in its early stages?

The logic of the Committee majority's position leads to a still more unacceptable conclusion. If it is true that nationalized economy is the sole and sufficient criterion of a workers' state, it then follows that the strength, extension and progress of nationalized economy is the sole and sufficient criterion of the strength, extension and progress of the workers' state. This was the view of many Marxists, even members of the Left Opposition, at the time of the announcement of the First Five Year Plan. Reasoning from this premise they considered it "inevitable"

The Revolution Betrayed

that the success, even the partial success, of the Plan would automatically strengthen, extend and make for the progress of the workers' state (that is, the form of society transitional between capitalism and socialism) was in point of fact greatly weakened and further degenerated during the period of the Plan, *in spite of* the great extension and expansion of the nationalized economy. This result *cannot* be explained on the basis of an acceptance of nationalized as a sole and sufficient criterion or condition of a workers' state. Such a basis can support only the Stalinist conclusion not ours.

These consequences of the position of the Committee Majority constitute a *reductio ad absurdum* of that position. The only way to avoid them (as well as to rid our position on the Soviet State from its internal contradictions and its utter inadequacy in explaining events) is to abandon that position. This means, first of all, to recognize that nationalized economy is *not* a sole and sufficient criterion or condition of a workers' state; to understand that other factors must be taken into account. It means that we do not settle the question of the nature of the Soviet State by appeal to "definition," but examine concretely not merely the economic foundation, but the actual relation of the state apparatus to that economy, its relation, its actual relation to the working class, the position, the actual position, of the working class in the Soviet regime. Such an examination of evidence, not of definition, can lead only to the conclusion that within the Soviet Union the working class is *not* the ruling or dominant class, and that therefore the Soviet Union is not a workers' state.

Why Defend the Soviet Union

The most frequently used argument of the Committee Majority against the Minority has been that our position if logically carried out, leads to the advocacy of defeatist policies, and undermines the theoretical basis for the defensist policy which we jointly claim to uphold.

It should be observed that this argument is not of the slightest weight with reference to the question at issue. The great English

Neither Capitalism nor Socialism

philosopher, David Hume, once remarked: "There is no method of reasoning more common, and yet none more blameable, than, in philosophical disputes, to endeavor the refutation of any hypothesis, by a pretense of its dangerous consequences to religion and morality. When any opinion leads to absurdities, it is certainly false; but it is not certain that an opinion is false, because it is of dangerous consequence." If a correct analysis of the nature of the Soviet State leads us to defeatism, then we must change our policies, not our analysis.

Nevertheless, the analysis of the Minority does *not* lead to defeatism.

Why Should We Be For The Defense Of The Soviet Union?

If we are defeatist, our position has nothing to do with whether or not we *call* the Soviet Union a "workers' state." Only a medicine man would base a policy on what things are *called*. We are defensists because we estimate that, in the light of the actual situation in the Soviet Union, the actual development there, such a policy is in the interests of the proletariat and of the world revolution.

We are for defense, primarily, because we - both of the Committee Majority and of the Committee Minority - consider that the socio--economic relations still obtaining in the Soviet Union are *progressive*, and are worth defending.

They are progressive for four major reasons:

Their *origin* is in the October Revolution, the first successful proletarian revolution. This is by no means a trivial point. A wage rise won by a successful strike is more progressive than a rise of the same amount handed down by the bosses to head of a strike.

The traditions and ideals of the Revolution, still carried - though forced far below the surface - in the hearts and minds of the Russian masses, are bound up with the socio-economic relations.

These relations provide the indispensable foundation for a workers' state; that is, once the workers' state is re-established, once the workers again make themselves the ruling class by ousting usurpers, they will be in a position to go forward decisively toward socialism

The Revolution Betrayed

without being forced to undertake a complete social and economic revolution. This is the precise focus of our positive policy: *to re-establish the class rule of the workers.* There is no other way to explain the meaning of the policies which we actually do advocate.

Most decisive of all in showing the necessity for a defensist policy is to compare the possible alternatives from the point of view of the workers' revolution - and this in general is how we decide whether we are for or against a policy. If the Soviet Union is defeated by an imperialist power, it will revert to the position of a semi-colonial nation (perhaps partly partitioned off into frank colonies) and the world revolution will be set back enormously. In the struggle against imperialism, the Soviet masses will have a genuine chance not merely to defeat the imperialist power (by itself progressive), but in the course of the struggle to cast off from their back the usurpers, regain class rule, and go triumphantly forward. The consideration of the alternatives leaves no doubt whatever that a defensist policy is mandatory, and this consideration of the alternatives leaves no doubt whatever that a defensist policy is mandatory, and this consideration alone suffices to refute all varieties of defeatists.

However, there is an ambiguity in the notion of "unconditional" defense of the Soviet Union. Events now make it necessary to point out certain distinctions which were formerly irrelevant, In reality, we stand for "unconditional defense of the revolution," and this imposes certain *conditions* on our defense of the Soviet Union. The first condition is the struggle against Stalinism, without which, in our opinion, *revolutionary* defense of the Soviet Union is impossible. Secondly, we must now recognize the possibility that the Soviet Union may engage in a *reactionary* war. (I have already mentioned how this might come about in connection with such events as those in Spain or China.) In such cases, far from being for support or defense we are for unconditional *opposition* to such a war. It is only when the war is itself progressive - e.g., is against imperialism - that we are for defense; and in those conditions we are for *unconditional* defense.

Neither Capitalism nor Socialism

Not all of the supporters of the Committee Majority will agree with these views on the problem of defense. Abern and Cannon, for example, have declared that *any* struggle in which the Red Army might be engaged would be, since it is the army of the workers' state, a progressive struggle, and therefore must be supported. They are, in my opinion, entirely consistent in their reasoning. And this is only another example of why the entire position is false.

Well Then; What Kind of State?

In the first place, we cannot decide this question, as I have already shown, by *identifying* the state with the economy. In that case, the whole theory of the state becomes meaningless. Even comrade Trotsky is guilty here. After agreeing that the "state" is a "political category," he slips into the identification by repeating an aphorism: "However, this very politics is only concentrated economics." This aphorism, however illuminating when considered as a metaphor, is a most questionable step in an argument. We must decide what kind of state it is by analyzing the *relationship* of the political institutions (army, bureaucracy, GPU, courts, prisons) - that is, the state itself - to the economy and to the classes and social groups within the Soviet Union, and internationally.

By such an analysis we are trying to *describe* a very complicated set of events which are in a process of rapid change. Our description will, on that account, be at least partially inadequate and distorting (since it will suggest more finality than is to be found in the changing process itself), but it can be reasonably accurate. In such a description the Committee Minority can, it believes, come to virtual agreement with *some* of the supporters of the position of the Committee Majority.

From many points of view it would be well to stop with such a description, and to forbear at this time the attempt to sum the description up in a single formula, which, in the light of the rapidity of change now going on, is doomed to be misleading to one or another degree. This description is altogether adequate as a guide to action and for further understanding, and nothing further is really needed. To

The Revolution Betrayed

stop with the generalized description and to refuse to be tied down to scholastic formulas: that is how I understood the quotation from *The Revolution Betrayed* with which I began this article.

Our description will show us, in my opinion, beyond any doubt, that the Soviet Union is at the present time *neither a bourgeois state nor a workers' state*: that is, neither the working class nor a consolidated bourgeois class is the ruling or dominant class within the Soviet Union in any intelligible sense that can be given to the conception of a ruling or dominant class. Not a single piece of evidence to the contrary has been advanced in the current discussion.

This may surprise us, and may upset previously formed ideas; but history has a way of surprising us, and we must avoid acting like political ostriches. However, there is in general nothing unprecedented in such a conclusion. The cry of "revisionism" raised against us has no foundation in Marxist theory. Nothing whatever in the theory of the state limits types of states to "bourgeois" or "proletarian." For many years Lenin anticipated a state in Russia which would be a "dictatorship of the proletariat and peasantry"; he may have been wrong, but no one attacked him as a revisionist for this conception of the state which was neither bourgeois nor proletarian. If he was wrong, he was so because things didn't turn out in that way, not because such a state is theoretically inconceivable. Not merely the possibility but the historical existence which were neither bourgeois nor feudal nor proletarian were frequently discussed by Marx and Engels. Engels definitely provided a place for a state which was in direct conflict with the economy - that is, for a state in which the ruling class was *not* the economically dominant class (how much more obviously he would have recognized this possibility in the case of nationalized economy which is not a form of economy giving property rights specifically to one class !) - C.F. , for example, his letter to Conrad Schmidt, October 27,1890. Of course such a state would be extremely unstable, and would not endure for long - "in [this] case nowadays the state power in every great nation will go to pieces in the long run..." But no one pretends that the present type of state in the Soviet Union will endure

Neither Capitalism nor Socialism

for epochs: it is above all characterized as unstable, transitory, in permanent crisis.

The specific analysis of various states, an analysis exact enough to enable us to work out correct policies, absolutely requires us to recognize "intermediary" forms of the state; it would be fatal to limit our "states" to feudal, bourgeois and proletarian. How could we possibly handle the analysis, for example, of the English state from 1500 to 1832 with only these simple categories? Of course, looking back, we can see that during all that time the bourgeoisie by and large advanced along with the advance and expansion of bourgeois economy. But such a general and after all abstract view would have been of little use to the bourgeoisie in solving the complex problems of state power. And what was the U.S. Civil War fought over if not to destroy a coalition *state* (not a coalition government - the form of government was not changed), established under the constitution of 1787, and replace it by an unambiguous bourgeois state?

If I were forced to choose between the single alternative, bourgeois or proletarian, I should unhesitatingly call the Soviet State bourgeois. At the present time the interests it *primarily* defends are bourgeois: the bourgeois interests within the mixed Soviet economy, and international bourgeois interests. Its defense of proletarian interests (unlike its function up until a few years ago) is now clearly *secondary* - though it may on occasion be nonetheless real for all that. But there is no reason whatever to make such a choice.

Is a single formula required? Very well: let all of us who agree on the *description* unite to agree on the clearest and most acceptable formula. In future history I think Comrade Carter is probably right in saying that it will be known as a "Stalinist state," distinguished as a specific state form; and there may be other examples of such a state in the future. If we look at the facts, and not at words, the most accurate formula is probably a "semi-bourgeois state" or an "embryonic bourgeois state." The Soviet State at present is primarily the instrument of the privileged strata of Soviet society - the bureaucracy, Army (particularly the upper ranks), the GPU, the richer collective peasants,

The Revolution Betrayed

the technicians, intellectuals, better-paid Stakhanovites, etc.; and the instrument also of the sections of the international bourgeoisie toward which the State gravitates. Is this not the *fact*?

Is this a "no-class" state? Of course not. It is simply not, primarily, the instrument of either of the two *major* classes in contemporary society. But it *is* the instrument of the "new middle class" striving to become a consolidated bourgeois class within the Soviet Union itself; and it plays its own extremely important role in the international class struggle taken as a whole. Such a state, clearly, is to be expected to be most unstable, transitory, torn by crisis; and this is just what we find. It is theoretically to be expected to be in irreconcilable conflict with its own "economic foundations" (the conflict would *not* be *irreconcilable* if it were in truth a workers' state - any kind of workers' state); and this is certainly the case. It must go, or the economic foundation must go., And this must happen precisely because it is *not* a workers' state, but nevertheless has the economic foundation *for* a workers' state.

Only such an explanation - whether or not put in just these terms - can provide us with a means for answering, without confusion or contradiction, *all* of the major problems, both theoretical and practical, which the Soviet Union in the present stage of its development poses to the revolutionary movement. And, in addition, only such an approach can provide a proper basis for *all* of our specific policies - which, in my opinion, cannot be justified any longer on the basis of the Committee Majority position.

"A Question of Terminology"

It is doubtful whether any dispute which enters into the life of a political organization can ever retain a "purely scientific" character. At the Council of Nicea, the debate resolved apparently around a single letter in the word used to describe the Son of God; but the historically significant issue veiled by the words of the debate was the split between the Eastern and the Western Church. We are also, in part at least, disputing over what kind of party we wish to form, and how we think it can best be built in the period ahead. The debate over the

Neither Capitalism nor Socialism

"Russian Question" in part opposes, or tends to oppose, conflicting tendencies within our own organization.

From a scientific point of view, the question of whether or not the Soviet Union is a workers' state is to a considerable degree a "terminological question"; the question, namely, of what words are most suitable and useful in describing and communicating what we mean. This does not mean that, even from a purely scientific point of view, the question is trivial. Words are social in their functioning. It is necessary not merely that our ideas be correct in our own heads, but that we succeed in communicating them to others; the words we use make possible or impossible such communication; but the words are not *our* property but rather the property of the society in which we live. Words are one of the chief - perhaps the chief - instruments of revolutionary struggle. Therefore it is well to take them seriously.

The verbal habit which leads the Committee Majority to continue calling the Soviet Union a workers' state - and it is nothing more than a verbal habit - has become an obstacle to the progress of our movement. It stands in the way of the successful communication of our ideas to the masses. It begins to enshrine a *bureaucratic* conception of the road towards socialism, which, if solidified, will be fatal to the revolution. It deifies economy in such a manner as to obscure the dialectical inter-relationship between economy and politics, and between both and psychology, intelligence and moral enthusiasm. It serves to justify in the minds of Stalinists and semi-Stalinists their slavishness to the bureaucracy - since do not even we tell them that after all the economy is "all"? It drives independent-thinking workers and intellectuals, who have broken with Stalinism, away from us and towards disillusion and defeatism; for we offer them an explanation in words which, when interpreted as men normally interpret words is false. It obscures in the minds of the masses the real goal which we propose to them. That goal, we must remember, is not a "nationalized economy." Cannon, and others among the Committee Majority, have been telling us, rather scornfully: Democracy! democracy is merely an instrument... How much more fully must we realize, and make others

The Revolution Betrayed

realize, that nationalized economy is merely - an instrument. If not - then, Stalin is the better choice.

Internal Bulletin of the Socialist Workers' Party 1937

THE FOURTH INTERNATIONAL
AND THE RUSSIAN COUNTERREVOLUTION — Yvan Craipeau

For many long years now, the Russian proletariat has lost any hope of political power, any control over the economy, any right to organization and expression, both in the Stalinist party and in the trade unions and soviets. In fact the latter have just been juridically liquidated by the new constitution, which officially puts an end to the dictatorship of the proletariat. Thus, under the pretext that the USSR has become a "classless society," the dictatorship of the proletariat - which in fact was no longer anything but a juridical fiction - is replaced by the plebiscite of the bureaucracy, by the "whole people," including the priests, the czarist police, the speculators and the rich peasants. But at the same time, in "the most democratic state in the world," the terror is intensified over the proletarians, on whom the internal passport is imposed, as in the czar's time, and who are sent to concentration camps on any suspicion. And the GPU deports, and shoots as "Trotskyists," tens of thousands of revolutionary workers, plus the entire old Central Committee of the Bolshevik Party.

As for Soviet society, it is developing in such a way as to give reassurance and enthusiasm to the worst bourgeois, like Mercier and the Croix de Feu deputy Robbe;[5] the army is readopting the external forms of the czarist army with its marshals and Cossacks: the soldier is being inculcated with the most vulgar nationalism. The factory is oppressed under the whip of the Stakhanovists and of piecework, spied on by an army of informers. Divorce is forbidden, the family and bourgeois morals reinstated in good standing; religion is encouraged, private property restored; inheritance re-established; inequality

Neither Capitalism nor Socialism

growing, while the school children, who have been put back in uniform as in the czar's time, are taught to be faithful and loyal subjects.

Social differentiation has reached unprecedented proportions (70 rubles up to 10,000). It has become stabilized. The new aristocracy now can wallow in expensive luxuries, amass fortunes, acquire fixed property, accumulate and pass on its wealth. Besides, today the Stalinist oligarchy has a collective, but exclusive, control over production, hiring and firing of labor, and the division of capital and surplus value.

Thus, it is for the benefit of this new class of exploiters, and through it, that the Russian reaction is carried on. Yet comrade Trotsky and the International continue to deny a specific class character to the ruling Russian oligarchy, and to portray them as an excrescence on the dictatorship of the proletariat, as badly trained functionaries who appropriate too great a proportion of the surplus value. Trotsky asks: take the functionaries of reformist trade unions or English clergymen, who swallow up a huge portion of the surplus value - do they however constitute an independent class?

> Always and under all regimes, the bureaucracy absorbs a rather large part of the surplus value. It would be interesting to calculate, for example, how much of the national revenue is eaten up in Italy and Germany by the fascist locusts. But this fact is entirely insufficient to transform the fascist bureaucracy into an independent ruling class. It is an agent of the bourgeoisie.. What has just been said can be applied also to the Stalinist bureaucracy. (*The 4th International and the USSR.*)[6]

But in *The Revolution Betrayed* Trotsky himself gives a decisive rejoinder: "One cannot deny that it [the bureaucracy] is something more than a simple bureaucracy; the very fact that it has taken power in a country where the most important means of production belong to the state creates entirely the new relations between it and the nation's wealth. The means of production belong to the state; the state in some respect belongs to the bureaucracy."

And that is the key to the enigma. Jouhaux, Citrine and Green (not to mention the English clergymen) have no economic power. They get fat on the crumbs dropped by the bosses, but only their masters, the bosses, dispose of the surplus value. One can say almost the same about the fascist servants of capital, even though the latter, controlling as they do a huge police apparatus, can at times give trouble to their masters. But it is an entirely different matter with the "Soviet bureaucrats." They hold in their hands all the levers of the national economy, all the means of production. All this is a long distance away from simple parasites or English clergymen.

"The clergy of the Middle Ages were a class," writes Trotsky, "to the extent that its rule rested on a definite system of landed property and serfdom."[7] Precisely this is the difference between American clergymen who live by collecting money from Christian simpletons, and the class of the medieval clergy who lived by exploiting the labor of the Christians themselves. In other words: "Classes are defined by their place in the social economy and, above all, by their relation to the means of production."[8] Today comrade Trotsky recognizes that in the USSR the means of production belong to the state and the state belongs to the bureaucracy. Thus the rule of the ruling Russian oligarchy does not depend only on the fact "that it has Rolls Royces at its disposal," but on the fact that it has unqualified control of the means of production, capital, and surplus value. That is what makes it the ruling class of the Russian society.

The Film of the Stalinist Counterrevolution

Comrade Trotsky senses that this means the definitive suppression of the conquests of the proletarian revolution. He tries to put off the day of reckoning: "If these relations became stabilized, legalized, normalized without resistance or against the resistance of the workers, they will end with the complete liquidation of the conquests of the proletarian revolution."[9] Thus comrade Trotsky envisages (in the

Neither Capitalism nor Socialism

future) the possibility of a transition *without military intervention* from the workers' state to a capitalist state. In 1933 that was called unreeling the film of reformism backwards. Well, now the same film can be unreeled "without resistance by the workers" and they don't even have to change anything essential *at bottom* in the relations of production and wealth. It would be enough if the existing relations became stabilized, legalized and normalized!

The International theses of July 1936 explain that it is the new constitution which permits gradual transition to "the economic counter-revolution, that is to say, to the reintroduction of capitalism by the dry route." All that by the power of a new constitution! Marxist language, on the contrary, says that a new Stalinist constitution only reflects "the dictatorship of the privileged strata of Soviet society over the working masses," that is, the economic counter-revolution which has dispossessed the proletariat for the benefit of the ruling oligarchy.

And this Stalinist counter-revolution is far from having triumphed "by the dry route." The Stalinist oligarchy had to have recourse to a surgical operation in order to subdue working-class resistance. They have temporarily broken the advanced workers through deportations, jail, prison camps, and shootings. Does it follow that the counter-revolution has been carried out without the aid of thousands of executions and hundreds of thousands of deportations, that is, without a large-scale class collision? That depends on the extreme exhaustion of the Russian proletariat, who have been deceived, divided, demoralized, terrorized; on the tight solidarity of the ruling oligarchy; on the privileged strata on which they base themselves; on the international counter-revolution, and on the support of world capitalism.

> [Next Craipeau replies to some Majority arguments: *The fact that the oligarchy hides its revenues and conceals its true social physiognomy like every ruling class, this only shows its class consciousness. It constitutes a class which is not as closed as the ruling class of the old*

The Revolution Betrayed

capitalist countries. The frequency of "accidents" in the career of bureaucrats does not at all stand in the way of their constituting a class, any more than "accidents" to individual capitalists stand in the way of the existence of the capitalist class. The bureaucrats can as yet transmit his "right" to exploit the state only indirectly, thanks to nepotism. It is probable that one day he will obtain the right to transmit it directly by inheritance. Besides, it is not the title-deeds to property that count:]

Ownership is control. The bureaucracy - as a collectivity - has unqualified control over all the means of production, all the accumulated capital, and it freely divides up the surplus value. As a collectivity, obviously; for just as the big stockholders and boards of directors are really the only ones who have a voice in running business, to the exclusion of the small and middle-sized stockholders, so also the right to unchecked control over the means of production becomes smaller and smaller the further one gets from the bureaucratic summits.

Let us come to this conclusion: even if it were established that the new masters were willing to have their rights over the means of production sanctioned directly by an official transferable and negotiable document, it is very clear that by the presence or absence of such a notarized writ in their strong-boxes can change nothing in the real class relations. Then it follows that they have exclusive control over the means of production, over hiring and firing, the wages of labor, over the division of capital and surplus value. No notarized writ will have the validity of this essential fact written down by comrade Trotsky:

"All the means of production belong to the state, and the state belongs in some respect to the bureaucracy."

The Planned Economy

[Can such a state be called a workers' state? The Bolshevik-Leninist[14] theses continue to say yes, though not without reservations and a certain reticence. To the end they base themselves on one argument:

Neither Capitalism nor Socialism

the existence of a planned economy. But the class character of a state is not defined by the existence of an economic plan. The USSR was indisputably a proletarian state at a time when the economic plan did not yet exist. In a pinch, one could conceive of the nationalization of a whole economy by a bourgeois state without anything being changed in the nature of the state (see the analysis by Engels in Anti-Duehring[10]). Planned economy is proletarian only if the proletariat is its master and if it is oriented toward socialism.

Nowadays, many capitalist states strive to resolve their contradictions by putting economic plans into effect. However, these plans are nothing but partial and timid ones, fettered by private property in the means of production. Therefore the Minority reporter makes note of the important difference between the role of the fascist bureaucracy, which is a lackey of finance capital, and the Russian oligarchy, which is its own master:]

Historically, the fascist bureaucracy uses the police power to save the regime of private property and to maintain capitalist anarchy by curbing it. Historically, the Russian oligarchy inherited a planned economy, which gives it, as the ruling class, unprecedented powers over the exploitation of labor, but which likewise will facilitate the exercise of economic power by the proletariat. The Russian economy is neither working-class, nor socialist, but rather economically progressive.

Russia and the Trade Unions

[The minority report next criticizes the comparison of the Russian state with a trade union:]

"The Soviet union," the Majority theses go on to say, "can be called a workers' state in nearly the same sense - in spite of the enormous difference in scale - that a trade union which is led and betrayed by opportunists, i.e. by agents of capital, can be called a workers' organization." An astonishing comparison!

The Revolution Betrayed

A workers' trade union in a capitalist regime is a combination of exploited workingmen for the purpose of reducing their rate of exploitation, particularly in order to raise their wages and thus decrease the surplus value which remains in the hands of the ruling class. The bourgeoisie succeeds in corrupting the leadership of the unions and of putting its own agents in. The result is that such unions - which have bourgeois agents at their head - inadequately fulfill their task as against the ruling class. While struggling to put in charge a proletarian leadership which will not betray, revolutionaries obviously struggle to safeguard the existence of these workers' organizations (even though inadequate) whose aim is to reduce the rate of exploitation of the workers. And how is it in Russia? The bureaucracy *itself holds all the means of production*, itself divides up the capital and the surplus value without any other control, itself determines the rate of exploitation of the workers *in its own interest* (the theses of the International conference). Nothing that resembles a combination of workers to reduce their rate of exploitation. The comparison comes down to comparing a trade union with a trust! It seems that there is an "enormous difference in scale" between them. Indeed, what "scale" could lead from one to the other? And it is on such images - a simple play on words on the term "bureaucracy" - that the "working class" character of the USSR rests!

The Russian State is no Longer a Workers' State

Thus it is that the formal property relations remain those that were created by the proletarian revolution, while the real property has passed into the hands of the Russian oligarchy. The latter use it in their own interests and in the interests of the new privileged strata, to the exclusion of proletarian interests. To proclaim that this state which is in their hands is a "workers' state" is like proclaiming that Hitler's state is "democratic" simply because it has largely retained "the form" of the Weimar constitution, the shadow of a Reichstag, and the illusion of the secret ballot. We ourselves prefer the definition given in April

Neither Capitalism nor Socialism

1930 by Rakovsky (then leader in the USSR of the Bolshevik-Leninist opposition) together with Kossior, Muralov, and Kasparova.

"From being a proletarian state with bureaucratic deformations, as Lenin defined the political form of our state, we are developing into a bureaucratic state with proletarian Communist survivals. Before our eyes there has been formed, and is forming, a large class of rulers with growing internal subdivisions, multiplying through partisan co-optation, through direct or indirect appointment (bureaucratic promotions, fictitious electoral system). As the supporting basis of this peculiar class, one finds a kind - a peculiar kind - of private property, namely, the possession of state power. The 'bureaucracy' possess the state as its private property, said Marx."[12]

We are told that "the workers will not have to make a social revolution in the USSR, that they will only have to give the existing organizations new life and democracy." Let us be clear about this. It is true that in Russia there still remains a part of the old framework of the workers' state: monopoly of foreign trade, planned economy, collective (oligarchic) character of the division of capital and surplus value, as well as certain social conquests (regarding hygiene, urban development, protection of children and maternity), although more and more these conquests have been monopolized by the ruling oligarchy (see Yvan and Trotsky). From this one can conclude that when the Fourth International takes power in the USSR, its job will be facilitated by the USSR's economic structure, which is progressive in relation to the capitalist countries.

But does this mean that this seizure of power will not be a social revolution? Suppose, for example, that the workers of a big capitalist trust take over their factories, or indeed that these French railway workers take over the (nationalized) railways: they *will be satisfied* to replace the board of directors (representatives of the stockholders' oligarchy) by representatives of the workers. It is possible they will keep a part of the personnel of superintendence. The overturn will consist in this: instead of the division of capital and surplus value being carried out by the stockholders' oligarchy and in their interests,

The Revolution Betrayed

this division will henceforward be carried out under the effective control of the workers and in their interests.

On the national plane, it is a revolution of this order that the Russian workers will make. They will tear out of the hands of the ruling oligarchy the management of the factories, of the trusts, of the planned economy; they will carry on this management no longer in the interests of the oligarchy, but in their own interest. They will decide themselves (through their representatives) the division of capital: the part assigned to the producers, to the employees, to the renewal of fixed capital, etc. It will be up to them to rebuild the proletarian social order by smashing the social order which the Stalinist oligarchy built up little by little, by abolishing the privileges, the new private property, inheritance, the reactionary laws on the family, divorce, army ranks, the cult of nationalism, etc.

In spite of the deceptive Soviet labels (many of which, anyway, have now been liquidated even on paper), it will be up to them to make a complete reconquest of political power by smashing the state cadres of the Stalinist bureaucracy, which they will be able to sweep out only by the armed insurrection of the proletariat. It seems that the "defense of the conquests of October" is, in reality, their reconquest, and necessarily leads through the proletarian revolution in Russia. To refuse to give the name of social revolution to this proletarian revolution comes under the head of casuistry.

Defense of the USSR?

[Next Craipeau passes on to the question of the defense of the USSR. There can be no question about the solidarity of the international proletariat with the USSR, as the advance bastion of the Proletarian Revolution, in attack as in defense :– EH]

For us, who see in the USSR a new form of the exploitation of man by man, it is obviously impossible for us to consider Voroshilov's victories as equivalent to victories of the World Revolution.

Neither Capitalism nor Socialism

Besides, even the Majorityites justify the defense of the USSR not as the "socialist fatherland," but (a) because its economy is progressive; (b) because the defeat of the USSR would mean the return of private property and capitalism; (c) because only the world revolution can be a faithful ally of the USSR; (d) through the comparison with the reformist trade unions.

To this the Minority reporter replies: (a) A progressive economy defends itself by itself, as is shown by all the examples from the past (the restoration of 1814-15 in France, the annexation of Finland etc.).

...If the present economy of Russia is progressive in relation to the economy of individual capitalism - even if we admit a bourgeois military victory - capitalism would no longer move to push this economy back to a more backward stage, indeed one which it is itself striving to transcend. The absolute retardation in the output of Russian production would, besides not permit the Russian ruling class to resist international finance capital. And what we would see would be, not a return to individual capitalism, but the colonization of the statified industry by the finance capital of the imperialist countries. Let us take a concrete look at the problem: the Italian and especially the German capitalists see in Russia, above all, an inexhaustible reserve of raw materials which they lack (oil, minerals, etc.), as well as an immense outlet for their manufactured products and their machines, mainly with an eye to the exploitation of the raw-materials resources. Imagine a German victory (or a French victory, for that matter). If Russian planned economy establishes its economic superiority, then finance capital, which already holds the upper hand in Germany, will obviously refuse to dismantle it in order to introduce a more backward system which will lessen the profit on capital. In the same way that a business man would refuse to dismantle his machines in order to replace them with older machines. German finances capital will make itself master (militarily or economically) of the whole state machine, will transform the bureaucrats into its employees, and will turn the state production to its own profit. The surplus value will go to new masters with different modes of division, but the statified and planned industry will remain in existence. Thus once more this law will be confirmed: a more advanced economy defends itself by itself...

... But, it is said, wouldn't defeat mean the triumph of the bourgeoisie and even, without doubt, the triumph of its fascist wing? The same fallacious reasoning is used against revolutionary defeatism in general and its Bolshevik Leninist protagonists, by the Comintern: "the defeat of democratic France would mean the victory of fascism." Which means: if the workers are bound up with the defeat of bourgeois democracy, the victors can only be the fascists. But the point is: the defeat of our bourgeois has a progressive meaning for us only if it is bound up with international revolutionary action for proletarian victory. Same thing in Russia: revolutionary defeatism is no more bound up with the victory of capitalism in Russia than with the victory of fascism in France and Germany. In proportion as the political and economic power of the ruling oligarchy weakens, the workers will begin to rise up. Without doubt, a part of the peasants - maintaining the tradition of individual property - will welcome the invader as the liberator who will re-establish individual in the fields. But the other part of the peasants - for whom collectivization means tractors - will join the workers in order to re-establish the workers' and peasants' power. As for the bureaucracy, it is possible that one part of them will try to prolong their rule by a compromise with the workers, while the other part will try to sell themselves to the foreign capitalism as their functionaries.

The USSR and World Imperialism
   [Finally, Craipeau brings up the international role of the USSR: an integral part of the system of imperialist alliances and one of the principal counter-revolutionary factors – EH:]

... They have, a long time ago, even rejected the cast-off clothing of bourgeois pacifism, disarmament and the petty-bourgeois tinsel of the Briand-Kellog type. They still talk about peace, no doubt, as do Eden, Blum, Hitler and Mussolini. But at the same time they push the

Neither Capitalism nor Socialism

frightened democratic governments - especially England, made timid by its slowness in rearming - to oppose their own audacity to the audacity of the Berlin-Rome axis; they push these governments to understand that delays can only accentuate the disintegration, of the Versailles bloc and that it is necessary to take advantage of the opportunities without being afraid of war. It is necessary for them to prepare the allies for war materially and morally: they order their lackeys to [attack] pacifism in the allied countries, to sound the chauvinist note, to destroy all class struggle in the name of "Union of the whole nation" against the foreign menace. They strive to unleash an arms race in the Allied countries, to multiply General Staff conferences, to seal new military alliances and to strengthen existing alliances. It is in this sense that they have rendered serious aid (often underestimated by us) to the Spanish government: on the sole condition that they keep Spain under the capitalist regime and crush attempts at proletarian revolution. With them it is a matter of keeping a strong military place of the first importance for the French-Russian-English coalition.

In this systematic work of Sacred Union, the Stalinists run into two enemies: a conjunctural enemy, fascism, which would prefer most often to avoid the Russian alliance but which, it may be hoped, can be brought back into the straight and narrow path: and an irreconcilable enemy, the revolutionary "Trotskyists," proletarian defeatists. Since the latter are irreconcilable, the only way to settle matters with them is violence. It is therefore significant that the USSR takes the lead in the bloody repression against "Trotskyism, agent of Germany and Japan."

Under these conditions, one can understand the danger of the "unconditional defense of the USSR." The question is all the more serious since our theses on war explain our defeatism by the necessity to denounce our capitalist government, allied to the USSR, as a perfidious ally that will betray the USSR, which we have to replace with a workers' state, the only faithful ally of the USSR. The Russian counter--revolution itself gives us a scathing reply: it supplies arms, planes and officers to the Spanish government on the sole condition that it

The Revolution Betrayed

maintain capitalism and destroy the working-class opposition (POUM, FAI, etc.).[13] Whether we like it or not, the faithful allies of the USSR (that is, of the Russian counter-revolution) are imperialism, and only its lackeys can be for "unconditional defense of the USSR."

Given this tight solidarity between today's Russia and imperialism and its decisive role in the imperialist conflict, the solidarity of the world proletariat with the Russian state could not but find itself in perpetual contradiction with its revolutionary action in its own country (just the contrary of what happens in the case of solidarity with a proletarian state or with a country oppressed by imperialism). Under these conditions all equivocation is a grave danger. That is why the theses presented to the conference have this conclusion:

To the slogan of the defense of the USSR it is necessary to counterpose revolutionary defeatism by the Fourth International and fraternization with the Soviet revolutionaries.

Quatriéme Internationale 1937

NOTES

1. Leon Trotsky, *The Revolution Betrayed*, tr. Max Eastman. Pathfinder Press (New York 1972.)

2. Max Shachtman, *The New International*, "Revolution and Counter-Revolution in Russia" (January 1938)

3. Jay Lovestone was an American socialist and trade unionist who joined the Communist movement in the early twenties. He was expelled in 1929 shortly after he had helped expel Trotsky's supporters. During the Popular Front period he and his group (which included the writer Bertram Wolfe among its better known members) argued that Stalin was right to attempt an accommodation with the Western Powers. This "moderation" in external affairs was in contrast to the growing terror inside Russia.

4. Daniel Guerin, *Fascism and Big Business*. Pioneer Publishers (New York, 1939).

Neither Capitalism nor Socialism

5. The reference is to a right wing French politician and a right wing French political organization. This article was written at a time when the French government was allied with Russia. It was the first Western power to do so. For a memoir of this period which describes the blow delivered by the Stalin-Laval pact to the reawakened French labor movement see Daniel Guerin *Front Populaire, revolution manquée* (Paris, René Julliard, 1963)

6. This citation is not accurate. It actually appears in *The Class Nature of the Soviet State,* Lanka Samasamaja Pulications (Ceylon, 1952) p. 12.

7 . Ibid., p. 13.

8 . Leon Trotsky, *The Revolution Betrayed,* p.280

9 . Ibid., p. 249.

10 . "Bolshevik-Leninist" was the term used by the adherents of Trotsky to describe themselves.

11 . See Frederick Engels, *Herr Eugen Dühring's Revolution in Science*, Marxist Library Vol. XVIII (International Publishers, New York). Craipeau is probably referring to the discussion of the role of the state in Part III, Section II.

12 . Christian Rakovsky, "Declaration of the Bolshevik-Leninist Opposition at the Central Committee and to all Party Members" *Biulleten Oppozitsii* No. 17-18, pp 11-19. This quote can be found on page 16. An English translation of this declaration which omits this passage, and curiously enough only this passage, can be found in *Christian Rakovsky, Selected Writings on Opposition in the USSR 1923-1930,* Edited by Gus Fagan (Allison & Busby Limited, London, 1980)

13 . See Burnett Bolleton, *The Spanish Revolution* (The University of North Carolina Press, Chapel Hill, 1979) for the most thorough description of this process. The FAI was the *Federacion Anarquista Ibérica* (Spanish Anarchist Federation), the anarchist non-party which was organized on totalitarian lines and functioned as a disciplined caucus inside the *Confederacion Nacional de Trabajo* (National Federation of Labor) one of two major labor federations. The POUM was the *Partido Obrera de Unification Marxista,* (Workers' Party of

The Revolution Betrayed

Marxist Unity) which was an amalgamation of a number of communist opposition groups.

Neither of these two groups acted as, or thought of themselves as, an alternative to the Popular Front government even though they protested its attempt to role back the revolutionary movement that rose to defend the Republic against Franco's insurrection. Hence, the quotes around the word trotskyist. Trotsky's insistence on an open political break with the Popular Front government was accepted by a very small minority of militants.

Chapter II
THE HITLER STALIN PACT

One consequence the signing of the pact between Stalinist Russia and Nazi Germany was the proliferation of "wave of the future" theories.

The book bearing this title by Anne Morrow Lindberg set the general tone. The author, taking note of Anglo-Saxon sensitivities, made clear that she herself regretted the excesses of the new totalitarian regimes and was only observing a phenomenon not necessarily approving of it. Fascism was a nice place to visit, but she wasn't sure she wanted to live there herself.

Nevertheless, the work in general exuded admiration for the vigor of the new regimes as compared to the lethargy and drift of capitalism mired in the depression.

On the left it was James Burnham who captured this spirit in his book the **Managerial Revolution**. *A synopsis of this book appeared in* The Partisan Review, *a literary and political review then generally sympathetic to Trotsky and left socialism in general. This article is reprinted here. It speaks for itself and demonstrates how Trotsky's insistence on the progressive role of statification and national planning could become the basis of an apology for Stalinism and fascism. Ironically, it was Burnham, when he was still a Trotskyist, who had warned against such a development.*

Dwight MacDonald's article in the same issue of Partisan Review *is of interest because it was one of the few serious attempts to explain how Nazi Germany had ceased to be capitalist even though no outright seizure of private property took place.*

The last selection attempts to refute this "new wave" analysis. Max Shachtman's "Is Russia a Workers' State?" while recognizing the futility of trying to show that either the working class or the capitalist class has any power left in Stalin's Russia still clings to Trotsky's emphasis on the historically progressive role played by the bureaucracy in defending nationalized property.

Shachtman refuses to follow Burnham in awarding similar honors to the fascist bureaucracy by emphasizing that Hitler halted before challenging the "juridical detail" of private property. The question of whether such a confiscation by the fascist party would be progressive just as Stalin's was is effectively dodged. In the section of Poland occupied by the Russians the capitalist class was expropriated and, simultaneously, every working class

Neither Capitalism nor Socialism

organization including the Communists was wiped out. This certainly placed in doubt the claim that all Stalin was doing, or was capable of doing, was preserving the achievements of the Russian Revolution. This issue is not discussed.

THE THEORY OF THE MANAGERIAL REVOLUTION–

James Burnham

It is remarkable that the catastrophic events of the past decade have not stimulated a positive and systematic revision of our general ideas about what is happening in the world. Surely no previous decade has ever crowded within its brief limits developments of such magnitude as the consolidation of Stalinism, the rise of Nazism, the New Deal, the invasion of China, and the second world war. If we are honest, we must recognize that no one anticipated, with any plausible concreteness, these events. In any field of scientific inquiry other than history, such a lack of correspondence between expectation and fact would have led to the conclusion that the theories upon which the expectations had been founded were false or at least inadequate. But, apparently, we are not very anxious to be scientific about history. We seek from history salvation rather than knowledge, forgetting that genuine salvation can be based only on knowledge.

Orthodox bourgeois and orthodox Marxist thinkers alike take note of events - after they have happened - and are content to "reaffirm" principles which have failed to meet the test of actual experience. We ought to begin to suspect that orthodox bourgeois and Marxist thinkers have been driven together into a corner their only remaining effort is to escape from reality.

It is true that during recent years a number of ex-Marxists - Eastman, Hook, Corey, Utley are examples - have been trying to break new ground. Their negative critique of Marxist theory has been astute and, much of it, convincing. Nevertheless, in their work so far - and this is perhaps not unnatural - there have been two deficiencies. None of them has yet tried, in any but the sketchiest way, to present a substitute for, or reformulation of, Marxist theory. And, second, they

The Hitler–Stalin Pact

have failed to separate, with the clarity plainly required, the moral problem of desirable political program from the descriptive problem of what actually seems to be happening in the world. It is this later problem which alone concerns me here; and with respect to it, new ideas seem to be emerging at the present time neither from Marxist nor bourgeois thought, but, so far as they are present at all, from a quite different source: from the anarchist tradition, and from the tradition - by no means unrelated to anarchism - of such writers as Pareto whose historical origins are perhaps to be found in Machiavelli.

I believe that we now have at our disposal enough evidence to answer, at least roughly and with a fair probability, this question of what is happening in the world, the question of the character of the present period of major social transition and its probable outcome. To give such an answer in detail cannot be the work of single individuals; it requires a cooperative effort. It may, however, be possible to reach some measure of agreement about the general direction in which the answer is to be sought.

During the past several generations, most of the writers in the fields of sociology, politics and economics who have abandoned the exceedingly naive assumption that the capitalist organization of society is eternal have accepted, implicitly or explicitly, a second assumption that is often expressed as follows: capitalism and socialism are "the only alternatives" for modern society; either capitalism will continue or socialism will replace it. It should be remarked that the two terms in this presumed alternative have an unlike status. What "capitalism" means we are able to know from experience, by generalizing the chief characteristics of post-Renaissance society, which we are all agreed in calling capitalism. What "socialism" means, on the other hand, we know only from definition, since there has never been a socialist society. Nevertheless, almost everyone agrees on the definition: socialist society is economically classless, politically democratic, and international (or at the least internationalist).

The assumption that capitalism and socialism are the sole alternatives is by no means confined to Marxists and others who *favor*

Neither Capitalism nor Socialism

socialism from a programmatic and moral standpoint. It is shared by many who oppose socialism and who fight against it. The most ardent defender of capitalism will usually agree with the firmest revolutionary that if capitalism goes it will be socialism that takes its place.

The acceptance of this assumption dictates the broad lines of the interpretation of contemporary events, and the expectations of the future. The significance of events is found in their relation to one or another of the alternatives. What happens is understood as of capitalism or from capitalism, as toward or away from socialism, as strengthening or weakening capitalism, bringing socialism nearer or pushing it farther off.

During the past generation, and especially during the past decade, this mode of interpretation, based upon and required by this assumption, has become more and more inadequate, less and less able to answer plausibly the problems raised by what is happening. To an ever increasing extent it becomes confusing, distorting, and sterile. It demanded that we regard the Russian Revolution of 1917 as a socialist revolution, and predict that it would move further toward socialism or back toward the restoration of capitalism. In fact, the post-1917 Russian social organization has done neither; but we are compelled by our assumption to say that it has done one or the other, and to waste time in such altogether fruitless disputes as that over whether Russia is today a "workers' (socialist) state" or a "capitalist state" - since these are the only terms admitted by our assumption. Germany did not become socialist through Nazism, and we are therefore compelled to distort terminology, sense and facts into caricatures in order to "explain" that Nazism is a "new form" of capitalism. In our interpretation of the New Deal in this country, we have at our disposal only the same narrow alternative. We can say, as many say, that the New Deal is "disguised socialism" - and no one should doubt the impenetrability of the disguise; or we can argue that it is merely a special form of "finance-capitalism," in which case we lapse into mysticism when asked why nine-tenths of the capitalists of the nation oppose it. Above all does the second world war leave us floundering. From its beginning, from the day of the Nazi-Soviet Pact, in the military, diplomatic, political, social-economic developments, our assumption makes the second world war unintelligible, and makes impossible an even roughly accurate anticipation of future events.

When an assumption is made explicit, it becomes possible to examine it critically, and, if this seems advisable, to reject it. If the assumption of "either capitalism or socialism" is merely verbal - that is, if it means only that we are resolved to call any possible change in social organization either "socialism" or "capitalism" - then of course the assumption cannot be disproved. we can at most suggest this verbal restriction is likely to be confusing.

But this particular assumption may easily be re-interpreted. We can understand its content not as an assumption, but as two different descriptive theories or hypotheses about what is probably going to happen, to be judged by the available evidence. Thus translated, the assumption divides into: the theory that capitalism will continue for the next historical period (let us say, at least several generations); the theory that capitalism will be replaced by socialism in the near future (let us say in the next decade or so).

These theories are not contradictories but contraries. That is, though one of them must be false, both of them may be false. It is logically possible that neither of them is true, and that a third hypothesis may be formulated which, on the basis of the evidence, is more probable than either of them.

What is at issue here is not, we should note, a question of program. Neither of these hypotheses - nor any additional alternative hypotheses - raises any problem of what "ought to be," of whether the continuance of capitalism would be "good" or "bad," whether we "ought" to fight for socialism, or what program "ought" to be adopted by men of good will. The problem is simply one of fact, of what, on the basis of the evidence now at our disposal, is most likely to happen

By now, the theory that capitalism is going to continue much longer is, from the scientific point of view, hardly worth the bother of refuting. Capitalism, considered on a world scale, is already half gone,

Neither Capitalism nor Socialism

and completing its disappearance before our eyes. In Russia, with a sixth of the earth's surface and about a twelfth of its population, nearly everyone grants that capitalism is already pretty well eliminated. And in all other nations, even those which we can still justifiably call capitalist, new institutional structures are well on their way toward the replacement of the institutions of capitalism. Mass unemployment, an impasse in agriculture, idle capital funds, the inability to exploit subject territories profitably, the inability to use the productive plant and new inventions and technological improvements, the disorganization of the financial system, the loss of confidence by the capitalists themselves, and the loss of mass appeal by the capitalist ideologies, all signalize the end of the capitalist organization of society in a manner similar to that in which analogous symptoms have signalized the end of other social orders in other times.

The theory that socialism is going to replace capitalism, in spite of its being widely believed, has seldom had much evidence presented in its favor. Belief in the theory has been based ordinarily on the following syllogism: Capitalism is going to end soon (which we may grant); capitalism and socialism are "the sole alternatives"; therefore socialism is going to come. Formally, this syllogism is valid. The trouble with it is the second premise, which is once more our assumption. Rejecting the assumption, as assumption, the syllogism has no relevance to the actual problem: whether, on the evidence, it is probable that socialism is coming.

Most of those who believe that socialism is coming, including most Marxists with the exception, perhaps, of Marx, have tended to accept another assumption, with the help of which their case has been given a coating of strength. This is the assumption that the elimination of private property rights in the instruments of production is a guarantee, a sufficient condition, of socialism. Since it is manifest that private property rights in the instruments of production are being rapidly eliminated, and since there is no reason to expect any reversal of this world trend, these facts, together with the new assumption, are enough to prove that socialism is coming.

The Hitler–Stalin Pact

But the new assumption is not in the least more justified than the other. We have in history numerous examples of exploiting or class societies, and non-democratic societies, where there have not been private property rights in the instruments of production. Control over (that is, property rights in) the instruments of production has been vested in a corporate body (for example, the body of priests or ancients), not in individuals as such. Nor are the examples confined to ancient or primitive history. Present day Russia shows plainly, to anyone who wants to see, that there is no necessary connection between private property rights and exploitation or class divisions. The Russian events *prove* that the elimination of private property rights in the instruments of production is not a guarantee, a sufficient condition, of socialism, since in Russia these rights are eliminated and there is not socialism - that is, a society which is economically classless and politically democratic.

With these two question-begging assumptions dropped, the case for the hypothesis that socialism is coming is extremely weak, almost non-existent. The fact that many of us would like it to come, think it the best possible form of society, consider it the only "rational solution" to the major social problems and conflicts, does not, as we know from historical experience, have any particular weight as evidence that it will come. It is not at all true that socialism and socialists have "never had a chance." On the contrary, socialism, and all branches of the movements professing socialist society as an ideal and aim have had many chances. And all of these chances have resulted in either betrayal or failure, usually both. Each branch will admit this of all the other branches; together their admissions cover the lot.

The Leninist wing has taken state power by revolutionary means and held it (Russia), but has not built socialism or toward socialism; and it has taken state power and lost it (Hungary), not to speak of failing to take it when it might have done so (Germany, China, Spain). The reformist wing has often been in charge of the government (Germany, Denmark, Sweden, Norway, Austria, France, England,

Neither Capitalism nor Socialism

New Zealand) but socialism has not appeared or even been approached. The anarchists have had their chance in Spain.

During the past generation, the working class, which must be presumed to be the main social force active in any possible transition to socialism, has had its social position progressively undermined. This has resulted from a falling off of its relative numbers, the presence of large-scale unemployment, and technological changes which reduce the relative importance of the working class in production. In addition, the development of new techniques of production, of propaganda and political rule, of military technique and strategy, all decrease the elements of potential power available to the working class.

During the past decade, a large part of the Marxist and other socialist-inspired movements has been wiped out. The only important section remaining is the Stalinist, which experience has proved to be an influence in no way moving toward socialism.

At the same time, the socialist ideologies have lost their power to move the masses, as is proved by their inability to make headway against rival ideologies - Stalinist and especially fascist.

There does not, in general, seem to be any positive evidence worth mentioning in the events of the past generation that substantiates the hypothesis that socialism is coming.

Both the theory that capitalism will continue and the theory that socialism will come are, on the basis of the available evidence, in extremely poor shape. However convincing they may once have been as speculation, historical developments since 1914 simply do not bear either of them out; on the contrary, actual historical developments have run counter to both of them. This by itself, would not be enough to prove both of them false. If there were no alternative theory, more probable on the evidence than either of them, then we should still have to accept the more probable of the two. But there is a third alternative (or rather a third group of alternative theories), Which needs little more than to be formulated to be recognized as far more probable than either, much more plausible in the interpretation it permits of the data of the past, and more convincing in its predictions of the future.

The Hitler–Stalin Pact

This third alternative I call "the theory of the managerial revolution," though naturally the name is of no importance. My own formulation must be understood as only one among several possible variants of a more general type of hypothesis that might be more exactly presented in somewhat different terms. This theory, or type of theory, is not at all an arbitrary speculation. It is based upon what has actually been happening in the world, especially since the beginning of the first world war. It explains, with reasonable and reasonably systematic plausibility, what has been happening; and through this explanation predicts, roughly, what is going to happen.

The theory may be summarized briefly as follows: We are now in the midst of a major social transformation (revolution), during which, as in other major transitions, the chief economic and political institutions in society, the dominant ideologies, and the class relations, are being sharply and rapidly altered. This transition is from the structure of society which we call capitalist - that is, a structure characterized economically by "private enterprise," the owner -"wage worker" relation, production for individual profit, regulation of production as a whole by "the market" rather than by deliberate human control, and so on; characterized politically by the existence of numerous sovereign national states, strong in their own political sphere but limited as to their intervention into other spheres of life, especially the economic sphere, and by typical parliamentary institutions; characterized in terms of class relations through the position of private capitalists as the ruling class; and characterized ideologically by the prominence of individualist and "natural rights" notions in widespread social beliefs.

The transition, which it is well to emphasize is already in mid--course, is to a type of society that I call "managerial." The economic structure of managerial society is to be based upon state ownership of the chief means of production, in contrast to the predominantly private ownership of the means of production in capitalist society. The new economy will be an exploiting (class) economy; but, instead of exploitation's taking place directly, as in capitalism, through owner-

Neither Capitalism nor Socialism

ship vested in individuals, it takes place indirectly, through control of the state by the new ruling class, the state in turn owning and controlling the means of production.

Some of the possible mechanisms of this new mode of exploitation, as they have been developed in Russia, are clearly shown in Freda Utley's very interesting recent book *The Dream We Lost*. Trotsky, committed to the view that Russia is a "workers' state," was forced to hold that Russia's rulers got their heavy share of the national income through fraud and graft, that Russia has a "fraud economy" - since, by definition, there could not be "exploitation" in a workers' (socialized) state. Miss Utley's analysis shows how superficial was this opinion to which Trotsky was driven by his unshakable faith in the "either capitalism or socialism" assumption.}

Through the new economic structure, as we have already seen from the examples of Russia and Germany, mass unemployment can be done away with, capital funds released from idleness, foreign trade carried on (by, for example, barter methods) at what would be an intolerable loss for capitalism, exploitation of backward territories and peoples resumed and stepped up, and the *capitalist* type of economic crisis eliminated. What is in question here is not whether we approve of the means whereby these ends are achieved (we might, from a moral standpoint, prefer unemployment to state labor camps), but merely the observation that they are achieved. They are achieved, moreover, not through the cleverness of individual leaders, but through new institutional arrangements which remove the private profit requirements that have brought a dying capitalism to mass unemployment, idle funds and dried up trade. There is thus every reason to believe that the achievements are not episodic, but a consequence of the newly rising structure of society.

Within any society, primary social power is in general held by those persons who have the chief measure of control over the instruments of production. Nevertheless, in the political order, power or "sovereignty" cannot simply float in the air; it must be concretized or "localized" in some definite human institution which is recognized

The Hitler–Stalin Pact

and accepted by the given society as the body from which laws, decrees, and rules properly issue. There is a natural enough tendency for each major structure of society to develop its own typical sort of institution to serve this function of the localization of sovereignty. All historians recognize the great symptomatic importance of what might be described as the "shift in the localization of sovereignty" which occurs as a phase of every social transition (revolution). As the old order decays, sovereignty departs from the institution where it has been localized, and comes to rest in a new type of institution which, though it exists as a rule within the old order, is there secondary in influence and in reality representative of the new order that is on its way up.

Under capitalism, political sovereignty has been most typically "localized" in parliaments (or some similar sort of institution, by whatever name it may have been called). Parliaments have been the "law-makers" of capitalism. During the generation since the first world war, sovereignty has been quickly shifting away from parliaments, and in most nations today parliamentary sovereignty has ended. In the new, managerial society, we can already see that sovereignty is to be localized where it has been in fact coming to rest, in the administrative commissions, boards, bureaus, of the new *unlimited* state.

In place of the dominant ideologies of capitalism, focusing around the concepts and slogans of "natural rights," "free enterprise," "private initiative," "life, liberty and the pursuit of happiness," and other offspring of "individualism," the ideologies of managerial society will focus around such concepts and slogans as the collectivity ("state," "race," "proletariat," "people"), "human rights v. property rights," "discipline," "order," "sacrifice," and so on. As examples of early of managerial ideologies may be cited Leninism-Stalinism (Bolshevism), fascism-Nazism, and, at a still more primitive level, New Dealism.

The managerial society will mean the reduction to impotence, and finally the disappearance, or virtual disappearance of the class of

Neither Capitalism nor Socialism

capitalists (to say that capitalist institutions will disappear is at the same time to say that capitalists will disappear). Within the new structure, the new ruling class - that is, those who have the principal control over the instruments of production and who get the principal differential rewards from the products of those instruments (for such persons are what we mean by the ruling class in any society) - will be the managers together with their bureaucratic colleagues in the strictly political movement. Under the institutions of managerial society, with the unlimited state at once the sovereign political and the controlling economic apparatus, these two latter groups (managers and bureaucrats) will be on the whole fused.

By "managers" I mean those who for the most part are already actually managing production nowadays, whether within the narrowing sphere of private enterprise or the expanding arena of state enterprise: the production executives, administrative engineers, supervisory technicians, plant co-ordinators, government bureau heads and commissioners and administrators. Under modern technological conditions, these managers (or administrators) are seldom identical as persons (as they used to be) with the capitalists, are not themselves capitalists; and in any event there is no necessary connection of any kind between the managerial and the capitalist functions in the total economic process.

To employ for a moment the metaphorical language of the class struggle: Just as once the early capitalists built up their power "within the womb of feudal society," but found that their power could not be consolidated and extended without smashing the foundations of feudalism; so the managers have built up their power within the womb of capitalism - more and more de facto power coming into their hands as the capitalists proper, pushed by technological, social and moral changes, withdraw from production to finance to economic idleness. For more than six hundred years,
from the fourteenth century until the first world war, the curve of capitalist social domination rose without interruption. The end of every decade found a greater percentage of the total economy subject

The Hitler–Stalin Pact

to capitalist rule and capitalist social relations than the beginning. During the course of the first world war, the curve turned catastrophically downward. The Russian Revolution snatched at one stroke a sixth of the world's surface and a twelfth of its population away from the capitalists and capitalism. The Nazis, it turns out, though more slowly are bringing about the same result in an even more decisive section of world economy. And in all nations, rapid structural changes are reducing everywhere both the area of the economy subject to capitalist relations as well as the degree of control exercised by the capitalists. The continuous economic process is abruptly accentuated, but not altered in direction, by political explosions.

The managers cannot consolidate their power without smashing the foundations of capitalism. Whether the managers themselves realize it or not, their problem can be solved only by doing away with "private enterprise" and parliamentarism, and replacing them by state economy and government by boards and bureaus. In the process, the managers do not, of course, do the actual fighting or construct the appropriate ideologies, any more than did the early capitalists. The masses do the fighting and intellectuals construct the ideologies. The result is what counts, and the result is already apparent: a society in which the class of managers, together with a group of political allies with whom the managers largely fuse in the apparatus of the new unlimited state, are the ruling class.

I am unable, in this article, to discuss the difficult and humanly most important problem of the relations among the managerial institutional structure, democracy, and totalitarianism. This much seems clear: Rapid advance toward the managerial structure has so far been accompanied by totalitarian politics. Nevertheless, totalitarianism is no more identical with the managerial structure than is democracy with the capitalist social structure. It is certainly at least possible that managerial society, when consolidated, will develop its own kind of democracy - though not, it would seem, a parliamentary democracy, and certainly not capitalist democracy; it is even possible that the

Neither Capitalism nor Socialism

transition to managerial society could be accomplished democratically.}

The achievement and consolidation of the managerial revolution faces a triple problem: the reduction to impotence of capitalist institutions (and thus of the capitalists) at home, and in the end also abroad; the curbing of the masses in such a manner that the masses accept the new order of managerial society; competition among various sections of the managers for dominant positions in the world.

The second step, it should be remarked, though it requires at certain intervals the use of force, above all demands a change of ideological and institutional allegiance. The masses must be led to accept one or another variant of the managerial institutions and the ideologies built upon the basis of managerial concepts and slogans; they must, we might say, come to see the (social) world in managerial terms. When that happens, the general structure of managerial society is reasonably assured; conflicts remain possible and likely, but they take place within the framework of managerial society, do not endanger its foundations, do not threaten to move toward the restoration of the capitalist structure or toward the overthrow of all forms of class structure - that is, toward socialism.

There is no pre-arranged temporal order in which these three parts of the managerial problem must be solved. Many different patterns or combinations are possible, and several are already being witnessed. Local social , political, cultural circumstances and even the specific influence of local leaders and organized political groups may rightly be expected to affect the patter which we discover in any given instance. For example:

The Russian Revolution we must understand not as a socialist but as a managerial revolution. As soon as we make this shift, the general course of Russian events becomes intelligible. Instead of spending all our time "explaining " why Russia has "deviated" from the socialist course, has failed to develop as expected, has constantly done the opposite of what theory demanded, we are able to show through the theory of the managerial revolution how Russia has developed consis-

The Hitler–Stalin Pact

tently along the lines to be deduced from theory, granted the specific circumstances of the Russian position. The triple managerial problem in Russia was worked out as follows: First, in a rapid and drastic fashion, the capitalist institutions and the capitalists at home were reduced to impotence; and, after an armed defense, a temporary truce was reached with capitalist institutions and capitalists abroad. Then (though this second step began during the solution of the first step), more gradually, the masses were curbed in such a manner as to lead them to accept the new exploiting order. The curbing of the masses began long before the death of Lenin (Lenin's and Trotsky's leadership in the smashing of the power of the Factory Committees and of the autonomy and rights of the trade unions and local soviets were decisive early moves, for instance); Stalin's definitive victory and the Moscow Trials merely symbolized the completion of the second part of the triple managerial problem. The Nazi-Soviet Pact and the inability of Britain to move against Russia during the Finnish war showed that capitalism from abroad was no longer capable of overturning the new order. The third part of the managerial problem remains: the competition with other sections of the managers for first fruits in the managerial world system. In this competition, the Russian weaknesses indicate that Russia will not be able to endure, that it will crack apart, and fall toward east and west.

Russia has today advanced furthest, from a structural or institutional point of view, toward the managerial goal. The rest of the world, however, plainly moves in the same general direction, though the specific route being followed need not be the same as the Russian. In Germany, for example, the pattern for the solution of the triple managerial problem is different, though the problem and the outcome are the same. The order of the first two stages in Germany is on the whole the reverse of what we found in the case of Russia. In Germany, the curbing of the masses, their redirection into managerial channels, by and large preceded the reduction of the home capitalists and capitalist institutions to impotence; and the undermining of the capitalists abroad proceeds along with the process of completing the

55

Neither Capitalism nor Socialism

reduction of the capitalists at home. This account is, however, too rigidly schematicized. In actual fact, the reduction of the home capitalists began, by a partial voluntary abdication, along with the curbing of the masses - the capitalists themselves seeing in this partial abdication their sole desperate chance of avoiding the more immediate and drastic Russian pattern (which it did, but as it turns out with no long term difference in the process as a whole, except for the better chance it gives individual capitalists to integrate themselves into the new order). The exile of Thyssen and the earlier retirement of Schact signify the recognition by German capitalism of the error in the original hope that Nazism was the savior of German capitalism, the understanding that Nazism is merely a variant pattern in the liquidation of capitalism.

As in the case of Russia, so with Germany, the third part of the managerial problem - the contest for dominance with other sections of managerial society - remains for the future. First had to come the death blow that assured the toppling of the capitalist world order, which meant above all the destruction of the foundation of the British Empire (the keystone of the capitalist world order) both directly and through the smashing of the European political structure which was a necessary prop of the Empire. This is the basic explanation of the Nazi-Soviet Pact, which is not intelligible on other grounds. The future conflict between Germany and Russia will be a managerial conflict proper; prior to the great world-managerial battles, the end of the capitalist order must be assured. The belief that Nazism is "decadent capitalism" (which is besides prima facie implausible in that not Nazi Germany but France and England have displayed all the characteristics which have distinguished decadent cultures in past historical transitions) makes it impossible to explain reasonably the Nazi-Soviet Pact. From this belief followed the always-expected war between Germany and Russia, not the actual war to the death between Germany and the British Empire. The war between Germany and Russia is one of the managerial wars of the future, not of the anti-capitalist wars of yesterday and today. In the United States , by virtue of relative geographical isolation and enormous resources, the revolution lags somewhat behind, but it is already well enough advanced to indicate the same general direction and outcome. New Dealism, both in its practical measures and in its ideology, can now be seen to be a managerial movement and belief, at a more primitive level, with more capitalist hangovers, than Bolshevism or Nazism. This the "Tories" (that is, the capitalists) have, from shortly after the beginning, recognized and attested in 1940, by overwhelming and "principled" opposition to Roosevelt's re-election. How ridiculous to attribute this opposition to failure on the part of the Tories to understand "their own true interests"! The Tories include many shrewd and intelligent men. They oppose New Dealism because they see that New Dealism in its consequences is directed against capitalism and thus against themselves. And already, plainly, the power is shifting from the capitalist hands into those of the managers and administrators, and their bureaucratic colleagues. The locus of sovereignty, already, has nearly completed its shift from parliament (Congress) to the administrative boards and bureaus. Private enterprise - necessarily the decisive basis of capitalism, for the capitalist is the private owner - gives way to the state. New Dealism is not Nazism, any more than Nazism is Bolshevism. There is not a formal identity among the three; but they are nonetheless linked historically. They are, all three, variant patterns of the way toward the same goal, differing in their stage of development as well as in their local background; they are three of the possible routes from capitalist society to managerial society. And in the war to come - which has, in reality, already started - the social transformation in the United States will leap forward.

We may, from the point of view of the managerial revolution, discover the historical significance of the first two world wars. In brief: the war of 1918 was the last great war of capitalism; the present war is the first great formative war of managerial society.

The first world war, we might say, was a final convulsive effort by capitalism to find a cure for the diseases which were already, below the skin, eating its substance away. Instead of a cure, as so often

Neither Capitalism nor Socialism

results from such desperate efforts, the disease was only spread and made mortal. The course of the war itself showed that capitalism was ending its days, by: the outright breaking off of an important section of the world (Russia) from the capitalist structure; the cumulative weakening of capitalist institutions in all nations together with the growth of new (managerial) institutions; the fact that, unlike the previous wars of capitalism, the war of 1914-18 was unprofitable for both victors and losers, whereas earlier wars were invariably profitable for the victors and often for the losers as well; the demonstrated inability to devise a workable peace.

From 1928 on, a renewed and far more devastating crisis set in, as shown not merely by the unparalleled economic depression but equally plainly by the consolidation of Stalinism and Nazism, the rupture of the state from its traditional capitalist limits in all other nations, and the beginning of the breakup of the political order (Manchuria, Ethiopia, Spain, the spread of Germany, and finally the new war).

The political division of the world into a comparatively large number of sovereign states, each with its armies and forts and currencies and tariffs and civil bureaucracies, is no longer workable for modern society with its complex division of labor and its needs for wider planning, control and trade exchanges. But in the Versailles peace, capitalism demonstrated that it was unable to smash the traditional political structure. The preservation of capitalism in the victorious powers (above all ion England, the heart of capitalist society) meant the continuation of capitalist-nationalist divisions, indeed their exaggeration; but such divisions, the last generation has proved, cannot any longer endure. The process of changing the world political structure involves also a change in the world social structure. The second world war comprises major initial steps in both these changes.

Already the world system of managerial society emerges: a comparatively small number of "super-states," fighting for and dividing the world among themselves. An economic map suggests the probable

The Hitler–Stalin Pact

outcome will be three great super-states, each based on one of the three main areas of advanced industry: north central Europe; the United States, especially the northeastern United States; Japan together with the east coast of China. In the future conflicts the managerial super-states of tomorrow cannot, in reality, hope to achieve a definitive military conquest of each other. The struggle will actually be, not for control over the central areas of advanced industry - the European area will already be ruled by Europeans, the East Asian by Asiatics, the United States area by Americans - but for prime shares in the rest of the world.

The world conflict, however, is not at all divorced from the internal social transformation. On the contrary, as so frequently in history, war speeds up and spreads the revolution. Those nations (Russia, Germany) which have gone furthest toward the managerial structure, carry their new institutions with their tanks and bombs. Their influence acts also by contagion in the nations which they have not conquered by direct military means. Within their own borders, they are forced to speed the rate of social change in order to keep going - a fact well symbolized by the increasing "radicalization" of Hitler's speeches during the course of the war. And the opposing nations are compelled to adopt the managerial methods in order to meet the challenge.

The United States, for example, approaches the world conflict socially unprepared. Already it is discovering that the institutions of capitalism do not permit it to compete adequately with its great rivals on the economic, military and ideological fronts. The economic integration of Latin America, essential to the survival of the American super state, is blocked by the fact that from a capitalist point of view such integration is not profitable. The building of an adequate military machine is prevented by the same cause. And, ideologically, the concepts and slogans and beliefs of capitalism are unable to arouse the masses. Since it is unlikely that the United States will decline its potential place in the new world system, as the isolationists in effect advise, we may feel sure that at an ever-increasing rate the United

Neither Capitalism nor Socialism

States will take those means necessary for the fulfillment of its "destiny": that is, will move evermore rapidly toward the managerial social structure. The managerial revolution is a world social revolution. Against a world revolution, even a six-ocean Navy would doubtless prove not enough.

Partisan Review Vol. 8, No. 3, 1941

THE END OF CAPITALISM IN GERMANY - Dwight Macdonald

The aim of this article is to show that the present German economy cannot be called 'capitalistic,' that it is a new and different kind of system (which I call, for lack of a better term, 'bureaucratic collectivism'). This view is, at present, rejected by most Marxists. It is more than a quarrel over terminology. For if the Nazi economy is still basically capitalistic, then we may expect it to be weakened in the future by the classic 'contradictions' of capitalism, then we may look for future revolutionary movements against fascism to assume the traditional proletariat vs. bourgeois form, then this war is essentially a repetition of the last war and the issue is merely whether Germany this time will be able to challenge successfully the Anglo-American domination of the world market. If, however, Germany is not capitalist, then all these future developments may be expected to take on quite different forms. I should add that, as I wrote in "National Defense: the Case for Socialism" (PARTISAN REVIEW, July-August, 1940), the non-capitalist nature of German economy, far from being a reason for supporting the present British and American governments in this war, seems to me to make more imperative than ever the establishment first of a democratic socialist government through the revolutionary action of the working class.

Let me begin with a very brief statement of just what I conceive 'capitalism' to be. (For a more detailed treatment, see my article, "What is the Fascist State?" in *The New International* for February 1941.) In his introduction to *The Living Thoughts of Karl Marx,* Trotsky writes:

The Hitler–Stalin Pact

In contemporary society, man's cardinal tie is exchange. Any product of labor that enters into the process of exchange becomes a commodity. Marx began his investigation with the commodity and deduced from that fundamental cell of capitalist society those social relations that have objectively shaped themselves on the basis of exchange, independently of man's will. Only by pursuing this course is it possible to solve the fundamental puzzle - how, in capitalist society, in which each man thinks for himself and no one thinks for all, are created the relative proportions of the various branches of economy indispensable to life ...

This means that, after all, chaos is not chaos at all, that in some way it is regulated automatically, if not consciously ... By accepting and rejecting commodities, the market, as the arena of exchange, decides whether they do or do not contain within themselves socially necessary labor, and thereby determines the ratios of the various kinds of commodities necessary for society.

Marx's *Capital* begins:"The wealth of those societies in which the capitalist mode of production prevails presents itself as an 'immense accumulation of commodities." A commodity Marx describes as a very queer thing, abounding in metaphysical subtleties and theological niceties." This is because commodities are "both objects of utility and, at the same time, depositories of value," that is, they exist as both "use values" and "exchange values." Since they obviously posses use value under slavery, feudalism or any non-capitalist form of economy, it is their exchange value which gives them their specifically capitalist character.

This seems to me a reasonably accurate description of how capitalism works. There are two main elements: production is regulated by exchange, that is, by the prospect of the individual and corporate property owners making a profit by selling their goods on the market;

Neither Capitalism nor Socialism

this market regulates "not consciously" but as an impersonal, autonomous mechanism working "independently of man's will."

In Germany today the market still exists, but it has lost its autonomy: it does not determine production, but is used merely as a means of measuring and expressing in economic terms the production which is planned and controlled by the Nazi bureaucracy. The old capitalist forms exist, but they express an entirely new content. Since 1936, production in Germany has not been determined by the market but by the needs of *Wehrwirtschaft*: guns, tanks, shoes, steel, cement are produced in greater or lesser quantities not because there is more or less prospect of making profits on this or that commodity, but because this or that is considered more or less useful for making war. Economically, this is production for use, the use being, of course, a highly undesirable one from the social point of view. Nor is this production controlled by a market mechanism working "independent of man's will" but by a bureaucratic apparatus which plans production (as against the well-known "anarchy" of capitalist production) and which consciously and willfully works out the best solution to the particular problem. No individual producer "thinks for himself"; on the contrary, if not one man, at least a small group of top bureaucrats, "think for all". Trotsky speaks of each individual producer having "his own private plan," but Dr. Ley of the Labor Front says: "There are no longer any private people. All and everyone are Adolph Hitler's soldiers, and a soldier is never a private person."

For many years now, capitalism in every advanced country has faced two great problems: how to overcome the increasingly deep contradiction between the forms of private property and the socialized nature of large-scale industrial production, enough to at least permit the survival of organized society; how to prepare adequately for war, the only way that these internal economic contradictions can obtain even a temporary solution.

The two problems are closely connected: war is the supreme test of any modern nation, for in war its very existence is staked; and war is a *social* undertaking, demanding far more centralized control and

The Hitler–Stalin Pact

planning, far more subordination of private property interests to national interests than peacetime production does; the disorganization of the economy characteristic of advanced capitalism makes impossible the effective prosecution of modern war. The only power which can control, if not solve, these contradictions, whether in peace or in war, is the State power. The economic crisis which began in 1929 gave a tremendous impulsion to State control of economy throughout the world. Our own New Deal, for example, was forced to take measures which a few years earlier would have been denounced as socialistic - but which even Wall Street (as witness the Wilkie campaign) today recognizes as permanent and necessary. But if economic crisis stimulates large-scale State intervention into the economy, war gives an enormously greater stimulus. To prepare for a modern war, which demands that production not only be raised to maximum capacity but also that it be directed into new channels and coordinated on a national scale - to do this, the State power must intervene decisively to free the objectively 'socialized' instruments of production from the fetters of archaic property forms. This in turn means that both the bourgeoisie as a class and also bourgeois property relations increasingly lose their validity, an a new ruling class, the State bureaucracy, capable of controlling production on a national scale, arises. In Germany, where for various well-known historical reasons, the problems both of economic crisis and of war economy facing modern capitalism presented themselves in a far more intense form than in any other advanced capitalist nation, in Germany the solution has taken on a correspondingly acute form. But in all capitalist nations, the bourgeoisie face the same dilemma faced by the German bourgeoisie: they cannot survive without war, but in order to make war, they must allow the State to destroy the basic forms of capitalism. There is only one historical alternative to this development: socialism. The fate of our civilization depends on whether the working class is able to turn history into this channel in the next period.

This process is going on in all advanced capitalist nations, and it will continue throughout the next historical period, until and unless

Neither Capitalism nor Socialism

socialist revolution intervenes. This is not a matter of 'just a war economy' or of a 'long-term investment by the bourgeoisie' - what a ridiculous shop-keeper's mentality to think in such terms in a period when the very bases of post-1800 society are dissolving before our eyes! For the great fact of the epoch we are now entering on is that war is no longer as interruption of the 'normal' peacetime development of capitalism, but has become, as Trotsky came to recognize in the last months of his life, *the normal mode of existence of our society.* As he wrote in his last article:

We should understand that the life of this society, politics, everything will be based upon war ... In this epoch, every great question, national or international, will be resolved with arms.

The new 'military' program he proposed, in taking the army as well as the factory, as a *normal* arena of class struggle henceforth, recognizes pragmatically - however reluctant Trotsky was to make any explicit revisions of basic theory - that the old concepts of class struggle must be reshaped.

We should read again, with the Nazi economy in mind, Marx's description of the death agony of capitalism:

> The monopoly of capital becomes a fetter upon the mode of production, which has sprung up and flourished along with it and under it. Centralization of the means of production and socialization of labor at last reach a point where they become incompatible with their capitalist integument. The integument is burst asunder. The knell of capitalist private property sounds. The expropriator are expropriated.

Marx expected the working-class to break the shell. It is one of the bitterest ironies of history that the workingclass proved incapable of doing so, and that this economically progressive and historically necessary task has been accomplished by a political movement reactionary to the point of barbarism, and working in the interest of a more effective prosecution of war. It is unpleasant and disheartening

The Hitler–Stalin Pact

to have to recognize that the Nazis and not the proletariat have shattered the structure of capitalism, and that the result has not been the social progress anticipated by Marxists but instead war and reaction in their most hideous forms. Yet how can one read such a passage and not see that the totalitarian State has done, *economically*, just what Marx and Lenin looked to the proletariat to do, namely, created new economic forms which correspond more closely to the 'socialization of production' than do the old private property forms?

From Schact's NRA to Goering's Four Year Plan

No one denies that there have been profound economic changes in Germany since 1933; no one denies that there has been considerable friction between the German big bourgeoisie and the Nazi bureaucracy. The historical problem is whether these changes, these conflicts involve issues fundamental to the continuance of capitalism itself, or whether - as in the case of our own New Deal era - they have taken place within the general framework of capitalism. It is my belief that, in both internal and foreign policy, the struggle of the last five years between the German business community and the Nazis involved basic issues, that the very existence of capitalism is at stake, and that the Nazis have by now decisively won the battle. In this section I want to sketch the main outlines of this historical development.

Three main periods may be defined: March, 1933 to June, 1934: struggle between the petty-bourgeois 'plebeians' or 'radicals' in the Nazi ranks and the big bourgeoisie, ending in the crushing of the former, once and for all,[1] by the top Nazi leadership in the June, 1934 'blood purge;' July, 1934 to September, 1936: supremacy of the big bourgeoisie, expressed in the 'economic dictatorship' exercised by Dr. Schact as Minister of Economics and head of the Reichsbank; this domination challenged by the Nazi bureaucracy with increasing strength all through the period. October, 1936 to the present: inauguration of the Second Four Year Plan; elimination, by the beginning of 1938, from key posts of the representatives of the big bourgeoisie, the Junkers, and the traditional army leaders;[2] concentration of all power

65

Neither Capitalism nor Socialism

- economic, political, military - into the hands of the bureaucracy; creation of a non-capitalist, planned, totalitarian, production-for-use economy.

Of the first period (1933-1934), I need only say here that I agree in general with the analysis of such Marxists as Dutt and Guerin: that big business put the Nazis into power, that the petty-bourgeois masses who followed Hitler were dupes, and that, in the first year of State power, the Nazi top leadership was primarily the tool of finance capital.

The second period began with the appointment, a month after the 'blood purge,' of Dr. Schact as Minister of Economics. (He retained his presidency of the Reichsbank, thus controlling the two key posts in the economy.) For the next two years Schact, in closest collaboration with the Army, heavy industry and finance capital, directed and reshaped the German economy. The "New Plan" he evolved represented the kind of economic policy these conservative groups wanted. Its most radical departures were in the field of foreign trade, where Schact was forced to take the first giant step towards a totalitarian economy: the creation of what was, in effect, a State monopoly of foreign trade. Inside Germany, the 'New Plan' was much less drastic. It resembled the contemporaneous New Deal recovery program in many ways: vast sums were spent on roads and public buildings; jobs were 'made' by using as much hand labor as possible; the decisive control was in the hands not of the politicians but of Schact and the still powerful trade associations. The conservative nature of the Plan is indicated in *Fortune's* comment on it: "Hitler only took longer steps where his predecessor had taken shorter ones." Thus much of the public works program had been planned by the preceding governments of Bruning, Schleicher and Papen, and the crucial sector of price control was left to the same official who had been Bruning's Price Commissar - which is to say prices were not effectively controlled.

Schact's "New Plan" failed to solve Germany's economic problems precisely because it was conservative. Writing in 1935 in Palme Dutt's *Labour Monthly*, a Marxist economist, R. Brown, predicted the Plan's

The Hitler–Stalin Pact

collapse because:(1) "The State planning of foreign trade is impossible under a system based on anarchic private capitalist production." (2) "The Fascist State is endeavoring to control prices but is actually powerless even to carry out a real system of rationing war materials and foodstuffs." Brown's prediction was accurate: the "New Plan" did collapse, and for the reasons he gave. He was also correct when he noted: "Finance capital is completely opposed to any State control of production or markets." As he pointed out, the Nazis faced a dilemma: a great deal *more* State intervention was necessary, and yet their big bourgeois 'masters' were insisting on *less*. Hence, Brown concluded, logically enough in his terms, that the "New Plan" would not be extended but curtailed, and that economic breakdown would follow. He was, of course, unable to foresee that the dilemma would be resolved by the dethronement of the 'masters' by the 'puppets,' and that the relatively mild 'New Plan' would be succeeded by the totalitarian Second Four Year Plan.

When the New Deal's economic program collapsed, also because it was a conservative *capitalist* measure where much sterner remedies were needed, the only effect was the severe depression of 1937-38. In Germany, however, the failure of Schact's program had more serious results, for three reasons: the economic crisis in Germany was so severe as to make it politically impossible to permit a depression; both the politicians and the big bourgeoisie, for reasons of foreign policy which did not then obtain here, agreed that an extensive rearming program was immediately necessary; political power was held not by a reformist government of the traditional democratic-capitalist type but by a totalitarian party with a large mass base, a "radical" (demagogically) program, and a ruthless and opportunist leadership which was not particularly interested in preserving capitalism, or indeed in any general principles. This party was able to take the drastic social and economic measures necessary to meet the situation.

These measures received their formal expression in the Second Four Year Plan, a turning-point in the German economy comparable to the Moscow Trials in the political evolution of Stalinism. Hitler

Neither Capitalism nor Socialism

proclaimed the Plan in an appropriate setting: at the annual Party Congress in Nuremberg. In his speech of September 9,1936 Hitler outlined the objectives of the Plan: to organize the nation at once on a war footing, to produce arms in huge quantities, above all, to make Germany independent of the world market for foodstuffs and industrial raw materials.

The magnitude of the last task - making Germany self-sufficient in raw materials - may be indicated by the fact that , in 1936, Germany produced no rubber, nickel or sulphur; practically no oil or tin; and much less iron ore, copper lead and timber than she needed. The only important industrial raw materials she produced in sufficient quantities for her (peacetime) needs were coal, zinc, manganese and potash. The Four Year Planners proposed that, instead of continuing to depend on the world market for these materials, ersatz materials be synthetically produced top replace them. This has meant fantastic expense - buna rubber costs four to six times what the natural product costs on the world market - but this expense was more than outweighed, in totalitarian economics, by the political advantages. So in the last four years Germany has developed quantity production of oil by hydrogenation from coal, of 'cell' wool from wood, of buna rubber from coal and limestone, and of a hundred lesser synthetic products, not to mention the exploitation by the State-owned Hermann Goering Iron Works of large deposits of low-grade iron ore (which private business had refused to work on the grounds of unprofitability). These technological miracles have been achieved in expensive plants for which the State has forced private business to put up most of the capital.

The Four Year Plan Authority became the supreme dictator of German economy. Its six major branches were concerned with:increasing the production of raw materials; distributing all raw materials on the basis of military utility; distributing the nation's labor power in the same way; increasing agricultural production; keeping prices and wages stable; controlling foreign exchange and foreign trade.

The Hitler–Stalin Pact

The only comparable system, in scope and completeness of control, was the Five Year Plan inaugurated in Russia in 1929. No capitalist 'war economy' - not even Britain's today after eighteen months of war - is of the same order.

The business community protested violently against the Second Four Year Plan because it clearly meant: greatly increased State control of business; enormous 'unproductive' and 'uneconomic' expenses for an even bigger bureaucracy and the creation of whole new *ersatz* industries; cutting off Germany once for all from the world market and international capitalism, rejecting all compromise and preparing for war.

Their protest, however, could take no very formidable shape: they had their chance to solve Germany's problems their way, under Schact, and had failed. A new power, largely of their creation, had now arisen and was soon to demonstrate the economic superiority of its non-capitalist methods.

Neither Schact nor the business community he represented was consulted in the matter of creating the new Plan. Schact's program - "economy in government, retardation of the Four Year Plan, and concentration on export trade" - speedily became only a memory as the Nazis drove ahead on the road of autarchy and rearmament.

There is no space to detail the history of the next four years. The main trend may be suggested:

October 19, 1936: Hitler appoints Goering chief of the Four Year Plan and supreme economic dictator of the Reich.

November 26, 1936: The Nazi bureaucrat, Josef Wagner, newly appointed Price Commissar under the Plan, issues general price-freezing decree. Henceforth all price, increases are forbidden, except on special authorization from his office.

December 1, 1936: Goering decrees the death penalty for all Germans who evade the restrictions on taking money or property out of the country.

February 13, 1937: The Reichsbank, hitherto the quasi-independent fortress of German finance capital, is 'coordinated' - "placed under

Neither Capitalism nor Socialism

Chancellor Hitler's direct authority as an organ of the German Government."

November 26,1937: Schact resigns as Minister of Economics, is replaced by Funk, Goering's man.' The N.Y. Times comments on "this final step in a long drawn-out careful program whereby Schact has been let out of active direction of the Reich's economic affairs. The problem from the first has been how Dr. Schact could be removed from authority, and control could be centralized in General Goering's hands, without too great a shock to the home and foreign business communities."

February 4, 1938: The Nazis execute a 'bloodless purge' of the conservative opposition in all spheres.

Economic: "The complete reorganization of the Ministry of Economics into the executive organ of Field Marshal Goering's Four Year Plan was announced today. Nothing is left of the old departments of the Ministry ..."

Foreign Policy: Purge in the Foreign office. The Nazi extremist, Von Ribbentrop, becomes Foreign Minister, replacing the ultra-conservative Von Neurath, the last of the old pre-1933 cabinet ministers to go.

The Army: The long struggle between the Nazis and the traditional Army generals ends in victory for the former. Fifteen generals retire, twenty-two get new commands. The two leading personalities in the Army, the pro-Nazi War Minister Von Blomberg and the openly anti--Nazi Commander in Chief Von Fritsch, both retire. The Army high command goes to two, obscure, colorless and non-political generals, Keitel and Brauchitsch. Goering is made Field Marshall, ranking him above all other generals. Von Blomberg has no successor as War Minister; Hitler assumes "personal and direct command over all the armed forces."

March 11,1938: Hitler occupies Austria. (It is now clear that the February 4 purge was in preparation for this move, which was widely opposed in Army and big business circles)

The Hitler–Stalin Pact

January 20, 1939: Schacht is suddenly removed by Hitler from the presidency of the Reichsbank, shortly after 'appeasement' visit by Montagu Norman, of the Bank of England, to Schacht in Berlin. Funk becomes new Reichsbank head.

September 5,1939: Goering appoints Nazi leaders as regional 'Reich Defense Commissars' in war economy.

December 28,1939: Four Year Plan Authority is superseded by the 'Economic General Staff' as supreme dictator of Reich economy. This Staff made up entirely of Nazi bureaucrats and State officials, no businessmen.}

The orthodox Marxist view of the relationship between big business and the State is well formulated in Hilferding's *Das Finanzkapital:* "Economic power is also political power ... The rule over the economy means control over the means of power of the State...Finance capital in its perfection is the highest stage of economic and political power in the hands of a capitalist oligarchy. It completes the dictatorship of the capitalist magnates." [This quotation, from the 1920 edition (p. 510), is taken from a forthcoming book by Guenter Reimann, "The Myth of the Total State," the manuscript of which the author very kindly allowed me to read.] As things have actually worked out in Germany, this formulation needs to be stood on its head: political power is also economic power; control over the State means rule over the economy. The German big bourgeoisie no longer 'use' the Nazi bureaucracy, the relationship is reversed. Schacht, the responsible representative of heavy industry and finance capital, has been deprived even of his control of the Reichsbank. His policies have been reversed. The National Economic Chamber and the other once powerful business associations have been stripped of the policy making powers they held up to 1936, and have been reduced to the role of administrative agencies through which the policies decided upon by the bureaucracy are transmitted to the business community. The various bodies set up since 1936 to decide national economic policy have included few, if any, representatives of the business community. [Three such bodies may be noted. First, the Second Four Year Plan Board, composed

Neither Capitalism nor Socialism

exclusively of Nazi bureaucrats and Army officers, with not even Schact on it. Second, the Privy Council Hitler set up after the February 1938, 'purge', whose eight members included not a single business spokesman. Third, the Economic General Staff set up by Goering, after the war began, to run the national war effort. Of its thirteen members, one was an Army officer, three were Nazi politicians, and nine were State secretaries in various ministries. There were jokes in business circles about the 'dictatorship of the secretariat' - and not only jokes.] In a word, the bourgeoisie have been displaced by a new ruling class, the bureaucracy; capitalism has yielded to bureaucratic collectivism.

2. Inside Germany: State Capitalism or Bureaucratic Collectivism ?

So much for the historical evolution of the present German economy. It has been shown that there was a basic policy conflict between the Nazis and the business community, that the policies of the former have triumphed, and that the groups and individuals representing the big bourgeoisie have been removed from the key economic controls since 1936. The question must still be answered, however: why isn't this simply the transition to 'State Capitalism,' the logical last stage of monopoly-capitalistic development? First there was the monopolization of individual branches of production - steel, coal, etc. - by powerful finance-capital groups. Now these monopolistic powers have united to form a 'super-trust' embracing the entire national economy, with the Nazis in political control as the famous 'executive committee of the bourgeoisie.' The rise of monopolies, the argument continues, has neither destroyed capitalism nor moderated the economic contradictions of capitalism, but on the contrary has intensified these contradictions. So why cannot we look for the development of the 'State-capitalist trust' to work the same way?

Such, in fact, has been the expectation of most Marxists during the last quarter-century. The early congresses of the Third International were well aware of the trend towards 'State Capitalism' which set in during the last war, and Lenin correctly predicted the future rise of "vast State-capitalist and military trusts." The crucial error of Marxist thought on this subject, however, was that it was expected that this historical trend would intensify the social and economic contradictions of capitalism - whereas it has actually resulted in the destruction of capitalism itself and, consequently, in the transposing of these contradictions into quite different terms. (To say that fascism is not threatened by the contradictions of capitalism is not to say that it hasn't its own contradictions, in some ways more serious than the capitalist ones.)

Consider, for example, Bukharin's *Imperialism and World Economy*. First published in 1915, this book is more to the point today than Lenin's better known *Imperialism*, since it deals mostly with the question which is so crucial today: State intervention into the capitalist economy. Bukharin's is an extraordinarily prescient book in some ways, and an extraordinarily short sighted one in others. Both in its vision and in its blindness it is typical of the twentieth century Marxist tradition.   Bukharin predicts in detail the rise of the 'State-capitalist trust':

> Competition reaches the highest, the last conceivable state of development. It is now the competition of State-capitalist trusts in the world market... The remnants of the old laissez-faire ideology disappear, the epoch of the new 'mercantilism', of imperialism begins... With the growth of the importance of State power, its inner structure also changes. The State becomes more than ever before an 'executive committee' of the ruling class... Thus the government is de facto transformed into a 'committee' elected by the representatives of entrepreneurs' organizations...

A remarkable passage to be written in 1915! Yet the really amazing thing is that Bukharin, like the other great Marxists, could have seen so clearly the line of development world capitalism was to take after the war without apparently recognizing, even as a theoretical possibility, the rise of 'State capitalism' might seriously affect and even

Neither Capitalism nor Socialism

destroy the capitalist system itself. It seems not to have occurred to either Lenin or Bukharin, even as a subject for speculation, that there might be profound differences between the economic monopolistic control, by private capitalist groups, of branches of production and the political ("totalitarian") monopoly exercised by politicians over the entire national economy. In his entire book, Bukharin touches on this theme only once, in a footnote:

> Were the commodity character of production to disappear - for instance through the organization of all world economy into one gigantic State trust, the impossibility of which we tried to prove in our chapter on ultra-imperialism - we would have an entirely new economic form. This would be capitalism no more, for the production of *commodities* would have disappeared; still less would it be *socialism*, for the power of one class over the other would have remained (and even grown stronger). Such an economic structure would, most of all, resemble a slave-owning economy where the slave market is absent.

This is such an interesting adumbration of what actually has come about in Germany that one regrets all the more keenly that Bukharin did not carry it further. It is worth noting, in passing, that Bukharin can conceive of production losing its commodity character and hence ceasing to be capitalist if a single *world* trust should arise - the reason being, of course, that in that case international competition would cease and the world market would have no meaning. But he fails to see that likewise, once a *national* monopoly has been established within a single nation, those same market-commodity relations are also destroyed and for the same reasons as would be the case on the world market.

The defects of the traditional Marxist conception of the coming 'State capitalist trust' as merely a mechanical extension of *private* monopolism may be seen if we compare the economic effects of the two developments. It is now generally agreed that, while monopolistic

The Hitler–Stalin Pact

(or, more accurately, in most cases, 'oligopolistic') trusts establish a more orderly and 'planned' kind of economy within their own particular sectors of production, the effect on capitalistic economy as a whole is to intensify its contradictions. Far from moderating the swings of boom and depression, as Bernstein and the pre-1914 'revisionists thought would be the case, the rise of finance-capital monopolies has had the effect that Lenin and Luxemburg predicted it would have: greatly *intensified* crises.

The effect of the State-controlled national monopoly in Germany, however, has been the reverse: it has weakened, if not eliminated, the economic contradictions of capitalism. For a long time now, bourgeois and Marxist observers have been predicting imminent catastrophe in Germany, and yet the economy seems stronger today than ever: there is one-hundred percent production and employment, the State experiences little difficulty in maintaining its huge expenditures, inflation seems more remote today than in the early years of the Nazi regime.

[It would be interesting to compile a register of prophecies of disaster, from 1933 to 1939, made by economists outside Germany. Even, Dr. Schact, Reichsbank head and Economics Minister, became convinced that financial disaster lay ahead if spending were not reduced and finally came into such sharp opposition on the point that he had to be stripped of all his powers. His prophecies have not come true. Schact's case is a particularly striking example of the 'cultural lag' observable in thinking on this subject both in Marxists and in bankers, and for the same basic reason, that both think in terms of a capitalistic economy. Although Schacht himself created much of the ingenious economic machinery by which the Nazi State controlled the contradictions of capitalism, he was, after all, by training a banker and this proved more decisive than his recent experiences as a bureaucrat.]

Why this difference in the economic effects of private as against State monopoly? The chief economic advantage enjoyed by private trusts is that they exist in a predominantly market economy and hence are able to levy tribute with the iron hand of monopoly on the

Neither Capitalism nor Socialism

relatively weak and unorganized non-monopoly sections of the economy. "Monopoly organizations," writes Bukharin, "can overcome the tendency towards lowering the rate of profit by receiving monopoly super-profits at the expense of non-trustified industries." Private monopolies thus throw the national economy still further out of balance and bring on ever more severe crises because their whole strategy, their *raison d'etre* in fact, lies in taking advantage of and intensifying the disproportion between the monopolized and non-monopolized parts of the whole economy. As Lenin describes it in *Imperialism*: "At the same time monopoly, which has grown out of free competition, does not abolish the latter but exists alongside it and hovers over it, as it were, and, as a result, gives rise to a number of very acute antagonisms, friction and conflicts."

In the case of a 'State capitalist trust,' however, the whole economy is controlled by the State, and there exists no longer any free-market sector. Hence the kind of unbalances created by the growth of private monopolies do not arise. Furthermore, the State controls not only all branches of the national economy, but also all the main economic factors: prices, wages, production, investment, profits, consumption, foreign trade, bank rates. These are thus robbed of their primary character as the determinants of economic development and become secondary instruments manipulated by a new 'prime mover,' the State bureaucracy. And they therefore lose their power to determine decisively the course of the economy. Private monopolism *perverts* the capitalist market economy, State monopolism *negates* it.

"When a government has complete control over the man power and the material resources of a country," writes Stolper in his recent *German Economy*, "the only limit to the expansion of production is precisely this man power and these national resources." In such an economy, Marx's famous "laws of motion of capitalism" are of little practical importance. The State can solve its economic difficulties - so far as these are caused by the workings of capitalist factors - by almost any means it chooses, including, if necessary, a proclamation by the Fuhrer that the moon is made of green cheese, followed by a decree by the Four Year Plan Authority that all banks and corporations must subscribe a certain percentage of their capital to finance the Hermann Goering Cheese Works to exploit lunar food resources.

The well-known Social-Democratic economist, Rudolf Hilferding, author of the classic *Das Finanzkapital*, has formulated the problem of 'State capitalism' in a masterly way. [In an article published over here last year in *Proletarian Outlook*, a mimeographed political paper, and originally printed in the Russian Social-Democratic organ. the *Sotsialistichesky Vestnik* of Paris. It may be noted that the press recently reported that Hilferding has been turned over to the Nazis by the Vichy government.] The essential passages of his argument are as follows:

> The concept of 'State capitalism' does not stand any analysis from the economic point of view. Once the State has become the sole owner of all the means of production, it renders impossible the functioning of capitalist economy, it abolishes the very mechanism which keeps going the process of economic circulation. The capitalist economy is a market economy. The price which is determined by competition between property owners - 'in the last analysis' if only as a result of this competition that the law of value operates - in turn determines what is produced, the part of profit which is accumulated, the branches of industry in which all of this takes place, and how finally, in the continual process of overcoming of crises, there is established a certain balance between the various branches of industry. The capitalist economic system is governed by the laws of the market whose analysis was given by Marx, and the *autonomy* of those laws constitutes the determining characteristic of the capitalist system of production.
>
> However, what a government economy does is precisely to abolish the autonomy of the economic laws; it is not a market economy, but an economy for use. What is produced, and how it is produced, is no longer determined by the price but by the State planning commission which fixes the character and extent

Neither Capitalism nor Socialism

of production. To outward appearance, prices and wages still exist, but their function has changed entirely. They no longer determine the march of production. That is directed by the central government, which alone fixes both prices and wage scales. Prices and wages are now only instruments of distribution determining for every one his share in the sum total of what the central government allots to the population. They have now become the technical means of distribution, a method which is simpler than would be a direct order stipulating the amounts of various products (which have ceased to be 'commodities') to be received by each individual. The prices have become symbols of distribution, but they are no longer the regulators of the nation's economy. While the form has been maintained, the function has been completely changed.

Now it is true that in this passage Hilferding is concerned mainly with the Soviet economy, which he believes to be 'totalitarian' and not 'State capitalist.' (Hilferding, in fact, denies the theoretical possibility of the existence of *State* capitalism.) It is also true that in Germany you still have private property, at least in form, whereas in the Soviet Union you have instead collectivized property (again, however, I must insist,'at least in form'). This difference, however, is not very important because: private ownership of the means of production is not an exclusive feature of the capitalist system (since in the slave states of antiquity you also had private ownership, to name only one example), but rather, as Marx, Trotsky and Hilferding all agree, production for the *market* is the distinguishing feature; and
in any case, in Germany private property exists in form only, not in reality, since the State determines what use the 'owner' shall make of his 'property' - as must be the case once the State has brought under its totalitarian control the very foundation-stone of capitalist property relations, namely, the market.

In any case, Hilferding later on explicitly links up the above analysis with the present German and Italian economies:

The Hitler–Stalin Pact

One of the essential characteristics of the totalitarian government is the fact that it subordinates the economy to its aims. Economy no longer has its own laws, for it is now subject to direction from above. In proportion as this subjection is being carried out, market economy is transformed into an economy for use, the character and the extent of the needs being determined by the State administration. The example of German and Italian economy shows how in a totalitarian state such a management of economy, once it has been started, assumes greater and greater proportions and endeavors to become all-embracing, as was the case in Russia from the very beginning. Notwithstanding the great differences in the points of departure, the economic systems of the totalitarian regimes present an increasing similarity to each other. In Germany, too, the government, intent upon maintaining and strengthening its power, determines the character of production and accumulation; the prices lose their regulating function, become a means of distribution. Like the economy itself, those who are engaged in the management of the economic activities are more or less subordinated to the State; they become its assistants. Economy loses the priority which it possessed under a bourgeois system.

This does not mean, of course, that the economic spheres do not exert a considerable influence upon the government both in Germany and Russia. But they do not determine the contents of politics. The general policy is determined by a small circle of those who hold power. Their interests, their ideas about what is needed for the preservation, application and strengthening of their own power are the determining factors of their policy which they impose, as a law, upon the economic life that is subordinated to them. Hence the importance which the subjective element, the element of the 'unforseen' of the 'irrational' in political development has acquired in politics.

The believer knows only of heaven and hell. The Marxist sectarian knows only Capitalism and Socialism, he knows only of classes - the

Neither Capitalism nor Socialism

bourgeoisie and the proletariat - as determining forces. He cannot conceive the idea that modern State power, having become independent, develops its enormous strength according to its own laws, that it subjects the social forces and compels them to serve it.

In this remarkable analysis. Hilferding not only demonstrates the non-capitalist nature of a 'Statified' economy, but also suggests the general political conclusion to be drawn from this: that the decisive controls today are political and not economic. The world crisis of capitalism has reached such proportions that economics has become 'politicized', so to speak. Politics dominates economy, rafter than, as in the last century, the opposite. The great, perhaps the fatal, error made by Marxists in the post 1918 period was to attach too much significance to economic forms, whether capitalist or socialist, and too little to new methods of political control which have arisen and which have been used to manipulate these forms in such a way as to negate their content.

3. Outside Germany: Nazism and World Capitalism

The internal policies of the Nazis flowed logically from their conception of the relationship of Germany to world capitalism. It was on the field of foreign policy that the decisive struggle took place between the Nazi bureaucracy and the German business community. As in the conflict over internal economic policy, the Nazis won because their conceptions were closer to the realities of modern power politics than were those of the bourgeoisie. And the Nazi economic policies have had the same destructive effect on the world market and the world capitalist system as they have had on the capitalist structure of Germany itself.

By the year 1936, it was clear that Germany would have to choose between two possible foreign policies: to try to fit Germany into the world market, obtaining from the 'have' powers concessions of colonies and access to raw materials, coming to some agreement with them on tariffs and trading areas, and generally attempting to gain enough of an outlet in the world market for profitable use of Ger-

The Hitler–Stalin Pact

many's tremendous productive capacity; to turn away from the world market and international collaboration, concentrating the entire national energies on building up a war machine powerful enough to smash the rival imperialisms so as to take by force what Germany needed and, above all, to establish a political dominance over Germany's beaten enemies that would guarantee her future.

The first course meant, in essence, to attempt to reconstruct the depression-damaged world market and to create, through coming to a peaceful agreement with the other great imperialisms, a stable new world capitalist order in which Germany would have a position truly reflecting her economic power. This policy was favored by practically the entire business community, which saw clearly the dangers of revolution and economic ruin even a victorious Germany would run in a second world war, and which also realized the kind of internal economy which the alternative course would mean. There were appeasers inside as well as outside of Germany, and, as was also the case in other countries, they represented primarily the big business forces. In the years of his power, Schacht was the leading proponent of colonies, trading concessions, and international collaboration as the key to Germany's economic problem. The sad case of Dr. Rudolf Brinkmann, Schacht's successor at the Reichsbank, may also be cited. Dr. Brinkmann summed up the businessman's objections to autarchy thus: "A well-planned internal economy depends on exports...Let us beware of arrogance. It is wrong to proclaim to the rest of the world: "You want us, you are dependent on us." We should rather say: "We are all mutually interdependent." It may be relevant to note that, within a few weeks of his taking over the presidency of the Reichsbank, Dr. Brinkmann went into retirement, suffering from "a nervous breakdown with loss of memory."

The second course, that of autarchy, meant, internally, more State intervention than ever, enormous State expenditures, and, as Schact well knew, the replacement of the old capitalist profit economy by a bureaucratic production-for-use planned economy; externally, it meant abandonment of the perspective of a peaceful collaboration of

Neither Capitalism nor Socialism

world capitalism, war as soon as the economy was ready for it, and, in the event of a German victory, the extension of this new kind of economy to - in the first instance - the whole European continent. The worst fears of the German business community have been realized.

Inside Germany, the Nazis' policies won out over those favored by the business community because they were better adapted to gearing a highly industrialized society for a supreme *social* effort, namely, war. So too in the field of foreign policy, the Nazi policies also triumphed over those of the conservatives because they were based on a more realistic and profound understanding of the condition of world capitalism in the thirties than the German big bourgeoisie had. The Nazis realized that the perspective of international cooperation, of a reconstitution of the world market and some kind of a 'deal' between the major capitalist powers (perhaps at the expense of Russia) - that this was a bourgeois Utopia. They saw clearly that world capitalism was in desperate straits, that the great 'have' imperialisms could not afford the concessions that would have integrated Germany once more into the world economy, that the world market had been wrecked by the 1929 depression, and that international competition in a dwindling market - whatever pious hopes the bankers and rentiers of London and Paris might have of a peaceful settlement - was bound to become more and more cut-throat. For Germany, therefore, the only course of safety lay in autarchy, rearming, and territorial expansion as rapidly as her armed strength - and the weakness of her enemies - permitted. The German bourgeoisie underestimated the decadence of world capitalism in general, of the great 'have' capitalist powers in particular. The Nazis made neither mistake.

Now it is true that the fact that the Nazis' war program was better *realpolitik* than the bourgeoisie's appeasement program does not prove its non-capitalist character. It would be quite possible that the war aims of the Nazi bureaucracy were the traditional ones of capitalist imperialism, and that it was simply a case of the Nazis understanding better than their own bourgeoisie how to achieve these aims. This is not the case, however. The war aims of Germany - and the kind of

The Hitler–Stalin Pact

economic and political order that will be created if she wins the war - are radically different from those of all the great powers in the last war and from those of America and England in this war.

[Perhaps I should make it clear that, in my opinion, these aims are primarily *economic* and not an expression of the German soul (Rauschnig) or the expansive force of the German ego (Mumford). But to say that the Nazis are fighting for *economic* reasons is by no means to say that they are fighting for *capitalistic* reasons. The whole question is whether they will exploit their war gains within a capitalist or a non-capitalist framework.] In *Imperialism and World Economy*, Bukharin defines "three fundamental motives for the conquest policies of modern capitalist states: increased competition in the sales markets, in the markets of raw material, and for the spheres of capital investment." Imperialist war he sees as an effort to use force against competitors in these three fields. I think we can take this as a fair summary of the orthodox Marxist definition of capitalist war aims today. These aims presume the existence of a capitalist world market - international exchange of commodities, settlement of trade balances in gold, an international price structure, the international division of labor, etc.

Bukharin, by the way, admitted that possibly 'State capitalist trusts' would establish *national* monopolies, but not that the world market itself might be destroyed. Thus he deduced that, just as the effect of the establishment *within a single industry* of a stable, non-market economy by private monopolies was merely to increase the contradictions and anarchy of the *national economy as a whole*, so these *national* State monopolies would merely aggravate the chaos of the *world* market. His calculation, however, went astray for the same basic reason as his predictions as to the nature of the 'State capitalist trust' went astray: because when monopoly reached *national* proportions, the decisive factor in the economy changed from the capitalist market to the State bureaucracy - that is, political controls arose which displaced capitalist market laws as the primary determinants of economy, both national and world.

Neither Capitalism nor Socialism

Nazi trade methods on the world market have had the effect of destroying that market itself (instead of merely gaining for one nation a larger share at the expense of other nations). As we have seen, the Nazi bureaucracy in 1936 decided to cut German economy loose from the world market. Autarchy flew in the face of the international division of labor. The international price structure also lost much of its meaning as far as Germany was concerned, since the State, controlling foreign trade completely, was able to use Germany's buying and selling on the world market as a political weapon; the Nazis preferred to pay more for Bulgarian wheat than they would have had to pay for, say Canadian wheat, since it was politically desirable to draw Bulgaria closer to Germany. Finally, the whole complex apparatus of the capitalist world market - internationally determined prices, settlement of unfavorable trade balances in gold, three- or four-cornered trade - was short-circuited by the introduction by the Nazis of State barter deals.

These non-capitalist trading methods were evolved precisely because the disintegration of the world market - expressed in rising tariff walls, ever-increasing concentration of the world's gold in the United States, drastic cuts in imports by all nations - made it impossible for Germany, financially weakest of all major nations, to get via the world market the raw materials she needed. Is there any reason to believe that after this war the world market will be in a better state? How can it be reconstructed as long as eighty percent of the world's gold supply is held by the United States? In point of fact, the evolution is all the other way: Nazi trade methods have forced other nations to adopt them, as in the proposed Inter-American Cartel, whereby the United States government would extend its control over Latin America by the same kind of barter and subsidy deals Germany for years has been using in Central Europe. World trade has become a *political*, rather than an *economic* matter.

Thus two of Bukharin's three "fundamental motives for the conquest policies of modern capitalist states" - "increased competition in the sales markets" and "in the markets of raw materials" - are ruled out. His third "fundamental motive" Is "competition for the spheres of capital investment." Both Lenin and Bukharin saw the *export of capital* (i.e., investments by the bourgeoisie of an imperialist nation in mills, factories, railroads, utilities of colonial and backward nations) as characteristic features of 20th century imperialism. "Under the old type of capitalism, when free competition prevailed, the export of *goods* was the most typical feature," wrote Lenin. "Under modern capitalism, when monopolies prevail, the export of *capital* has become the typical feature." Unhappily - or happily, depending on your point of view - the fatal basic contradiction of capitalist imperialism - that the market itself, the mechanism through which the more advanced imperialist nations must exploit the backward and colonial nations, works so as to bring the backward nations up to the level of the advanced ones - this appears in its most extreme form in the typical form of 20th century imperialism: the export of capital. For to export capital means no more and no less than to put into the hands of the 'subjugated' nation not merely the products of modern industry but the very machines and factories and capital goods that produce these products. In a word to give them the instruments, in an era of war, to challenge ultimately their imperialist masters. (Thus, for example, the rebuilding and rationalizing of German industry in the twenties, the economic foundation of the Nazi war machine, was financed chiefly by huge loans - i.e., 'capital exports ' - from the United States.

And so we find the export of capital figuring not at all in Germany's postwar calculations. Even in the Balkans, a comparatively primitive region with plenty of openings for capital export, Germany is trying to lower, not raise, the level of production. Thus the first provision in an economic treaty forced on Yugoslavia in October and designed to integrate that country with the Nazis' "New European Order," was summarized by the *N.Y. Times* (October 15): "Yugoslavia must concentrate almost exclusively on increasing her agricultural production at the expense of any industrial development." And in the more advanced European nations Germany has conquered, where there is little room for capital export anyway, there have been many

Neither Capitalism nor Socialism

indications that in the "New European Order" Germany will try to create if she wins the war, the rest of Europe will be de-industrialized (i.e., there will be an export of capital *to* - not from - Germany!) as much as possible to permit the concentration of the more advanced types of industry within the borders of Germany. This is the long term perspective.

In the next few years - again if Germany wins - her economic relations with the conquered nations of Europe will have a different - but also a non-market - basis: the systematic stripping of the rest of Europe of the food, gold, raw materials and other property urgently needed by Germany for the continuance of her war effort. This is what Marx called 'primitive accumulation' - acquiring property not by exchange but by force. But was not this also practiced by the Allies on Germany after the last war? Not in the terms that Germany is now practicing it. It is significant that

> Germany never paid most of the reparations bill, and most of what she did pay was paid with money borrowed from American bankers.

That is, the Allies did not have the political control to force payment (the Ruhr occupation was a fiasco), and the conquered nation was actually able to borrow from one of the victors the means to pay the indemnity. In a word, the whole transaction took place not in the sphere of armed force but within the framework of peacetime capitalist market relations. This time, however, the victorious armies are in physical occupation of the conquered nations. And this time it is not a question of "indemnities" or "reparations" - conceptions of an *exchange* economy, so much gold and coal and ships being paid for so much destruction of enemy property, after which the payer is free from all obligation - but of a *permanent* adjustment of the political and economic structures of the occupied nations to fit the needs of the victor. And this time Germany, if she emerges victorious, is in a position not only to strip the defeated nations far more thoroughly than the Allies (not being in armed control of Germany;) could do in 1918, but also to reorganize the entire continent into an economic hinterland of Germany - as against the Balkanized *status quo* attempted by the Allies at Versailles.

Partisan Review - May-June 1941

IS RUSSIA A WORKERS' STATE - Max Shachtman

That the "Russian Question" should continue to occupy the attention of the revolutionary movement is anything but unusual. In the history of modern socialism there is nothing that equals the Russian Revolution in importance. It is indeed no exaggeration to write - we shall seek to reaffirm and demonstrate it further on - that this revolution does not have its equal in importance throughout human history.

For us, the historical legitimacy of the Bolshevik revolution and the validity of the principles that made its triumph possible, are equally incontestable. Looking back over the quarter of a century that has elapsed, and subjecting all the evidence of events to a soberly critical re-analysis, we find only a confirmation of those fundamental principles of Marxism with which the names of Lenin and Trotsky are linked, and of their appraisal of the class character and historical significance of the revolution they organized. Both - the principles and the appraisal - are and should remain incorporated in the program of our International.

Our investigation deals with something else. It aims to re-evaluate the character and significance of the period of the degeneration of the Russian revolution and the Soviet state, marked by the rise and triumph of the Stalinist bureaucracy. Its results call for a revision of the theory that the Soviet Union is a workers' state. The new analysis will be found to be, we believe, in closer harmony with the political program of the party and the International, fortifying it in its most important respects and eliminating from it only points which, if they correspond to a reality of yesterday, do not correspond to that of today.

In our analysis, we must necessarily take issue with Leon Trotsky; yet, at the same time, base ourselves largely upon his studies. Nobody has even approached him in the scope and depth of his contribution to understanding the problem of the Soviet Union. In a different way, to be sure, but no less solidly, his work of analyzing the decay of the Soviet Republic is as significant as his work of creating that Republic. Most of what we learned about Russia, and can transmit to others, we learned from Trotsky. We learned from him, too, the necessity of critical re-examination at every important stage, of regaining, even in the realm of theory, what was once already gained, or, in the contrary case, of discarding what was once firmly established but proved to be vulnerable. The garden of theory requires critical cultivation, re-planting, but also weeding out.

What new events, what fundamental changes in the situation, have taken place to warrant a corresponding change in our appraisal of the class character of the Soviet Union? The question is, in a sense, irrelevant. Our new analysis and conclusions would have objective merit or error regardless of the signature appended to them. In the case of the writer, if the question must be answered, the revision is the product of that careful re-studying of the problem urged upon him by both friends and adversaries in the recent dispute in the American section of the International. The outbreak of the second world war, while it produced no fundamental changes in the Soviet Union in itself, did awaken doubts as to the correctness of our traditional position. However, doubts and uncertainties cannot serve as a program, nor even as a fruitful subject for discussion. Therefore, while putting forward a position on those aspects of the disputed question on which he had firm opinions, the writer did not take part in what passed for a discussion on that aspect of the question which related to the class character of the Soviet Union. The founding convention of the Workers' Party provided for the opening of a discussion on this point in due time, and under conditions free from the ugly atmosphere of baiting, ritualistic phrase-mongering, pugnacious ignorance, and factional fury that prevailed in the party before our expulsion and the split. The writer has, meanwhile, had the opportunity to examine and reflect upon the problem, if not as much as would be desirable then at least sufficiently. "Theory is not a note which you can present at any moment to reality for payment," wrote Trotsky. "If a theory proves

The Hitler–Stalin Pact

mistaken we must revise it or fill out its gaps. We must find out those real social forces which have given rise to the contrast between Soviet reality and the traditional Marxist conception." We must revise our theory that Russia is a workers' state. What has up to now been discussed informally and without order, should now be the subject of an ordered and serious discussion. This article aims to contribute to it.

Briefly stated, this has been our traditional view of the character of them Soviet Union:

> The character of the social regime is determined first of all by property relations. The nationalization of land, of the means of industrial production and exchange, with the monopoly of foreign trade in the hands of the state, constitute the bases of the social order of the USSR. The classes expropriated by the October revolution, as well as the elements of the bourgeoisie and the bourgeois section of the bureaucracy being newly formed, could re-establish private ownership of land, banks, factories, mills railroads, etc., only by means of counter-revolutionary overthrow. By these property relations, lying at the basis of the class relations, is determined for us the nature of the Soviet Union as a proletarian state. (Trotsky, *Problems of the Development of the USSR.*, p.3. 1931)

But it is not a workers' state in the abstract. It is a degenerated, a sick, an internally-imperilled workers' state. Its degeneration is represented by the usurpation of all political power in the state by a reactionary, totalitarian bureaucracy led by Stalin. But while politically you have an anti-Soviet Bonapartist dictatorship of the bureaucracy, according to Trotsky, it nevertheless defends, in its own and very bad way, the social rule of the working class. This rule is expressed in the preservation of nationalized property. In bourgeois society, we have had cases where the social rule of capitalism is preserved by all sorts of political regimes - democratic and dictatorial, parliamentary and monarchical, Bonapartist and fascist. Yes, even under fascism, the

Neither Capitalism nor Socialism

bureaucracy is not a separate ruling class, no matter how irritating to the bourgeoisie its rule may be. Similarly in the Soviet Union. The bureaucracy is a caste not a class. It serves, as all bureaucracies do, a class. In this case, it serves - again, badly - to maintain the social rule of the proletariat. At the same time, however, it weakens and undermines this rule. To assure the sanitation and progress of the workers' state towards socialism, the bureaucracy must be overthrown. Its totalitarian regime excludes its removal by means of more or less peaceful reform. It can be eliminated, therefore, only by means of a revolution. The revolution, however, will be, in its decisive respects, not social but political. It will restore and extend workers' democracy, but it will not produce any fundamental social changes, no fundamental changes in property relations. Property will remain state property.

Omitting for the time being Trotsky's analysis of the origin and rise of the Stalinist bureaucracy, which is elaborated in detail in *The Revolution Betrayed*, we have given above a summary of the basic position held by us jointly up to now. So far as characterizing the class nature of the Soviet Union is concerned, this position might be summed up even more briefly as follows:

To guarantee progress towards socialism, the existence of nationalized property is necessary but not sufficient - a revolutionary proletarian regime is needed in the country, plus favorable international conditions (victory of the proletariat in more advanced countries). To characterize the Soviet Union as a workers' state, the existence of nationalized property is necessary and sufficient. The Stalinist bureaucracy is a caste. To become a new ruling class it must establish new property forms.

Except for the slogans of revolution, as against reform, which is only a few years old in our movement, this was substantially the position vigorously defended by Trotsky and the Trotskyist movement for more than fifteen years. The big article of Russia written by Trotsky right after the war broke out, marked, in our opinion, the first - and a truly enormous - contradiction of this position. Not that Trotsky abandoned the theory that the Soviet Union is a degenerated workers' state. Quite the contrary, he reaffirmed it. But at the same time he advanced a theoretical possibility which fundamentally negated his theory - more accurately, the motivation for his theory - of the class character of the Soviet state.

If the proletariat does not come to power in the coming period, and civilization declines still further, the immanent collectivist tendencies in capitalist society may be brought to fruition in the form of a new exploiting society ruled by a new bureaucratic class - neither proletarian nor bourgeois. Or, if the proletariat takes power in a series of countries and then relinquishes it to a privileged bureaucracy, like the Stalinist, it will show that the proletariat cannot, congenitally, become a ruling class and then " it will be necessary in retrospect to establish that in its fundamental traits the present USSR was the precursor of a new exploiting regime on an international scale." The historic alternative, carried to the end, is as follows: either the Stalin regime is an abhorrent relapse in the process of transforming bourgeois society into a socialist society, or the Stalin regime is the first stage of a new exploiting society. If the second prognosis proves to be correct, then, of course, the bureaucracy will become a new ruling class. However onerous the second perspective may be, if the world proletariat should actually prove incapable of fulfilling the mission placed upon it by the course of development, nothing else would remain except openly to recognize that the socialist program based on the internal contradictions of capitalist society, ended as a Utopia. It is self-evident that a new "minimum" program would be required - for the defense of the interests of the slaves of the totalitarian bureaucratic society.

But are there such incontrovertible or even impressive objective data as would compel us today to renounce the prospect of the socialist revolution? That is the whole question.[3]

That is not the whole question. To that question, we give no less vigorously negative a reply as Trotsky. There is no data of sufficient weight to warrant abandoning the revolutionary socialist perspective. On that score, Trotsky was and remains quite correct. The essence of the question, however, relates not to the perspective, but to the theoretical characterization of the Soviet state and its bureaucracy.

Up to the time of this article, Trotsky insisted on the following two propositions:

> Nationalized property, so long as it continues to be the economic basis of the Soviet Union makes the latter a workers' state, regardless of the political regime in power;

and,

> So long as it does not create new property forms unique to itself, and so long as it rests on nationalized property, the bureaucracy is not a new or an old ruling class, but a caste.

In the "USSR in War," Trotsky declared it theoretically possible - we repeat: not probable, but nevertheless theoretically possible -

> for the property forms and relations now existing in the Soviet Union to continue existing and yet represent not a workers' state but a new exploiting society;

and

> for the bureaucracy now existing in the Soviet Union to become a new exploiting and ruling class without changing the property forms and relations it now rests upon.

To allow such a theoretical possibility, does not eliminate the revolutionary perspective, but it does destroy, at one blow, so to speak, the theoretical basis for our past characterization of Russia as a workers' state.

To argue that Trotsky considered this alternative a most unlikely perspective, that, indeed (and this is of course correct), he saw no reason at all for adopting it, is arbitrary and beside the point. At best, it is tantamount to saying: At bottom, Russia is a workers' state because it rests on nationalized property and... we still have a social-revolutionary world perspective; if we abandoned this perspective, it would cease being a workers' state even though its property forms remain fundamentally unaltered. Or more simply: it is not nationalized property that determines the working class character of the Soviet state and the caste character of its bureaucracy; our perspective determines that.

If Trotsky's alternative perspective is accepted as a theoretical possibility (as we do, although not in quite the same way in which he puts it forward; but that is another matter), it is theoretically impossible any longer to hold that nationalized property is sufficient to determine the Soviet Union as a workers' state. That holds true, moreover, whether Trotsky's alternative perspective is accepted or not. The traditional view of the International on the class character of the USSR rests upon a grievous theoretical error.

Property Forms and Property Relations

In his writings on the Soviet Union, and particularly in *The Revolution Betrayed*, Trotsky speaks interchangeably of "property forms" and the "property relations" in the country as if he were referring to one and the same thing. Speaking of the new political revolution against the bureaucracy, he says: "So far as concerns property relations, the new power would not have to resort to revolutionary measures."[4] Speaking of the capitalist counter-revolution, he says: "Notwithstanding that the Soviet bureaucracy has gone far toward preparing a bourgeois restoration, the new regime would have to introduce into the matter of forms of property and methods of industry not a reform, but a social revolution."[5]

When referring to property forms in the Soviet Union, Trotsky obviously means nationalized property, that is, state ownership of the means of production and exchange continues to exist. It is further obvious that no Marxist will deny that, when the proletariat takes the helm again in Russia, it will maintain state property.

However, what is crucial are not the property forms, i.e., nationalized property, whose existence cannot be denied, but precisely the

Neither Capitalism nor Socialism

relations of various social groups in the Soviet Union to this property, i.e., property relations! If we can speak of nationalized property in the Soviet Union, this does not yet establish what the property relations are. Under capitalism the ownership of land and the means of production and exchange is in private (individual or corporate) hands. The distribution of the means or instruments of production under capitalism puts the possessors of capital in command of society, and of the proletariat, which is divorced from property and has only its own labor power at its disposal. The relations to property of these classes, and consequently the social relations into which they necessarily enter in the process of production, are clear to all intelligent persons.

Now, the state is the product of irreconcilable social contradictions. Disposing of a force separate from the people, it intervenes in the raging struggle between the classes in order to prevent their mutual destruction and to preserve the social order. "But having arisen amid these conflicts, it is as a rule the state of the most powerful economic class that by force of its economic supremacy becomes also the ruling political class and thus acquires new means of subduing and exploiting the oppressed masses," writes Engels. Under capitalism, "the most powerful economic class" is represented by its capitalist class state.

What is important to note here is that the social power of the capitalist class derives from its "economic supremacy," that is, from its direct ownership of the instruments of production; and that this power is reflected in or supplemented by its political rule of the state machine, of the "public power of coercion." The two are not identical, let it be noted further, for a Bonapartist or fascist regime may and has deprived the capitalist class of its political rule in order to leave its social rule, if not completely intact, then at least fundamentally unshaken.

Two other characteristics of bourgeois property relations and the bourgeois state are worth keeping in mind.

Bourgeois property relations and pre-capitalist property relations are not as incompatible with each other, as either of them are with socialist property relations. The first two have not only lived together

The Hitler–Stalin Pact

in relative peace for long periods of time but, especially in the period of imperialism on a world scale, still live together today. An example of the first was the almost one-century-old cohabitation of the capitalist North and the Southern slavocracy in the United States; an outstanding example of the second is British imperialism in India. But more important than this is a key distinction between the bourgeois and the proletariat. The capitalist class already has wide economic power before it overthrows feudal society and, by doing so, it acquires that necessary political and social power which establishes it as the ruling class.

Finally, the bourgeois state solemnly recognizes the right of private property, that is, it establishes juridically (and defends accordingly) that which is already established in fact by the bourgeoisie's ownership of capital. The social power of the capitalist class lies fundamentally in its actual ownership of the instruments of production, that is, in that which gives it its "economic supremacy," and, therefore, its control of the state.

How do matters stand with the proletariat, with its state, and the property forms and property relations unique to it? The young bourgeoisie was able to develop (within the objective limits established by feudalism) its specific property relations even under feudalism; at times, as we have seen, it could even share political power with a pre-capitalist class. The proletariat cannot do anything of the kind under capitalism, unless you except those utopians who still dream of developing socialism right in the heart of capitalism by means of "producers' cooperatives." By its very position in the old society, the proletariat has no property under capitalism. The working class acquires economic supremacy only after it has seized political power.

> We have already seen (said the *Communist Manifesto*) that the first step in the workers' revolution is to make the working class the ruling class, to establish democracy. The proletariat will use its political supremacy in order, by degrees, to wrest all capital from the bourgeoisie, to centralize all the means of production into the hands of the state (this meaning the proletariat orga-

nized as the ruling class), and, as rapidly as possible, to increase the total mass of productive forces.

Thus, by its very position in the new society, the proletariat still has no property, that is, it does not own property in the sense that the feudal lord or the capitalist did. It was and remains a propertyless class! It seizes state power. The new state is simply the proletariat organized as the ruling class. The state expropriates the private owners of land and capital, and ownership of land, and the means of production and exchange, become vested in the state. By its action, the state has established new property forms - nationalized or statified or collectivized property. It has also established new property relations. So far as the proletariat is concerned, it has a fundamentally new relationship to property. The essence of the change lies in the fact that the working class is in command of that state-owned property *because* the state is the proletariat organized as the ruling class (through its Soviets, its army, its courts and institutions like the party, the unions, the factory committees, etc.), There is the nub of the question.

The economic supremacy of the bourgeoisie under capitalism is based upon its ownership of the decisive instruments of production and exchange. Hence its social power; hence, the bourgeois state. The social rule of the proletariat cannot express itself in private ownership of capital, but only in its "ownership" of the state in whose hands is concentrated all the decisive economic power. Hence, its social power lies in its political power. In bourgeois society the two can be and are divorced; in the proletarian state, they are inseparable. Much the same thing is said by Trotsky when he points out that in contrast to private property, "the property relations which issued from the socialist revolution are indivisibly bound up with the new state as their repository."[6] But from this follows in reality what does not follow in Trotsky's analysis. The proletariat's relations to property, to the new, collectivist property, are indivisibly bound up with its relations to the state, to the political power.

We do not even begin to approach the heart of the problem by dealing with its juridical aspects, however. That suffices, more or less,

The Hitler–Stalin Pact

in a bourgeois state. There, let us remember, the juridical acknowledgment by the state of private ownership corresponds exactly with the palpable economic and social reality. Ford and Dupont own their plants...and their Congressmen; Krupp and Schroeder own their plants...and their Deputies. In the Soviet Union, the proletariat is master of property only if it is master of the state which is its repository. That mastery alone can distinguish it as the ruling class. "The transfer of the factories of the state changed the situation of the worker only juridically," Trotsky points out quite aptly.[7] And further: "From the point of view of property in the means of production, the differences between a marshal and a servant girl, the head of a trust and a day laborer, the son of a peoples' commissar and a homeless child, seem not to exist at all."[8] Precisely! And why not? Under capitalism, the difference in the relations to property of the trust head and the day laborer is determined and clearly evidenced by the fact that the former is the owner of capital and the latter owns merely his labor power. In the Soviet Union, the differences in the relations to property of the six persons Trotsky mentions is not determined or visible by virtue of ownership of basic property but precisely by the degree to which any and all of them "own" the state to which all social property belongs.

The state is a political institution, a weapon of organized coercion to uphold the supremacy of a class. It is not owned like a pair of socks or a factory; it is controlled. No class - no modern class - controls it directly, among other reasons because the modern state is too complicated and all-pervading to manipulate like a 17th century New England town meeting. A class controls the state indirectly, through its representatives, its authorized delegates.

The Bolshevik revolution lifted the working class to the position of ruling class in the country. As Marx and Engels and Lenin had foreseen, the conquest of state power by the proletariat immediately revealed itself as "something which is no longer really a form of the state." In place of "special bodies of armed men" divorced from the people, there rose the armed people. In place of a corrupted and bureaucratized parliamentary machine, the democratic Soviets

Neither Capitalism nor Socialism

embracing tens of millions. In the most difficult days, in the rigorous period of War Communism, the state was the "proletariat organized as the ruling class" - organized through the Soviets, through the trade unions, through the living, revolutionary proletarian Communist Party.

The Stalinist reaction, the causes and course of which have been traced so brilliantly by Trotsky above all others, meant the systematic hacking away of every finger of control the working class had over its state. And with the triumph of the bureaucratic counter-revolution came the end of the rule of the working class. The Soviets were eviscerated and finally wiped out by decree. The trade unions were converted into slave-drivers cracking the whip over the working class. Workers' control in the factories went a dozen years ago. The people were forbidden to bear arms even non-explosive weapons - it was the possession of arms by the people that Lenin qualified as the very essence of the question of the state! The militia system gave way decisively to the army separated from the people. The Communist Youth were formally prohibited from participating in politics, i.e., from concerning themselves with the state. The Communist party was gutted, all the Bolsheviks in it broken in two, imprisoned, exiled and finally shot. How absurd are all the social-democratic lamentations about the "one-party dictatorship" in light of this analysis! It was precisely this party, while it lived, which was the last channel through which the Soviet working class exercised its political power.

"The recognition of the present Soviet state as a workers' state," wrote Trotsky in his thesis on Russia in 1931, "not only signifies that the bourgeoisie can conquer power in no other way than by an armed uprising but that also the proletariat of the U.S.S.R has not forfeited the possibility of submitting the bureaucracy to it, of reviving the party again and of mending the regime of the dictatorship - without a new revolution, with the methods and on the road of reform."[9]

Quite right. And conversely, when the Soviet proletariat finally lost the possibility of submitting the bureaucracy to itself by the methods of reform and was left with the weapon of revolution, we should have

The Hitler–Stalin Pact

abandoned our characterization of the U.S.S.R. as a workers' state. Even if belatedly, it is necessary to do that now.

That political expropriation of the proletariat about which the International has spoken, following Trotsky's analysis - that is nothing more nor less than the destruction of the class rule of the workers, the end of the Soviet Union as a workers' state. In point of time - the Stalinist counter-revolution has not been as cataclysmic as to dates or as dramatic in symbols as was the French Revolution or the Bolshevik insurrection - the destruction of the old class rule may be said to have culminated with the physical annihilation of the last Bolsheviks.

A change in class rule, a revolution or counter-revolution, without violence, without civil war, gradually? Trotsky has reproached defenders of such a conception as "reformists in reverse." The reproach might hold in our case, too, but for the fact that the Stalinist counter-revolution was violent and bloody enough. The seizure of power by the Bolsheviks was virtually bloodless and non-violent. The breadth and duration of the civil war that followed were determined by the strength and virility of the overturned classes, and not least of all, by the international imperialist aid furnished to them. The comparative one-sidedness of the civil war attending the Stalinist counter-revolution was determined by the oft-noted passivity of the masses, their weariness, their failure to receive international support. In spite of this, Stalin's road to power lay through rivers of blood and over mountains of skulls. Neither the Stalinist counter-revolution nor the Bolshevik revolution was effected by the Fabian gradualist reforms.

The conquest of state power by the bureaucracy spelled the destruction of the property relations established by the Bolshevik revolution.

The Bureaucracy: Caste or Class

If the workers are no longer the ruling class and the Soviet Union no longer a workers' state, and if there is no private-property-owning capitalist class ruling Russia what is the class nature of the state and what exactly is the bureaucracy that dominates it?

Neither Capitalism nor Socialism

Hitherto we called the Stalinist bureaucracy a caste, and denied it the attributes of a class. Yet, Trotsky admitted September a year ago, the definition as a caste has not "a strictly scientific character. Its relative superiority lies in this, that the makeshift character of the term is clear to everybody, since it would enter nobody's mind to identify the Moscow oligarchy with the Hindu caste of Brahmins." In resume it is called a caste not because it is a caste - the old Marxian definition of a caste would scarcely fit Stalin & Co. - but because it is not a class. Without letting the dispute "degenerate into sterile toying with words," let us see if we cannot come closer to a scientific characterization than we have in the past.

The late Bukharin defined a class as "the aggregate of persons playing the same part in production, standing in the same relation toward other persons in the production process, these relations being also expressed in things (instruments of labor)." According to Trotsky, a class is defined "by its independent role in the general structure of the economy and by its independent roots in the economic foundation of society. Each class ... works out its own special forms of property. The bureaucracy lacks all these social traits."

In general either definition would serve but not as an absolutely unfailing test for all classes in all class societies. Although, for example, the merchants would fail to pass either of the two tests given above, Engels qualified them as a class.

> A third division of labor was added by civilization: it created a class that did not take part in production, but occupied itself merely with the exchange of products - the merchants. All former attempts at class formulation were exclusively concerned with production. They divided the producers into directors and directed, or into producers on a more or less extensive scale. But here a class appears for the first time that captures the control of production in general and subjugates the producers to its rule, without taking the least part in production. A class that makes itself the indispensable mediator between two producers and exploits them both under the pretext of saving them the trouble and risk of exchange, of

extending the markets for their products to distant regions and of thus becoming the most useful class in society: a class of parasites, genuine social ichneumons, that skim off the cream of production at home and abroad as a reward for very insignificant services; that rapidly amass enormous wealth sand gain social influence accordingly; that for this reason reap ever new honors and ever greater control of production during the period of civilization, until they at last bring to light a product of their own - periodical crises in industry.[10]

The Marxian definition of class is obviously widened by Engels to include a social group "that did not take part in production" but which made itself "the indispensable mediator between two producers," exploiting them both. The merchants characterized by Engels as a class are neither more nor less encompassed in Trotsky's definition, given above, or in Bukharin's, than is the Stalinist bureaucracy (except in so far as this bureaucracy most definitely takes part in the process of production). But the indubitable fact that the bureaucracy has not abolished state property is not sufficient ground for withholding from it the qualification of a class, although, as we shall see, within certain limits. But it has been objected:

> If the Bonapartist riffraff is a class this means that it is not an abortion but a viable child of history. If its marauding parasitism is "exploitation" in the scientific sense of the term, this means that the bureaucracy possesses a historical future as a ruling class indispensable to the given system of economy.[11]

Is or is not the Stalinist bureaucracy "a ruling class indispensable" to the system of economy in the Soviet Union?

This question - begs the question! The question is precisely: what is the given system of economy? For the given system - the property relations established by the counter-revolution - the Stalinist bureaucracy is the indispensable ruling class. As for the economic system and the property relations established by the Bolshevik revolution (under

Neither Capitalism nor Socialism

which the Stalinist bureaucracy was by no means the indispensable ruling class) - these are just what the bureaucratic counter-revolution destroyed! To the question, is the bureaucracy indispensable to "Soviet economy"? one can therefore answer, yes and no. To the same question put somewhat differently, Is the bureaucracy an "historical accident", an abortion or viable and a necessity, the answer must be given in the same spirit. It is an historical necessity - "a result of the iron necessity to give birth to and support a privileged minority so long as it is impossible to guarantee genuine equality."[12] It is not an "historical accident" for the good reason that it has well-established historical causes. It is not inherent in a society resting upon collective property in the means of production and exchange, as the capitalist class is inherent in a society resting upon capitalist property. Rather, it is the product of a conjunction of circumstances, primarily that the proletarian revolution broke out in backward Russia and was not supplemented and thereby saved by the victory of the revolution in the advanced countries. Hence, while its concrete characteristics do not permit us to qualify it as a viable or indispensable class in the same sense as the historical capitalist class, we may and do speak of it as a ruling class whose complete control of the state now guarantees its political and economic supremacy in the country.

It is interesting to note that the evolution and transformation of the Soviet bureaucracy in the workers' state - the state of Lenin and Trotsky - is quite different and even contrary to the evolution of the capitalist class in its state.

Speaking of the capitalist manager into capitalists and managers of the process of production, Marx writes:

> The labor of superintendence and management arising out of the antagonistic character and rule of capital over labor, which all modes of production based on class antagonism have in common with the capitalist mode, is directly and inseparably connected, also under the capitalist system, with those productive functions, which all combined social labor assigns to individuals as their special tasks ... Compared to the

The Hitler–Stalin Pact

money-capitalist the industrial capitalist is a laborer, but a laboring capitalist, an exploiter of the labor of others. The wages which he claims and pockets for this labor amount exactly to the appropriated quantity of another's labor and depend directly upon the rate of exploitation of this labor, so far as he takes the trouble to assume the necessary burdens of exploitation. He can easily shift this burden to the shoulders of a superintendent for moderate pay...Stock companies in general, developed with the credit system, have a tendency to separate this labor of management as a function more and more from the ownership of capital, whether it be self-owned or borrowed.(Capital III)

Even thought this tendency to separate out of the capitalist class (or the upper ranks of the working class) a group of managers and superintendents is constantly accentuated under capitalism, this group does not develop into an independent class. Why? Because to the extent that the manager (i.e., a highly-paid superintendent-worker) changes his "relations to property" and becomes an owner of capital, he merely enters into the already existing capitalist class. He need not and does not create new property relations. The owning class remains the ruling class; the managers remain its agents.

The evolution has been distinctly different in Russia. The proletariat in control of the state, and therefore the economy, soon found itself unable directly to organize the economy, expand the productive forces and raise labor productivity because of a whole series of circumstances - its own lack of training in management and superintendence, in bookkeeping and strict accounting, the absence of help from the technologically more advanced countries, etc.,etc. As with the building of the Red Army, so in industry, the Russian proletariat was urged by Lenin to call upon and it did call upon a whole host and variety of experts - some from its own ranks, some from the ranks of the class enemy, some from the ranks of the bandwagon-jumpers, constituting in all a considerable bureaucracy. But, given the revolutionary party, given the Soviets, given the trade unions, given the factory committees, that is given those concrete means by which the

Neither Capitalism nor Socialism

workers ruled the state, their state, this bureaucracy, however perilous, remained within the limitations of "hired hands" in the service of the workers' state. In political or economic life - the bureaucracies in both tended to and did merge -the bureaucracy was subject to the criticism, control, recall or discharge of the "working class organized as the ruling class."

The whole history of the struggle of the Trotskyist movement in Russia against the bureaucracy signified, at bottom, a struggle to prevent the crushing of the workers' state by the growing monster of a bureaucracy which was becoming increasingly different in quality from the "hired hands" of the workers' state as well as from any kind of bureaucratic group under capitalism. What we have called the consummated usurpation of power by the Stalinist bureaucracy was, in reality, nothing but the self-realization of the bureaucracy as a class and its seizure of state power from the proletariat, the establishment of its own state power and its own rule. The qualitative difference lies precisely in this: the bureaucracy is no longer the controlled and revocable "managers and superintendents" employed by the workers' state in the party, the state apparatus, the industries, the army, the unions, the fields, but the owners and controllers of the state, which is in turn the repository of collectivized property and thereby the employer of all hired hands, the masses of workers, above all, included.

The situation of the young Soviet republic (the historical circumstances surrounding its birth and evolution), imposed upon it the "division of labor" described above, and often commented on by Lenin. Where a similar division of labor under capitalism does not transform the economic or political agents of the ruling class into a new class, for the reason given above (primarily the relations to capitalist property), it does tend to create a new class in a state reposing on collectivized property, that is, in a state which is itself the repository of all social property.

Trotsky is entirely right when he speaks of "dynamic social formations (in Russia) which have no precedent and have no analogies." It is even more to the point when he writes that "the very fact of its (the

The Hitler–Stalin Pact

bureaucracy's) appropriation of political power in a country where the principal means of production are in the hands of the state creates a new and hitherto unknown relation between the bureaucracy and the riches of the nation." For what is unprecedented and new, hitherto unknown, one cannot find a sufficiently illuminating analogy in the bureaucracies in other societies which did not develop into a class but remained class-serving bureaucracies.

What Trotsky calls the indispensable theoretical key to an understanding of the situation in Russia is the remarkable passage from Marx which he quotes in *The Revolution Betrayed*. "A development of the productive forces is the absolutely necessary practical premise (of communism), because without it want is generalized, and with want the struggle for necessities begins again, and that means that all the old crap must revive."

Both Lenin and Trotsky kept repeating in the early years: in backward Russia, socialism cannot be built without the aid of more advanced countries. Before the revolution, in 1915, Trotsky made clear his opinion - for which Stalinism never forgave him - that without state aid of the western proletariat, the workers of Russia could not hope to remain in power for long. That state aid did not come, thanks to the international social democracy, later ably supplemented by the Stalinists. But the prediction of Lenin and Trotsky did come true. The workers of the Soviet Union were unable to hold power. That they lost it in a peculiar, unforseen and even unforeseeable way - not because of a bourgeois restoration, but in the form of a seizure of power by a counter-revolutionary bureaucracy which retained and based itself on the new, collectivist form of property - is true. But they did lose power. The old crap was revived - in a new, unprecedented, hitherto-unknown form, the rule of a new bureaucratic class. A class that always was, that always will be? Not at all. "Class", Lenin pointed out in April 1920, " is a concept that takes shape in struggle and in the course of development." The reminder is particularly timely in considering the struggle and evolution of the Stalinist bureaucracy into a class. Precisely here it is worth more than passing notice (because of its profound significance), that the counterrevolution, like the revolution that preceded it, found that it could not, as Marx said about the seizure of power by the proletariat in the Paris Commune, "simply lay hold of the ready-made state machinery and wield it for its own purposes." The Russian proletariat had to shatter the old bourgeois state and its apparatus, and put in its place a new state, a complex of the Soviets, the revolutionary party, the trade unions, the factory committees, the militia system, etc. To achieve power and establish its rule, the Stalinist counter-revolution in turn had to shatter the proletarian Soviet state - those same Soviets, the party, the unions, the factory committees, the militia system, the "armed people", etc. It shattered the workers' state and put in its place the totalitarian state of bureaucratic collectivism.

Thereby it compelled us to add to our theory this conception among others: Just as it is possible to have different classes ruling in societies resting upon the private ownership of property, so it is possible to have more than one class ruling in a society resting upon the collective ownership of property - concretely, the working class and the bureaucracy.

Can this new class look forward to a social life-span as long as that enjoyed, for example, by the capitalist class? We see no reason to believe that it can. Throughout modern capitalist society, ripped apart so violently by its contradictions, there is clearly discernible the irrepressible tendency towards collectivism, the only means whereby the productive forces of mankind can be expanded and thereby provide that ample satisfaction of human needs which is the pre-condition to the blooming of a new civilization and culture. But there is no adequate ground for believing that this tendency will materialize in the form of a universal "bureaucratic collectivism." The "unconditional development of the productive forces of society comes continually into conflict with the limited end, the self-expansion of the existing capital." The revolutionary struggle against the capitalist mode of production, triumphing in those countries which have already attained a high level of economic development, including the development of labor productivity, leads rather to the socialist society. The circumstances which left Soviet Russia isolated, dependent upon its own

The Hitler–Stalin Pact

primitive forces, and thus generated that "generalized want" which facilitated the victory of the bureaucratic counter-revolution, will be and can only be overcome by overcoming its causes - namely, the capitalist encirclement. The social revolution which spells the doom of capitalist imperialism and the release of the pent-up, strangled forces of production, will put an end to the want and misery of the masses in the West and to the very basis of the misery of Stalinism in the Soviet Union.

Social life and evolution were slow and long-drawn-out under feudalism. Their pace was considerably accelerated under capitalism. World society which entered the period of world wars and socialist revolutions, finds the pace speeded up to a rhythm that has no precedent in history. All events and phenomena tend to be telescoped in point of time. From this standpoint, the rise, and the early fall, of the bureaucracy in the Soviet Union necessitates an indication of the limits of its development, as we pointed out above, precisely in order to distinguish it from the fundamental historical classes, this is perhaps best done by characterizing it as the ruling class of an unstable society which is already a fetter on economic development.

Stalinist Bureaucracy - Fascist Bureaucracy

What has already been said above should serve to indicate the similarities between the Stalinist and Fascist bureaucracies, but above all to indicate the profound social and historical differences between them. Following our analysis, the animadversions of all species of rationalizers on the identity of character of Stalinism and Fascism, remain just as superficial as ever.

Trotsky's characterization of the two bureaucracies as "symmetrical" is incontrovertible, but only within the limits with which he surrounds the term, namely, they are both products of the same failure of the western proletariat to solve the social crisis by social revolution. To go further, they are identical but again within well defined limits. The political regime, the technique of rule, the highly developed social demagogy, the system of terror without end - these are essential features of Hitlerite and Stalinist totalitarianism, some of them more

Neither Capitalism nor Socialism

fully developed under the latter than under the former. At this point, however, the similarity ceases.

From the standpoint of our old analysis and theory, the Soviet Union remained a workers' state despite its political regime. In short, we said, just as the social rule of capitalism, the capitalist state, was preserved under different political regimes - republic, monarchy, military dictatorship, fascism - so the social rule of the proletariat, the workers' state could be maintained under different political regimes - Soviet democracy, Stalinist totalitarianism. Can we then, even speak of a "counter-revolutionary workers' state"? was the question posed by Trotsky early this year. To which his reply was, "There are two completely counter-revolutionary workers' Internationals" and one can, therefore, speak also of "the counter-revolutionary workers" state. In the last analysis a workers' state is a trade union that has conquered power." It is a workers' state by virtue of its property forms, and it is counter-revolutionary by virtue of its political regime.

Without dwelling here on the analogy between the Soviet state today and the trade unions, it is necessary to point out that thoroughgoing consistency would demand of this standpoint that the Soviet Union be characterized as a Fascist workers' state, workers state, again, because of its property forms, and Fascist because of its political regime. Objections to this characterization can only be based upon the embarrassment caused by this natural product of consistency.

However that may be, if it is not a workers' state, not even a Fascist workers' state, neither is it a state comparable to that of the German Nazis. Let us see why. Fascism, resting on the mass basis of the petty-bourgeoisie gone mad under the horrors of the social crisis, was called to power deliberately by the big bourgeoisie in order to preserve its social rule, the system of private property. Writers who argue that Fascism put an end to capitalism and inaugurated a new social order, with a new class rule, are guilty of an abstract and static conception of capitalism; more accurately, of an idealization of capitalism as permanently identical with what it was in its halcyon period of organic upward development, its "democratic" phase. Faced with the imminent prospect of the proletarian revolution putting an end both to the contradictions of capitalism and to its capitalist rule, the bourgeoisie preferred the annoyance of a Fascist regime which would suppress (not abolish!) these contradictions and preserve capitalist rule. In other words, at a given stage of its degeneration, the only way to preserve the capitalist system in any form is by means of the totalitarian dictatorship. As all historians agree, calling Fascism to political power - the abandonment of political rule by the bourgeoisie itself.

But it is argued, after it came to political power, the Fascist bureaucracy completely dispossessed the bourgeoisie and itself became the ruling class. Which is precisely what needs to be but has not been proved. The system of private ownership of socially-operated property remains basically intact. After being in power in Italy for over eighteen years, and in Germany for almost eight, Fascism has yet to nationalize industry, to say nothing of expropriating the bourgeoisie (the expropriation of small sections of the bourgeoisie - the Jewish - is done in the interests of the bourgeoisie as a whole). Why does Hitler, who is so bold in all other spheres, suddenly turn timid when he confronts the "juridical detail" represented by private (or corporate) ownership of the means of production? Because the two cannot be counterposed: his boldness and :radicalism" in all spheres is directed towards maintaining and reinforcing that "juridical detail," that is, capitalist society, to the extent to which it is at all possible to maintain it in the period of its decay.

But doesn't Fascism control the bourgeoisie? Yes, in a sense. That kind of control was foreseen long ago. In January 1916, Lenin and the Zimmerwald Left wrote: "At the end of the war a gigantic universal economic upheaval will manifest itself with all its force, when, under a general exhaustion, unemployment and lack of capital, industry will have to be regulated anew, when the terrific indebtedness of all states will drive them to tremendous taxation, and when state socialism - militarization of the economic life - will seem to be the only way out of difficulties." Fascist control means precisely this new regulation of industry, the militarization of economic life in its sharpest form. It controls, it restricts, it regulates, it plunders - but with all that it main-

Neither Capitalism nor Socialism

tains and even strengthens the capitalist profit system, leaves the bourgeois intact as the class owning property. It assures the profits of the owning class - taking from it that portion which is required to maintain a bureaucracy and police spy system needed to keep down labor (which threatens to take away all profits and all capital, let us not forget) and to maintain a highly modernized military establishment to defend the bourgeoisie from attacks at home and abroad and to acquire for it new fields of exploitation outside its own frontiers.

But isn't the Fascist bureaucracy, too, becoming a class? In a sense, yes, but not a new class with a new class rule. By virtue of their control of the state power, any number of Fascist bureaucrats, of high and low estate, have used coercion and intimidation to become Board Directors and stockholders in various enterprises. This is especially true of those bureaucrats assigned to industry as commissars of all kinds. On the other side, the bourgeoisie acquire the "good will" of Nazi bureaucrats, employed either in the state or the economic machinery, by bribes of stocks and positions on directing boards. There is, if you wish, a certain process of fusion between sections of the bureaucracy and the bourgeoisie. But the bureaucrats do not thereby become a new class, they enter as integral parts of the industrial or financial bourgeois class we have known for quite some time!

Private ownership of capital, that "juridical detail" before which Hitler comes to a halt, is a social reality of the profoundest importance. With all its political power, the Nazi bureaucracy remains a bureaucracy; sections of it fuse with the bourgeoisie, but as a social aggregation, it is not developing into a new class. Here, control of the state power is not enough. The bureaucracy, in so far as its development into a new class with a new class rule of its own is concerned , is itself controlled by the objective reality of the private ownership of capital.

How different it is with the Stalinist bureaucracy! Both bureaucracies "devour, waste, and embezzle a considerable portion of the nationalized income"; both have an income above that of the people, and privileges which correspond to their position in society. But similarity of income is not a definition of a social class. In Germany,

The Hitler–Stalin Pact

the Nazis are not more than a bureaucracy - extremely powerful, to be sure, but still only a bureaucracy. In the Soviet Union, the bureaucracy is the ruling class, because it possesses as its own the state power which, in this country, is the owner of all social property.

In Germany, the Nazis have attained a great degree of independence by their control of the state, but it continues to be "the state of the most powerful economic class" - the bourgeoisie. In the Soviet Union, control of the state, sole owner of social property, makes the bureaucracy the most powerful economic class. Therein lies the fundamental difference between the Soviet state, even under Stalinism, and all other pre-collectivist states. The difference is of epochal historical importance. Of epochal historical importance, we repeat, for our analysis does not diminish by an iota the profound social revolutionary significance of the Russian proletarian revolution. Starting at a low level, lowered still further by years of war, civil war, famine and their devastations, isolated from world economy, infested with a monstrous bureaucracy, the Soviet Union nevertheless attained a rhythm of economic development, an expansion of the productive forces which exceeded the expectations of the boldest revolutionary thinkers and easily aroused the astonishment of the entire world. This was not due to any virtues of the bureaucracy under whose reign it was accomplished, but in spite of the concomitant overhead waste of that regime. Economic progress in the Soviet Union was accomplished on the basis of planning and of the new, collectivist forms of property established by the proletarian revolution. What would that progress have looked like if only those new forms, and property relations more suitable to them, had been extended to the more highly developed countries of Europe and America! It staggers the imagination.

Fascism, on the other hand, has developed to its highest degree the state as regulator, subsidizer and controller of a social order which does not expand but contracts the productive forces of modern society. The contrary view held by those who are so impressed by the great development of industry in Germany in the period of war economy, is based upon superficial and temporary phenomena. Fascism, as a motor or a brake on the development of productive

Neither Capitalism nor Socialism

forces, must be judged not by the tons of war-steel produced in the Ruhr, but on the infinitely more significant policy it pursues in the conquered territories which it seeks to convert, from industrially advanced countries, into backward agricultural hinterlands of German national economy.

Both bureaucracies are reactionary. Both bureaucracies act as brakes on the development of the productive forces of society. Neither plays a progressive role, even if in both cases this or that act may have an abstractly progressive significance (Hitler destroys Bavarian particularism and "liberates" the Sudetens; Stalin nationalizes industry in Latvia). In the Soviet Union, however, the Stalinist bureaucracy is the brake, and its removal would permit the widest expansion of the productive forces. Whereas in Germany, as in other capitalist countries, it is not merely the Fascist bureaucracy who stand in the way, but primarily the capitalist class, the capitalist mode of production.

The difference is between increased state intervention to preserve capitalist property and the collective ownership of property by the bureaucratic state.

How express the difference summarily and in conventional terms? People buying canned goods want and are entitled to have labels affixed that will enable them to distinguish at a glance pears from peaches from peas. "We often seek salvation from unfamiliar phenomena in familiar terms," Trotsky observed. But what is to be done with unprecedented, new, hitherto-unknown phenomena, how label them in such a way as to describe at once their origin, their present state, their more than one future prospect, and wherein they differ from other phenomena? the task is not easy. Yet, life and politics demand some conventional. summary terms for social phenomena; one cannot answer the question - What is the Soviet state? by repeating in detail a long and complex analysis. The demand must be met as satisfactorily as is possible in the nature of the case.

The early Soviet state we would call, with Lenin, a bureaucratically deformed workers' state. The Soviet state today we would call - bureaucratic state socialism, a characterization which attempts to

The Hitler–Stalin Pact

embrace both its historical origin and its distinction from capitalism as well as its current diversion under Stalinism. The German state today we would call , in distinction from the Soviet state, bureaucratic or totalitarian state capitalism. These terms are neither elegant nor absolutely precise, but they will have to do for want of any others more precise or even half as precise.

The Defense of the Soviet Union

From the foregoing analysis, the basis is laid not only for eliminating the discrepancies and defects in our old analysis, but for clarifying our political position. *Political or Social revolution?* Here, too, without falling into a game of terminology or toying with abstract concepts, it is necessary to strive for the maximum exactness. As distinct from social revolution, Trotsky and the International called up to now for a political revolution in the Soviet Union. "History has known elsewhere not only social revolutions which substituted the bourgeois for the feudal regime, but also political revolutions which, without destroying the economic foundations of society, swept out an old ruling upper crust (1830 and 1848 in France, February 1917 in Russia, etc.). The overthrow of the Bonapartist caste will, of course, have deep social consequences, but in itself it will be confined within the limits of political revolution." (The Revolution Betrayed.)[13] And again, on the same page: "It is not a question this time of changing the economic foundations of society, of replacing certain forms of property with other forms."

In the revolution against the Stalinist bureaucracy the nationalization of the means of production and exchange will indeed be preserved by the proletariat in power. If that is what is meant by political revolution, if that is all it could mean, then we could easily be reconciled to it. But from our whole analysis, it follows that the Stalinist counterrevolution, in seizing the power of the state, thereby changed the property relations in the Soviet Union. In overturning the rule of the bureaucracy, the Soviet proletariat will again raise itself to the position of ruling class, organize its own state, and once more change its relations to property. The revolution will thus not merely

Neither Capitalism nor Socialism

have "deep social consequences," it will be a social revolution. After what has been said in another section, it is not necessary to insist here on those points wherein the social revolution in Germany or England would resemble the social revolution in Russia and wherein they would differ from it. In the former, it is a question of ending capitalism and lifting the country into the new historical epoch of collectivism and socialism. In the latter. it is a question of destroying a reactionary obstacle to the development of a collectivist society towards socialism.

Unconditional Defense of the U.S.S.R.?

The slogan of "unconditional defense of the Soviet Union" assumed that, even under Stalin and despite Stalin, the Soviet Union could play only a progressive role in any war with a capitalist power. The Second World War broke out, with the Soviet Union as on of the participants, now as a belligerent, now as "non-belligerent." But, "theory is not a note which you can present to reality at any moment for payment." Reality showed that the Soviet Union, in the war in Poland and in Finland, in the war as a whole, was playing a reactionary role. The Stalinist bureaucracy and its army acted as an indispensable auxiliary in the military calculations of German imperialism. They covered the latter's eastern, northern and southeastern flank, helped in the crushing of Poland (and along with it of the incipient Polish Commune), and for their pains, received a share of the booty. In the conquered territories, it is true, Stalin proceeded to establish the same economic order that prevails in the Soviet Union. But this has no absolute value, in and of itself - only a relative value. One can say with Trotsky that "the economic transformations in the occupied provinces do not compensate for this by even a tenth part!"

From the standpoint of the interests of the international socialist revolution, defense of the Soviet Union in this war (i.e., support of the Red Army) could only have a negative effect. Even from the more limited standpoint of preserving the new economic forms in the Soviet Union, it must be established that they were not involved in the war. At stake were and are what Trotsky calls "the driving force behind the

The Hitler-Stalin Pact

Moscow bureaucracy...the tendency to expand its power, its prestige, its revenues."

The attempt to exhaust the analysis of the Stalinist course in the war by ascribing it to "purely military" steps of preventive-defensive character (what is meant in general by "purely military" steps remains a mystery, since they exist neither in nature or society), is doomed by its superficiality to failure. Naturally, all military steps are...military steps, but saying so does not advance us very far.

The general political considerations which actuated the Stalinists in making an alliance with Hitler (capitulation to Germany out of fear of war, etc.) have been stated by us on more than one occasion and require no repetition here. But there are even more profound reasons which have little or nothing to do with the fact that Stalin's master ally is German Fascism. The same reasons would have dictated the same course in the war if the alliance had been made, as a result of a different conjunction of circumstances with the noble democracies. They are summed up in the lust for expansion of the Stalinist bureaucracy, which has even less in common with Lenin's policy of extending the revolution to capitalist countries than the Stalinist state has with the early workers' state.

And what is the economic base of this lust for expansion, this most peculiar imperialism which you have invented? we were asked, sometimes with superior sneers, sometimes with genuine interest in the problem. We know what are the irrepressible economic contradictions that produce the imperialist policy of finance capitalism. What are their equivalents in the Soviet Union?

Stalinist imperialism is no more like capitalist imperialism than the Stalinist state is like the bourgeois state. Just the same it has its own economic compulsions and internal contradictions which hold it back here and drive it forward there. Under capitalism, the purpose of production is the production of surplus value, of profit, "not the product, but the surplus product." In the workers' state, production was carried on and extended for the satisfaction of the needs of the Soviet masses. For that, they needed not the oppression of themselves or of other people but the liberation of the peoples of the capitalist

Neither Capitalism nor Socialism

countries and the colonial empires. In the Stalinist state, production is carried on and extended for the satisfaction of the needs of the bureaucracy, for the increasing of its wealth, its privileges, its power. At every turn of events, it seeks to overcome the mounting difficulties and resolve the contradictions which it cannot really resolve, by intensifying the exploitation and oppression of the masses.

We surely need not, in a serious discussion among Marxists, insist upon the fact, so vehemently denied a year ago by the eminent Marxologist at the head of the S.W.P., that there are still classes in the Soviet Union and that exploitation takes place there. Not capitalist exploitation - but economic exploitation nonetheless. "The differences in income are determined, in other words, not only by differences of individual productiveness, but also by a masked appropriation of the product of the labor of others. The privileged minority of shareholders is living at the expense of the deprived majority." (The Revolution Betrayed) The driving force behind the bureaucracy is the tendency to increase this "masked [and often not so masked] appropriation of the product of the labor of others'" Hence, its penchant for methods of exploitation typical of the worst under capitalism; hence, its lust to extend its dominion over the peoples of the weaker and more backward countries (if it is not the case with the stronger and more advanced countries, then only because the power, and not the will, is lacking), in order to subject them to the oppression and exploitation of the Kremlin oligarches. The de facto occupation of the northwestern provinces of China by Stalin is a case in point. The occupation and then the spoliation of eastern Poland, of the three Baltic countries, of southern Finland (not to mention the hoped-for Petsamo nickel mines), of Bessarabia and Bukovina, tomorrow perhaps of parts of Turkey, Iran and India are other cases in point. We call this policy Stalinist imperialism.

But are not imperialism and imperialist policies a concomitant only of capitalism? No. While crises of overproduction are unique to capitalism, that does not hold true either of war or imperialism, which are common to diverse societies. Lenin, insisting precisely on the scientific, Marxist usage of the terms, wrote in 1917:

Crises, precisely in the form of overproduction or of the "stocking up of market commodities" (comrade S. does not like the word overproduction) are a phenomenon which is exclusively proper to capitalism. Wars, however, are proper both to the economic system based on slavery and the feudal system. There have been imperialist wars on the basis of slavery (Rome's war against Carthage was an imperialist war on both sides) as well as in the Middle Ages and in the epoch of mercantile capitalism. Every war in which both belligerent camps are fighting to oppress foreign countries or peoples and for the division of the booty, that is, over "who shall oppress or plunder more," must be called imperialistic.[14]

By this definition, on which Lenin dwelled because comrade S. had made an "error in principle," it is incontestable that the Stalinists in partnership with Hitler have been conducting an imperialist war "to oppress foreign countries or peoples," "for the division of booty," to decide "who shall oppress more and who shall plunder more." It is only from this standpoint that Trotsky's statement late in 1939 - "We were and remain against seizures of new territories by the Kremlin" - acquires full and serious meaning. If the Soviet state were essentially a trade union in power, with a reactionary bureaucracy at its head, then we could not possibly oppose "seizures of new territories" any more than we oppose a trade union bureaucracy bringing unorganized workers into the union. With all our opposition to their organizing methods, it is we, the left win, who always insisted that Lewis or Green organize the unorganized. The analogy between the Soviet state and a trade union is not a very solid one...

The theory that Soviet economy is progressive and therefore the wars of the Stalinist bureaucracy against a capitalist state are, by some mysticism, correspondingly and universally progressive, is thus untenable. As in the case of a colonial or semi-colonial country, or a small nation, we defend the Soviet Union against imperialism when it is fighting a progressive war, that is, in our epoch one which corresponds to the interests of the international socialist revolution. When it

Neither Capitalism nor Socialism

fights a reactionary, imperialist war, as did "little Serbia" and China as in the last world war, we take the traditional revolutionary position: continue implacably the class struggle regardless of the effects on the military front.

Under what conditions is it conceivable to defend the Soviet Union ruled by the Stalinist bureaucracy? It is possible to give only a generalized answer. For example, should the character of the present war change from that of a struggle between the imperialist camps into a struggle of the imperialists to crush the Soviet Union, the interests of the world revolution would demand the defense of the Soviet Union by the international proletariat. The aim of imperialism in that case, whether it were represented in the war by one or many powers, would be to solve the crisis of world capitalism (and thus prolong the agony of the proletariat) at the cost of reducing the Soviet Union to one or more colonial possessions or spheres of interest. Even though prostrated by the victors in the last war, Germany remained a capitalist country, whose social regime the Allies did their utmost to maintain against the revolutionary proletariat. In the present war, we find victorious Germany not only not undertaking any fundamental economic changes in the conquered territories but preserving the capitalist system by force of arms against the unrest and revolutionism of the proletariat. There is no reason to believe that victorious imperialism in the Soviet Union would leave its nationalized property intact - quite the contrary. As Germany now seeks to do with France, imperialism would seek to destroy all the progress made in the Soviet Union by reducing it to a somewhat more advanced India - a village continent. In these considerations, too, the *historical significance* of the new collectivist property established by the Russian Revolution, again stands out clearly. Such a transformation of the Soviet Union as triumphant imperialism would undertake, would have a vast and durable reactionary effect upon world social development, give capitalism and reaction a new lease on life, retard enormously the revolutionary movement, and postpone for we don't know how long the introduction of the world socialist society. From this standpoint

The Hitler–Stalin Pact

and under these conditions, the defense of the Soviet Union, even under Stalinism, is both possible and necessary.

To revise one's position on so important a question as the class character of the Soviet union, is, as the writer has himself learned, no easy matter. The mass of absurdities written against our old position only served to fix it more firmly in our minds and in our program. To expect others to take a new position overnight would be presumptuous and unprofitable. We did not arrive at the views outlined above lightly or hastily. We neither ask nor expect others to arrive at our views in that way. It is, however, right to ask that they be discussed with the critical objectivity, the exclusive concern with the truth that best serve our common interests, and the polemical loyalty that are the best traditions of Marxism.

The New International 1941

NOTES

1. This is overstated. For a discussion of the *continuing* conflict among Nazi hierarchs, the Officer corps, remnants of the Imperial and Weimar bureaucracies, the representatives of industrial and finance capital and the plebeian rank-and-file of the Nazi movement see Guerin, *Fascism and Big Business*.

2. For a discussion of the officer corps' resistance to the Nazi attempts to eliminate all independent control over the army see Gordon A. Craig, *The Politics of the Prussian Army 1640-1945* (Oxford University Press, New York) 1964. Craig himself bemoans the pusillanimity of the officer corps. However, since the standard he uses to measure their behavior is that of the army reformers at the time of the Napoleonic wars who for a while acted as a kind of *ersatz* opposition his criticism cannot be taken too seriously. Nothing like Stalin's purge of the officer corps took place in Germany.

3. Trotsky, "The USSR in War," *The New International*, Nov. 1939, p. 327)

4. Leon Trotsky, *The Revolution Betrayed*, p. 252.

Neither Capitalism nor Socialism

5 . Ibid., p. 253.

6 . Ibid., p. 250.

7 .. Ibid., p. 241.

8 . Ibid., p. 238.

9 . Leon Trotsky, "Problems of the Development of the USSR" *Writings of Leon Trotsky (1930-31)*, (Pathfinder Press, New York) 1973.

10 . Frederick Engels, "The Origin of the Family, Private Property and the State", *Karl Marx and Frederick Engels Selected Works*, Vol. 3 (Progress Publishers, Moscow) 1970. p. 323.

11 . Leon Trotsky, "Again and Once More Again on the Class Nature of the USSR", *In Defense of Marxism* p.24.

12 . Leon Trotsky, *The Revolution Betrayed*. P. 55.

13 . Ibid., p. 288.

14 . I have not been able to find this quote in the English collected works.

Chapter III
THE DEFENSE OF COLLECTIVIST PROPERTY

The German invasion of Russia in June of 1941 put those anti-Stalinist socialists who still had faith in the progressive role of the bureaucracy that was defending nationalized property in a very difficult position.

Stalin was defending nationalized property in this instance and any attempt to exploit the popular antigovernment fury that boiled over in the first few months after the invasion clearly ran the risk of aiding the Nazi invader. Behind the involved Marxistical argumentation the participants in this debate were trying to find the answer to a difficult question: should socialists suspend their opposition to Stalin for the duration? This question was to become even more difficult in the period of the Cold War when Stalinism's opponent was not Nazi Germany but liberal capitalism.

The lesson all socialists, and many liberals and pacifists, had drawn from World War I was that calling a halt to the class struggle in the interests of the war effort was a disaster for the labor and progressive movements.* The governing classes in all belligerent countries simply took advantage of the situation to undermine all the gains won in decades of bitter struggle. The contending countries all moved at a faster or slower pace in the direction of military dictatorship.

Did such an analysis apply also to Russia? Should socialists continue to oppose Stalin and his government and indeed put themselves at the head of

---

*. The reader should be warned here that considerable confusion was introduced into this debate in left and socialist circles generally by the tendency of all participants to use as part of their theoretical equipment Lenin's World War I slogan of "Revolutionary Defeatism". That slogan seemed to imply that the choice was support of your own government to the point of abandoning all opposition or favoring the victory of the enemy.

Liberals and Stalinists, of course, emphasized Lenin's slogan because in the face of Nazism it was clear which choice should be made. They emphasized that, unlike World War I, in this war there really were significant differences between both sides.

For a discussion of the origins and disastrous consequences, in World War I itself, *of this misleading slogan see Hal Draper's* The Myth of Lenin's Revolutionary Defeatism *(Humanities Press 1995).* This same series of articles also examines the other, more successful, attempts of Luxemburg and Trotsky to work out a political approach that more effectively dealt with this dilemma.

Neither Capitalism nor Socialism

the popular opposition to the bureaucracy or should they, for the duration, ally themselves with Stalin's war effort?

The first article in this section, basing itself on Shachtman's emphasis on the progressive role of nationalized property opted for the later course.

Joseph Carter, in the second article, for the first time argued that nationalization per se was not progressive and that the working class had nothing to defend in Stalin's government.

Shachtman's reply, in the form of a resolution, denounced Carter's view as an apology for capitalist restoration and emphasized that, under some conditions, it might be necessary for socialists to "fight with the army of Stalin."

THE BASIS FOR DEFENSISM IN RUSSIA - Ernest Erber

Long and violent polemics were waged between Trotsky and his supporters on the one hand and ourselves on the other during the Russian invasions of Poland and Finland over the relation between the economy of a state and the character of its wars.

Trotsky insisted, in the case of Russia, upon an automatic relationship - "Progressive economy equals progressive war" was what his formula boiled down to. This resulted in the contradiction of simultaneously denouncing the invasion as a "blow at the world revolution" but characterizing them as "progressive wars."

We answered that no war that dealt a blow at the revolution could be progressive since it was precisely the effect of the war on advancing or retarding the proletarian revolution that determined whether it was progressive or reactionary.

We did not, however (nor could anyone who considered himself a Marxist), say that there was no connection between the economy of a state and the character of its war. What we insisted on was that certain states could, on the basis of the same economy, fight *both* progressive and reactionary wars. Factors in addition to the economy would have to be weighed in connection with a specific war to determine its character. These would be rooted in the political, diplomatic and military policies that preceded that war.

The Defense of Collectivist Property

The war between Britain and Germany was an imperialist war on both sides because the economy of both countries forced them to fight for markets, raw materials and outlets for surplus capital. It was a war over the redivision of the world.

The war between Japan and China was imperialist on Japan's side and national defensive on China's side because the economy of Japan forced her to expand into China while the latter was struggling to create a unified national existence.

In the war between Germany and Russia we must begin by asking "What is the nature of Russian economy?"

A defensist cannot discuss the character of the war with those who hold that Russia is a capitalist state. The discussion with them can only revolve around the question of the nature of Russian economy. If Russian economy is no different from that of Germany's or Britain's, then, obviously, the matter of defeatism or defensism requires no discussion.

With those, however, who hold that Russian economy is basically different from the economy of the capitalist world, as does Shachtman, there is common ground on which to discuss an attitude towards the character of the war.

The Economic Conflict Between Russia and World Imperialism

The Russian Revolution dealt world capitalism a double blow. First, it established a workers' state to act as both a beacon and a spur to the revolution in the rest of the world. We can refer to this as a *political* blow to capitalism. Second, it wrested one-sixth of the earth from world imperialism and threw up a monopoly of foreign trade to keep it free from imperialist penetration. We can refer to this as an *economic* blow to capitalism.

The Stalinist counter-revolution has effectively wiped out the existence of Russia as a *political* threat to capitalism. Far from remaining merely passive, Stalinist Russia did its utmost in Spain, China, Germany, France and elsewhere to reassure the capitalist states that it desired nothing else than the status quo - to be left alone.[1] There was no political concession too treacherous or revolting for Stalin. He

123

Neither Capitalism nor Socialism

buried revolutions with an effectiveness that surpassed anything the capitalists themselves could do.

But he could not purchase peace and security! Neither from the Anglo-French imperialists nor from Hitler. For the new exploiting class in Russia was forced to exist upon the nationalized economy they had appropriated from the revolution. The existence of the nationalized economy was possible only as long as a monopoly of foreign trade kept Russia beyond the reach of world imperialism. *Economically*, therefore, the Russia of Stalin remained as much a problem on the agenda of world imperialism as the Russia of Lenin. As capitalism declined, the problem became ever more acute.

It is in this that the irrepressible conflict between Russia and world imperialism existed.

In speaking of "world imperialism" it is necessary to bear in mind that the term refers to *both* a generalized economic law and to definite national states. Economically imperialism is the same system, no matter which capitalist state carries it out. But politically, imperialism is the diplomatic and military activity of each particular imperialist state.

Thus we speak of the law of imperialist expansion into economically backward states. Yet, in connection with a specific expansion, for instance Ethiopia, it was undertaken by Italian imperialism in the face of resistance by British imperialism. Not love for the Ethiopians, but their own imperialist interests motivated the British.[2]

The above must be borne in mind when discussing the conflict between Russian economy and world imperialism.

Why the Concerted Imperialist Attack Did Not Occur

The years following the revolution in 1917 saw feverish activities on the part of the imperialists against the Soviet Union. The first activities consisted of small scale intervention - Americans at Archangel, Japanese at Vladivostok, French in the Black Sea - and material assistance to the White Guard armies. As long as the war lasted, the Germans were also active against the Soviets in Finland and the Ukraine.

The Defense of Collectivist Property

Following the German revolution, the German bourgeoisie was unable to act against the Soviets on its own and unwilling to act as the agents of French and British imperialism. To do the latter would have only established Anglo-French imperialism on both of Germany's frontiers and make the resurrection of German military strength all the more difficult.

Following the failure to successfully utilize Poland against the Soviet Union in 1921, the British imperialists made preparations for a direct intervention. The militant response of the British working class with a general strike put an end to these moves.

The German bourgeoisie answered the anti-Soviet agitation of Anglo-French imperialism with the Treaty of Rappollo, a German-Soviet pact for diplomatic and military collaboration. The pact was not the inspiration of the German Social Democracy but of the Reichswehr general staff, the stronghold of the most aggressive German nationalists. Russian collaboration represented to the Germans both a weapon against Anglo-French imperialism and a means of blackmailing them. This tactic foreshadowed the policy of Nazism, which was nothing else but the national chauvinist element in complete control.[3]

From 1921 until 1933 the existence of a strong revolutionary movement in Central Europe and the anti-war sentiments of the British and French working classes prevented any further imperialist adventures against Russia. However, the victory of Hitler opened a new epoch. Beginning in Germany, the proletarian movements of Central Europe were smashed one by one. In their place arose the new military might of German imperialism. But German imperialism was not only a threat to the Soviet Union. It was also a threat to Anglo-French hegemony. Even if Germany struck at Russia first, Anglo-French imperialism would have little consolation. For the German organization of Russian resources would again make her the first military power on the continent and place France at her mercy. The result was he feverish and contradictory diplomacy of England and France from the advent of Hitler to the outbreak of the war. First, efforts to placate Germany with loans, permission to rebuild its navy, etc. - then the Stalin-Laval

Neither Capitalism nor Socialism

Pact - then the Munich Peace - then feverish efforts for a British-Russian Pact - then the war.

From this review it becomes apparent that the nature of the conflict between Germany and Anglo-French imperialism was such that a joint imperialist attack became ever more improbable. (The conflict between Anglo-American imperialism and Japan in the Far East had the same result.) History had cast Stalinist Russia for the role of an ally of one of the imperialist camps.

Had England been willing to sign a second Munich Pact over the body of Poland, it is highly probable that German imperialism would have launched its first offensive against Russia. But another appeasement would have cost Britain every continental ally, with the possible exception of France. When Hitler realized that a second Munich was out of the question, he chose the pact with Stalin and the war against Britain first.

But the war against Britain has bogged down. The Channel could not be blitzed. The prospect is a long war. Russian supplies now became imperative for Germany. The economic organization of Russia by German imperialism would solve both its historic objective and its immediate military needs. The long awaited imperialist attack on Russia is taking place.

The Hitler-Stalin Pact and Russian Imperialism

For the Kremlin, the pact with Hitler promised two advantages: (a) another chance to escape involvement in the war and (b) the opportunity of sharing in the conquests of German imperialism. But did not the Russian participation in the division of Poland, the conquest of the Baltic states, etc., prove that Russian participation in the war was identical with that of Germany? Superficially it was identical. In both cases armies attacked and occupied territories. But fundamentally it was different.

The imperialism of Russia was of that primitive kind found in embryonic form in every exploiting class and awaiting but the opportunity to become active. Every exploiting class seeks to perpetuate itself against internal and external foes. This requires military and

The Defense of Collectivist Property

economic strength. An opportunity to increase its military and economic strength is therefore eagerly accepted. Parts of Poland and Finland, Bessarabia and the Baltic states were to be picked up, practically, for a song. The Russian rulers would truly have been altruists had they declined the invitation.

But is this the same as modern finance imperialism with its "expand or die"? Has anyone yet proven that Russian expansion was forced by internal economic pressures? Has anyone yet explained why Russia took such modest slices of Finnish territory when she could have extracted more if Finnish rsources were vital to her? Or why she has relinquished the nickel mines? Or why she chose territory that had primarily little economic value?

Russian imperialism has perhaps something in common with Chinese imperialism in Tibet but nothing in common with modern finance imperialism.

Stalin's War Against Finland and Stalin's War Against Germany

The invasion of Poland and Finland was an attempt by the Kremlin to strengthen its own reactionary rule. Since it made the workers of the occupied countries victims of nationalist illusions and agents of their own national bourgeoisie and through them of world imperialism, the Soviet occupation lowered their revolutionary consciousness and retarded their class development. This constituted a blow at the world revolution. The revolts in the Baltic states have revealed that Stalin had not turned them into fortresses but rather into prisons with inmates who were prepared to mutiny at the first opportunity. This has justified our position that military occupation of buffer territory at the expense of alienating the support of the workers of the world would be a loss, not a gain, to the defensive efforts of the Kremlin. The purposes, the execution, and results of the Soviet occupations were thoroughly reactionary.

Can we, however, say the same for the Kremlin's attempts to defend Russia against German imperialism?

In the case of the conflict between Germany and the British empire with who is waging a defensive war and who an offensive war. All

Neither Capitalism nor Socialism

finance imperialism is, by its very nature, aggressive. If Germany attacked first, it only meant that the solution to her economic problems could not bear as long a postponement as those of Britain and France.

But can we also say that the conflict between Germany and Russia is basically an attempt to re-divide the world. We can say that on Germany's side it was caused by the pressure of German economy upon the frontiers of Russia. But can we say that it was also caused by the pressure of Russian economy on the frontiers of Germany?

Germany's attack on Russia is so obviously a predatory imperialist raid against Russian economic resources that no one - no one - has yet tried to attribute it to anything else.

Is the reactionary war against Poland and Finland - undertaken on the initiative of the Kremlin - being repeated in the attempt of the Kremlin to resist German imperialism? The answer is so obviously no that it seems a bit childish to have to deal with the question in these terms.

Russia is participating in this war because the Kremlin is fighting for its life. Further concessions to Hitler would have so lowered its prestige and strength within the country as to make it vulnerable to its internal enemies - ither of the right or the left.[4] True, it turned down Hitler's demands and chose to fight because its own neck was at stake. But why did Negrin fight? Why did Haile Selassie fight? Why does Chiang Kai-shek fight?[5] Stalin can save his own neck only by resisting German imperialism. In doing this his interests coincide with those of the world proletariat. Russia's defense against Germany is a progressive war.

How the Outcome of the Russo-German War Will Effect World Revolution

Victory or defeat for either Germany or the British Empire will offer the proletariat as great or as small a perspective for revolution. The destruction of the British Empire will open up an epoch of colonial revolutions in Asia and Africa which might prove to be the Achilles' heel of "victorious" German imperialism. The defeat of Germany will liberate Europe and once more offer the proletariat an opportunity to play its historic role.

The Defense of Collectivist Property

What will Hitler's conquest of Russia offer the world proletariat? The only answer that might be given - we hope never in our ranks - is that it will destroy Stalinism. This program has long ago been written for "Trotskyism" - not by revolutionists but by the GPU and Stalin's pen prostitutes. The destruction of the Stalin regime by the *Russian proletariat* would of course mean the destruction of Stalinism everywhere. The destruction of the Stalin regime by *Hitler* would - aside from its other reactionary consequences - forever prevent history from putting the Stalinist lies about the Soviet "paradise" to the test. The Stalinist dupes would not become revolutionists because Hitler destroyed Stalinism. They would carry their illusions about the Soviet Union to their grave.

The effect of an imperialist conquest of Russia was very ably described by Max Shachtman in the December 1940 issue of *The New International*:

(The author here quotes the passage which appears above in which the reduction of Russia to "a somewhat more advanced India" is predicted. EH)

Comrade Shachtman, however, would defend Russia against the above consequences only in case of a *combined* imperialist attack in which Russia would have no allies. Why such a combined attack became virtually impossible was dealt with above.

But there are those who argue that Hitler is not invading the Soviet Union primarily to destroy the nationalized economy and make it a German colony. His primary concern, they say, is to defeat Great Britain. The Russian campaign is merely (!) a raid to secure the resources with which to continue his main war. True, perhaps. But how absurd when used to define the character of the war! Hitler, likewise, was not primarily interested in expropriating the German Jews. He only wanted their resources for his war against Britain. True, perhaps, but of little comfort to the Jews.   But what would the effect of a Russian victory be? The possibility of a Russian victory without

129

Neither Capitalism nor Socialism

the support of proletarian revolutions in the West is extremely hypothetical.[6] But we can be sure that news of serious German reverses tomorrow would set the wheels in motion in Britain for an understanding with Germany. Is anyone so hare-brained as to believe that Britain would turn over the task of organizing Central Europe to Stalin?

But if the European revolution breaks out before Hitler has smashed Stalin, will it not fall victim to Stalinism as did the Spanish revolution? Of this we have no guarantee. All we can say is that with the rise of the revolutionary current, the revolutionary Marxists can again swim with the stream and seek to win it for their program. We can ask for no more.[7]

Stalin's Relations with Anglo-American Imperialism

"War is a continuation of politics by other means," has long been accepted as a guide-rule by Marxists. But progressive politics in time of general imperialist war often become inseparable from one of the imperialist camps and, thereby, lose their progressive character.

In the last war the struggle of the Arabs against the Turkish Empire became merged with the reactionary struggle of British imperialism to control the Near East. The struggle of Serbia for national unity and independence became merged with the struggle of Russia to break up the Austro-Hungarian Empire and control the Balkans. The struggle of Belgium to maintain its national independence became merged with the struggle of Anglo-French imperialism to control the continent. China was ordered by the Allied imperialists to declare war on Germany. The nationalist revolutionary movement of the Czechs was enlisted by the Allies against Germany. The fighting organizations of the Polish nationalists were enrolled by the Central Powers.

The Irish revolutionary movement entered into military relations with the Germans. Submarines landed arms on the Irish coast and conveyed information between Ireland and Germany. But revolutionary Marxists hailed and supported the uprising of the Irish nationalists against British rule in 1916.

The Defense of Collectivist Property

These examples illustrate the fact that the mere alliance with a reactionary force for military reasons does not affect the progressive nature of a struggle. What is important is the extent to which the progressive side in the war can maintain its independence.

Had the Ethiopians risen in revolt against Italian rule at the outbreak of the war and accepted British arms, would this have changed the revolutionary content of their struggle? The fact that they rose at a time when Italy was occupied in a war with Britain would have attested to their perspicacity but would not have changed the character of their struggle. But their current role as auxiliaries of the British army in conquering Ethiopia for British imperialism has no progressive content whatsoever. Chiang Kai-shek has long been acting as an ally of British and American imperialism in China. American imperialism has already given him more financial, material and diplomatic support than it will ever give Russia. American engineers, military advisers, aviators and other specialists have long been part of the Chinese forces. Roosevelt seeks volunteers for China's army by offering to accept service there as equivalent to service in America's own army and therefore release them from the draft obligation. Has this changed the character of China's war? No. Will an American declaration of war against Japan alter the situation? It might. We would have to wait and see. Naval struggles in the Pacific between Japan and America and military operations on the Phillipines would not affect the character of China's war. Those who would become defeatists in China at such a time would, in effect, be punishing China for remaining at war with Japan while the latter was being attacked by a third power. Was the American Revolution any less historically progressive because it was accomplished with the aid of Louis XIV's army and navy?

If, however, the Chiang Kai-shek government were reduced to a mere facade for American imperialism, the character of the war would obviously change. Its outcome would only determine whether Japanese or American imperialism would exploit China. The world proletariat has no interest in this question. It rejects both imperialism.

Neither Capitalism nor Socialism

The argument that Russia takes part in the war in a reactionary manner because she is allied to Anglo-American imperialism becomes at first incomprehensible and then ludicrous. She has merely "switched sides" is the argument. That she has "switched sides" is incontestable. But this would only have validity if we had been defeatists during the Finnish war on grounds that Russia was allied to Germany. This was not the case. We were defeatists because the alliance with Germany had a reactionary purpose, the conquest of new territory by the Kremlin. Is this the purpose - *today* - of the alliance with Anglo-American imperialism? How utterly absurd! What the Kremlin may do tomorrow we will leave until tomorrow. No one has yet asked us to be defeatists in China on the ground that Chiang Kai-shek has designs upon Japan which he will realize after crushing the Japanese army. The argument that the alliance with Anglo-American imperialism makes Russia's war reactionary is nothing but the other side of the coin from the Stalinist argument that the same alliance makes the war of Anglo-American imperialism progressive.

Those who hold that it is possible for Russia to fight a progressive war against imperialist encroachment upon her territory and who refuse to be for Russian defense today can only do so on one basis - that Stalin has already become a mere facade for the Anglo-American imperialists and turned the country over to them. That this *might* take place is improbable but not impossible. In that event it will be immaterial whether Russia becomes a colony of German or of Anglo--American imperialism. But since when do we base our strategy of today on the *possibility* of tomorrow?

Stalin's alliance with Anglo-American imperialism today does not give the latter one-tenth as much entree to Russia as the Anglo--American alliance with China gives it entree to the latter country. To be consistent, those who hold that Russia is fighting a reactionary war by virtue of her alliance must certainly say the same for China.

The Lines of Defeatism and Defensism Tested in Action

An attitude toward the character of a war must be based on the fundamental factors - strategy of the world revolution, nature of

The Defense of Collectivist Property

imperialism, character of the Russian economy, etc. But the position based on these considerations must also coincide with the obvious tactics of the revolutionary struggle. If they do not, something is wrong with the position. It was in this test that the line of Trotsky on the Polish and Finnish events bogged down worst. It bogged down so badly that a Finnish civil war had to be discovered to bolster it.

The revolutionary defeatist in Russia today must tell the workers to continue the class struggle without regard for its effect on the military front against Germany. This could only be justified with the argument that a German conquest of Russia is no different for the world proletariat than a German conquest of France. The quotation from Shachtman has already pointed out the significant difference. Or the defeatists would have to become preposterous and tell the Russian worker that the country was already in the hands of imperialism - Anglo-American imperialism - and that resistance to German imperialism is only in the interest of Wall Street and London investments.

(Or would the defeatist tell the Russian worker that there are only three camps in this war - two imperialist camps and the revolutionary camp, and that Russia is part of one of the imperialist camps? If it is the slogan of the Third Camp that has led our defeatist astray then the motion of Comrade Coolidge of a year ago to expunge all reference to the Third Camp from our documents was absolutely correct. The "Third Camp" as an agitational slogan was very much in order. But the "Third Camp" in the sense of military line-ups which precludes the possibility of a military alliance between a progressive and a reactionary force - this is a snare and a delusion. The sooner Marxist education roots it out of our movement, the sooner will the damage be undone.)

Basing himself on this line, the defeatist would seek to institute a mass movement against the Kremlin on the demand that it cease its imperialist war against Germany - the slogan of "peace" in time of war is very revolutionary. But what would our movement say tomorrow if Stalin made peace which could only take place on Hitler's terms? We would denounce him as a capitulator and a traitor. Why? We did not do it when he made peace with Finland. As true defeatists, we

Neither Capitalism nor Socialism

welcomed the latter. Would we welcome peace with German imperialism?

Would the defeatist ever be able to explain to a Russian worker why he should take the manufacture and transport of supplies to China into account when waging the struggle against Stalin but not the needs of the Russian front against Germany? How explain to the Russian worker that the conquest of China by Japan is of direct consequence to him, but the conquest of Russia by Germany does not matter sufficiently to require defensive efforts?

The program of the Russian revolutionary defensists would be along the following lines:

> No political support to the Stalin regime. Only a democratically constituted workers' regime can victoriously defend the Soviet Union. Continue the struggle for the overthrow of the bureaucratic exploiters as the first step in the organization of defense against German imperialism. On guard against the tendency of the Kremlin to capitulate to Hitler.
>
> "War at the front - revolution in the rear!" support to all mass movements against the Kremlin, on a defensist basis, i.e., choice of those weapons of struggle that will not weaken the front.
>
> Election of committees in the shops, villages and armed forces as first step toward reconstituting Soviets. Freedom of press, speech and organization. Dissolution of the GPU and creation of workers' vigilance committees. Release of all political prisoners held for revolutionary activity against the Stalin regime.
>
> For a free and independent Soviet Ukraine! For self--determination for all national minorities oppressed by the Kremlin regime.

New International - August 1941

BUREAUCRATIC COLLECTIVISM - Joseph Carter

Hitler's invasion of Russia brought sharply to the fore the conflicting views on the class character of the Soviet Union. Until then those holding diverse positions on this question were all united by a common conception of the reactionary character of Russia's role in the Second World War and common political conclusions. However, the new turn in the war once again raised the problem: Is Stalin conducting a progressive or reactionary war? Should we retain our position of revolutionary opposition to all camps in the Second World War or become supporters of Russia in the war?   For us these questions necessarily raise the fundamental problem of the class nature of the Soviet Union. Only on this basis can we establish clear and consistent criteria for deciding the character of Russia's war and our political tasks. Even more: the dispute on this question has already revealed confusion and uncertainty on fundamental concepts of Marxism which far transcend in importance the "Russian question" itself. There is little doubt that in this problem, as in other matters, our generation of Marxists has failed to analyze adequately the new phenomena of our times, to examine critically our old doctrines in the light of new experiences , to revise the views found wanting, and thus failed to prepare ourselves for the rapidly moving events and tasks. Not only have the old movements failed, but the new movement for a Fourth International has likewise not met the theoretical and practical tests which the social crisis and the war have created.

It is imperative that this fact be frankly acknowledged; so that starting from a clear recognition of the existence of a crisis of Marxism - for it is nothing less than that - we can proceed collectively to re-evaluate our old views and thus sharpen the theoretical and practical instruments indispensable for socialist victory. So far as the present author is concerned, the basis of such re-examination remains the great scientific teachings of Marx and Engels, which, employed in the critical spirit advised by the masters themselves, alone furnish the guide for our present needs and for working class emancipation.

In the present article I propose to discuss the class character of the Soviet Union, particularly the views of Leon Trotsky, and present my own position in positive form.

Neither Capitalism nor Socialism

Trotsky's Analysis of Stalinism

Trotsky once wrote: "You will agree that a theory is in general valuable only in so far as it helps to foresee the course of development and influences it purposefully." (*The Defense of the Russian Revolution*) Let us apply this sound concept to Trotsky's analysis of Stalinism.

The origin of the Russian Trotskyist Opposition dates back to the sharp factional fight which broke out in the Bolshevik Party after the death of Lenin. Trotsky analyzed this struggle as follows: In view of the fact that the Bolshevik Party had a complete monopoly of political power (that is, excluded all rival parties), the interests of the conflicting classes sought expression through factions of the ruling party. The Right Wing represented the Thermidorian faction; the pressure of the capitalist restorationist elements (the kulaks, Nepmen, the old petty-bourgeois specialists) and the labor aristocracy (the better paid workers, white collar employees, and trade union officialdom). On the other hand, the left opposition represented the interests of the working class. In between these two class forces was the Stalin faction, the "bureaucratic Centrist" wing of the party, representing no independent class, but wavering between the two fundamental factions, veering in the long run towards the right, viz., towards bourgeois restoration. The defeats of the West European socialist revolutions strengthened both the Right and the Center; these two united against the Left on the basis of "socialism in one country alone."

The main internal danger, continued Trotsky, came from the capitalist elements, and politically the Right Wing. The later favored a slow tempo of industrialization and collectivization, and increased concessions and conciliation with the rich and middle peasants. The Stalinists were attacked primarily for constantly conceding to the Right Wing. Trotsky spoke of the existence of elements of dual power in Russia, bourgeois and proletarian. He warned that the destruction of the proletarian wing of the party would spell the victory of the Russian Thermidor, that is, the destruction of nationalized property and the establishment of capitalism. Such, according to Trotsky, was the objective meaning of the factional fight in the Bolshevik party and the logic of its development.

The Defense of Collectivist Property

Early in 1928 Trotsky wrote:

... the socialist character of industry is determined and secured in a decisive measure by the role of the party, the voluntary internal cohesion of the proletarian vanguard, the conscious discipline of the administrators, trade union functionaries, members of shop nuclei,etc. If we allow that this web is weakening, disintegrating and ripping then it becomes self-evident that within a brief period nothing will be left of the socialist character of state industry, transport, etc. The trusts and individual factories will begin living an independent life. Not a trace will be left of the planned beginnings, so weak at the present time. The economic struggles of the workers will acquire a scope unrestricted save by the relation of forces. The state ownership of the means of production will be first transformed to a juridical fiction and later on even the latter will be swept away. (*The Third International After Lenin*.)

Trotsky's prognoses were refuted by history. The First Five Year Plan, put into effect a few months after he had penned the above lines, strengthened and centralized state ownership and control over the trusts and factories and extended the planned economy on a scale never reached before. The Bolshevik Party was destroyed, both its Left Wing and Right Wing liquidated politically and physically. The proletarian "web" was broken, but the Stalinists extended their totalitarian control over the economy. At the same time the bureaucracy destroyed virtually all the old capitalist elements in the economy. Contrary to Trotsky's predictions, the destruction of the Bolshevik party did not mean the end of state property and planning; Russia did not travel the road of Thermidorian, capitalist restoration. On the contrary the Stalinist counter-revolution took a new, hitherto unknown path, the road of bureaucratic absolutism.

Yet Trotsky in the above quotation (and on innumerable other occasions) stated that "the *socialist* character of industry is determined and secured in a decisive measure by the role of the party, the

Neither Capitalism nor Socialism

voluntary internal cohesion of the proletarian vanguard, etc." That is, the socialist character of state industry was determined by the domination of the proletarian party in the state and through it in the economy. Or, put in another way, the economic power of the proletariat rested on its political power.

Confronted by the unexpected development of the destruction of the political power of the working class *and* the strengthening of state power and planning, Trotsky faced the dilemma: either to maintain his old criterion and affirm that Russia is no longer a workers' state and its economy no longer "socialist"; or to revise completely the Marxist conception of the workers' state. He chose the latter course, and thereby abandoned the Marxist view he had held until then. He now affirmed that it was the state-owned character of property which determined the socialist character of the economy and the proletarian nature of the state. The bureaucracy's expropriation of the political power of the working class, he added, only signified that Russia was a "degenerated" workers' state, politically dominated by a Bonapartist bureaucracy.

Unfortunately, Trotsky never subjected his old analyses to a thorough critical examination. He never sought to explain why, contrary to his predictions, Russia did not travel the Thermidorian, capitalist road of counter-revolution even though the political power of the working class was destroyed. It is true that he often declared that "the bureaucracy after a stubborn resistance, found itself compelled by the *logic of its own interests* to adopt the program of industrialization and collectivization." (*The Kirov Assassination* emphasis in original) But this would only indicate that the logic of the bureaucracy's own interests was not capitalist restoration (or socialism) but its own absolutist rule in state and economy.

And in retrospect, was the Right Wing of the Bolshevik Party the "Thermidorian" faction? Here again Trotsky never re-examined this question in great detail. However, he did write in 1938:

The latest judicial frame-ups were aimed as a blow *against the Left*. This is true also of the mopping up of the leaders of the Right Opposition, because the Right group of the Bolshevik Party, seen from the viewpoint of the bureaucracy's interests and tendencies, represented a *Left* danger. (*Program and Resolutions of the Founding Conference of the Fourth International,* Emphasis in original)

This correct appraisal of the relation between the Right Wing and the Stalinists involves a serious revision of the old view as to the "class struggle" in the Bolshevik Party. It is strange indeed that the Right Wing, the "Thermidorian" faction, whose policy was that of resistance to rapid industrialization, was to the left of the bureaucracy which "by the logic of its own interests" adopted the program of rapid industrialization and collectivization. Strange, that is, from the viewpoint of those who hold that Russia is a workers' state. It should be recalled that in 1929 there were Russian Oppositionists who advocated a bloc with the Right Wing against Stalinism. Trotsky at that time wrote a vitriolic attack on this proposal as "unprincipled" because it would mean a united front of the Left and Right against the "Centrists." In this case, as in others, the false analysis led to incorrect politics.

Stalinism and Bonapartism

Trotsky defended his new position, that the Stalinist state is a workers' state though the working class has no political power, by citing the bourgeois Bonapartist regimes. Under Bonapartism (and fascism) the bourgeoisie is deprived of all political power and is in fact politically oppressed. Despite this, the bourgeoisie remains socially the ruling class and the regime is bourgeois in character. Stalinist Bonapartism, according to Trotsky, has an analogous relation to the Russian working class.

The analogy would be valid only if the political expropriation of the working class had been accompanied by the strengthening of its economic and social power, its domination of society. Such was the case under all Bonapartist regimes: the political expropriation of the bourgeoisie was accompanied by (or more exactly, was the precondition for) the strengthening of its economic and social power. (In a more complex form this holds true for fascism.) Marxists have adduced abundant empirical evidence to prove this contention.

139

Neither Capitalism nor Socialism

But what does the evidence show as regards Russia? Simply this: that the working class has been deprived of all economic and social power as well as political power. The strengthening of state property and planning, which allegedly signifies the social rule of the proletariat, resulted in the increased economic, social and political oppression of the working class. Here is a process which is the exact opposite of what occurs under Bonapartism!

By this analogy, however, Trotsky revealed an important methodological error which permeates his writings on Stalinist Russia. In seeking to explain the different forms of bourgeois rule, Trotsky failed to give adequate recognition to the decisive, qualitative differences between proletarian and bourgeois rule. In other contexts, for example in his theory of the permanent revolution, Trotsky proceeded from the basis of the totally new character of proletarian rule as compared to all previous class rule, to wit, the working class must first conquer political power, and through its own state organize the economy. (And with successful socialist revolutions internationally, build a world socialist economy which would lead to the dissolution of the workers' states and the proletariat as a class, to the triumph of a world socialist classless society.)

Every ruling class has its own laws of development and its own forms of economic, social and political domination. The bourgeoisie, for example, first develops its economic power (capitalist ownership of the means of production and exchange) in the womb of feudalism, and then struggles for political and social power. In bourgeois society, in other words, the rule of the capitalist class rests basically on bourgeois private property. The state power defending this property may be in the hands of a semi-feudal aristocracy, a military clique, a parliamentary government controlled by the big bourgeois or petty-bourgeois parties, a Bonapartist bureaucracy, a fascist bureaucracy, etc. Quite the contrary is the case of the proletarian revolution and proletarian state. The proletariat is a propertyless class. Its control over the economy and its domination in society is possible only through first winning political power. It is through state power that the working class becomes the ruling class and develops the conditions

The Defense of Collectivist Property

for the abolition of all classes, the socialist society. Without political power the working class cannot be the ruling class in any sense.

Of course, the workers' state may assume different forms. But whatever the form the state must express the political power of the proletariat. Once it is acknowledged, as Trotsky and everyone in our movement has, that the Russian workers have no political power whatsoever, that is tantamount to saying that Russia is no longer a workers' state.

But can there not be a sick, degenerated workers' state? History has given the answer: the regime of Lenin and Trotsky was a sick, bureaucratized. revolutionary workers' state - as Lenin and Trotsky themselves often affirmed. In a healthy workers' state there would be complete democracy, the working class exercising its power democratically through Soviets, trade unions, rival parties. This state of affairs, as is known, never existed in Russia. The political rule of the working class was expressed almost exclusively through the dictatorship of the proletarian party, the Bolsheviks (with extreme limitations on Soviet and union democracy from the earliest days). The administration of the state and the economy in culturally backward and isolated Russia, while controlled by the Bolsheviks, was in the hands of a bureaucracy. The Bolsheviks expected, and worked for, the extension of the Russian Revolution into the more advanced industrial countries which would break the capitalist encirclement, raise the Russian industrial and cultural level, and thus create the preconditions for complete workers' democracy.

When these conditions did not materialize the Stalin faction which controlled the party apparatus expressed the dominant desire of the bureaucracy for a peaceful and stable national existence. The old Bolshevik (and bourgeois) elements of the bureaucracy were eliminated, and a new bureaucracy created. The theory and practice of national socialism, "socialism in one country alone," was developed as the great social rationalization ("ideology") of the bureaucracy. With the Stalin faction as its representative it utilized its centralized administrative control of the state and economy to conduct a civil war to destroy its internal opponents, proletarian and bourgeois. On the

Neither Capitalism nor Socialism

one hand, it destroyed the limited workers' democracy that had existed, liquidated the old Bolshevik Party and converted the Communist International into the world detachment of Stalin's Foreign Office and GPU. On the other hand, it wiped out virtually all remnants of the old capitalist elements in the economy, strengthened state property and extended the industrialization and collectivization of the country. Thus when the Stalinists announced "the complete and irrevocable victory of socialism," they were indeed proclaiming to the world the triumph of bureaucratic collectivism.

Bureaucratic Collectivism: What Kind of New Society

Stalinist Russia is thus a reactionary state based upon a new system of economic exploitation, bureaucratic collectivism. The ruling class is the bureaucracy which through its control of the state collectively owns, controls and administers the means of production and exchange. The basic motive force of the economy is the extraction of more and more surplus labor from the toilers so as to increase the revenue, power and position of the bureaucracy. The economy is organized and directed through state totalitarian planning and political terrorism. The toilers are compelled by the state (as well as economic necessity) to labor in the factories and fields. Forced labor is thus an inherent feature of present-day Russian productive relations.

The relations within the ruling class - the share which individual bureaucrats receive of the wealth produced, their relative power and position, the manner in which persons enter or are forced out of the ruling class - are determined by non-economic, primarily political factors.

Through the state monopoly of foreign trade the bureaucracy has a complete monopoly over the internal market; for the exploitation of the abundant material and human resources of the country, for the investment and for sale of goods. This monopoly is indispensable for the Stalinist imperialist exploitation and oppression of the national minority peoples of the Soviet Union (the Ukrainians, the Georgians etc.)

The Defense of Collectivist Property

While bureaucratic collectivism has succeeded in raising the industrial level of the country, its productive relations are tremendous obstacles to the real growth of the social productivity of labor, the raising of living standards of the masses, and the economic and political freedom of the workers and peasants. Despite the organizational advantages of state-owned monopoly and the vast internal market, and totalitarian planning (aided by the importation of advanced capitalist technique), Stalinist Russia has experienced a growing decline in the annual rate of increase of industrial output and an increasing disproportion between the income of the bureaucracy and the "new intelligentsia" on the one hand, and the income of the mass of workers and peasants on the other. (In recent years the yearly rate of increase of industrial production has been, according to official figures, only twice the rate experienced under Czarism.) The terroristic regime which is an integral part of bureaucratic planning (the bureaucratic productive relations) leads to constant disruptions in production; disproportions in the output of the various industries dependent on one another and therefore large-scale economic waste; low efficiency of production. The constant purges of the bureaucracy leads to vast disruptions of planning and production. The low wages, speed-up and poor housing have led to such large turnovers of labor, despite laws restricting labor mobility, that far stricter laws carrying penalties including the death sentence, had to be proclaimed to maintain production. The progressive, organic and long-range development of the productive forces, the real growth of the social productivity of labor, and the raising of the standard of living of the masses demand scientific planning, that is, democratic planning by and of the masses. This is the antithesis of Stalinism.

Then again, bureaucratic collectivism is a nationally limited economy (or, more accurately, confined to a single backward "empire," Stalinist Russia). In relation to the capitalist imperialist states, Russia occupies the position of a huge national trust which by monopolizing the home market intensifies the contradiction existing within these countries between the tendency for unlimited increase of the capitalist productive forces and the growing limitations of the

Neither Capitalism nor Socialism

markets for capital investment and the sale of commodities. From the standpoint of Russian industrial and cultural development, the overthrow of world capitalism is an indispensable condition for the liberation of its own nationally confined productive forces, so that it could benefit fully from advanced Western technique and take its place as an integral part of a progressive world economy. Here also, bureaucratic collectivism reveals its socially reactionary character in its role as an assistant of outlived capitalist imperialism in the task of destroying the independent working class movement for socialism.

Thus, from the day of its birth the new Stalinist society is a reactionary obstacle to the development of Russian and world society toward socialist freedom and security. From a historical viewpoint, Russia has taken a bastard path backward from the regime established by the Bolshevik Revolution. It is from the start torn by contradictions and antagonisms which exclude its assuming a progressive road comparable to early bourgeois society. It arrives on the scene of history as an expression of world social reaction; at a time when the world economic conditions already exist for a great leap forward from class exploitation to socialist freedom and plenty; and when the working class is the only social power which can bring about the progressive transformation of society.

The class conscious workers have no interest in common with this new system of exploitation and oppression, bureaucratic collectivism. In wartime as during peace the revolutionary socialists must not give any support to the Stalinist state. Our task is that of awakening the working class to socialist struggle against bureaucratic collectivism, fascism and democratic imperialism; and for working class power and socialism.

[Revolutionary socialists, therefore, are not defensists with respect to the Stalinist state either in peacetime or in war, any more than they are in capitalist states. They advocate and support only those measures which lead towards the independent organization and action of the working class against the bureaucracy, for socialist revolution and workers' power. They will seek allies among the peasantry and

The Defense of Collectivist Property

oppressed minorities within the Stalinist state. In the course of the struggle against Stalinism, there will inevitably arise both progressive and reactionary movements, both under the banner of democracy. Revolutionary socialists, while advocating socialist democracy, will support all progressive democratic movements against Stalinism and seek to gain leadership in such movements. They will oppose all reactionary movements, in particular those connected with bourgeois imperialist powers. Such movements have as their aim the restoration of capitalism. Revolutionary socialists are as opposed to capitalist restoration in Russia as they are against the maintenance of Bureaucratic collectivism.

In no case do we accept the alternatives - Stalinist reaction or capitalist-imperialist reaction as the determinant of the struggle of the working class, any more than we do in the case of the alternative fascism or imperialist democracy. Revolutionary workers must take the third road: the struggle against both types of reaction and against the exploitative and oppressive societies from which they spring, the struggle for the political power of the proletariat and for socialism. No other victory can lead to the emancipation of the working class and the progress of humanity.

Hitler's invasion of Russia is an integral part of the Second World War. The immediate aim of the German attack is the conquest of Russian territory primarily for economic and military advantages in the struggle to defeat British and American imperialism; and the seizure of the rich Russian resources as a step toward complete world domination. The Anglo-American alliance with, and aid to, Russia are aimed at the defeat of German imperialism. Stalin's defense of Russia is a defense of the bureaucracy's dictatorial rule over the Russian people and the oppressed nationalities (Ukraine, etc.), and a defense of his imperialist conquests since 1939 in the Baltic, Balkans, etc. As against both imperialist camps - Berlin-Rome-Tokyo and

Neither Capitalism nor Socialism

Washington-London-Moscow - we remain the party of the third camp of labor and the oppressed peoples.]*

Shachtman's Theoretical Confusion

What are Shachtman's views on Russian society? A quick reading of his article, "Is Russia a Workers' State?" (New International, December 1940[8]) would suggest that he is in fundamental disagreement with Trotsky on the nature of Russian economy and society; and in basic accord with those who hold that Russia is a new, reactionary, exploiting society. However, as I propose to show, the appearance belies the reality. While accepting the latter position in "form," Shachtman has adopted the former position in "essence." The result is an illogical, eclectic combination of incompatible ideas which is called a third position.

Let us see. Shachtman has declared that in our movement only two contributions (aside from Trotsky's) had been made to the clarification of the Russian question. First, that introduced by Carter on the

---

*. The material in brackets is taken from a resolution introduced by Carter and his supporters. This article is in defense of that resolution and all the other sections of the resolution are included in the article. In fact, the whole section titled "Bureaucratic Collectivism: What Kind of Society?" is a paraphrase of the resolution.

It is strange that this section was left out of the article since Shachtman was accusing Carter of supporting pro-capitalist popular movements. Shachtman argued that *only* a *consciously* socialist movement could be supported. The paragraphs in brackets sum up Carter's answer to that charge.

The issue is important because the revolts in Eastern Europe against stalinism have not always been *consciously* socialist although none have been for returning heavy industry back to private ownership. Shachtman's position would, to take a contemporary example, seem to rule out support for a movement like Polish *Solidarity* while Carter's position would clearly make such support the center of a socialist political strategy.

The Defense of Collectivist Property

qualitative differences between the state rule of the proletariat and the state rule of the bourgeoisie. (Already discussed in the first section of the present article.) Second, the distinction between "property forms" and "property relations" introduced by Shachtman himself.

On the latter question, Shachtman writes in his article: "...Trotsky speaks interchangeably of the 'property forms' and the 'property relations' in the country as if he were referring to one and the same thing." It is true that under Stalin "state ownership of the means of production and exchange continue to exist... However, what is crucial are not the property forms, i.e., nationalized property, whose existence cannot be denied, but precisely the relations of the various social groups in the Soviet Union to this property, i.e., property relations!" The state owns the property but the bureaucracy controls the state and is "the ruling class of an unstable society which is already a fetter on economic development."

Thus summarized it would appear that there is complete agreement between Shachtman and those who declare that Russia is a reactionary bureaucratic collectivist state. What is "crucial" are the property relations writes Shachtman. But what are "property forms" as distinct from property relations? Shachtman defines them by giving examples: private property forms - as under capitalism and other class societies; state or collectivist property form of property as under Leninist Russia and Stalinist Russia.

Now, it is true that Trotsky identified Russian state property (the "property form") with the property relations established by the Russian workers' revolution. But he did this not only "as if he were referring to one and the same thing," as Shachtman writes, but because he was consciously referring to one and the same thing. In other words, his error was not terminological - a confusion of phrases - but an error in analysis. When Marxists speak of the "form of property" they invariably mean *social* form of property, that is, property relations; as feudal form of property (and economy), capitalist form of property (and economy), socialistic, transitional form of property (and economy), etc.

147

Neither Capitalism nor Socialism

If for the sake of greater clarity on the new Russian phenomenon Shachtman chooses to introduce a terminological distinction between "form of property" and "property relations" he can do so but only on one condition: By making clear that by "form of property" he does not mean "social form of property." Otherwise the result is not clarity but confusion; otherwise property forms *are* property relations.

If property forms are to be distinguished from property relations then the only meaningful distinction is that between the *general manner* in which property is owned (privately or through the state) and *who* owns the property. So that one can say, on the basis of private property, you can have feudal property relations and bourgeois property relations. This would be a distinction the technical organizational form of property (and economy) and the *social* form of property (and economy).

This is what Shachtman *appears* to say in the section "Property Forms and Property Relations".[9] To repeat once again: The property relations are "crucial" in determining the character of Stalinist society. Stalin, while retaining the state property forms, destroyed the property relations established by the Russian Revolution. This was a social counter-revolution.

Yet we find Shachtman writing in a later section of the same article:

> In the Soviet Union, control of the state, sole owner of social property, makes the bureaucracy the most powerful economic class. Therein lies the fundamental difference between the Soviet Union, even under Stalinism, and all other *pre-collectivist states*. The difference is of epochal importance.

Shachtman, of course, did not mean to write that the fundamental difference "between the Soviet Union, *even* under Stalinism," is that the bureaucracy is the most powerful economic class, for he does not hold that this was so in Leninist Russia. But his error in composition, due to hasty writing, has a deeper significance. Without submitting it to Freudian analysis, it is clear from the context of the entire section

The Defense of Collectivist Property

that Shachtman slides back to Trotsky's view on the "epochal historical importance" of present-day Russian society; that despite his lengthy polemic with Trotsky on property forms and property relations he considers that Stalinist Russia is a *socio-economic continuation* of the economic system under Lenin; a continuation of the progressive economy, transitional from capitalism to socialism, established by the Russian Revolution. Immediately following the paragraph quoted above, Shachtman adds:

> Of epochal importance, we repeat, for our analysis does not diminish by an iota the profound social revolutionary significance of the Russian proletarian revolution. Starting at a low level, lowered still further by years of war, civil war, famine and their devastations, isolated from the world economy, infested with a monstrous bureaucracy, the Soviet Union nevertheless attained a rhythm of economic development, an expansion of the productive forces which exceeded the expectations of the boldest revolutionary thinkers and easily aroused the astonishment of the entire world. This was not due to any virtues of the bureaucracy under whose regime it was accomplished, but in spite of the concomitant overhead waste of that reign. Economic progress in the Soviet Union was accomplished on the basis of planning and the new, collectivist forms of property established by the proletarian revolution.

Trotsky's Concept of Soviet Economy

Here in full bloom is *Trotsky's* basic analysis of present-day Russian economy. The Russian Revolution is not dead, according to both Trotsky and Shachtman; it exists in the "progressive" collectivist forms of property. To deny this, it would appear from the above, is to "diminish ... the profound social revolutionary significance of the Russian proletarian revolution" - no less. But Shachtman had written that "what is more crucial" in determining the character of Russian economy (and any economy) "are not the property forms, i.e., nationalized property ... but precisely the relations of various social

Neither Capitalism nor Socialism

groups in the Soviet Union to this property, i.e., *property relations!"* (Emphasis, including the triumphant exclamation point, is Shachtman's). If these property relations (bureaucratic class exploitation of the workers) are "crucial," why did not Shachtman compare them to capitalist property relations and show why the former are "more progressive" than the latter? The fact is, that despite Shachtman's painstaking insistence on the basic distinction between Russian "property forms" and "property relations" his collectivist forms of property look like, feel like, and act like, that is, *are* what Trotsky called interchangeably property forms and property relations. Shachtman, then, agrees with Trotsky on the social and historical significance of Stalinist Russia - as a progressive economy and society transitional from capitalism to socialism. He follows Trotsky's method of comparing the superiority of nationalized property over bourgeois private property, and citing the economic progress experienced under Stalinism as evidence of this superiority.

Thus in his attempt to combine the position that Russia is a new, reactionary economic system with the opposite view that it is a progressive economy established by the Russian workers' revolution but distorted by bureaucratic domination, Shachtman adopts arguments and terminology from the first position up to the point when he reaches the crucial problems of the concrete social and historical significance of Russian economy - the core of the dispute. He then employs Trotsky's arguments and essential theoretical conclusions, without, however, drawing other inescapable, theoretical and political conclusions which necessarily follow from them.

Several years ago Trotsky quite correctly wrote that anyone who holds that Russia is a new economic system of exploitation and agrees with what he (Trotsky) considered the criteria as to what constitutes a progressive society - and Shachtman fits this description - must be in essential agreement with him. In a polemic against a French comrade he stated that for the sake of the argument he would concede that Russia is a new class society and the bureaucracy a new exploiting class. He continued:

The Defense of Collectivist Property

But that does not prevent us from seeing that the new society is progressive in comparison with capitalism, for on the basis of nationalized property the new possessing "class" has assured a development of the productive forces never equaled in the history of the world. Marxism teaches us, does it not, that the productive forces are the fundamental factor of historic progress. A society which is not capable of assuring the growth of economic power is still less capable of assuring the well-being of the working masses, whatever may be the mode of distribution. The antagonism between feudalism and capitalism and the decline of the former has been determined precisely by the fact that the latter opened up new and grandiose possibilities for the stagnating productive forces. The same is true of the USSR. Whatever its mode of exploitation may be, this new society is by its very character superior to capitalist society. There you have the real point of departure for Marxist analysis.[10]

Shachtman agrees with Trotsky as to what is the "real point of departure for Marxist analysis" of the historical significance of Russian society. He agrees with Trotsky's appraisal of Russian economic progress under Stalinism. He agrees with Trotsky's estimate of the relation between present-day Russia and capitalism. That is, he is in complete accord with Trotsky's basic position on Russian economy and society.

But why the repetitious insistence that Shachtman agrees with Trotsky? one may ask. The simple reason is Shachtman's article itself: His arguments against the view that Russia is a "workers' state", his emphasis that what is "crucial" are property relations and not nationalized property, his characterization of the economy as a new system of class exploitation and the bureaucracy as a new ruling class - all these suggest that Shachtman does reject the fundamental position of Trotsky on Russian economy. In the not-very-brief article, he several times repeats the phrase about the "historical significance" of the collectivist form of property, devotes only a few lines as to what this significance is, and nowhere *explicitly* declares that he agrees with

Neither Capitalism nor Socialism

Trotsky that Russian society is progressive as against capitalism. Trotsky's view nonetheless, is the basic premise of the final section of his article, "The Defense of the Soviet Union."

The Basic Contradiction of Shachtman

Shachtman writes that: "The theory that Soviet economy is progressive and therefore the wars of the Stalinist bureaucracy against a capitalist state are, by some mysticism, correspondingly and universally progressive, is thus untenable." (Note that Shachtman here does not commit himself on the question of whether or not "Soviet economy is progressive." He is saying: even if Soviet economy is progressive it does not follow, etc.)

He continues:

When Russia fights a war which corresponds to the interests of the international socialist revolution, we will defend Russia just as we defend a similar progressive war of a colonial country. If it wages a reactionary war we will be revolutionary anti-war oppositionists. We would become defensists in the present war should its character change "into a struggle of the imperialists to crush the Soviet Union when the interests of the world revolution would demand the defense of the Soviet Union by the international proletariat." Why? Because a victory of the imperialists would (a) reduce Russia to a colony for capitalist investment; (b) destroy nationalized property.

Shachtman adds:

In these considerations, too, the *historical significance* of the new, collectivist property established by the Russian revolution stands out clearly. Such a transformation of the Soviet Union as triumphant imperialism would undertake *would have a vast and durable reactionary effect upon world social development, give capitalism and reaction a new lease on life, retard enormously the revolutionary movement, and postpone for we don't know how long*

The Defense of Collectivist Property

the introduction of the world socialist society. From this standpoint and under these conditions, the defense of the Soviet Union, even under Stalinism, is both possible and necessary.(My emphasis. J.C.) [11]

There you have, in the most graphic language, Shachtman's conception of the place of the new, bureaucratic exploiting society in contemporary world politics and economics.

What importance, then, have lengthy discourses on property forms and property relations, new, exploiting economy and new, bureaucratic ruling classes for one who holds the traditional conclusions of our movement on the significance, the meaning, the place of Russian society in "history" and in the present-day world? None whatsoever!

But Shachtman today is not for the defense of Stalinist Russia. This is all to the good. But why is he not a defensist? When comrades agreeing with Shachtman's article (as, for example, Erber) today quote it against him, his answer is simple: The character of the war has not changed. Russia is a junior partner of the imperialist democracies. Just as we subordinate the defense of the national independence of Ethiopia in the present war because Ethiopia is a tool of Anglo-American imperialism, so we subordinate defense of the "progressive" Russian collectivist property.

This is mere sophistry. Would the defeat of Ethiopia in the present war have as its consequence the opening up of a long epoch of world reaction which, according to Shachtman, would follow a defeat of Russia? Obviously not. Or does Shachtman hold that such a heavy blow at world socialism such as he depicts in his article would not be the result of a Russian defeat in the war *because* Stalin is allied to Anglo-American imperialism? An affirmative answer makes no sense. If Shachtman's view on the significance of Stalinist Russia is true, then the consequences he foretells would follow in any *major* war with the capitalist imperialists in which Stalin is engaged and defeated. There is no escape from this conclusion - once Shachtman's false premises are accepted.

Neither Capitalism nor Socialism

It should be added that Shachtman's analogy between backward colonial Ethiopia (or China) and his "progressive collectivist" imperialist Russia is also false from another viewpoint. We defend Ethiopia (and China) against imperialism because we are for its national independence. However, when Ethiopia is involved in the present war it loses its national independence to Anglo-American imperialism. (The same would be the case with China, if the war in the Far East becomes an integral part of the Second World War.) In other words, that which we were fighting for, the national independence of the colonial people, is no longer involved in the war; has already been destroyed. The contrary is the case with Russia. Stalin, in his alliance with the imperialist democracies, has not given up nationalized property, i.e., what Shachtman wants to support. A Russian victory in the war does not necessarily mean the destruction of Shachtman's "progressive" collectivist form of property - that is precisely what Stalin is fighting for since that is the basis of his class rule. The analogy therefore is a hasty, ill-considered argument which may sound good but is, on analysis, deceptive and false.

Shachtman, therefore has no consistent theoretical or political basis for his present position on Russia in the war. (all his other arguments are subsidiary to the main points considered above.) Once Trotsky's fundamental position on the significance of Russian economy and society is accepted - as Shachtman does and I do not - his *basic* theoretical and political conclusions necessarily follow. But the re-evaluation of the Russian question, the establishment of clear and consistent criteria for revolutionary politics on Stalinist Russia, requires the rejection of Trotsky's position along the lines indicated by those who hold that Russia is a reactionary, bureaucratic collectivist society.

The New International - September 1941

THE RUSSIAN QUESTION - Max Shachtman

(What follows is the conclusion of a resolution written in response to Carter's characterization of Russia as a reactionary social and economic order and especially his denial that nationalization and state planning by a bureaucratic ruling class was progressive and a step towards socialism. The preceding sections which are not included here sum up the previous discussions on the historical origin of the system as a product of the decay of the Russian revolution.)

What is the Class Character of the USSR?

The class character of a state is determined fundamentally by the property relations prevailing in it, that is, those relations which are at the bottom of the existing production and social relations. In any social order based upon private , the prevailing form of property, be it in slaves, in feudal land holdings, or in capital determines the property relations, is inseparably linked with them, may be used interchangeably with them. The social domination of the ruling class in states based upon one or another form of private property - although not necessarily or at every stage the political domination of such a class - is represented primarily by its ownership of property. The state, i.e., the machinery of coercion, is then the instrument for preserving the existing property relations, for preserving the domination of the economically most powerful class from assaults by classes it oppresses and exploits.

When, however, the epoch of private ownership of social property comes to an end and the epoch of collectivist property is inaugurated, as was done by the Bolshevik revolution of 1917; when private property is abolished and the means of production and exchange become the property of the state - it is impossible to apply the same criterion as is legitimately applied to states based on any form of private property. It is then no longer possible to determine the class character of the state by establishing which class owns the property, for the simple reason that no class owns property under such a social system. The state is the repository, the owner of all social property. The state, however, is not a class but a political instrument of classes.

Neither Capitalism nor Socialism

Property relations in a collectivist system are therefore expressed, so to speak, in state relations. The social rule of the proletariat - which, unlike all preceding classes, is and must remain a propertyless class - lies in its political rule and can lie only in its political rule, which it employs to destroy all private property and private-propertied classes as a precondition for safeguarding its own rule, and, eventually, for its own dissolution into a classless socialist society.

When the Russian proletariat, through its various organizations and institutions controlled the Soviet state, in the period of Lenin-Trotsky and for some time thereafter, the Soviet republics were a workers' state with bureaucratic and even capitalistic deformities. The Stalinist counter-revolution consists precisely in the destruction of all semblance of working-class control over, or influence in, the state, and the usurpation of all political and therefore economic power by the bureaucracy. The final triumph of the Stalinist counter-revolution coincided with is represented by - the complete destruction of the last representative proletarian organization in the country, the Bolshevik Party, and its replacement by the party of the bureaucracy bearing the same name. Like the proletariat, the social rule of the Stalinist bureaucracy, which is also a private-propertyless class, lies in its political rule and can lie only in its political rule which it employs to destroy all private-propertied classes in order to preserve its own class domination - to preserve it also from the proletariat it exploits and oppresses.

Inequality and Bureaucracy

Irrespective of his refusal to accord the rulers of the Soviet Union the status of a class, it is Leon Trotsky in whose [writings the most complete analysis is] made of the origins and rise of the Stalinist bureaucracy to its position of domination. The bureaucracy rose to power as the universal Soviet gendarme in the midst of "generalized want" - traceable in turn to the isolation of the original workers' state. "The basis of bureaucratic rule is the poverty of society in objects of consumption, with the resulting struggle of each against all." Yet, the growth of the productive forces under Stalinism did not result in a

The Defense of Collectivist Property

relaxation of the totalitarianism of the "gendarme" (the bureaucracy) but rather in its accentuation. "The present state of production is still far from guaranteeing all necessities to everybody. But it is already adequate to give significant privileges to a minority, and convert inequality into a whip for the spurring on of the majority. That is the first reason why the growth of production has so far strengthened not the socialist, but the bourgeois features of the state." But not the only reason. The bureaucracy is "the planter and protector of inequality." In distributing the wealth of Soviet society, its guide is its own interest and no other. "Thus out of a social necessity there has developed an organ which has far outgrown its socially necessary function, and become an independent factor and therewith the source of great danger for the whole social organism."

However, it is precisely in this process of becoming "an independent factor" that its development into a class may be established. "With differences in distribution," says Engels, "*class differences emerge.*" Society divides into classes: the privileged and the dispossessed, the exploiters and the exploited, the rulers and the ruled... Distribution, however, is not a merely passive result of production and exchange; it has an equally important reaction on both of these. The development of each new mode of production or form of exchange is at first retarded not only by the old forms and the political institutions which correspond to these, but also by the old mode of distribution; it can only secure the distribution which is essential to it in the course of a long struggle. But the more mobile a given mode of production and exchange, the more capable it is of expansion and development, the more rapidly does distribution also reach the stage in which it gets beyond its mother's control a comes into conflict with the prevailing mode of production and exchange." The "old mode of distribution" prevalent in the workers' state was based, essentially, on the equality of poverty. A truly socialist mode of production could be based only on equality in the midst of abundance. Abundance was possible only with a tremendous socialist development of the productive forces and of labor productivity.

Neither Capitalism nor Socialism

But it is precisely such a development that was impossible on the basis of one country alone, and a backward country like Russia at that. "...A real upward swing of socialist economy will only be possible after the victory of the proletariat in the most important countries of Europe" (Trotsky, 1923). It is therefore inadmissible, from the Marxian standpoint, to apply decisively the principal criterion of social progress, i.e., the development of the productive forces, to a workers' state (concretely, to *the* workers' state of Lenin-Trotsky) *in one country alone*. The national limitedness of the workers' state prevented the "real upward swing of socialist economy"; so also did the "old mode of distribution," i.e., the equality of poverty. The demands of Soviet economy for development could not be satisfied by a capitalist restoration - quite the contrary. they were satisfied by an unforseen social development.

The System of Bureaucratic Collectivism

The bureaucracy arose and it organized and developed the productive forces, including the principal productive force of society, the proletariat, to an enormous degree. It accomplished "a real upward swing" of Russian economy, but not of *socialist economy*. With barbarous, anti-socialist, bureaucratic methods, by introducing and constantly accentuating inequality, it lifted backward Russia to the position of one of the economically most advanced countries of the world, expanding the productive forces at a rate unknown in any contemporary capitalist or semi-capitalist country, right in the midst of a raging world capitalist crisis, in a period of a violently contracting world market and without the benefits of the world market enjoyed in the past by every capitalist country. But it is precisely at that point that one of the fundamental differences between bourgeois Bonapartism and Stalinist "Bonapartism" must be established. Whereas the Stalinist bureaucracy undermined and finally destroyed the social rule of the proletariat in Russia and established in its place a reactionary system of social relations, the class rule of bureaucratic collectivism, traditional Bonapartist and Bismarckian regimes were political regimes established to preserve the rule of the bourgeoisie. The Stalinist regime

The Defense of Collectivist Property

rose as a new social system which destroyed the rule of the proletariat. For a *socialist* development of the productive forces, i.e., for a development based upon the planned collaboration of a number of workers' states in which are included technologically advanced countries, a democratic political regime and a steady growth of equalitarianism are sufficient. For the *bureaucratic-collectivist* development of the productive forces in the Soviet Union, a new ruling class was necessary, that is, a particularly brutal gendarme converting "inequality into a whip for the spurring on of the majority," and steadily accentuating the inequality in favor of the ruling class.

Under the social system of bureaucratic collectivism, this inequality can manifest itself economically only, or at least primarily, in distribution, since in the field of property-ownership, *all* classes are equal - none of them owns social property. With the new mode of distribution, the bureaucracy developed a new mode of production, production for the swelling needs of the bureaucracy, based upon state property and the enslavement of the working class. It was this new mode of production which was, in Engels, words, "at first retarded not only by the old forms and the political institutions which corresponded to these, but also by the old mode of distribution." Classes are the product of struggle against "the old forms and the political institutions which corresponded to these (and also) the old mode of distribution" - that is, against production for the needs of the masses, against the democratic working class political institutions (the soviets, the revolutionary party), and the more or less equalitarian system of distribution - it was in the course of he struggle against these that the bureaucracy developed as a class and consolidated itself as the ruling class.

Limitations of the New Order

The perspectives of the new social order in Russia and the new ruling class are narrowly limited by the specific and unique historical circumstances which gave birth to it. It is not, of course, possible to set down dogmatic and categorical laws of historical development for this new phenomenon; unlike capitalism, for example, it has no long

Neither Capitalism nor Socialism

history behind it which permits of a conclusive historical analysis. Political economy, observed Engels, "as the science of the conditions and forms under which the various human societies have produced and exchanged and on this basis have distributed their products - political economy in this wider sense has still to be brought into being. Such economic science as we have up to the present is almost exclusively limited to the genesis and development of the capitalist mode of production." So far as it has been possible to observe and analyze the phenomenon of Stalinist bureaucratic collectivism, however, its essential characteristics may be established even now.

Bureaucratic collectivism is a nationally-limited phenomenon, appearing in history in the course of a singular conjunction of circumstances, namely, the isolation and decay of a proletarian revolution in a backward country and a world-capitalist encirclement. Its ideology is not merely nationalist in general, but Russian-nationalist; its theory and banner is not so much "socialism in one country alone" as "socialism" in this particular country, Russia. Its expansion beyond the frontiers established by the revolution has been, thus far, episodic, conjunctural. But a far more fundamental consideration is this: *Russian* capitalism was ripe in 1917 for a socialist revolution but not for socialism; *world* capitalism was ripe in 1917, and is over-ripe today, not only for the socialist revolution but for the complete socialist reorganization of society. On a *world* scale, there is already a class, fully matured socially, capable of putting an end to the anarchy of capitalist production and capable of developing the productive forces *socialistically*, that is capable, once it is in power, to do on a world scale what the proletariat in Russia proved incapable of doing by itself, in one country alone.

The bureaucracy in Russia became the ruling class because capitalism in the rest of the world remained in power; in turn, the Stalinist bureaucracy has prolonged the term of power of capitalism. The bureaucracy in Russia is a byproduct of the delay of the world proletarian revolution; it will not continue in power with the advent of the revolution. As a new ruling class, in a new, exploitative society, it has come on the historical scene belatedly, as an anti-capitalist

The Defense of Collectivist Property

anachronism; its belatedness and transitoriness are underscored by the existence on a world scale of a matured, socially-qualified roletariat. From the day of its birth, it is torn by mounting contradictions, which make impossible the firm and durable consolidation of bureaucratic collectivism "in one country." Genuine planned economy on the basis of state property is impossible in one country, in a hostile capitalist world environment. Planned economy conflicts at every turn with bureaucratic management and appropriation of surplus products. The rate of development of the productive forces, made possible by the existence of state property, is decelerated after a period of time precisely by the increase of inequality which was the initial spur to this development, that is, by a swollen bureaucratic stratum. The totalitarian Great-Russian oppression of the peoples of the national republics engenders disintegrative centrifugal tendencies at the periphery of the bureaucratic empire. The anti-revolutionary nationalism of the bureaucracy conflicts with the "internationalist needs" of the economy, that is, its need of fructification by a rational world economy; this in turn facilitates the destruction of the whole economy by world capitalism, its reduction by the latter to the status of a colony or colonies.

The Second World War will therefore be the supreme test of Stalinist collectivism. Should world capitalism gain a new lease on life and be spared defeat at the hand of world revolution, Russia cannot, in all likelihood, escape integration into the capitalist system as a colony or series of colonies of imperialism. Should world capitalism collapse under the blows of proletarian revolution, the weight of the latter would crush Stalinism to the ground and precipitate the third, final proletarian revolution in Russia.

The Future of this Order

However, just what stages of development will be passed before bureaucratic collectivism in Russia is destroyed either by the proletarian revolution or capitalist counter-revolution, cannot be established categorically in advance. Bureaucratic collectivism is still in power and

Neither Capitalism nor Socialism

it is necessary to have as clearly as possible in mind the revolutionary proletarian attitude toward it and the political problems it raises.

Classes and social orders are historically conditioned; so also are the bureaucracy and bureaucratic collectivism in Russia. Product of reaction, both the ruling class and the social order it dominates are reactionary. The proletariat and its revolutionary vanguard therefore are uncompromisingly opposed to the politics of the regime and strive to overthrow it with all means consistent with the struggle for socialism. But the Marxist proletariat recognizes that while this new social order represents a reaction from the workers' state established by the Bolshevik Revolution the forces producing this reaction were not strong enough or not of such a nature as to hurl Russia still further back to capitalism.

Russia remains a collectivist society, differing fundamentally from the workers' tate of Lenin-Trotsky in that it is a *reactionary* collectivist society. But it has not been integrated into the system of world capitalism. Bureaucratic collectivism is closer to capitalism, so far as its social relations are concerned, than it is to a state of the socialist type. Yet, just as capitalism is part of the long historical epoch of private property, bureaucratic collectivism is part - an unforseen, mongrelized, reactionary part, but a part nevertheless - of the collectivist epoch of human history. The social order of bureaucratic collectivism is distinguished from the social order of capitalism primarily in that the former is based on a new and more advanced form of property, namely, state property. That this new form of property - a conquest of the Bolshevik revolution - is progressive, i.e., historically superior, to private property is demonstrated theoretically by Marxism and the test of practice.

The proletarian revolution in a capitalist country would abolish the reactionary social relations by abolishing private property; the proletarian revolution in Russia would abolish the reactionary social relations of bureaucratic collectivism primarily by destroying the political (and therefore the social) power of the bureaucracy but not the property form on which the bureaucracy and the social relations it established are based, namely, state property. This fundamental

The Defense of Collectivist Property

difference is not calculated to distinguish the two social orders from the standpoint of where it is "easier" to carry through the proletarian revolution. It is calculated, however, to indicate the essential difference between the two social orders - bureaucratic collectivism and capitalism - and the historical superiority of the one over the other. In both cases, the prevailing social relations are based on the prevailing property forms. In the one case, the property form would have to be abolished by the proletariat in order to advance toward socialism; in the other, the property form would have to be preserved. In the case of capitalism, the establishment of state property would be an historical step forward, it would be progressive, in comparison with private property. In the case of bureaucratic collectivism the restoration of private property would be an historical step backward, it would be reactionary, in comparison with state property. "An enormous mistake is made in counterposing state capitalism only to socialism, when, contrariwise, it is absolutely necessary in the given economic-political situation to make a comparison between state capitalism and petty-bourgeois production." (Lenin 1921) In the same Marxian sense, it may be said that it is a mistake to compare bureaucratic collectivism only with a workers' state or socialism; it must be compared also with what is the *main enemy* of the *world* (not merely the Russian) proletariat, namely, world capitalism. From the standpoint of socialism, the bureaucratic collectivist state is a reactionary social order; in relation to the capitalist world, it is on a historically more progressive plane.

The progressivism of bureaucratic collectivism is, however, *relative* and not absolute, even in relation to the capitalist world. Thus, for example, in conflicts between the Stalinist regime, on the one side, and a colonial or semi-colonial country, which is part of the capitalist world, on the other, the revolutionary proletariat takes its position by the side of the colonial or semi-colonial country; the revolutionary struggle for colonial independence is a decisive part of the struggle against the main enemy of the proletariat, world imperialism. Thus, for example, in a struggle between Stalinist Russia and capitalist imperialism, on the one side, and another section of capitalist imperial-

Neither Capitalism nor Socialism

ism on the other, the revolutionary proletariat takes its position against both camps, refusing to subordinate or mitigate in any way its struggle against the main enemy, imperialism, and imperialist war, to the defense of the Stalinist sector of one capitalist imperialist camp, any more than it would in a similar case with regard to a small nation or a colonial country, big or small, that became an integral part of an imperialist camp. The relative progressivism of bureaucratic collectivism is not of greater significance to the world proletariat than, with all its social differences, is the struggle for colonial independence. Under all circumstances, it is subordinated to the interests and strategy of the world proletarian revolution.

Under What Conditions is Defense Possible?

The revolutionary proletariat can consider a revolutionary (that is, a critical, entirely independent, class) defensist position with regard to the Stalinist regime only under conditions where the decisive issue in the war is the attempt by a hostile force to restore capitalism in Russia, where this issue is not subordinate to other, more dominant, issues. Thus, in case of a civil war in which one section of the bureaucracy seeks to restore capitalist private property, it is possible for the revolutionary vanguard to fight with the army of the Stalinist regime against the army of capitalist restoration. Thus, in case of a war by which world imperialism seeks to subdue the Soviet Union and acquire a new lease on life by reducing Russia to an imperialist colony, it is possible for the proletariat to take a revolutionary defensist position in Russia. Thus, in case of a civil war organized against the existing regime by an army basing itself on "popular discontent" but actually on the capitalist and semi-capitalist elements still existing in the country, and aspiring to the restoration of capitalism, it is again possible that the proletariat would fight in the army of Stalin against the army of capitalist reaction. In all these or similar cases, the critical support of the proletariat is possible only if the proletariat is not yet prepared itself to overthrow the Stalinist regime.

On the other hand, it must be borne in mind that at their inception the inevitable, progressive mass movements of the workers and

The Defense of Collectivist Property

peasants *against* the reactionary regime, particularly those movements which arise in the oppressed national republics, will be politically immature and confused, and influenced by nationalist, federalist,[12] democratic and even reactionary prejudices. The Fourth Internationalists count heavily, however, on the decisive revolutionary influence that can and will be exerted on such movements by the hundreds of thousands of revolutionary militants who are imbued with the still living traditions of October and who would be the guarantee that the popular mass movements would take a proletarian direction. That is particularly true of such movements in republics like the Ukraine, White Russia, Georgia, Armenia, Azerbaidjan, etc., where the people's hatred of Stalinism has been cunningly and systematically exploited by reactionary imperialist forces from abroad. However, in the event of a civil war, especially in a totalitarian country like Russia, when the contending movements take the clearly defined form of *armies*, with clearly discernible social and political aspirations, the Fourth International must be free to choose, depending on the concrete conditions, between support of one armed camp or the other, or, if neither is possible for the revolutionary proletariat, to work for the completely independent victory of the Third Camp.

What We Reject

We reject the theory that the Soviet Union is a degenerated workers' state which must be unconditionally defended against any capitalist country regardless of conditions or circumstances, This theory covers up the class nature of the Stalinist bureaucracy and the reactionary character of the regime. By the same token , it tends to underestimate the full, reactionary significance of the bureaucracy. It disseminates the notion, discreditable to socialism, that a regime which is a prison for the working class and in which the latter does not have one iota of control, nevertheless has something "proletarian" about it - indeed, decisively proletarian - about it, simply because of the existence of state property. It conflicts with the revolutionary Marxian criteria for establishing a collectivist state as a workers' state. By the policy of "unconditional defense," it has already, in the Second

Neither Capitalism nor Socialism

World War, been compelled to give objective support first to one imperialist camp (the Axis, in the invasions of the Baltic, the Balkans and Finland) and, in the second stage of the war, to another imperialist camp (the Allies, in Iran, in the Pacific and in the Arctic). The theory denies, further, the existence of Stalinist imperialism, as the policy of bureaucratic aggression and expansion, and thus objectively covered the invasions of 1939-1941 while declaring contradictorily at the same time its opposition to "the seizure of new territories by the Kremlin." The Party therefore rejects also the policy of unconditional defensism with regard to the reactionary Stalinist state.

We reject the theory that the Soviet Union is a fascist capitalist state and the political line flowing from it. The bourgeois elements in Russia are an unsubstantial social grouping. The principal basic characteristics of capitalism are absent in the Soviet Union - private property, wage labor and commodity production. The ruling class in Russia is not composed of capitalists, that is, of owners of capital; the income of the members of the ruling class in Russia is not derived from profit accruing from the ownership of capital. Free labor in the Marxian sense of the term long ago ceased to exist in the Soviet Union. Neither is there the prevalence of commodity production, that is, production for the market. We also reject the policy, flowing from this theory, of support of democratic capitalism against the "fascist capitalism" of Russia[13] as a disguised form of support for capitalist restoration.; and on the same grounds, reject the petty bourgeois utopia of a struggle for a "Constituent Assembly."[14] Finally, we reject the policy, flowing from this theory, of no united fronts under any conditions in this country with the "fascist" Communist Party, as only a new version of the old Stalinist theory of "social fascism";[15] we reaffirm the admissibility of united fronts, under certain conditions, with the Communist Party as a party.

We reject the theory that capitalism and bureaucratic collectivism are "equally reactionary" and the political line flowing from it. This theory implies the superiority of "democratic capitalism" to totalitarian collectivism,[16] which can only open the road in practice to supporting reactionary movements of capitalist restoration. the

The Defense of Collectivist Property

Russian proletariat could take power in 1917 only when backed by the revolutionary-democratic peasant masses. Capitalist democracy can struggle for power again in Russia only if backed by reactionary world imperialism; that is, Russia can be reintegrated into the capitalist world only in one of two forms - either under a savage, fascist or semi-fascist dictatorship, or as a group of colonies of imperialism, with the latter as the more likely form. The theory of a "bourgeois--democratic" or a "democratic" revolution against the Stalinist dictatorship which "will not restore capitalism" but "only" establish "democracy" under the rule of a "Constituent Assembly" is a reactionary dream propagated for years by Kautsky.[17] The reactionary liquidation of Stalinism can be accomplished only by means of the most brutal military dictatorship of the bourgeoisie; the revolutionary liquidation of Stalinism can be accomplished only under the leadership of the proletariat fighting under the banner of international socialism. Any intermediate choice is an illusion, a trap, a dream, a petty-bourgeois Utopia. The theory of the "equally reactionary" character of the two mutually hostile and irreconcilable classes and regime can only have the objective effect of disarming the Russian proletariat in the face of capitalist restorationism, by preaching the lie that it is a matter of indifference to the workers if the present regime is liquidated by capitalist reaction and the bourgeoisie restored to power...

New International 1941

NOTES

1. See Bolleton, *The Spanish Revolution* for a discussion of Stalin's single-minded determination to subordinate everything to the attempt to build an alliance with Britain and France.

2. The Italian invasion of Ethiopia was a source of great confusion for the left in the pre-war period. On the one hand, the regime of Haille Selassie was not one that inspired the average progressive. On the other hand, a victory for Mussolini would not only strengthen fascism internationally it would increase

Neither Capitalism nor Socialism

the danger of war. On the third hand, the official British opposition to the Italian action was clearly motivated by its own imperialist aims in Africa. On the fourth hand, the Russian government was covertly aiding Mussolini by shipping the Italians oil.

It wasn't a good situation for those who, as Trotsky put it, considered that all that was required of a progressive was to open your mouth as wide as possible and shout "down with fascism."

3. German diplomacy in WWII was more complicated than is represented here.

4. The record seems to indicate that the Russian government and Stalin in particular clung to the Hitler-Stalin pact even *after* it became clear that the German army was invading. See "The Hitler Stalin Pact" by R. Saunders in *The New International*, February 1948, p. 42 and Ernest Erber in the same issue p. 50. An unsigned article titled "Stalin's Role in
the Nazi Pact" appeared in March of the same year on p.80.

5. Juan Negrin was the right wing socialist who became the last premier of the Spanish Republic with Communist Party support because the previous premier Largo Caballero was too independent and too tied to his working class base to be easily manipulated. Haile Selassie was the emperor of Ethiopia at the time of Mussolini's invasion. Chiang-Kai-Shek was the nationalist dictator who crushed the working class in 1925-1927 and in the thirties led the resistance against the Japanese invaders.

What all of these characters have in common is that they were politically despicable but found themselves at the head of a progressive struggle against fascist reaction or foreign aggression. The attempt here is to compare Stalin's role in 1941 to that of these equally distasteful political figures.

6. See Gabriel Kolko, *U.S. Foreign Policy:1943-1945*, Random House (New York, 1968) for a discussion of the actual attitude of the Russian government towards the resistance. Stalin saw it as a threat.

7. Kolko describes the effect of Russian victories on anti-Stalinist and non-Stalinist socialists in some detail. They were treated much as Stalin had treated the left in the Spanish Civil War.

8. See previous chapter.

9. See previous chapter.

10. Leon Trotsky, *Internal Bulletin of the Socialist Workers' Party 1938*.

The Defense of Collectivist Property

11. See "Is Russia a Workers' State" in this collection.

12. See Moshe Lewin, *Lenin's Last Struggle*, Pluto Press (London, 1975), for a discussion of Lenin's emphasis on the progressive significance of nationalist struggles against Great Russian chauvinism.

13. The advocates of the views of C. L. R. James referred to here nowhere called for support to "democratic capitalism".

14. C.L.R. James partisans didn't advocate this either.

15 In 1944, Shachtman himself was to argue against such fronts. See *New International*.

16. Again Shachtman imputes to his opponents a position they did not hold.

17. There is no indication where the statements in quotes came from. Kautsky did not use these phrases.

Chapter IV
THE THIRD CAMP

The events of the year 1948 made clear that the Russian experience was not going to be an isolated one. One could no longer claim with Trotsky that Stalinism was only defending what was left of the October Revolution.

In Czechoslovakia the Communist Party expropriated what was left of the bourgeoisie politically and economically. While the presence of the Red Army in the wings certainly aided the Communists it was the internal situation of the country that made their victory possible. Capitalism was discredited and the working class exhausted. As had happened earlier in Russia, the Communist Party filled the vacuum.

In China, it was clear to all that Mao's victory owed nothing to Russian help. Most political observers were aware that Stalin and the Russians were not sympathetic to Mao's attempt to seize power; they preferred a sharing of power with the Kuomintang.

In Yugoslavia, Tito's break with Stalin raised the possibility of a bureaucratic collectivist state hostile to Russia and allied to the capitalist states diplomatically.

Clearly, this new system, neither capitalist nor socialist, was not going to be remain a peculiar byway of history. For socialists, the issue that had been debated for ten years inside the Trotskyist movement became an issue all had to take a stand on. This new system was anti-capitalist. It was also clearly oppressive and based on the intensive exploitation of the working class. Did socialists have to support it because of its anti-capitalism? Trotsky had tried to dodge the issue by arguing that the progressive aspect of Russia, nationalized property, was a result of the October revolution and could not be defended for long by the bureaucracy. That dodge would no longer work. Indeed, Trotsky himself had qualified his position. He stated that his thesis would no longer hold if the bureaucracy lasted through the war. The extension of its power over more than a quarter of the world's population he did not even anticipate.

Trotsky was not alone. Few political analysts, bourgeois or socialist, expected the rapid collapse of the capitalist system in as large a part of the world. Those socialists who had rejected support for the bureaucracy in any circumstances had used the term "Third Camp" to describe their position. It was not just a case of rejecting the two military alliances that temporarily

Neither Capitalism nor Socialism

formed during the Hitler-Stalin pact nor the latter alliance of the capitalist democracies and Stalin's Russia. For them the future of socialism, and civilization, depended on an independent, popular movement opposed to both systems.

It was from this perspective that the articles reprinted here analyzing the events of 1948 were written. They demonstrate the ability of such an approach to deal with the complex reality of the post war world in a way that those who saw it in simpler terms of socialism versus capitalism were unable to.

THE TRIANGLE OF FORCES — Notes on the Czech Coup
Hal Draper

The Stalinist coup de force in Czechoslovakia has had a double impact. On the one hand, it has greatly sharpened the tension between Washington and Moscow and raised a new wave of war fears. On the other hand, it has posed new questions about the nature of Stalinism and its potentialities outside Russia itself.

It is the second of these that we wish to discuss here. In doing so, we necessarily face the difficulties of analyzing a phenomenon which is still in the process of developing; one thing which is certain is that Stalinism, both inside and outside Russia, is not a finished social formation. It is not yet ready to sit for a leisurely portrait, as capitalism did for Marx in his time, but must be examined through snapshots taken in motion.

So also the full significance of fascism did not appear the day after Mussolini's "march on Rome." That event did, however, destroy a great many illusions — as even a snapshot can — and it brought about a fair amount of unlearning which is a precursor of knowledge.

In this sense, one aspect of the Czech events is perfectly clear. The view hitherto held by some Marxists that the Stalinist parties are merely a variety of working-class social-reformism — parties whose mode of betrayal is capitulation to their own bourgeoisie at critical junctures — this view is given its quietus. It does not matter that the Socialist Workers Party (the official-orthodox-canonical Trotskyists), in its *Militant,* still writes that the Czech CP was "capitulating" to Beneš and Masaryk.[1] Such paranoiac politicians can now be left to their own hashish pipes without disturbing them with polemics.

Our own analysis of the Stalinist parties as both antiworking class and anticapitalist, as representatives of the new bureaucratic-collectivist exploitative system of Russia, more than ever is confirmed as the starting point. This does not mean that it exhausts the problems raised by Stalinism in the modern world. The advantage of a Marxist analysis is that it is not thrown into a theoretical crisis of confusion by new events but rather given new material for its further development and clarification.

The mistake of the bewildered theoreticians of the Fourth International is curiously reflected in the Benes-Masaryk *Realpolitiker* who touched off the coup. The National-Socialist and People's Party representatives who precipitated the events by resigning from the government obviously expected that the parliamentary crisis so evoked would naturally be resolved according to the consecrated rules of the parliamentary game. They too (like our unfortunate SWP) thought they were playing with just another gang of bourgeoisified reformist politicians of unconventional origin.

What was revealed, instead, was the pitiful impotence of the bourgeois democracy to stand up against Stalinism's march to full power.

Democratic capitalism is simply not viable in Europe today. Masaryk mirrored its fate: its only elbow room even for a courageous gesture is in choosing the manner of its passing away. Only armed force remains available for European capitalism to stem the advance of Stalinism — armed force organized internally in a militaristic Bonapartism merging into outright fascism (such as De Gaulle is preparing for France),[2] or the direct employment of armed force such as may unleash the First Atomic War.

A western capitalism, so armed to the teeth and so maintained in artificial existence while Washington pumps Marshall plans through its veins (keeping it alive like the famous Carrel-Lindbergh chicken heart) — such a capitalism can gain even a historical reprieve only if eventually the capitalist colossus of the West defeats the colossus of

Neither Capitalism nor Socialism

the East at Armageddon. The legions of the degenerating Roman Empire also regularly defeated the encroaching barbarians but only because the victorious legions were legions of barbarians.

The theory of the lesser evil itself degenerates with capitalism. Is capitalist democracy Europe's "lesser evil" as against totalitarian Stalinism? For the theory of the lesser evil to make even its usual sense, there must be two practical alternatives; for the lesser-evildoers are nothing if not "practical." But capitalist democracy is not now a practical alternative even in the sense in which that notorious phrase is used by short sighted opportunists.

Capitalism can remain democratic in form only as long as there is some remnant of social dynamism left in the old system. In Europe it is spent, and is now overdrawing its account. There is only one social force in old Europe whose interests are both anticapitalist and anti-Stalinist and which therefore has the social power to cut itself loose from the symmetrical totalitarianisms on east and west. That is the working class

Everything hinges on the fighting capacity of the European working class. That is why one examines the Czech events for the play of forces within the working class during the crucial period of Stalinism's reaching-out for power, though we will see why the picture so gained cannot yet be a definitive one.

What is perfectly clear, again, is negative. Those sections of the Trotskyist movement which, in the past couple of years especially have put forward the slogan "Communist Party to power!" as a correct strategy for Europe; which have maintained that this slogan is not different from nor less correct than the British version "Labor Party to Power!" — these face the complete bankruptcy of their politics.

The theory behind this slogan was that it was a mere repetition of Lenin's "Oust the capitalist ministers!" in 1917. The theory was that the Communist Parties of Europe, being basically social-reformist, would certainly "expose themselves" either by refusing to take power (like the Mensheviks and SRs of 1917) or, if they were compelled to take power (like the German Social-Democrats of 1918-19), by merely administering the capitalist machinery in a compromise with the bourgeoisie.

The Czech CP took power and "ousted the capitalist ministers." If the SWP therefore deduces that the Stalinists "must be" capitulating to Benes and Masaryk, it is because the events of life cannot contradict deductions from "first principles" — in theology.

What is more important is a second corollary of the "CP to power!" slogan. This was the claim that the taking of power by the CP would produce such a wave of responsive enthusiasm and revolutionary elan (due to the workers' illusions about the Stalinists' revolutionary character) that the resulting mass upsurge from below would build up an insurrectionary wave from the grass roots which would roll over the heads of the Stalinists themselves, which the Stalinists would be powerless to stem. Indeed, for this reason the CP would be unwilling to take power in the first place, for fear of awakening the sleeping giant. So the theory went.

The slogan was wrong and the theory was false: the Stalinists are not simply social reformists but anticapitalist and totalitarian as well as antisocialist. The tactics that applied to Kerensky and Ramsay MacDonald could not be mechanically applied to Gottwald and Thorez.[3] The Czech experience now demonstrates in life that the second corollary was false also. There was no such revolutionary wave from below unleashed by the Stalinist coup.

But did not the press reports indicate that what took place in Czechoslovakia was indeed a revolutionary rising resembling the great October Revolution in Russia in 1917? So went the intimations of the bourgeois press. Wasn't there a general strike. Weren't there "soviets," didn't the working class support the Stalinist coup? In short, wasn't the CP road to power in Czechoslovakia essentially the same as that of Lenin and Trotsky in Russia?

It is easy to see why the bourgeois commentators should be unable to understand, or be uninterested in, the differences between the Czech coup and the proletarian revolution: both are anticapitalist, and the bourgeoisie is less concerned with the motivation of its despoiler than with the fact of its spoliation, like other victims. But among

Neither Capitalism nor Socialism

radicals the question has led to two quite opposite interpretations of the events. These are: The Czech CP was losing influence among the workers; the masses were turning against Stalinism to such an extent that the coup de force was necessary in order to forestall its ouster from power. (See Rudzienski's article in this issue.) The overwhelming majority of the of the working class actively and enthusiastically supported the CP; and this must make us question the role of the working class in the struggle for socialism. [The article by Irving Howe in *Labor Action* of March 8, "Observations on the Events in Czechoslovakia," is a crass enough example of this reaction. Howe does not draw any theoretical conclusion about the role of the working class — he substitutes an exhortation to nourish the "flickering but still beautiful socialist dream" — but his view of the relation between the working class and the Stalinist coup is there. It is that "the pattern of recent events makes quite clear that the Stalinists had the active support of the bulk of the workers and unions. *Otherwise they could not have seized power.*" (My emphasis.) If on the one hand the Stalinists cannot seize power *against* the working class, and on the other hand *did* seize power with the active support of the workers, what we have here is not a "Stalinist coup" but a proletarian revolution unfortunately led by the CP — to be sure a bureaucratic-collectivist revolution. Howe's analysis is false, both factually and politically, in closing the door ("Otherwise they could not have taken power") to that which is precisely the Stalinists' aim: to take power from above. Whether we, in turn, can close the door to the opposite — the possibility of the Stalinists taking power on the swell of a real revolutionary upsurge — will be considered below.]

The evidence available does not justify either of these views. But whether one surmises that the CP was losing proletarian support or had it tucked away in a vestpocket, it is not this question which leads to the greatest insight into the play of class forces in Czechoslovakia. It is quite possible, to say the least, that the majority of the working class was still overwhelmingly pro-CP in sentiment, in the sense and for the reasons discussed in the next section. But from the viewpoint of examining the nature of Stalinism, what deserves attention is the

The Third Camp

fact that the actual role of the working class mass in the events was essentially a passive one.[4]

The Marxist views of proletarian revolution have been so overlaid by Stalinism that this comment requires explanation today.

In the first place, there is no evidence of the entrance en masse of the Czech working class onto the stage of action in the fashion that has characterized every real proletarian revolutionary upsurge — whether one that was more or less spontaneous or one that was organized and planned (like the Russian October). The first two installments of Victor Serge's book now running in the New International,[5] are enough to show the vital difference.

What has characterized them all is the fact that — all the way down to layers of the working class that may not have previously known even elementary organization, all the way down to raw, backward, even unpoliticized strata — the working class in its mass became not merely spectators of the doers and movers on top (applauding or disapproving, i.e., "supporting" or "not supporting") but themselves became the doers and actors, the movers and shakers, a class in motion. That is the meaning of Trotsky's remark, in his biography of Stalin, that during the October days that shook the world, the Bolshevik Central Committee lagged behind the masses' action; that is why Lenin felt it was so desperately urgent that the insurrection not be delayed lest the floodtide of the masses' upsurge be missed. For Lenin it was not he who was "setting the date" for the revolution.

The proletarian never has been ridden like a bridled horse but only like a whirlwind. It has unleashed wild energies, which the revolutionists have tried to "lead". It is a bureaucratic view of the relation between proletarian revolution and the revolutionary party which finds it merely in the fact that the masses "support" the latter. Before October the Russian masses supported Kerensky and therefore, insofar as they did, did not exercise their class strength from below, did not seize arms, did not seize the land, did not demonstrate. The Bolshevik victory was not sealed merely because the masses switched their "support" but because the masses did throw off these shackles from

Neither Capitalism nor Socialism

on top and acted in their own name. When this happened they became Bolsheviks.

In the Czech coup of the Stalinists there was not a whiff of this heart and soul of the proletarian socialist revolution, the characteristic moreover which gives the revolution its overwhelmingly democratic impulsion.

Gottwald's Action Committees had no more resemblance to soviets than the elections in Stalinist Russia have to soviet democracy. The soviets were revolutionary rank-and-file councils, representative institutions whose function was precisely to involve the broadest strata of the masses in the tide of action. The Czech Action Committees were apparatus shock troops of carefully picked Stalinist supporters, whose function was to seize levers of control behind the backs of the masses, and turned on and off like a faucet.

Of this mold are the cadres of a putsch or the stormtroops of a counter-revolution. If the Action Committees had the slightest resemblances to soviets, they could not have been packed up the day after the coup like a fire brigade that is no longer needed.

So also with the rest of the CP's "mass action from below" — the union resolutions, delegations and herded demonstrations; and the hour long general strike (whether it was complete as some reports say, or ragged as do others) after which the workers went back to their benches, to read about the "revolution" in the evening papers.

The Czech Stalinists did not topple the bourgeois power from below but snatched at the top, against the background of staged demonstrations. Indeed, they had the main levers of power in their hands since the "liberation," though a minority in the cabinet. In this sense it was even less of an overturn than the Nazi seizure of power in Germany; and the CP's methods were fitted to the task.

Side by side with the extra-legal force of the Action Committees and the terrorism of the Security Police went the maintenance of parliamentary forms. While a coup de force in actuality, it was carefully and systematically kept by the Stalinists within the forms of a constitutional change in government.

The Third Camp

It would be quite wrong to believe that this was done only to deceive or placate Czech morons, foreign liberals, Wallaces or Archbishops of Canterbury.[6] The preservation of parliamentary forms, and even of bourgeois captives and turncoats in the cabinet, served the far more important purpose of limiting the elbow room for the initiative of the masses, maintaining the air of "business as usual" rather than of revolution in the handing-over of the state machine to the new caretakers, keeping the masses from taking the center of the stage — avoiding precisely the outburst of that revolutionary elan which neither the new nor the old masters desired.

What accounted for this ability of the Stalinists to keep the working masses on the sidelines, to shepherd them to and from demonstrations in the midst of a power struggle, in the first place to gain the pro-CP sympathies of their majority? The reasons are neither new nor obscure.

1) The starting point is the fact that the Czech workers, like the workers of most of Europe, have had their bellyful of capitalism and in their vast majority look with hope only to socialism. This is the rock bottom basis of the attraction of the working class toward the CP, as the only party of meaningful size which claims to be for socialism, as the party which still supports the mantle of the greatest revolution in the history of man. That illusion has not ceased to dazzle.

2) But still, after all that has happened, cannot the workers see through the CP? Cannot they see the horribly brutal totalitarianism of the Russian slave system and take warning? Can they really have any illusions about the "socialist" character of the earth's most monstrous prison house of the proletariat? Can they be that "stupid"?

It is only liberal snobs who can try to understand the complex situation in terms of the workers' "stupidity." Especially in Eastern Europe, where capitalism is not only bankrupt (it is that in America too in another sense) but visibly in shambles and putrefying at a terrific rate, where it has not only no attractive power but where no class-conscious worker can dream of anything but burying it, where all this is not merely a matter of theory or opinion but of what is to be done today and tomorrow morning — what alternative is there for a

Neither Capitalism nor Socialism

worker who is attracted by the socialist protestations of Stalinism but repelled by its Russian reality?

Cling to the bourgeois politicians — Benes & Co., forever protesting their love for the Slav brother in the Kremlin? The whole impetus of the workers' struggles in the past decades had been directed against these bourgeois politicians and against their known and old evils, and not against the new, still mooted, less tried evils of Stalinism. Throw up hands in futility and relapse into a non-political coma? It is easier to do this in America. A real socialist alternative? There can be no doubt of the great numbers who looked for one and the greater numbers who would; but there was no revolutionary socialist party in Czechoslovakia and none in sight before the bend in the road.

In such an impasse arises, if not enthusiastic support for the Stalinists, then at least bewildered toleration of it or the sheer immobilization of uncertainty and confusion, Until a revolutionary socialist party of democratic Bolshevism takes root there is no way of squeezing out of the cul-de-sac.

3) All that is common to much of Europe. In Czechoslovakia the Stalinists' strength rested on more than their appeal as an alternative to capitalism. The country since the end of the war had been fully in the Russian orbit, a dependency of Russia. Every section of Czechoslovakia was aware of that; even the pro-Western bourgeois-democratic politicians gritted their teeth and vowed that "we have to get along with Russia," "we cannot fight Russia," etc. Up to now Russia has kept the country on a long leash; in one way, all that has happened now is that the Kremlin has shortened the leash into a noose.

But in Czechoslovakian reality, "we cannot fight Russia" became "we cannot fight the CP." Or rather, that was a task which involved more than merely one's opinion of the CP's "brand of socialism," but also the whole precarious and internationally complicated foundation of the country's very existence.

4) "We have to get along with the CP — can't we perhaps use it?" This question arises quite apart from the opportunism of mere bandwagon jumpers, numerous as such are. If one cannot even try to fight it to a standstill, in a country where Russian power looms over

The Third Camp

all, then the best thing to do is to attempt to ride it and salvage what one can. In their own way and for bourgeois interests this is what Benes and Masaryk tried to do: this forlorn hope has its impress on working class attitudes too. Besides — who knows? — maybe the Russians are slavedealers and butchers and maybe that is the way communism had to develop in that backward country, but — cannot we hope that our Stalinists (who, after all, are Czechs and not Muscovites) may be different and "not so bad"?

5) There are other ways of rationalizing support of Stalinism in spite of at least a partial appreciation of its nature. Especially where the only alternative seems to be the impossible one of a revived capitalism (and not a democratic one, to boot) the atmosphere is also created for the growth of the vicious concept of the "totalitarian stage of socialism": Stalinism is bad, but maybe it is the necessary road through which we must pass to real socialism, through the progressive democratization of a Stalinist regime no longer threatened by capitalist encirclement.

6) On the one hand, then, there is the tendency of sections of workers to support the CP because they believe the CP is for some kind of socialism. On the other hand, the socialist ideals held by such workers are themselves insensibly penetrated by the poison of Stalinism itself.

First among these poisonous concepts is the notion that the nationalization of industry is ipso facto socialistic, and that, given this much, complete socialism can follow if the regime is allowed to develop in peace. If the official theoreticians of the Fourth International can put forward their own variant of this syphilitic notion — nationalization equals workers' state — rank-and-file workers may understandably fall victim to its cruder forms.

The other concept of Stalinism which is at hand to overlay the socialist thinking of the masses is the abandonment of the fundamental Marxist principle that socialism can be achieved only through the self-activity of the masses themselves and never handed to them by "leaders." The ideology of Stalinism encourages the passivity of the mass in preparation for their coups.

Neither Capitalism nor Socialism

What we have touched upon in these six points are not finished phenomena; the relative weight of each is still indeterminate. They are, however, forces at work in the absence of an organized revolutionary Marxist vanguard which indubitably played a role in a situation, such as that in Czechoslovakia, where the events took place under the shadow of Russian power, whether the Russian army was in the country or not. To generalize the potentialities of Stalinism from this specific situation is quite a leap in the dark, more useful for rationalizing a preconceived conclusion than for scientifically exploring new ones. The Czech coup — to use a military figure — was essentially the straightening out of a salient in the Russian front in Eastern Europe, not a new advance into Europe.

There is no reason for Marxists to follow the panic-stricken impressionists who have just about decided that the working class is doomed to accept the Stalinist counterfeit as the good coin of socialism. We cannot close the door to fresh understanding of Stalinism as it develops; but it is necessary to understand how workers, aspiring to socialist democracy, fall into bewilderment, uncertainty and uneasy passivity when they see before them no way to turn in order to effectuate their socialist ideals; while meanwhile the Stalinists assail their ears with a barrage of propaganda about their "new democracy." Those who seize the opportunity to reject a working class in such an impasse for its "stupidity" are ten times more bewildered by events than the workers they scorn and a hundred times more impotent.

On the basis of such a state of passive acceptance, the Stalinists are in a position to do that at which they are past masters — to manipulate the masses. Their success is not due to in the first place to mere skill and apparatus-juggling; it works only on the basis of a class which is not yet in motion, not in upsurge.

That is why the Stalinists themselves, for all the necessity they are under to gingerly use the club of working class action against the bourgeoisie, do not themselves want to arouse the class in the manner of the Russian October. Like the bourgeoisie itself, they may be compelled to call on working class action to take the stage to a greater or lesser extent, while seeking to keep it within limits. They can

The Third Camp

usually do so all the more freely in proportion as there is no organized working class opposition to crystallize the anti-Stalinist democratic revolutionary forces. Insofar as this is true, and in circumstances vital for them, the Stalinists may be readier to take the long chance on being able to control the masses in movement than they showed themselves to be in Czechoslovakia. Where no alternative threatens, even the most reactionary bourgeois will most freely do likewise. The Czech events show that the CP's perspective is to avoid unleashing the revolutionary initiative of the masses.

Rather their aim is to manipulate the workers' movement as a kind of Greek chorus in the wings. Their aim is no clean sweep of the old bourgeois state machine; on the contrary they have a real need to try to integrate into their own regime as many of the old political figures as possible, to put them into new jobs as bureaucrats of the Stalinist power.

For the old bureaucrats (even for amenable bourgeois who are willing to accept careers as factory managers and technical intelligentsia) there is a personal "way out" in the Stalinist revolution which does not exist for the bourgeoisie as such — a personal way out which a proletarian socialist revolution does not offer, in its need to smash the old state machine and build a new one on a basis of proletarian democracy.

Thus the Stalinist bureaucracy in the new satellites is recruited from and absorbs the adaptable elements of the old regime. To this limited degree (again, we are speaking of a situation where it is impossible for capitalism to go on in the old way) the Stalinist revolution is the "lesser evil" for the bourgeoisie as compared with the socialist revolution.

The bourgeoisie has little interest in trying to mobilize the masses against the Stalinist usurpers — they still have reason to fear the masses even more. At no time, therefore, during the Czechoslovakian crisis did the "democratic" politicians dream of appealing to the people over the heads of Gottwald and Noske; at no time did they stop counseling order, quiet, and reliance on the top parliamentary maneuvers.

Neither Capitalism nor Socialism

This, to be sure, is exactly what should have been expected from these "defenders of democracy"; but the Czech situation itself raises the question, speculative but not farfetched in given circumstances, of what the working class problem would be if the bourgeoisie had decided to take a stand.

What if Beneš had resisted the Stalinist coup — or if not Beneš, then DeGasperi in Italy or Schuman in France, perhaps pressed to resist by American imperialism? What if civil war were to break out — bourgeois democracy formally ranged on one side, totalitarian Stalinism on the other?

The speculative problem deserves discussion not mainly in order to anticipate the future but for the light it throws on the class relationships engendered by the Stalinist advance. Just as the situation itself obviously recalls the line-up of the Spanish civil war, so also the main lines of the answer are provided by that experience.

In the Spanish civil war, behind each camp — the Loyalist bourgeois democracy (Azana) and totalitarian fascism (Franco) — loomed a rival foreign imperialism in the background., Trotsky and our movement took the stand of material support (not political support) to the Loyalist camp, while recognizing that such a policy could last only as long as the international imperialist rivalry remained a subordinate element and did not actually convert the Spanish war into a world war in which the former would be absorbed (like the case of Serbia in World War I).[7]

But meanwhile, we said, the task of the socialists is twofold: to defend democracy against fascism, but to seek to defend it by our own (i.e., revolutionary methods — by building a proletarian power in the democratic camp and fighting behind the banner of that proletarian power, not under the political banner of the bourgeois democrats. The programmatic aim of the revolutionists in Spain was to turn the civil war into a revolutionary war, through the defense of democracy against fascism — in order to defend democracy against fascism, since in the last analysis only the proletarian socialist revolution could actually defeat the totalitarian threat. This last point was even truer in Czechoslovakia than in Spain, given the thin hair by which bourgeois

The Third Camp

democracy was already suspended.[8] The very comparison with Spain, however, raises the vital difference. In the Spanish civil war, the whole of the working class was actively, enthusiastically and consciously on the side of the Loyalist government. On the other side was capitalist reaction in its starkest form — fascism.

Not so in Czechoslovakia. At best the decisive sections of the working class were actively in neither camp, at worst at least passively supporting or at least tolerating the Stalinist coup — disoriented precisely by that characteristic of totalitarian Stalinism which blinds so many socialists who are far better educated than the Czech worker-in-the-street; namely, the fact that Stalinism is not only antisocialist and anti-working-class but also anticapitalist.

Not only is this no small difference, it is precisely this difference which makes the present situation in Europe so crucial a test of the necessity for Marxist reorientation, which characterizes the three-cornered social struggle of our day, and which we discuss in the next section.

In Czechoslovakia, the "Spanish policy" would mean a conscious effort to swing at least a vanguard of the proletariat toward an active anti-Stalinist position and into the anti-Stalinist camp, to organize a vanguard in that camp under its own class banner, its own class slogans and aims and methods — to break through the working class passivity not by acting as the "left wing" of Stalinist totalitarianism (the SWP form of suicide) but by organizing the proletarian resistance and taking over the leadership and hegemony of the anti-Stalinist struggle.

The CP victory in Czechoslovakia was not completely different from the totality of Russian expansion since the end of the war, but so many of its features and effects show differences in degree that it may (looking back upon it in a future year) stand out as a divide.

For there was a difference worth noting between the rape of Czechoslovakia and the way in which Russia grabbed its other East European satellites, the Baltics, Poland, etc. The latter countries were openly taken at the point of the Russian army's bayonets (or in Yugoslavia, by Tito's Stalinist army) whereas there was no Russian

Neither Capitalism nor Socialism

army on Czech soil in February. The Czech CP was not handed the government by a Russian general; it took over complete control under its own steam. so to speak. All the Stalinists needed in Poland et al. was a military conquest, not a state coup. In Czechoslovakia the open Stalinist dictatorship was won from within, not imposed from without.

But isn't this a difference in superficial form only, in view of the factors already mentioned? The Stalinists had entrenched themselves at the levers of the real state power while the Russian occupation army was still in the country, and the relationship of forces was already fixed when the last soldier departed. The rest of the game was the working out of this gambit. And even after the Russians were gone, the shadow of the Kremlin determined the political climate of Prague; we have stressed that even the bourgeois politicians understood that Czechoslovakia was a dependency of Russia. Under these circumstances, does it make much difference whether or not a Russian regiment was around in the life?

The answer is clearly no, from the point of view of the Czech CP's ability to take over once it had decided to (or once the Kremlin had decided). It was no gamble for them. But was it a dress rehearsal? Was it an experiment, under conditions where fumbling would be inconvenient but not fatal, in the mechanism of the Stalinist coup, from which other Stalinist parties could learn? The field trial of a road to power which would be more necessary, and might be more dangerous, farther to the west?

It is enough to raise the question, since we are not crystal-gazing at the moment. Raising the question, not answering it, means politically that we recognize the emergence of the bureaucratic-collectivist empire as a bidder for the historic role of successor to a doomed capitalism. This much we have said before; if it is worth noting again, it is merely that Czechoslovakia has made the development a bit plainer.

The end of the Second World war has indeed ushered in a new stage in our epoch of wars and revolutions. In most of the world, and above all in Europe, it is no longer enough for working class revolutionists to chart the lines of class struggle against capitalism in the assurance that every blow struck against capitalism is a blow for the socialist future. They face two enemies: a capitalism which is anti-Stalinist and a Stalinism which is anticapitalist.

What has emerged into the light is a three cornered struggle for power; it was implicit in Czechoslovakia; it is this utterly new constellation of social forces which disorients and confuses the working class movement.

It is the recognition of this new stage which is the basis of the politics of the third camp. The alternative to it is support of capitalism (vide the reformists) or left-handed support of Stalinism (vide the Fourth International majority). From that dichotomy there is no escape to freedom.

That is why one of the frontiers of Marxism is today in the analysis of what is happening in Eastern Europe, where the old rulers and the new barbarism stand face to face, while the only force for a regenerated humanity. the working class, pauses in bewilderment.

Without the working class struggle, no socialism: this is truer than ever before. What is not true is that anticapitalist struggle automatically equals socialist struggle. The conscious planned intervention and leadership of a revolutionary Marxist party, anticapitalist and anti-Stalinist, which has not been poisoned at its source by a false conception of the relation between socialism and workers' democracy, is more than ever the key to a possibility of victory.

New International April 1948

THE ECONOMIC DRIVE BEHIND TITO - Hal Draper

The general driving motivation behind the Tito-Stalin split is fairly clear now — though naturally not to everyone.

It was not merely a personal spat between tinseled marshals, as some of our contemporaries put it in first reaction. It did not mean that the Yugoslavs were going over to Wall Street. There were other attempts at the "real lowdown" on Tito, ranging from the merely ignorant to the fantastic.

Neither Capitalism nor Socialism

There was Henry Wallace (at his press conference in Philadelphia on July 23) who opined that the Yugoslavs had been suffering from a "semi-feudal" land-ownership system and that the Cominform was wroth because Tito was slow in reforming it. This congenital blunderbuss simply did not know that wellnigh the last remnants of feudal relations had been wiped out after the First World War, even in Croatia where they hung on longest.

There was Louis Adamic, the Stalinist bedfellow who before June 29 was Tito's chief horn-tooter in the U.S. Torn between his Stalinoid fellow-traveler mentality and his Yugoslav nationalism, the best Adamic could do was this:

> Then, what is the rift? On the one side, poor manners which go with the idea on the part of some Soviet and/or Cominform leaders that Yugoslavia ought to do so-and-so and thus-and-thus; on the other side, resentment of such manners ... Essentially, the crisis between the Cominform and the Yugoslavs is not political but in human relations.[9]

There was the egregious Rebecca West, whose recent concern with world affairs has sadly deprived the literary world of her contributions without any visible benefit to politics: her theory was that the split was a jointly staged affair designed to give Stalin an excuse to march troops through Yugoslavia to Italy's gates...

There was the Spanish Anarchist underground radio which figured out on July 1:"Tito ... was in the Spanish [civil] war, and may well have contracted the shortcoming of Spanish indiscipline." We admit to throwing this in for comic relief.

In the first issue of Labor Action after the news broke, we put the stress on the driving force behind Tito's apostasy: his aim " to blackmail Russia into accepting him within the Russian war bloc with a status similar to that which, for example, Churchill hopes to attain for a Western Union within the American bloc."

"Tito is in reality asking for promotion from the status of branch manager to that of junior partner with Stalin." The question of national

The Third Camp

independence involved — and it is involved — is for him the independence of the native Yugoslav ruling bureaucracy from control by the Russian: the conflict between the Yugo and the Commissar is over who is to benefit from the exploitation of the masses.

Essentially, this is the same kind of impulsion that drives the rising bourgeoisie of a colonial country to seek increasing independence from the bigger capitalist nation that rules it. It has been demonstrated once again that this is not the era for the building of new stable empires over the bent backs of the peoples, and that Stalinist imperialism falls heir and victim to the same disintegrative forces which are also tearing capitalist imperialism apart.

This general impulsion means that there is an inherent conflict of interests between the Russian imperialist colossus and its satellites — an inherent contradiction leading to national resistance, which opens the door to the revolt of the masses against both the foreign and the home-grown oppressor.

But in what form did this general conflict concretize itself in Yugoslavia? It is precisely when we seek to inquire into the more immediate wellsprings of the Yugo-Stalinist heresy that the view clouds; the materials for an analysis are fragmentary and misleading. I certainly do not have the intention of putting forward any all-embracing hypothesis under the now-common title "The Real Truth Behind the Tito Break."

It is possible, however, to throw a spotlight on one aspect of the struggle as it took shape in Yugoslavia — its economic basis, the economic issues underlying the general motivation of national autonomy.

This is not the economic question which has come into most notice in the charges pro and con — the dispute over collectivization of agriculture — although there is a relationship. The issue in Yugoslavia was and is: the industrialization of the country.

Yugoslavia according to Robert St.John's books, is "The Land of the Silent People." The "silent people" are the peasants. It is their land par excellence.

Neither Capitalism nor Socialism

Yugoslavia is the most agrarian country of all Europe, the most thoroughly peasant land on the continent. Here in a mountainous area about the size of Oregon, 77-80 per cent of the population is engaged in agriculture. (Significantly as we shall see, the runner up — Bulgaria with 74 per cent — is the other country in Stalin's empire which first publicly raised the proposal for Balkan federation.)

This was the picture when Tito took over:

Among its 15 ½ — 16 million people (10 ½ million on the land) there are two million separate peasant holdings. It is a land of small peasants. Only every second one of them even owns a plow of his own. The overwhelming majority of them own the land they work — 92.5 percent of the area under cultivation belongs to the peasants who till it.

There are few large estates and still fewer "great landowners." Only 7 percent of the cultivated land is in farms of 200 acres or more, and many of these are worked by large peasant families. The average family holding is only 13 acres; two-thirds of the farms are smaller than this.

Among the Serbians, fully 80 per cent are peasants. Here, among the dominant nationality of this multi-national state, there is one city of over 100,000, one other of over 50,000 and a sprinkling of towns; the rest is village. In Macedonia there is a single more or less modern city. In Montenegro (which is, with Croatia, the basis of the CP's strength) there is nothing that can be called a city, and only two towns of 10,000. Croatia and Slovenia are the most industrialized sections, but still mainly village, farm, forest and countryside.

Now pre-1917 Russia, as is well known, was also a predominantly peasant land, but it would be deceptive to equate the two. Russia had its sector of big industry, its giant plants, in which the revolution incubated. Yugoslavia does not.

In all Yugoslavia there are only 475,000 industrial and transport workers, a majority of whom are in Croatia and Slovenia. In 1929 Charles A. Beard wrote that "according to recent figures only twenty-two [factories] employ more than one thousand workers." Ten years later the figure would be somewhat higher but not enough to change the picture. What manufacturing industries there are engage in producing mainly consumers' goods, but 75 per cent of the manufactured products required are imported.

Zagreb in Croatia is a big Balkan banking and financial center, but "the organization of domestic commerce in Yugoslavia could be compared more or less to that prevailing in the smaller communities or rural districts of the United States."

Of the less than a half million industrial and transport workers — constituting less than 3 per cent of the population — perhaps 63,000 belong to trade unions. (That was 1940; even today Tito's compulsory "trade unions" claim a membership of only 662,000.) And of this number a large proportion work in small family shops, or at handicrafts; others are semi-proletarians eking out miserable peasant incomes with miserable factory wages.

This then is the face of Yugoslavia, the country whose people first took up arms against the Nazi conqueror and which now is also the first to revolt against the new Russian conqueror.

It might seem that in this, the most economically backward country of all Europe, the question of industrialization is the most utopian or at least furthest removed from the top of the agenda, at any rate least pressing.

The contrary is true, for three reasons which point to a single end. The first of these reasons applies to most peasant countries; the second applies especially to a peasant country on the European continent; and the third applies to a European peasant land within the Stalin empire. All three are not merely "objective forces" at work but consciously held drives and motivations.

(1) Industrialization is the only basic solution of the key peasant problem of this peasant country. Western Marxists tend to think of the peasant question in the old world in terms of the slogan "Land to the peasants" — the breaking up of the large estates — as a result of the revolutions in Russia and Spain. But this program is almost irrelevant in Yugoslavia. The peasants already had the land. Yet they sank deeper and deeper into poverty and misery.

Neither Capitalism nor Socialism

The operative cause is the phenomenon of agrarian overpopulation, which "has been recently the most important economic problem of Yugoslavia... [and] agrarian overpopulation ... will remain the central economic problem of Yugoslavia in the near future." [10]

This phenomenon, common to backward peasant economies, arises from the tendency for the increase of population on the land to outstrip the capacity of the land to support them under the given technological conditions. Even where an excess can still be fed, they are not needed for production and depress the standard of living proportionately. Where the excess grows huge, the problem assumes overwhelming importance.

What is the way out of this automatic poverty producing mechanism? The Yugoslav economic study we have quoted comes to the conclusion that it lies only in intensified industrialization, other solutions being very limited in effect.

> Agrarian overpopulation came to an end in the countries of the Northwest only when they became strongly industrialized. Yugoslavia will have to look for a lasting solution in the same way.[11]

The conclusion was accepted among bourgeois specialists even before the war; it is not new. The fierce economic drive behind industrialization is, therefore, from this point of view, not peculiar to the Tito bureaucracy. The latter inherited it. On it, however, are superimposed two others.

(2) Industrialization is the key to national sovereignty.

The important point is not merely that this is true but that this truism plays a leading role in the thinking of the Yugo-Stalinists. Naturally they must recognize that even an industrialized country can enjoy only a limited national sovereignty in Europe these days, but an agrarian backwoods can enjoy little if any.

Back in 1944 Edvard Kardelj, No. 2 man in the Tito apparatus, was already laying stress on this point as a guide to post-war reconstruction. In an article in the then Tito organ *New Yugoslavia* he gives

The Third Camp

it first place among the "general questions concerning the present position of small nations."

The Nazis' economic penetration, he explains, meant —

> the "reorganization" of the economy of the small nations in accordance with the economy of the larger fascist countries such as fascist Germany. In practice this meant preventing the independent development of the industrialization of small countries and transforming the existing industries of the small countries into mere appendages of the industry of fascist Germany. Such a plan means keeping us down to the level of agrarian countries to feed the industrial countries, and in the first place Hitlerite Germany. According to this plan, therefore, the whole of Southeastern Europe would have become a sort of agrarian appendage to Germany.

This means, he concludes, reducing us "to the level of colonial countries." Change "Germany" to "Russia" and we have (as we shall see) the underlying economic basis of the dispute which later proved irrepressible. The general motivation of national independence is translated in economic terms into the aim of industrialization; and contrariwise, opposition to industrialization will raise fundamentally the question of national independence.

(3) The third reason behind the dynamic of Yugoslav industrialization concerns the nature of the new ruling group in Yugoslavia, the Titoist bureaucracy. We shall have more to say about this later. At this point, however, it is necessary to point out that the relationship between the bureaucratic-state economy and the goal of industrialization cuts both ways. Just as the bureaucratic collectivism of Titoist Yugoslavia makes possible a perspective of rapid industrialization as compared with private capitalism, so also the objective necessity of industrialization pushed even the pre-Tito bourgeois governments in the direction of the bureaucratization of the economy (statification specifically).

Neither Capitalism nor Socialism

Thus Mirkovic, the bourgeois editor of the *Jugoslav Postwar Reconstruction Papers*, concludes his "Problems of Industrialization":

> The public (the State in the first place) has played and will play an increasingly important role in all industrialization schemes (which is true of all countries of the East). The State (the public in general) remains the only significant investor in an economy where private savings are relatively insignificant and where the role of foreign investment is as yet uncertain. [Vol. 4, No. 1.]

The bourgeois state recognized that the road to industrialization lay through statification:

> Public planning will have to play an essential role in post-war reconstruction of the region. The fact that Eastern Europe is just at the beginning of its industrialization process will help toward that effect. Even prior to the war most of the essential enterprises (posts, telegraphs, railways, power plants, steel mills, forestry resources, steamships) were in the hands of the public (state, communities, cooperatives). [Vol. 1, No. 6.]

If for the bourgeoisie industrialization meant statification, then for the bureaucratic-collectivist ruling class under Tito, the terms of the equation are multiplied and transferred right to left: thorough statification requires thorough industrialization.

Otherwise the ruling bureaucracy can never transform itself into an indigenously rooted ruling class but is doomed to remain merely a proconsular apparatus for the foreign exploiter — even if the foreign exploiter is a bureaucratic-collectivist state.

When the Tito machine took power, it was not yet a class in its own right. What we are witnessing are its strivings to achieve the status of the ruling class of Yugoslavia, to become a Yugoslav class in the first place. It can achieve a distinctive role in the process of production only in proportion to the industrialization of the country. The rulers of a land of small-holding peasants can only be either bourgeois or tax-farmers for a foreign conqueror.

The dynamic social forces behind the question of industrialization should be clear. In this single economic question are wrapped up —

(1) the solution to the overriding economic problems of the country;

(2) the key to Yugoslav national-independence sentiments;

(3) the *sine qua non* for the transformation of the bureaucracy into an indigenous ruling class.

We shall be prepared, then, to see in its proper light the actual industrialization program which the Titoists put into effect leading up to the split with the Cominform.

The Yugoslav Five Year Plan was adopted on April 28, 1947. Its sweep and scope were unexpected.

The Stalinist Doreen Warriner (a British version of Louis Adamic), writing in the *New Statesman and Nation* for April 11 on the eve of its unveiling, rhapsodizes about the Polish Three Year Plan — why, this writer exclaims, it aims at increasing the total national income to sixteen per cent higher than pre-war, "a very ambitious target." And in contrast —

> Yugoslavia's industrialization will be a long process, for 75 per cent of the population are still in agriculture, as against 60 percent in Poland and 50 per cent in Czechoslovakia.

Three weeks later Yugoslavia announced its own target — an increase of the total national income over pre-war of 93 per cent!

Later, writing in the quarterly *Yugoslavia Today and Tomorrow*, the same author rhapsodizes about the way in which Yugoslavia's plan is different from those of other satellites:

> ... of all the East European plans, Yugoslavia's is the most ambitious. It aims, not as the other plans in the main do, at the restoration of production to pre-war levels, but at the complete transformation of the country from a backward and undeveloped area to a modern industrial economy. [Winter 1948]

Neither Capitalism nor Socialism

It is clear that Russia set its face against this perspective for Yugoslavia.

It thereby fell afoul of the feverish ambitions and hopes boiled up by the forces we have described, and unleashed the full fury of Yugoslav nationalism as filtered through the special needs and aims of the Yugo-Stalinist bureaucracy. (Like other national-resistance movements and tendencies today, this is not merely the continuation of the "old" Balkan nationalism but is the old spirit of nationalist resistance given new forms, motivations and drives.)

It is this conflict over industrialization which gives meaning to an otherwise most peculiar controversy which raged through the polemics between the Yugoslavs and their Cominform critics. It will be necessary to start with some representative quotations since this element in the dispute did not at all penetrate into the American press reports — the correspondents, no doubt, deeming it meaningless "Marxist" hair-splitting.

The subject of this controversy was: the possibility of building socialism in one country![12]

First, some samples from the Cominform mouthpieces:

> ... the leaders of Yugoslavia are distorting the Marxist-Leninist doctrine on the possibility of building socialism in one country alone. Socialism cannot be built in one or several countries without the aid of the popular democracies or against them ... [Georghiu Dej, general secretary of the Rumanian Stalinist party.]

> The draft program [of the CPY] ... follows the un-Marxist un-Leninist nationalist idea that Yugoslavia can supposedly build socialism by herself, and the question of aid from the other Communist Parties and the Soviet Union and from the popular democracies in building socialism in Yugoslavia is to all intents and purposes ignored. [Yudin, Russian representative in the Cominform.]

The Third Camp

Yugoslavia thinks that she is able to build socialism herself ... the Soviet Union built socialism alone in isolation, for she was surrounded by capitalist countries. Today, however, the countries of popular democracy which are building socialism are not isolated any longer. The cooperation with the Soviet Union ... constitutes one of the main stays of the planned economy, and the aid from the Soviet Union does not contain any political clauses. [Polish radio summary of article in *Glos Ludu*, Polish Stalinist organ.]

The main rejoinder for the Yugoslavs was made by Milovan Djilas, No. 4 man in the Tito hierarchy:

the question of the possibility of building socialism in one country surrounded by capitalism has already been worked out by Comrade Stalin. Comrade Stalin's teachings show that it is possible in one country but not in all countries. Such a country was the USSR. However, Comrade Stalin does not say that the USSR is the only such country.

Djilas delicately complains about the fact that the `Cominform` has hypocritically pitched the question on the "lofty" level of the theory of socialism-in-one-country when what is really at stake is a couple of other things: the Yugoslavs' tempo of industrialization, and whether "they should have renounced one thing or another for the sake of the realization of the common socialist [read: Russian] aim."

The defensive protestation quoted from *Glos Ludu* should also be noted: ":the aid from the Soviet Union does not contain any political clauses," it assures us. This merely reveals that the Yugoslavs are aware that it does, and don't like it.

It is in fact this question of "aid from the Soviet Union" which is the meaningful heart of the controversy, and not the question of socialism-in-one-country — which is only the theoretical mask conferred by the Cominformers. One needs only a slight acquaintance with Russian economic policy vis-a-vis its satellites to know what the Russians mean

Neither Capitalism nor Socialism

when they insist that the latter must "build socialism" only "with the aid of the Soviet Union."

To put it bluntly (as the Titoists energetically avoid doing in their public articles and speeches — while talking about the "degeneration of the Soviet Union" in private bull sessions) it means: reconstructing the native economy in dependence on the Soviet Union, adjusting the native economy to Russia's needs and its "higher interests."

This is also the content of the "political clauses" which the Yugoslavs fear. The relationship and reaction is, *mutatis mulundis*, analogous to that of the Western nations to the Marshall Plan.

We have questioned the meaning of the phrase "aid from the Soviet Union," which is used in practically all the Cominform fulminations on this subject, and have interpreted it. It is interesting to find that Yugoslav spokesman, Boris Kidric, raises the same suspicion about the cliche.

> Those comrades who accuse us of posing the building of socialism without the aid of and even against the socialist camp have nowhere defined what they actually mean by the term "aid." Let us therefore be permitted to define the question of aid ourselves ...
>
> Economic aid can be understood in various ways. One may understand aid to mean a gift without any counterservices — so to speak, aid on a silver platter. On the other hand, aid can be understood as increasingly closer mutual economic cooperation and mutual facilitation of economic development.

By the second, Kidric makes clear in his report he means the mutual aid which is the outcome of normal foreign-trade and exchange relations between friendly but sovereign states. What he rejects is — getting something for nothing! Surely a curious point to polemize about at some length, as Kidric does ... He continues:

The Third Camp

> As to the first kind of aid — aid on a silver platter — we can and must openly and clearly say that we never requested it either of the Soviet Union or of the popular democracies, not because we were hostilely inclined to the Soviet Union but ... because the Soviet Union for us is a too precious a means of international progress.

A touchingly generous reason, followed immediately by something less angelic:

> What would such aid mean from the Soviet Union? It would mean, for example, to request — without any of our own efforts, without the development of the forces of production in our country by our working people, without economic counter-services — that the Soviet Union, at its own expense, with the efforts of the Soviet people themselves, create a heavy industry, etc., in our country.

With the usual Aesopian language (although we must admit that Kidric is the most outspoken because of the nature of his subject) he neglects to add (but clearly conveys) that in the contingency described

(1) the industry so built by Russia "at its own expense" would naturally belong to Russia and not to Yugoslavia;

(2) it would be built and planned to conform to Russia's needs and economic pattern for Eastern Europe, and not to Tito's vision of an industrially self-sufficient Yugoslavia;

(3) it would be built at the tempo, and to the degree, and with the distribution of such categories as consumers' goods and heavy industry, as were convenient to the Kremlin; - that, in other words, it would mean the Russification of Yugoslav economy.

This is what "aid on a silver platter" means. The Russians offer a poisoned bonbon, and Tito politely demurs: "No, no, thank you, it would spoil my appetite, if you don't mind."

Neither Capitalism nor Socialism

Just as the economic drive behind Tito explains the meaning of the controversy over "socialism in one country," so also it must be taken into consideration in fitting another piece of the jigsaw puzzle into the picture. This is the demand raised by the Yugoslavs for a Balkan Federation.

To be sure, in this case the immediate visible motivations are sufficient to account for the demand without any deeper probing. Tito knows that there are two strikes against him if he tries to stand alone and isolated against powerful Russia; he knows too that the Stalinist bureaucracies of the other satellites are, like him, chafing at Russian domination, even if — unlike him — they dare do nothing about it. Nothing could be more natural, therefore, than that he should look to an alliance with his fellow sub-dictators for mutual defence of their national independence against Russification. In addition, in this split-up corner of Europe where the crisscrossing of national and ethnic lines is wellnigh unravelable, the idea of Balkan Federation has historically been the standard slogan of all socialists and Marxists and indeed of all enlightened elements.

The idea of Balkan Federation is, therefore, in any case an inevitable accompaniment of any movement for autonomy from Russia in this region. But in addition, given the specific economic drive behind Titoism, Balkan Federation also becomes an economic necessity and not merely a political weapon.

For the Cominform accusations of "adventurism" directed against Tito have more than a kernel of truth. The frenzied pace of industrialization and economic development which is set by the Yugoslav Five Year Plan has, as we have seen, the slim physical basis of a country which is quite small, is lacking in many critical raw materials (like oil), is short on capital and skilled labor, etc. The belief is widespread, even among foreign observers rooting for Tito's anti-Cominform resistance, that the Marshall is riding for a fall, that he will infallibly break his neck in this attempt to leap over his own head, now that the rest of the Russian empire is mobilized against him.

Backward Yugoslavia alone is too slim a base for such ambitions as Tito's; his economic aspirations demand a wider economic area on

The Third Camp

which to rest. The traditional slogan of Balkan Federation therefore, takes on new meaning as an economic necessity in proportion as a counterweight is sought to the Russification of Balkan economy.

The slogan of Balkan Federation is in any form inherently an anti-Russian slogan today, and it was by no mere whim of the Kremlin that Dimitrov of Bulgaria was slapped down when he breathed it in January. For Russia has its own solution to the "Balkanization" of the Balkans: namely, the integration of these states into the Russian empire (whether this means formal absorption into the USSR is immaterial). Balkan Federation solves nothing that "Russian federation" does not also solve; it therefore has meaning today only as an alternative to domination by Russia.

As long as capitalism ruled in the Balkans, the Stalinists could be the champions of Balkan Federation as a handy weapon which hit against each national group of rulers; now that Russian imperialism rules it is equally true that the slogan hits objectively at the current rulers. Thus the slogan which, before the war, expressed the negation of national sovereignty and Balkan separation, today means — separation from the Russian empire. The "traditional" slogan is only apparently traditional; its content is new.

To give a practical meaning to the adventurist program of hothouse industrialization and bureaucratization, Tito is, then, forced to look outside his own borders for a bigger and more viable ground of operations against the Russian overlordship. He can not find this by submitting to the West because his own social basis (bureaucratic economy) is thereby jeopardized. He therefore looks to the section of Europe already under bureaucratic collectivism. He seeks an "Eastern Union" which will bear to the Russian giant a relationship similar to that sought by Churchill in Western Union vis-a-vis the American giant.

But nowadays there is no fine line between imperialist oppressor and imperialist subject. Just as, under the hierarchic structure of feudalism, a landholder was a lord over his vassals and at the same time often himself the vassal of o more powerful lord, so today: the overlordship of American imperialism presently threatens the national

Neither Capitalism nor Socialism

sovereignty of and evokes the spirit of national resistance in states which are themselves the actual or would-be imperialist oppressors of other nations. So also Yugoslavian bureaucratic-collectivism, in the very process of attempting to mobilize the other satellites against Russia in the name of national independence, at the same time tries to dominate them. Tito dreams not merely of autonomy from Russian rule but of himself becoming No. 1 in Eastern Europe.

Dreams? More than that. His mouthpieces constantly insist that Tito-Yugoslavia is No. 1 in the world of "popular democracies." This is truly remarkable in view of the fact that this claim recurs in the midst of appeals to these states to support Tito against the Cominform. It does not sound like a very diplomatic tack to take! The appeal is not: "Let us both assert our independence"; it is: "Support me, your leader."

The reaction of the other satellite dictators to Tito's break was complicated by the existence of this tendency. On the one hand Dimitrov, Rakosi, Pauker, et al. have the same yearning for a free hand from Russian tutelage as Tito struck out for. On the other hand, however, Tito is a rival bidder for domination over them.

The matter went further in the relations between Yugoslavia and Albania, because of Albania's geographical position and size. It is well known that before the break Albania was practically a sub-satellite of Belgrade. Yet with the Cominform blast it was little Albania that went furthest in words and deeds in breaking off friendly relations. The day after the break, the Albanian CP statement flatly launched the accusation: "The leaders of the ... Yugoslav Communist Party tried to convert our country ... into a colony of their own. The Trotskyist leaders of the Yugoslav Communist Party have attempted ... to annihilate the independence of our country and our party."

On July 6 *Borba*, replying, unwittingly painted a detailed picture of a Yugoslavia engaged in as thorough a process of economic infiltration in Albania as characterizes Russian policy in, say, Rumania. Just as in the latter case the Russification of Rumanian economy has taken place largely through the formation of "mixed companies" in which Russian capital has the predominant control, so also were Yugoslav-Albanian

The Third Camp

mixed companies formed to develop the latter country. *Borba* itself underlines that this was done "on the model of Soviet mixed companies formed after the liberation of some popular democracies." The article reveals that — at a time when Yugoslavia itself is starving for machinery, technical equipment and personnel, and investment capital! — Tito poured quantities of these precious resources into Albania, just as if it were a province of his own. Thus were constructed or reconstructed Albania's naphtha industry, mining industry, the Durres-Pecin railroad the hydroelectric power station near Tirana, copper production, new chromium mines, and a long list of various kinds of factories.

Borba's main argument, of course, is that these sacrifices were made purely out of the generosity of the Yugoslav heart: "these facts ... serve to unmask the utter shamelessness of the lies about the mixed companies being a Yugoslav government instrument for the exploitation of Albania" — but the reader is reminded of Kidric's strenuous objections to getting "something for nothing" in the case of his would-be benefactor Russia.

One can see, concludes Tito's organ, that there is no basis for "the wretched and insane clamoring about new Yugoslav imperialism, about the enslaving intentions which were allegedly to turn Albania into a colony." But the parallel, between the Yugoslavs' protestations to the Albanians and Russia's to the Yugoslavs, is almost exact. And the Hoxha bureaucracy or its leading section obviously had the same thoughts about "aid on a silver platter."

Naturally, Tito's hopes of becoming the dominant power among the satellites was not based upon his claims to prowess during the "war of liberation." Such an exalted position could be secured and maintained by Yugoslavia only on the basis of superior economic power. Hence the frantic drive to refit Yugoslavia's economy for its sub-imperialist mission in Eastern Europe by outbuilding and outstripping all the other satellites in industrial construction. Tito is goaded to an adventuristic pace in the Five Year Plan not only by the desire for independence from Russian domination but also by the

Neither Capitalism nor Socialism

desire to substitute his own hegemony over the southeast portion of the bureaucratic-collectivist world.

Russia, however, has no desire to see its provincial gauleiters sink independent roots which inevitably give them a certain amount of independence from Moscow. If the over-all plan, from the point of view of Moscow's empire-wide integration of Eastern Europe in coordination with its own war economy, assigns to Yugoslavia the role of an "agrarian country [which] should deliver to industrially developed countries [Poland and Czechoslovakia] raw materials and food, and they to Yugoslavia finished industrial consumer goods," [see Kidric's remarks above] then the drive towards industrialization which arises from Yugoslavia's own needs raises all the questions of national sovereignty.

But the Tito regime seeks native social roots in Yugoslavia even before its industrialization has gotten far — in fact, in order to have a native base on which it can rest while asserting sufficient independence from Moscow to go ahead with its own plans. This base can only be among the peasantry, the Yugoslav proletariat being tiny. Tito can remain in power only by neutralizing (certainly, by not exacerbating) peasant resistance, which is a continual problem even at best. If Tito cannot depend on peasant support (more to the point: peasant toleration or passive acceptance), then he can rule Yugoslavia only a simple agent of the Kremlin.

Therefore, wherever the danger of an independent orientation raises its head (and this is true actually or potentially in every satellite) it is in the interest of Russia to drive its local Stalinist agency into collision with the popular masses so that the CP will have to fall back on its Russian master as its sole support and the sole insurance of its rule.

Paradoxically, Russia cannot afford to permit its satellite Communist Parties and their leaders to be "popular" — i.e., to gain independent support among the masses. As agents of a terroristic dictatorship, they must rule by terror alone. Russian imperialism must reproduce its own totalitarian image in each of its vassals. (We are reminded of the not improbable theory that Kirov, the Leningrad boss

The Third Camp

who was supposed to have stood for a "soft" policy, was assassinated by the GPU precisely because his greater popularity with the masses tended to make him less dependent for his political existence on the all-powerful Vozhd.)

This is the meaning of the Cominform demand that Tito "sharpen the class struggle in the countryside." It is not an economic directive — hence the lack of any specification — but a political injunction: break with your native mass support, rely only on the Kremlin!

It is curious to note how this was formulated into a specific charge in the case of Constantin Doncea, the Stalinist Vice-mayor of Bucharest who was recently purged. The AP dispatch of August 25 listed the accusations against him, and on the list is literally the following: "trying to make himself popular!" This comes next in line after: "neglecting the party line, surrounding himself with bourgeois [i.e., non-Stalinist?] elements, acting independently and taking no party advice ..."

The case of Wladislaw Gomulka in Poland raises the same question. Whether he was or was not actually guilty of "Titoism" or any other heresy, the fact is that Gomulka was the only figure in the regime who enjoyed an independent popularity of his own. This is impermissible in itself.

We began by inquiring into the specific national features of the Tito revolt, but have seen that these specific features account only for the fact that Yugoslavia led the way in the inherent tendency of the satellites to break away from Moscow's complete domination. If in Yugoslavia the specific economic content of the dispute is over industrialization, this is only one form of the general question of the Russification of economy in Eastern Europe which applies with full force to all the other "popular democracies."

Under Russian bureaucratic-collectivism, where political terrorism and the economic forms of complete statification are fused into an integral set of productive relations, planning (including planning for war) can take place only from above down, and only through

Neither Capitalism nor Socialism

totalitarian mechanisms; and this applies to its empire as to its home territories.

Within Russia the inherent contradiction between planning and totalitarianism (so vividly described by [13]) stands in the way of the development of the forces of production. In the empire, the extension of this social system stimulates the development of a native bureaucratic-collectivist class in the satellites and thus produces the disintegrative tendency directed at the totalitarian unity of the empire.

One is reminded of the way in which modern capitalist imperialism, driven by its internal needs to export capital, stimulates the development of a native capitalist class and a native proletariat — that is, a rival capitalism and a potential gravedigger of imperialism. The disease calls forth the antibodies.

Some wave-of-the-future theoreticians (like Burnham) have speculated about the "softening of the dictatorship" of Stalinism as its power increases.[14] This is one version of the familiar neo-Stalinist apologia for Russian terrorism: it is regrettable but temporary, and will disappear as the capitalist world ceases to be a threat to the dictator.

But events have shown that the terrorism of the Stalinist system is not a defense mechanism against capitalist encirclement but an inherent part of bureaucratic collectivism. Just as American capitalism shows its basically antidemocratic character more clearly in its imperialist adventures abroad than in its bailiwick at home, so the immanent driving forces of bureaucratic-collectivist totalitarianism show up even more starkly in its empire than in Moscow or even Irkutsk.

The dictatorship of the bureaucracy will not "soften" with the years; it can only grow brittle, before it is shattered by the irrepressible revolt of the people.

The New International October 1948

THE NATURE OF THE CHINESE STATE — Jack Brad

Throughout Asia the post-war period has been one of vast social upheaval. What happened in Europe after the First World War is now happening in Asia after the second.

Without the organizing technology of modern society which links together great areas and peoples and without extensive industry which creates a more homogenous and substantial working class, Asia's revolutions have taken varied forms.

In no case have these changes been organized by a socialist revolutionary party basing itself on the workers. Leadership has fallen to national bourgeois classes, social democrats (Burma) or to mixed elements of the bourgeoisie and nationalist landlords. Though in most instances these elements have sought and obtained mass support from the peasantry and the working class, the leadership has never passed to these latter. Thus the great transformation is taking place under conservative auspices and with limited objectives.

While Stalinist parties exist in almost all the countries of Asia, in only two of them is the nationalist movement operative in the name of Stalinism as such, and only here does Stalinism so completely dominate the movement as to clearly stamp its own character on it in exclusive fashion — in China and in North Korea. Elsewhere national bourgeois groups (India, Indonesia, Siam, Ceylon), social democrats (Burma) or landlord elements (South Korea) are in the forefront.

In several of these countries social-democracy is active (India, Indonesia, Vietnam). This is a new phenomenon which deserves examination, since Social Democracy in colonial areas on a large scale is something new. Trotskyist or left anti-Stalinist groups exist on a larger scale than they do anywhere in the West in Ceylon, India, Burma, Indonesia and possibly Indo-China.

The exception to the above pattern is Indo-China, where the CP is a leading but not exclusive or completely dominant force. The reason for this is the protracted struggle which forces Indo-Chinese nationalism to seek international allies; that is, the national struggle is forced into the inter-imperialist framework. If warfare is renewed in Indonesia, as seems likely, the movement there may also be forced onto the alien tracks of Stalinism. Wherever imperialism has been too weak an has made serious concessions Stalinism has had to take second place.

Neither Capitalism nor Socialism

Both China and Korea have this feature in common: in both countries the two world powers face each other directly, creating a fixed inter-imperialist limitation to the struggle — unless it took the road of social revolution. Without that alternative (and the reason for its failure in Asia needs to be studied) middle elements between the powers were doomed. In the revolt of Asia, which is one of the great new forces of the post-war period and which is the most dynamic progressive factor in the world today, only in China and North Korea has Stalinism become dominant; these two instances are deviations from the general pattern, for they represent a new tyranny and enslavement.

Thus in China, the U.S. supported Kuomintang rule, but at the same time tried to strengthen the "liberals." This was the essence of Marshall's proposals. But neither the Kuomintang nor the CP wanted the liberals as U.S. spokesmen, and the liberals were too weak to accept such a role. The dolorous fate of the Democratic League is the full history of Chinese liberalism.

The Kuomintang is no longer and has not been for many years the party of nascent capitalism. Unable to make headway against the continuous warfare and conquests of the Japanese, the bourgeoisie lost political power. Never fully emancipated from imperialism, part of it under Wang Ching-wei sold itself completely to Japan. Never fully divorced from usury and landlordism, it could not resist the growing dominance of feudalism over the Kuomintang during the war, when the state was in the interior removed from the seats of power of the bourgeoisie and dependent on the landlords.

The Kuomintang, during the Chungking period, became a narrow dictatorship resting on local landlord alliances in the distant provinces and on the Whampao clique of militarists who were personally sworn to Chiang. The top families of the state utilized their monopoly of political and military power to take over the nation's economy. When the government moved back to Nanking this economic power was extended to the entire country. This bureaucratic state capitalism was antibourgeois, its methods and practices were aimed at limiting and

The Third Camp

hampering the capitalist class. The Kuomintang had gone full cycle and become a break on capitalist development.

The Democratic League was largely representative of the intellectuals, the university professors and the students. The key program was prevention of civil war through establishment of a national congress in which all parties would be represented. This coincided with the program of the U.S. for China, and Marshall[15] later singled out these men of the Democratic League as "the splendid body of men" with whom alone he wished to work. Today the Democratic League is underground in Kuomintang China; its main center is in exile in Hong Kong. Its greatest aspiration is to enter a coalition with the CP in an attempt to win minimal conditions for the survival of the bourgeoisie.

The historic failure of Chinese capitalism is the fundamental underlying cause of the failure of American policy there. It was the only possible counterweight to socialist or Stalinist development. Its failure opened the dikes to Stalinism as the leader of the "national revolution." It is Stalinism which has fallen heir to the unfinished tasks of the bourgeois revolution begun in 1911. War since 1938 and five years under puppet rule have exhausted the capitalist class so that today, like the proletariat, it is a spectator in the civil war, unable to determine its own future. Neither of the two great classes of modern society is a leading factor in the present civil war.

Capitalism failed in China because it was unable to solve a single one of its pressing problems. It could not oust the imperialists; it could only shuttle between them to sell itself to the highest bidder. It did not unify the country geographically, politically or economically. It failed to develop a centralized state of representative character. It could not even begin to introduce the most moderate land reform because it was itself corrupted by usury-land relations. Nor did it succeed in achieving the basic requisite of modern national existence — industrialization. Having failed in every one of these essentials, it could not hold power against the landlords or the Stalinists; nor did it have the strength to effectuate a new alliance with U.S. imperialism independent of the Kuomintang.

Neither Capitalism nor Socialism

Chinese capitalism is not alone in this defeat. It is doubtful indeed if any native capitalism will succeed in making itself the dominant force anywhere in Asia. In none of the new states emerging out of the disintegration of capitalist imperialism is there a bourgeoisie strong enough to rule by itself; here this class tends to develop its power through state-controlled economy, and it is not likely that it will be able to assert itself on a purely economic basis. This is certainly one aspect of Trotsky's theory of permanent revolution which remains valid. It is unlikely that classical capitalism has any more of a future in Asia than anywhere else. What forms will arise out of the dissolution of Oriental society are not clear as yet.

Between Chinese feudalism and Stalinism, "liberal" capitalism is being crushed. (The same is true in Korea.) The inter-imperialist conflict is precisely what creates the greatest difficulties for the native capitalists in these two countries. Thus the inter-imperialist conflict establishes narrow limits for the national struggle, distorting it in its own interests. And where the U.S. intervenes it forces the national leadership into Stalinist channels.

All over Asia the desire for national freedom goes hand in hand with the struggle against feudalism and the creation of modern industrialism. These are the social aspirations of the rising classes. Chinese Stalinism is an indigenous movement in the sense that it has secured to itself a monopoly of the leadership for these ends in China. Its party, program and leadership are known and have established deep roots in the historic struggles of the last twenty years.

Its name is linked with the desires of the peasantry. Its armies are Chinese and nowhere in these armies is there an important amount of Russian power or Russian armaments — at least none has been revealed to this time. Like the Yugoslavs, the Chinese Stalinists are conquering without the Russian armies. They are establishing their own tradition of victories and their own patriotism.

This means that while the Chinese CP is part and parcel of international Stalinism and takes its lead in all matters from the Kremlin, it is not a movement of Russian expansion in a simple sense but the growth of a native Stalinism, which carries out the needs of Russian foreign

The Third Camp

policy on its own. It is more like the Yugoslav CP in this sense than, say, the Polish.

Its leadership has not been Russified by long years of residence in Moscow, although the Russians did bring their own Chinese commissars to Manchuria, who are now major factors in the leadership of the Chinese CP; and Chu The and Cho En-lai have been to Moscow. This party has fought its battles largely without Russian material or even diplomatic help. Not that it has had no help. But its kind and quantity is as nothing compared with U.S. help to the Kuomintang or Russian "aid" to the Polish CP. These distinctions are important for the future.

Thus while the Chinese civil war takes place within the context of the inter-imperialist struggle, this context distorts it but does not so dominate it as to replace or overshadow the elements of national and social conflict. Only if the U.S. altered its policy to one of full intervention and thus precipitated active Russian measures could the civil war become subordinated.

But the inverse is not true either. The CCP is part and parcel of world Stalinism. Its attitudes have always been governed by the latest requirements of Russian foreign policy just like every other CP. Its internal regime of hierarchy, discipline, bureaucracy and idolatry for the Leaders, including the entire Russian hagiography, as well as its slogans and foreign policy have followed every zig and zag of the Stalintern. When Trotskyists were being purged in Moscow they were also being purged in China. When the Bukharinists' turn came in Moscow, it came in China too.

One of the major crimes of Chinese Stalinism is its utilization of the great agony of the 400 million Chinese to the purposes of Russian foreign policy. Victory for the CP does not remove China from the inter-imperialist struggle, as a socialist victory would, but transfers the alliance to Russia. This is one of the major reasons why revolutionary socialists cannot support Chinese Stalinism any more than they can support it anywhere else. Far from bringing peace to China, the CP (no less than the Kuomintang) will involve China in vast international imbroglios and eventually in a war in which it has no possible interest. This is the terrible price Stalinism exacts for its conquests.

Neither Capitalism nor Socialism

The British historian R. H. Tawney has written that he who achieves an alleviation of the abysmal human degradation which is the lot of the Chinese peasant will win the support of half a million villages. This is the limitless source which feeds the Stalinist flood.

The CP has become a peasant party in that it seeks its base primarily in the countryside and that it has developed a theory which gives leadership of the Chinese social revolution to the peasant class through the instrumentality of the CP. It has not been connected with the struggles of the workers for over a decade. It has not had power in any sizeable city. It is a rural party and its entire outlook and membership is rural, as is most of its leadership. The problems of workers and cities are foreign to it.

Nowhere else in modern history has a national revolution been led by a party based on the peasantry. The unique Chinese experience is possible because Stalinism is that unifying ingredient which is absent in the peasantry as a class. With its discipline, ideology, leadership and indefatigable organizational labors it creates cohesion and gives unified direction.

An extremely revealing and frightening statement of the Stalinist theory of the Chinese revolution has been made by Liu Hsiao-chi, member of the Central Committee, and next to Mao Tse-tung, the leading theoretician; it is worth quoting at length.

A. L. Strong, the reporter of his remarks, para-phrases Liu: "Even the concept of the 'proletariat' [quotation marks in the original] as a base for the Communist Party is given a new meaning." And Liu says:

> All this [proletarian leadership] applies to the western world. But in China we have only a few such people. Of our 500 million people only two or three million can be called industrial workers, whom the imperialists and capitalists are training to be the reserves of the CP some day. Meanwhile Mao Tse-tung is training two or three million from another kind of people who are not only no less disciplined and devoted, but in fact perhaps even more disciplined and devoted than the industrial workers.

The Third Camp

China has only a few industrial workers to be the foundation but we have millions of kids [CP youth] like this. Such people have never known Marx, but they are brought up in the spirit of communism. Their discipline and devotion to public affairs is no less than that of the industrial workers. They give their lives to the fight against foreign imperialism and native oppressors even when very young. They fight now for the "new democracy" but if in the future it is time to build socialism, they will be ready to build it. If it is time for communism, they will be ready for that also. Only one thing they will not build or accept — the old forms of capitalism...

Today we are building capitalism but it is a "new capitalism"...As the core of this "new democracy" and "new capitalism" we have three million people — the army, the party and the government — who have lived for twenty years in what might be called "military communism." It is not the "military communism" they had in Russia, for here it is applied only to this leading group [the army, the party and the state of three millions]. [*Amerasia*, June 1947, page 162-3.]

In her comment on this statement, Anna L. Strong adds:

China's revolution is a peasant revolution. Its basic characteristic is that the peasants (not the workers) form the principal mass that resists the oppression of foreign capital and left-over medieval elements in the countryside. In the past Marxist analysis has not been applied to guide such a revolution.

Since 1927 Stalinism has not been a political party in China but an armed camp, an embryo state. Party members and leaders were equivalent to state officials. Sometimes the fortunes of the state party were low indeed, as after the Long March when it was reduced to 40,000. In those days, and even today, not only were and are party and

Neither Capitalism nor Socialism

state identical, but the two are coefficients of the army's power and are identical with it too.

Liu is exaggerating when he says "we have three million people who have lived twenty years in what might be called 'military communism'," for the present CP and army of two and one-half million to three million are post war developments. But the process he so clearly describes is important.

For twenty years this group, acting as a state, military and political power, isolated from the working class and the cultural influences of the coast cities, has developed a hard bureaucratic corp. Carefully selected through numerous purges the leadership is a tight homogenous hierarchy. Not part of the peasantry, its self-arrogated role is to lead, organize, discipline and provide policy for the peasant but never to become part of his class. While the peasantry remains the atomized mass it naturally is, the CP takes its best sons to itself and manipulates the real needs of the masses in its struggle for power. All this it does consciously. Relations between party and class are fixed from above.

The bureaucracy for the entire country is developed in advance, in isolation, almost in laboratory fashion. This is the cadre of the state, which advances with military victory, carries through the agrarian policy and organizes the new citadels of political power. It deals with social groupings as a separate entity and by retention of its social independence determines the relationship between classes on the basis of the needs of its own rule. Thus Liu inform us that the policy for today is construction of a "new capitalism" but that the party retains the liberty to move against this "new capitalism" and its economic classes when it decides the time has come for "socialism." It is the party — or more accurately, the state-party-army — which is the bearer of historic change, no matter in whose name it acts at the moment.

A close study of Mao Tse-tung's writings indicates, as Liu implies in the opening sentences above, that the CP considers itself the leader of the nation, of all classes in Chinese society and as such it fulfills a program which is above classes, i.e., in its own interests as the state power. This Bonapartist conception gives the CP great tactical

The Third Camp

flexibility. At the same time it is a theory of social revolution, but not of the bourgeois-democratic revolution nor of the proletarian socialist revolution; it is the theory of the bureaucratic-collectivist revolution.

The social revolution which is clamoring for birth in China, as elsewhere in Asia, is conquered and distorted. As Liu puts it: "Today we are building capitalism," but it is a "new capitalism" like the "new democracies" of Eastern Europe, and for this a national alliance of classes eases the ascent to power and also serves to keep the masses quiescent. But as Mao put it so succinctly: "The United Front must be under the firm leadership of the CP." (Turning Point, p. 20) But when "it is time to build socialism [read Stalinism]," after the consolidation of power, the CP "will be ready for that also." This is the answer to those who speculate about the Chinese CP following a path different from that of Stalinism elsewhere.

When placed against the background of the Great Revolution of 1925-1927 the most striking feature of current events in China is the absence of the working class in an active role. Where are Canton's millions who in 1925 challenged the might of foreign gunboats and Kwangtung warlords, gave power to the Kuomintang and forced their way into the CP by tens of thousands? Where are the heroic masses of workingmen who paved the way for the Northern Expeditions by their independent militancy?

The steel workers and coal miners of Hankow and Wuhan are silent today, but in the turbulent years two decades ago they performed miracles, defied the British gunboats, organized mass unions in the cities and organizations of the poor peasants in the countryside, and still had enough left to man the armies of the Kuomintang, later the "left" Kuomintang. And still later, when Chiang's terror had wounded and bled the aroused giant of China's revolution and Stalinism had eviscerated its spirit, this proletariat was still capable of the final defiance of the Canton commune.

It was under the leadership of this great urban class that the peasantry organized the struggle against medieval leftovers and militarist tyranny. The democracy of the upheaval was self-evident in the rise of local leaderships everywhere, freedom from traditional restraints, the enormously rapid progress in political education of millions of the submerged and illiterate. The people held the stage and the workers took the lead, allying themselves with and creating political groups which acted on the peoples' needs. The masses taught the leaders, very often marching far ahead of them. The revolution in the villages was not a peasant revolt in geographic or social magnitude but, under the advanced lead of the proletariat, it took on the radical character of an agrarian revolt, not reform. Ties between urban and rural masses were indissoluble in the common struggle.

This heroic popular social movement of twenty years ago is a measure of the conservative, manipulated, primarily military march of Stalinism today.

Today the Chinese proletariat does not have a party of its own; it is not an active, organized, cohesive social class. It does not have a program of leadership to express its desires in the present situation. The intervening decades have brought cumulative disasters. When the Canton commune was suppressed thousands of workers were slaughtered, and in the Kuomintang reaction in every city followed the massacre of the militants. Police terror, assisted by underworld hoodlumism and secret police, established a regime over the working class which did not permit widespread organization. With the best militants assassinated or in hiding, the proletariat was left leaderless and beheaded. The links with the peasantry were broken. Political organization was non-existent.

The treason of Stalinist policy culminated in the exodus to the South. The workers were abandoned to the Kuomintang; many of the surviving militants left with the CP peasant armies for the hills and mountains of South-central China.

The CP desertion of the cities was a betrayal from which the workers never recovered. After these shattering defeats even an underground of serious proportions could not develop. On occasions since 1927 the CP has raided the cities and universities for new leadership elements which had aroused the police of the Kuomintang. This has been the only relationship the CP has had with the urban workers.

The Third Camp

In addition to police terror and gangsterism the Kuomintang organized the workers into its own "blue unions." When after the war even these "unions" became restive, Chu Hsen-fan, Kuomintang-appointed president of the Chinese Federation of Labor, was driven to exile in Hong Kong. Chu joined with Marshal Li in the "Kuomintang-Revolutionary League" and is now a Stalinist front in their recently launched Labor Federation.

Under Japanese and puppet rule the workers were unable to raise their heads. They were cut off from the anti-Japanese struggle. It is a weakened class which has not recovered from the disasters of 1927 and the subsequent twenty years of oppression. These were the cumulative disasters which permitted the control of the revolution and its transformation into a new reaction by the CP.

The CP of 1948 is not the party of 1928. It does not look upon the workers as the leading class. Its attitude toward the workers is that they are necessary for production and to carry out directives, but its politics are not directed toward the workers.

Piece work and speedup have been made universal. Production quotas for the individual worker as well as for each productive unit are established. Payment is made according to achievement. The entire Stalinist incentive system has been introduced under oppressive conditions. Stakhanovism and "labor heroes" are the means of establishing fear on the job, for it is not well to fail to meet the goals set by the pace-setters. "Labor heroes" receive public awards and state recognition in the presence of their fellow workers. Congresses of "labor heroes" are held at which methods of speedup are discussed. The process of differentiation in the factory is begun with the new "labor heroes" being set up above their class.

Since the CP is tied to its agrarian base it will project the cost of industrialization onto the workers as the only class from which the tremendous burdens that are inevitable in such a program can be safely extracted. From this indicated assumption we may conclude that Stalinism will from the beginning be especially oppressive to the workers of China. With their first contact with cities, there are already reports of declining standards of living.

Neither Capitalism nor Socialism

In its relation to the working class the CP acts as a ruling bureaucracy exercising state power. Its separation from urban culture and urban classes and its complete Stalinization in the last twenty years has transformed it into a party alien to the proletariat; it is a bureaucratized agrarian party. It does not even manipulate the workers through detailed control of its organizations because its estrangement is so complete.

During August 1947 in the Manchurian city of Harbin the CP began to re-establish connections with the urban working class through an All-China Labor Congress. Delegates are supposed to have come from Kuomintang cities representing underground unions. It is significant that it is three years after the war and after almost an equal period of CP rule in Manchuria that such a congress is called. The scanty reports available on this meeting are all from official Stalinist sources. What comes through clearly is that the workers were given no role in the overthrow of the Kuomintang — except to "prepare to welcome the People's Liberation Army; and to support and take part in revolutionary movements of the people [that is, the CP J.B.]."

Relations to the capitalist class are carefully defined: "...workers should make a distinction between the 'comprador' capitalists of the ruling bureaucracy and national capitalists who are also oppressed. They should endeavor to win the latter for struggle against imperialism and the Kuomintang." (Above quotations from *China Digest*, August 24,1948.)

The final official resolutions of the congress established two programs for labor, one for Kuomintang areas and one for the "liberated areas." These statements are important statements of policy. In Kuomintang areas:

(1) The consolidation of their [workers'] own strength and the expansion of their fighting ranks so as to prepare for the arrival of the Liberation Army. (2) Cooperation with national industrialists in their common fight against the bureaucratic capitalists. (3) The dispatch of skilled technicians into the Liberated

The Third Camp

Areas...(4) The protection of all factories and machines. [*China Digest,* August 21, 1948].

The relation of the workers to the CP armies is clearly defined as a passive one of "preparing" for the CP armies to take power. If there is to be a "liberation" the CP will bring it, and this task is exclusively and uniquely the CP's.

In the directive on administration of newly conquered cities (*China Digest,* August 13, 1948) the Central Committee orders:

> All law-abiding enemy functionaries, personnel of economic and educational organs and policemen should not be taken prisoner or arrested. They must be given duties and remain at their original posts under the orders of definite organs and personnel, to watch over their original organs.

The directive very carefully states the role of each section of the bureaucracy and bourgeoisie but has not one single word on the part workers or their organizations are to have in their "liberation" and reorganization of the cities. On the contrary every effort is made, as the above quotation shows, to keep the administration intact until the CP political commissars arrive to take over. Those "who violate these policies must be thoroughly taken to task ..." The policy is fixed and imposed, and woe to him of any class who dares to struggle against it.

In relation to the civil war the CP pursues a conservative military policy. Popular activities independent of its own troops are frowned upon. There is no call for workers or peasants to rise in revolt in Kuomintang areas. Social policy is likewise a function arrogated by the CP and carefully imposed by prior bureaucratic determination of its limits, stages and methods.

Every last element of spontaneity or mass participation is strained out of the movement. In this way the entire direction of the real social revolution which is the profoundest desire of the people is transformed into a new tyranny of bureaucratic collectivism. The "new democracy" of Stalinism does not aim at eliminating the bourgeoisie

Neither Capitalism nor Socialism

or the agrarian rich at this time. The only group put out of the pale of acceptance by the CP is the Kuomintang itself. With all other classes it proposes a period of "joint reconstruction."

In order to carry through such a program the CP must guarantee the quiescence of the masses. However, this does not constitute a surrender by the CP to native capitalism. Nothing would be further from the mark. For the power of all classes is strictly defined and limited by the CP, which all real power. Through its control of the peasant unions and the village poor, the CP can and will launch an offensive against the new kulaks which its present policy is producing.[16] Through similar methods in the cities the CP will (when it is decided) be able to use the workers and the petty bourgeoisie against the capitalists.

The CP, by its position above the classes manipulates all of them for its own state needs. The class struggle is replaced by class manipulation.

This is the actual relationship which is emerging under the "new democracy." Instead of a pro-labor state we have the emergence of an antilabor state; instead of a peasant power, an antipeasant power; in the name of democracy the new tyranny of Stalinism arises out of the failure of capitalism and proletarian independence.

It is hardly likely, since no serious alternative exists, that the urban working class will be able to avoid the fatal embrace of the CP. Yet it will take a long time before this party's roots are secure among the workers. Memories of the betrayal of 1927 persist among older workers, and tendencies to reject the labor-capitalist collaboration policy of the CP are inevitable. A period of economic chaos is probable and restlessness with CP rule and with the bourgeoisie will develop. Also, Stalinism's labor policy is one of intensified work and increasing production at labor's expense. The agrarian policy of Stalinism tends to create a newly rich kulak in the villages who will threaten the food supplies of the cities. All this is in prospect and the sailing will not be easy for the new masters.

That the present Stalinist revolution in China is led from and gives prior leadership to the village is of enormous importance. Much of the peculiar political maneuvering in China today — the coalition program of the CP, its hesitancy to utilize the masses except under closest control, its slogan of "return the factories to their owners" — arise from this original difficulty. The CP may actually be unable to organize and administer all of China because of this alienation.

The key to the uprooting of feudalism, to a modern revolution in the village as well as national unification, lies in the cities. Unless modern transport and communications are constructed the country cannot be held together physically. Unless agriculture is reorganized to the needs of industry, city and country will not be integrated. Only an industrially-oriented agriculture can create the mentality which will accept sharp breaks from traditional peasant patterns and introduce new methods adapted to local use as well as deal with such otherwise "insoluble problems" as land fragmentation.

The lesson of the great revolution of 1927 is the very opposite of that stated by Liu above. The revolutionary urban masses, at the head of which was the working class, did prove sufficient to take and organize the power. The Stalinists have put this tremendous dynamic force in fetters, substituting themselves for it. It may well be that its alienation from the working class will prove to be the Achilles heel of Chinese Stalinism...

New International December 1948

PEKING VS. MOSCOW — THE CASE OF ANNA LOUISE STRONG

The Moscow dispatch announcing that Anna Louise Strong had been placed under arrest as a spy startled all observers of Stalinist political life. In its terse announcement Tass reported that: "Mrs. Strong is accused of espionage and subversive activity directed against the Soviet Union." She is described as "the notorious intelligence agent." It is indicated that she will be expelled shortly from Russia. Another amazing phrase of the dispatch declares that she made her way into the USSR "only through the negligence of certain foreign relations officials."

Neither Capitalism nor Socialism

Since her "notoriety" as a spy and certainly as an anti-Russian spy, is rather newly fabricated, the attack on "certain foreign relations officials" is surprising, unless it is possible that there were differences of opinion in the Foreign Office about the incident and unless the public announcement is at the same time a proclamation of victory for one faction.

From no direct observation does the charge make sense. The charge does not specify for whom she did this spying. Interestingly, she is accused also of "subversive activity." In the last accusation made against a U.S. newspaperman in Moscow last April, in the case of Richard Magidoff, the implication was clearly that he was a U.S. agent. In all other cases of such charges in Eastern Europe in recent years, whatever the particular verbal formula, the charge always accused the Western Powers. For some reason that is not clear, this implication is not present in the charges against Strong. One is forced to ask: for whom was she spying?

The idea of her being an American spy is slightly absurd from several points of view, although spying is a game in which the grotesque and incongruous are normal. There does not seem to be any surface evidence. But again it must be emphasized that this fact alone does not exclude the possibility. The U.S., like other states has its agents. However, if A. L. Strong is an American spy, she has done this work in remarkable fashion but the propaganda she has poured out for Russia probably outweighs any information she could have passed to her employers.

She is the author of about a dozen books in praise of Stalinism in a variety of countries — Russia, Spain, Poland and China. She has written hundreds of articles for scores of publications in support of Stalinism. She has been a standard name in innumerable respectable front organizations. In 1930 she founded the Moscow Daily News, a Russian government organ published in Moscow but circulated widely throughout the English-speaking world. She married a Russian official. In November 1944 she was obviously assigned to do a job on the Lublin puppet regime of the Russians for Poland and in 1946 published her unstinting praise in "I Saw the New Poland." In "The

The Third Camp

Soviets Expected It," she developed the Russian line that the Hitler-Stalin pact was a clever tactic essential to gain time for Russian defense against the inevitable attack — thus completely whitewashing the "fascism is a matter of taste"[17] Molotov-Ribbentrop agreements and the policy of collaboration with Hitler which helped launch World War II. If all this is the work of an American agent, then the U. S. Secret Service ought to demand its money back.

It is clear that her "notoriety" as claimed by Tass, had not yet percolated to local Stalinist circles, which were caught as surprised and flat-footed as the next man. When this reporter called the Daily Worker for comment the answer was extremely curt and definite: No statement!

In the recent period Miss Strong has been most closely identified with the American Committee for a Democratic Far Eastern Policy, which has published a number of her articles in its periodical, Spotlight, and only two weeks ago brought out her latest book "Tomorrow's China." (This book was serialized in the Daily Worker.) Miss Maude Russell, secretary of the group, had this to say: "Miss Strong's connections with our committee are as a reporter on China. Her writings are very valuable to the American people. We intend to continue to circulate her book." Confusion, chagrin and consternation were evident in the tone and content of this statement. Another perfectly good "front" has been stabbed in the back.

In the last two to three years, and on many previous occasions, Miss Strong has covered the Chinese Stalinist front for various agencies, most recently and currently for the world wide Stalinist news service, Allied Labor News. She is the only reporter to have interviewed Mao Tse-tung in recent months and the only reporter to be permitted to roam about Manchuria since the Russian occupation began in 1945. At one time, when Chinese CP headquarters was in Yenan, the welcome mat was out and Mao was always at hand to tell his romantic life story to every reporter who could break through the Kuomintang cordon. But this is no longer so.

Since 1945 Miss Strong is the only one to have made public interviews, not only with Mao, but with most of the other top Chinese CP

Neither Capitalism nor Socialism

leaders. Manchuria and Stalinist China are now closed to foreign correspondents. With the exit of Agnes Smedley and Gunther Stein and the departure of Edgar Snow for what appears to be semi--permanent New York residence, Miss Strong has been chief external propagandist for Chinese Stalinism. Since 1946 she has been identified not so much with Russia or Stalinism in particular as in her earlier exploits, but with the Chinese party.

In her latest book "Tomorrow's China," and in an essay published in the defunct magazine, "Amerasia," Miss Strong writes of the Mao and of the CP leadership with the adulation usually reserved for Stalin alone. What is more, she attributes to Mao the distinction of being the sole new contributor to Marxism-Leninism-Stalinism and of having developed a uniquely felicitous program for China which "extends" these theories to the special situation of that "backward country."

Incidentally, in a speech on January 17, 1949, which has been reprinted as a pamphlet entitled "Chinese Lessons for American Marxists," Earl Browder[18] points to the distinctiveness of Chinese CP theory, its "exceptionalism" as the reason for its success. He quotes from several of Miss Strong's articles in support of his thesis that Mao Tse-tung's policy has been to develop a particular line for Chinese Communism, to "Chinaize Marxism-Leninism." Browder quotes extensively from "The Thoughts of Mao Tse-tung," by A. L. Strong. Browder was purged for just such an exceptionalist approach in the U. S.

Now there have been rumors of serious differences in the top echelons of the Chinese Party. First there was reported to be discontent with the Russian looting of Manchurian industry — which today is an enormous obstacle to economic reconstruction, for which the Chinese CP must take responsibility. Also the Russians appear to have established "mixed companies" for control of the products of what remains of Manchurian industry and agriculture. Proposals of this kind were associated with the Tito-Stalin split.[19]

Miss Strong reports in her latest book that after striping the industry the Russians closed their Siberian frontier against the Chinese Stalinist armies and trade. Sections of the Chinese leadership are not

The Third Camp

at all happy about the stranglehold the Russians have obtained in the Northeast. From 75 to 80 percent of all Chinese industry was in Manchuria. Industrially all the rest of China is not a very great prize compared with this. Without Manchuria, efforts at reconstruction must start from what is practically zero.

There seems to be several other evidences of conflict between Russian and Chinese Stalinism. One can well imagine, for example, the dismay when the discredited Nanking government[20] was able to announce its negotiations with Russia, over the heads of the Chinese CP, to give Russia an economic monopoly over Sianking, largest province in Northwest China. For behind the screen of CP victories the Russians have been the real victors through a policy of dismemberment which makes it increasingly difficult for the Chinese party to parade as patriots without attacking Russia.

What is more important, Nanking has received an unearned respite through these stab-in-the-back tactics of the Russians. Much of the mystery of why the CP armies have deliberately refrained from taking Nanking and Shanghai is probably explicable in the light of these events. Russian policy seems to be to attempt to prevent a Tito-like development in this party, which, like the Yugoslavian, is capturing power under its own steam.

Anna Louise Strong has become the chief propagandist for this party and a close associate of its leadership. If she is not an American agent, and she is not charged with being one, she might be considered a Chinese agent. Perhaps not a spy; but then she is also accused of "subversive activity." This would also explain the public attack on "certain (Russian) foreign relations officials." For it maybe that Miss Strong was acting as a courier to groups in the Russian Foreign Ministry, from the Chinese party, who favor a different attitude toward that party. The Tass announcement would serve as a warning to such people.

It would also be a public demonstration of Russian displeasure and a warning to the Chinese leadership. It would serve as a signal to all Communist Parties to tone down and begin to be critical of the Chinese party and of Mao Tse-tung. This would also explain the peculiar nature of the action. Instead of treating the alleged spy as a spy — that is, trying her in court — she is denounced and expelled. Surely if she were a U.S. spy who had so thoroughly concealed herself these many years, she could not receive help from that quarter. Or, if a trial was inadvisable, she could have been disposed of quietly as was Julia Stuart Poyntz. Instead we have a great fanfare which is best explained at this moment as a deliberate and pointed warning to the Chinese party by means of ejecting its agent.

...The explanation of the Strong incident which seems to cover most of the known facts is that her arrest as a spy by the Russian police is an incident in the silent struggle between Russian imperialist objectives in China and the needs of the Chinese Communist Party. There have long been indications of difficulties between the two. The Strong incident is the first public declaration by Moscow of its determination, and a warning to the Chinese and all Communist Parties.

Russian expansion in Asia has already dismembered large parts of China: At Yalta it received special privileges in Manchuria. There are indications that the Russians have established a stranglehold over the Manchurian economy. But this also creates undue problems and difficulties for the Chinese Stalinists. For Manchuria, containing 75 to 85 per cent of all China's industries, is the biggest prize in China, and without it Chinese economy is reduced to complete dependency.

There have been rumors of conflict for several years now between Russian and Chinese Stalinist policies. So much so that when the Russians marched into Manchuria in 1945 they brought with them "their own Chinese" under the leadership of Li Li-san, one time head of the Chinese party, who has since taken a post in the top leadership and is a key liaison man with the Russians.

The rumor will not down that Gen. Lin Piao, chief of the Chinese CP armies in Manchuria is also part of the Russian group. Li is assigned to his staff. His army of 300,000 is the best equipped of all Chinese armies. He seems to have replaced the Chinese veteran Chu The, Mao Tse-tung's closest associate. Russian ambition seems to aim at a pan-Mongol and pan-Turk buffer zone extending from the Japan

The Third Camp

Sea to the Persian Gulf. As part of this vast and far-flung internal projection it comes into conflict with Chinese Stalinism in Manchuria, Sianking and possibly North China.

Miss Strong has been most closely identified with the Chinese CP in recent years. Indeed she is the only propagandist to have traveled throughout Manchuria in the post war period and the only one to have had frequent interviews with the entire top leadership of the Chinese party. In her essay "The Thought of Mao Tse-tung" and her book, "Tomorrow's China," she reports extensively on the Chinese leadership. Indeed, A. L. Strong had become the international publicist of the Chinese party.

If any more evidence of this were needed, the publication by *Borba*, the Yugoslav CP organ, of its exchange with the Soviet Information Bureau on Miss Strong's book would be enough. The Yugoslav release quotes a letter from Miss Strong as follows:

> I want to point out certain publishing changes that were made in Moscow by the editor of the Soviet Information Bureau. I do not have time to send you personally these changes but the Soviet Information Bureau will send you a copy through their representative in Belgrade.

Which means that up till a few months ago Miss Strong released her material on China through Russian propaganda agencies and her "notoriety," as Tass described it in its announcement of her arrest as a spy, is of rather recent origin.

We wonder what the Committee for a Democratic Far Eastern Policy, the U.S. front organization which published her book here, will have to say at this bold description of the book as a Stalinist handout. This particular organization has corralled some eminent persons — T.A. Bisson, Harrisan Forman, Stanley Isaacs, Michael Straight, Arthur U. Pope, Frieda Kirchwey, Leland Stowe and numerous other obvious non-Stalinists.

The Yugoslav release brings us back to the question for whom could Miss Strong have been an agent? Surely not for the U. S. She is not even accused of that. *Borba* printed its revelations in answer to

Neither Capitalism nor Socialism

implied accusations that Yugoslavia had been the source of Miss Strong's espionage...It is interesting that Moscow should be tainting her, ever so lightly it is true, with Titoism. For it is just this tendency in the Chinese party — its desire to organize a strong, unified China — that is at issue. This is not yet Titoism. It has a long way to go for that.[21] That is why Miss Strong's arrest must be viewed as a warning rather than as a broadside. Nationalist tendencies in the multi-form Russian empire may take more varied forms than Tito has shown and the single denotation as Titoism will not be broad enough to include them all.

An iron curtain has rung down over Manchuria. Correspondents are excluded; reports are scarce. A silent battle is raging there which may be of greater importance for the future of China than the Yangtze front. It is a war waged in camera between factions for strategic positions. But its ferocity should not be discounted. The prize is enormous. Like all differences in Stalinism, it is waged in the top committees only, in semi-conspiratorial fashion. That is the anatomy of Stalinist inner politics.

The New International February 1949

NOTES

1. Eduard Beneš and Jan Masaryk were the two leaders of the Czech government in the immediate post war period. The charge that the Communists were capitulating to them was, by the time this article appeared, ludicrous. Their government had been overthrown and they were under arrest. Masaryk died after jumping or being thrown from a window of the cell in which he was confined.

2. This statement may seem extreme. However, see Kolko, *U.S. Foreign Policy* for a treatment of the Anglo-American invasion of Greece which was only two years in the past when this article was written. Concealed in the velvet, democratic phrases of the Marshall Plan period was a fist. In Greece, the glove had come off.

The Third Camp

3 . Clement Gottwald and Maurice Thorez were the leaders of, respectively, the Czech and French Communist Parties.

4 . See Jon Bloomfield, *Passive Revolution*, (Allison & Busby, London, 1979) for a development of this analysis by an academic researcher who clearly does not look at this phenomenon from a third camp point of view.

5 . Victor Serge, *The Year One of the Russian Revolution*, tr. by Peter Sedgewick. Holt, Rheinhart & Winston (Chicago, 1972).

6 . The Wallace referred to her is Henry Wallace, Franklin Roosevelt's Secretary of Agriculture who ran as an independent candidate for president in 1948. Initially supported by segments of the labor movement frustrated with the Democratic
party's drift to the right, the campaign tended more and more to rely on a nostalgic appeal to the good old days of the war time alliance with Russia when all right thinking people agreed on the rhetoric if not the program of the president. As the pressures of the cold war pulled this coalition to pieces the campaign, and Wallace himself, degenerated into a CP front. The Archbishop of Canterbury shared the same nostalgia for the simplicity of war time slogans.

7 . The spark that ignited World War I was the assassination by a Serbian nationalist of Archduke Ferdinand of Austria. The fight for national liberation by the Serbs had in general been supported by the Socialist and progressive movements. The Tsarist government's demagogic appeals to this cause against Austro-German imperialism caused some confusion. The Serbian socialists won considerable respect from the international movement by refusing to be used in this way. They denounced the war as imperialist and rejected any aid from, or support of, one imperialist bloc against the other.

8 . Bloomfeld, in the work cited above, devotes a chapter to describing the collaboration of the bourgeois democracy and the Communist Party in dismantling factory committees which had sprung up when the German occupation collapsed. As usual this is described as a "spontaneous action of the class" meaning no one has taken the trouble to research the subject and discover the individuals and organizations responsible.

9 . Trends and Tides, July-Sept 1948.

Neither Capitalism nor Socialism

10 . Yugoslav Postwar Reconstruction Papers [JPRP], Vol. 3, No. 5, ed. by Nicholas Mirkovic; published 1942-43 by the Office of Reconstruction and Economic Affairs of the pre-Tito bourgeois Yugoslav government-in-exile; a 4-volume collection of studies of Yugoslav economy as a guide to post-war economic planning.

11 . JPRP, Vol 3, No. 5.

12 . The reference is to the debate in the Russian Communist Party and subsequently in the international movement over this slogan in the 1920's. The slogan encapsulated the new bureaucracy's desire to enjoy its privileges in peace. In a backward country like Russia, this meant consigning the hopes of the majority of the population for a better life to the next millennium. The slogan rallied the newly privileged against the socialist principles of the opposition.

13 . Victor Kravchenko, *I Chose Freedom, The Personal and Political Life of a Soviet Official*, (Charles Scribner's Sons, New York, 1952).

14 . See chapter two of this book.

15 . George C. Marshall is best known because he gave his name to the Marshall Plan. This program of aid and the complex system of trade agreements associated with it is usually credited with setting European capitalism back on its feet (and subordinating Europe economically to American capital) after the devastation of World War II had thoroughly discredited the capitalist system in its European heartland.
Marshall's reward was to be savaged by Senator Joseph R. McCarthy and tainted with the reputation of being at best a Communist dupe.

16 . "Kulak" is the Russian term to describe the new rich peasant of the twenties created by the expropriation of the great estates of the church and the nobility in the Russian Revolution. In the 20s this class of newly enriched peasants became Stalin's first source of popular support. In the early years of Mao's regime, similar support was sought in China. The fate of these original supporters of the new government was similar to that of their Russian predecessors.

17 . At the time of the pact with Hitler, the Russian ambassador Molotov is reputed to have claimed that "fascism is just a matter of taste."

The Third Camp

18 . Earl Browder was the general secretary of the American Communist party from 1934 to 1945. He became the symbol of the party's "Americanization" during the period of American-Russian collaboration in World War II. Mao's reputation as an "agrarian reformer" rather than a partisan of class warfare fit this rhetoric. But there was also the attraction for any non-Russian communist party leader who made it on his own without or even against the influence of the Russians.

19 . See the preceding article on "The Economic Drive Behind Tito."

20 . Chiang Kai-shek's Nationalist government based itself in this old capital in the last fight against Mao's armies.

21 . In fact, an open break did not come until 1963.

Chapter V
BEYOND THE THIRD CAMP

In the first article selected here the author begins his discussion of the significance of the post-World War II British Labour government by briefly summarizing the Marxist position on the possibility of a "parliamentary road to socialism", that is, on a constitutional, peaceful, transition to socialism as opposed to an insurrectionary one. The question was raised in the public mind by the serious, and unexpected, anticapitalist measures taken by a legally elected government. After stating his position that a socialist transformation requires the independent selfmobilization of the working class which, under certain circumstances, may confront the ruling class with the choice — either allow a popularly elected government to carry out the anticapitalist measures demanded by its working class base or resort to illegal insurrectionary methods; the author argues that this is not what happened in Britain. Instead, the Labour government made serious inroads on capitalist power while restraining independent working class activity. It was this that raised the "new question." Is there a third possibility? A non-working-class, bureaucratic "road to socialism."

In the event, this speculation by observers at all points of the political spectrum proved premature. The revival of capitalism in Western Europe stimulated by the Marshall Plan and the Korean War boom led to a corresponding revival of traditional (more or less) reformism. The anticapitalist trend in Britain and Europe reversed itself, at least temporarily, and the measures taken by the Labour government in the end came to little more than a large scale, and expensive, socialization of the losses of the capitalist class. Unprofitable but vital industries, such as coal, were nationalized, subsidized by taxes levied on the lower classes in particular and the investors pensioned off adequately even while they screamed about socialist tyranny. Once more, a socialist government carried out a necessary, but painful, reform of the capitalist system which no openly procapitalist party could summon up the courage to carry out.

Nevertheless,, the extent of the measures taken against particular sections of the capitalist class and the extent of nationalization required to stabilize postwar capitalism — on the continent and even in the United States as well as in Britain — represented a qualitative change in capitalism. If the anticapitalist measures taken by the Labour government did not lead to a new

Neither Capitalism nor Socialism

postcapitalist society, they still raised the question: How far can such "despotic inroads" go before we can say "this is not capitalism anymore"?

The next two articles by Hal Draper continue this discussion of the myriad, and influential, political tendencies towards this "bureaucratisation of capital-ism" in the post-WWII period. The significant point here is that these political and ideological tendencies were typically found on the right wing of the socialist movement and even among non- or anti-socialists.

The final selection, by Seymour Melman, is a selection, not only from a substantial book, but of a substantial body of material. The discussion was initiated, as far as we have been able to tell, by a 1944 article published in the magazine Politics *edited by Dwight MacDonald. The author was listed as Walter J. Oakes. This was the pseudonym of an economist employed by a Wall Street firm. The argument, briefly summarized, was that capitalism could only avoid a repeat of the Great Depression by heavy government subsidies. In the political context of the day that was only possible through military expenditures which, whatever their justification militarily, provided the kind of "pump-priming" that Roosevelt's New Deal had never been able to provide. This thesis was elaborated on by the same author using a different pseudonym, T. N. Vance, in* The New International *in the 1950s. We have chosen to ecerpt the Melman chapter because, being written twenty years later it has the advantage of being able to present in historical perspective a tendency which Oakes/Vance was analyzing on the fly.*

It would take us beyond the limits set for this collection of historical articles to comment on more recent developments such as the World Bank or the International Monetary Fund. These agencies, run by unelected and, with the exception of the occasional Paul Wolfowitz, unknown bureaucrats are instruments of bureaucratic planning which make a Stalinist GOSPLAN functionnary of the 1930s look like a small businessman.

ASPECTS OF THE LABOR GOVERNMENT — Max Shachtman

As the long postwar boom winds down with the consequent reemergence of chronic mass unemployment and stagflation, the growth of bureaucratic collectivist tendencies at the expense of classical reformist socialism is likely to continue.

The "New Question" posed by the experience of the Labor government is not, then, whether socialism can be established by parliamentary means or only by extraparliamentary means. It is this: Can the working class reach socialism only by its own efforts, by its direct class rule over the economic and political life of the country, or can socialism be attained without workers' control and simply by an expropriation of the bourgeoisie carried out, one way or another, under the control and direction of a more or less benevolent workers' bureaucracy? The spread of Stalinism has raised the same question in one way; the Labourite government in another way. If it is not the most vital question of our time, it is certainly one of the most vital. Not a few Marxists have abandoned the basic convictions of the founders and teachers of scientific socialism by replying, in effect, in the affirmative: Yes, the road to socialism lies or may lie through the domination of society by a workers' bureaucracy or a bureaucracy that arose out of the labor movement. They have concluded that the Stalinist revolution is the socialist revolution, that Stalinist society is progressive, that the Titoist state is socialist, and the like. As for ourselves, we remain unreconstructed in our belief that the emancipation of the working class, that is, socialism, is the task of the working class itself and no one else. The experience of the Labor government, especially when considered, as it must be, in the light of the social and historical significance of the rise of Stalinism, has not modified our belief in the slightest degree and we see no grounds in the realities of British society to warrant such a modification.

That the general position of the British working class has improved under the Labour government is undeniable. That the general position of the British bourgeoisie has deteriorated is equally undeniable. But what has been most significantly strengthened and improved is the economic and political position of the labor officialdom. It is they, first and foremost, who have benefited from the economic and political

Neither Capitalism nor Socialism

changes effected by the Labour government, just as it is they and not the working class itself that have effected the changes.

This implies that classical reformism itself has changed. That is correct. It corresponds to the profound changes that capitalism has undergone. Classical reformism — as exemplified by the old German Social DEmocracy and the Labor Party of the MacDonald days — not think of expropriating the bourgeoisie and actually abolishing the rule of capital in the economy; or if it did think of it, it never went further than to translate its thoughts into hollow public speeches and writings.

The German Social Democracy, when it had complete control of the country, published its findings in weighty scientific tomes, under the direction of Karl Kautsky himself; but it never nationalized the coal industry. If the MacDonald governments even talked about nationalization, the tones were too faint to be remembered today. The contrast with the present Labour government is clearly evident. The classical Social Democracy was a bureaucratically dominated product of the rise of capitalist imperialism. Its ideology and social interests were shaped in the period of that rise. It drew its economic sustenance from the vast super-profits accumulated by the big imperialist states. It acquired a stake — modest but nonetheless a stake — in the preservation of capitalism, that is, of private property in the last analysis. It opposed the extreme bourgeois reaction which would wipe out the labor movement that was the mass basis for its privileged economic and social position. It opposed the revolutionary overthrow of capitalism which would bring the workingclass to power and abolish, in a socialist way, the special bureaucratic privileges it enjoyed. Hence, its basic attachment to capitalism, to capitalist prosperity, to capitalist democracy, to capitalist colonial policy, to reforms which would solidify its mass basis and add to its own privileges.

A very excellent example of this reformism, in the life and in the flesh, and in a specific national form, of course, is to be found right here in the United States: the American labor officialdom. Its like exists nowhere else on earth today because there is no longer any capitalist power comparable to the American. The other capitalist regimes have collapsed or are always on the brink of collapse, economic and political. The British is included. The empire of old is at an end. At an end, too, are the huge super-profits which corrupted the British working class, primarily its officialdom, for generations (Britain is, for example, in debt to India today!). In one country after another — again Britain included — private property is less and less the basis for national economic strength and prosperity, and this becomes more and more obvious even to the labor aristocracy. Ideology lags notoriously behind social reality. In France, where capitalist decay is further advanced than in England, the ideology of the reformist officialdom, or what is left of it, has not changed significantly; it acts and thinks as if it still had the old stake in the preservation of private property. In England, however, the ideology of the labor officialdom has kept much more active pace with the changes in the historical position of British capitalism. Compare British capitalism of 1945 with British capitalism of 1924, and you get a fairly adequate measure of the change in the Labour Party (and, for that matter, in the working class as a whole) from the days of MacDonald's rule to those of Attlee and Bevin.

It is not of course a question of the personal sincerity and integrity of this or that official, which we would like to believe is of the highest quality. It is a question of social forces and interests and ideologies. The official slogan of "Socialism Now!" means, in practice, "Socialism for the Officialdom," or "Socialism Directed by the Officialdom in the Very Best Interests of Labour." This means no socialism at all. But it does mean a different attitude toward private property and capitalist rule of the economy. Yesterday's reformist officialdom, the Labourite bureaucracy of today, wants to dispossess the present property owners, wants to take over industry, wants economic and political control of the country, even if its training dictates Fabian prudence and gradualism in achieving its wants. It may think it wants it for the working class; it doubtlessly does think so. But Marx in his time, and Freud in his, taught us not to judge a man by what he thinks of himself — a man or a social group — but by what he does and by the objective effect of his acts. The present officialdom wants to dispossess the old property owners, but not in order to install the free rule of the working class. Socialist democracy, genuine proletarian democracy, would give

Neither Capitalism nor Socialism

the bureaucrats (we speak not of this or that individual, but of a specific social stratum) even less in the form of special position, privilege and power than it enjoyed in the heyday of capitalism. That is why in Britain today, unlike Russia in 1917, the undermining of the power of the capitalists is not accompanied by an extension of democratic, socialistic workers' power.

An adequate treatment of the foreign policy of the Labour government is of key importance. [As is the related question of the specifically Labourite "theory" (unformulated and unvoiced but nonetheless real) of "socialism in one country," which pervades the thinking and action of the British government.] But it must await another occasion. Here it must suffice to point out that the very nature of the change in British reformism determines the fact that its foreign policy is essentially imperialistic. It is no more the task of the labor officialdom to liberate the colonial peoples than to emancipate its own working class. Its task and concern are to reorganize Britain, and as much of the empire as its broken forces enable it to hold together, in its own interests. It is true that the Labourites agreed to grant India national independence. But that was imposed upon them by the Indians. In Malaya, Labourite foreign policy shows itself to be as outrageously imperialistic, rotten and barbarous as the French in Indo-China. It may be freely granted that the Labour government's foreign policy is, on the whole, much more democratic than Stalinist Russia's, but it is not one whit less imperialistic in its fundamental character. The new rulers and would be rulers have little interest in preserving the power of the British capitalist class; but they have shown active interest in preserving whatever colonial power they could in the interest of Britain, that is the British government, that is, themselves.

Five years of the new Labour government have brought the country and its working class to a fork in the road. If the present basic economic and political trend were to continue uninterrupted in Britain, the means of production and exchange would all end up in the hands of the state and the state in the hands of an all powerful bureaucracy. Beginning in a different way, with different origins, along different roads, at a different pace, but in response to the same basic social causes, Britain would then develop toward the type of totalitarian collectivism which is the distinguishing mark of Stalinist society, Mr. Attlee's denunciations of Russia as a "bureaucratic collectivist state" to the contrary, notwithstanding. Fortunately, we are a long way from that yet, a long, long way. Distinguishing periods of development and judging the pace at which changes take place, taking into account conflicting social forces and judging their interplay — these are of the essence of socialist politics. If we speak above of the present trend, it is only conditional, only as abstracted from other trends and forces, and in order to indicate what this particular trend is so that, knowing and understanding it, it is easier to resist it. It would be preposterous, and worse, suicidal, to take the beginning for the end, the thread for the strand. Is it necessary to mention more than this one fact: Stalinism not only took years to come fully to power but it was able to reach it only because the working class movement in Russia was so deeply crushed, demoralized, passive, exhausted, whereas the British working class movement is only beginning to feel its power, is strong and vigorous, is inspired with socialist hopes and convictions, is impatient with its government because it does not move fast and firmly enough toward workingclass socialism, and above all is still in a position to debate its problems freely, to express itself openly, to make changes, even basic changes, without having to fight a ubiquitous and omnipotent police state.

What is or should be overwhelmingly important for the socialist movement, for the serious British socialists in particular, is that there is a workers' government in power in Britain which is so constructed, and which is based on such a popular proletarian movement, as makes it possible by entirely democratic means to transform the government into a genuinely socialist workers' regime. If this were accomplished, the consequences would be breathtaking. The great wheels of history which have sunk so deeply into the mud of retrogression for a quarter of a century would be lifted on to a smooth dry road and race forward at a tremendous speed. The transformation is possible, the opportunity is golden...

New International 1951

Neo-Corporatists and Neo-Reformists — Hal Draper

> ...the application of joint-stock companies to industry marks a new epoch in the economical life of modern nations ... in joint-stock companies it is not the individuals that are associated, but the capitals. By this contrivance, proprietors have been converted into shareholders, i.e. speculators. The concentration of capital has been accelerated ... A sort of industrial kings have been created, whose power stands in inverse ratio to their responsibility - they being responsible only to the amount of their shares, while disposing of the whole capital of the society - forming a more or less permanent body, while the mass of shareholders is undergoing a constant process of decomposition and renewal, and enabled, by the very disposal of the joint influence and wealth of the society, to bribe its single rebellious members. Beneath this oligarchic Board of Directors is placed a bureaucratic body of the practical managers and agents of the society ... It is the immortal merit of Fourier to have predicted this form of modern industry, under the name of Industrial Feudalism. - Karl Marx, in *N. Y. Daily Tribune*, July 11, 1856.

The replacement of capitalism by a New Order is being discussed, even advocated or at least viewed with kindliness, by some very eminent and respectable thinkers in this country not usually associated with revolutionary ideologies. This trend, or school of thought, seems to have gained steadily in the last few years. Its meaning can best be understood in the context of a wider, a worldwide trend in relation to which it constitutes only one strain or national form.

The wider, international trend is the burgeoning of *bureaucratic-collectivist ideologies* in a broad-spread infiltration of all bourgeois thought today. By "bureaucratic-collectivist" I mean in this connection the ideological reflection or anticipation of a new social order which is neither capitalist nor socialist, but which is based on the control of both economy and government by an elite bureaucracy — forming a new exploitive ruling class — which runs the fused economic-political structure not for the private-profit gains of any individual or groups, but for its own collective aggrandizement in power, prestige, and revenue, by administrative planning-from-above. One premise of this conception is that the totalitarian statified economy developed under Stalinism in Russia, which is today consolidating its power over a good portion of the globe, is one well-developed form of bureaucratic-collectivism.

Whatever the label conferred on this system, however, it is less controversial that key elements characteristic of its structure have, in our own day, already had a massive impact on the capitalist world and its thought. The channels by which this society-wide pressure has been exerted are two related ones. First is provided by the contradictions and difficulties of capitalism itself, the solutions of which point to some type of collectivism and to some form of increased statification, whether under the Great Depression (with the New Deal as carrier) or under the Permanent War Economy of today. Second is the direct impact of the Russian advance-model on the system of the old world, in evoking emulation, triggering analogous patterns, enforcing imitation by the logic of rivalry.

1

The current - within the borders of this larger phenomenon - which this article proposed to investigate shares with all others a common desire to present itself as being "beyond capitalism or socialism ." In a key document to be discussed, W.H. Ferry, of the Center for the Study of Democratic Institutions founded by the Fund for the Republic at Santa Barbara, says for example:

> I think there is something brand new emerging here as well as in Europe which is certainly not capitalism. If you wish, you can call it socialism. Several of my less friendly critics suggested that the new fascism was being proposed here. Naturally, I don't agree to that statement.

Beyond the Third Camp

But what apparently distinguished it from the other, more typical bureaucratic-collectivist currents is its hostility to statification or "statism," which it aspires to replace with a more pluralistic constellation of corporate powers. *Thus it finds itself developing a new corporatism* — which naturally leads right back to bureaucratic statism by a different theoretical route.

A.A. Berle Jr. strikes this keynote in his foreword to the recent book edited by Harvard's E.S. Mason, *The Corporation in Modern Society*, whose several chapters by leading authorities convey many of the leading conceptions of this neo-corporatism. Berle is discussing the "two systems" of modern industrialism, the one in Russia and the "modern corporation" in the U.S. He calls the corporations "these non-Statist collectivisms" and sees them as "suggesting an eventual non-Statist socialization" of profits. In another place Berle says the present system is really "Collectivism" or "non-Statist Socialism," and though (being unafraid of labels) he also calls it "People's Capitalism," he makes clear he believes the social order is traveling beyond capitalism or socialism.[1]

These neo-corporatist ideas have their roots, in the immediate sense, not in a predilection for any of the older and more famous corporatisms which come to mind, but in a reaction to distinctively American conditions, in the soil of the one capitalism left in the world which seems to be a going concern.

One root is a wave of intensified soul-searching about the dominant institution of this capitalism, the corporation. "What Mr. Berle and most of the rest of us are afraid of is that this powerful corporate machine ... seems to be running without any discernible controls," writes Prof. Mason. Why does the system seem to them out of control?

It is certainly not controlled by the famous Invisible Hand of the Market, they agree. A new stage in the concentration of economic power has come into being. In *Power Without Property* Berle has laid great stress on the immense expansion of the fiduciary institutions (pension funds, mutual funds, etc.) and their economic consequences. These funds buy common stocks, i.e. formal shares in the ownership of the economy. They grow and their holdings proliferate. Then –

Neither Socialism nor Capitalsm

> A relatively small oligarchy of men operating in the same atmosphere, absorbing the same information, moving in the same circles and in a relatively small world knowing each other dealing with each other, and having more in common than in difference, will hold the reins. These men by hypothesis will have no ownership relation of any sort. They will be, essentially, non-Statist civil servants – unless they abuse their power to make themselves something else.

This, he argues, is creating "a new socio-economic structure," with basic political effects. "Then, the picture will be something like this. A few hundred large pension trust and mutual fund managers (perhaps far fewer than this number) would control, let us say, the hundred largest American industrial concerns ." Again: "In result, the greatest part of American economic enterprise, formerly individualist, has been regrouped and consolidated into a few hundred non-Statist, collective cooperative institutions ."

So, as noted, divorce between men and industrial things is becoming complete. A Communist revolution could not accomplish that more completely. Certainly it could not do so with the same finesse. When a Russian Communist government says to the workers that "the people" own the instruments of production but it will take care of them, it is assigning to its population a passive-receptive position closely comparable to the one we are studying. The difference lies in the fact that the criteria for reception are different, and that the political State exercised the power factor now gradually but steadily being aggregated under the American system is nonpolitical but equally impersonal fiduciary institutions.

This concentrated power of the fiduciary managers, a stage beyond the "America's Sixty Families" pattern, is only potential: in practice they eschew voting control. Thus, the lack of any control over the corporate managements becomes institutionalized. But whether they exercise their power or not, the result is a small oligarchy of uncontrolled managers, continuously making decisions which have a vital impact on the society as a whole.

2

Berle's next question is: What "legitimates" this uncontrolled corporative power? Not assignment of this power to the managements by the shareholders. Berle and Means took care of the fiction of shareholder control back in 1932; and even Adler and Kelso's *Capitalist Manifesto* only advocates that the shareholder *should* control, meaning that he does not now.

A second source of "legitimacy" could be the market, if one argues that it is the objective hand of the market which imposes decisions on the managers, not their whims. But our neo-corporatists do not believe this.

What then can legitimate the decisions of management? The solution of government control arises, of course, but to our subjects this means "state control," which means "statism" which means socialism, communism, totalitarianism, Sovietism and other unthinkable things. In general, they are in a flight from statism under the impress of the Russian horrible example. They grope for an alternative.

What then? Beardsley Ruml has suggested an appointed-trustee system: the Board of Directors co-opts a special member to act as "trustee" for a given interest-group (the company's customers, or suppliers, or employees, or the "community," etc.) protecting its interest against the board. I cite this mainly to illustrate what "groping" means.

The next grope is cited not only because it is Berle's but because it gives a proper sense of the hopelessness of the effort. This is the feudal analogy presented by Berle in *The 20th Century Capitalist Revolution* (1954), a much misunderstood book which does *not* present a Luce-type celebration of our economic system. In his strange chapter on "The Conscience of the King and the Corporation," Berle is trying to answer the question: How have absolute, uncontrolled powers been curbed in the past, not by upheavals from below but by organic dispensations from above? - for perhaps this will also apply to the absolute, uncontrolled power which is our present problem. He finds an answer in the medieval Curia Regis. Any man could throw himself before the king's feet and get justice dispensed on the spot by the kings' conscience. The custom became institutionalized. Hence the beginning of equity courts and (one gathers, in this Berlean history) eventually other democratic counterpoises to the absolute power. "It is here suggested," Berle concludes, "that a somewhat similar phenomenon is slowly looming up in the corporate field through the mists that hide us from the history of the next generation ."

The legitimation, therefore, is immanent in the historical process itself. The important thing, he is saying, is not whether the king's rule was legitimate but that this *was* the way the new system arose.

The approach stirs a reminiscence. It is our American school's analogue of the standard Stalinist "historical" justification of *its* absolute power: totalitarianism and terror are passing phenomena preparatory to a glorious morrow, mere flecks on the wave of the future. If it is dressed in feudal terms, this is partly because Berle has long been fascinated by the virtues of feudal society. (Compare his rather amazing paean of praise to medieval institutions, over 20 years ago in *New Directions in the New World*.) But this nostalgia for feudalism is not confined to Berle. In reaction to monolithic-statism, feudalism begins to appear "pluralistic," which in contemporary sociological jargon is high praise. Its integration of the individual in pre-capitalist community relationships looks good as against the alienation of man under capitalism. The feeling crops up especially in the neo-corporatists, as they view the "feudal" pattern of a society where overweening social power lumps up in a number of huge agglomerations, with a relatively small number of corporations lording it over their own "baronies," each one with vassals dangling after, like the auto dealers after the Big Three of Detroit.[2]

3

Berle's announcement in *The 20th Century Capitalist Revolution* that the big corporation not only has a soul but also a conscience was subjected to a good deal of understandable ribbing, even before those General Electric executives went to jail; but this discovery of the corporate conscience should be considered only one form of another

Beyond the Third Camp

grope, not yet examined. This is the proposal for the Statesmen-Managers. If the decisions made, without control, by the big corporation executives are so vital for society, these executives must be more than glorified shopkeepers.

Their decisive job cannot be simply to further the interests of the corporation, maximize profits, etc., with primary responsibility to the owners. They must train themselves to think in social terms, in terms of the impact of their decisions on the bigger world outside; in short, to be Statesmen rather than parochially profit-minded businessmen. This becomes also a solution, or part of a solution, to the problem of legitimacy. It may be soul-quaking to think that the fate of our whole society is in the hands of corporate overlords whose nearsighted eyes are fixed only on the shortest way to money-grubbing, but it is heartening to think that this fate is taken care of by Experts who, having proved their managerial skill in the rough-and-tumble of business, now blossom out as broadgauged Social Thinkers too. This is the meaning of the refrain in Philip Selznick's recent *Leadership in Administration*: "The executive becomes a statesman as he makes the transition from administrative management to institutional leadership ." The theme can also be found in some of the contributions to the Mason book.

In this approach, then, the new irresponsibility of the uncontrolled Institutional Leaders is no longer a thing to view with alarm but rather a necessary precondition to freeing them from the petty, distorting influences of short-range, profit-maximizing considerations.

In this context we get demonstrations (which once would have sounded like muckraking) of how our corporate barons are indeed making the vital decisions politically and socially, as well as economically: how the oil companies determine our foreign policy; how General Dynamics decides strategy in the struggle for the world, etc. The objection, of course, is not that this is done but that it is too often done by executives who are not also Statesmen.

But this line is inherently dangerous, as Mason points out:

> If equity rather than profits is the corporate objective,

one of the traditional distinctions between the private and public sectors disappears. If equity is the primary desideratum, it may well be asked why duly constituted public authority is not as good an instrument for dispensing equity as self-perpetuating corporate managements?

And Eugene V. Rostow warns that this trend invites the response that it is men elected to advance the general welfare who should make the decisions rather than uncontrolled oligarchs. But this implies *democratic control* of the decision-making apparatus, and democracy is the only way out which our neo-corporatists reject with unquestioning uncertainty.

4

Neo-corporatism presents itself, first of all, as another attempt to answer the problem of legitimacy. But this problem, after all, is only the current way in which its posers formulate to themselves the basic question of the underpinnings of the whole social system. Real solutions are bound to lie in radical, i.e., systemic, changes.

The outline of such a change appears under the name of "Constitutionalizing the Corporation" in the deliberations (already mentioned) of the Center for the Study of Democratic Institutions led by W.H. Ferry.[3] Ferry began with a number of complaints about the present system which could once have been part and parcel of a socialist propaganda pamphlet: against over-concentration of wealth, the "paradoxes and contradictions" of contemporary capitalism, alienation, the myth of the "self-regulating economy," the "greed of the affluent," economic individualism, "the messiness of the present economic arrangements," etc. This leads on to formulations favoring "a political economy based on the purposive use of law, politics, and government on behalf of the common good," "the primacy of politics" for "the rational control of our economic affairs," "bringing the economic order under political guidance," and so on.

These phrases seem to give the primacy to *political* power over the corporate power, subordinating the latter to the former, i.e. installing

Beyond the Third Camp

"statism," in the terminology previously referred to. This general "socialistic" approach gave way to something else as the discussions at the Center advanced, with the participation of an impressive panel of eminent thinkers: Robert Hutchins, Berle, Scott Buchanan, Reinhold Niebuhr, I.I. Rabi, J.C. Murray, Walter Millis, and others. At a month-long meeting—a sort of enlarged plenum—of the Center held last summer, Ferry presented a programmatic paper for discussion by the group.

The concrete idea that emerged is the foundling of a new political order on a "commonwealth of corporations." Ferry proposed (after raising the question of a "fourth branch of government" for economic questions):

> A less dramatic form of constitutionalization might be the formation by statute of a commonwealth of corporations, an "association of free, self-governing nations ." This would call for federal charters, or "constitutions," which would recognize the autonomy of the member-corporations but charge them collectively with specific powers and responsibilities ... Along some such route might also come the legitimacy that Berle believes the modern corporation is seeking. Establishing a commonwealth or federation of corporations would necessitate, for example, a review of corporate charters.

He explains further:

> ...we keep on thinking in the very limited terms of nationalization or non-nationalization, private ownership or national ownership. It is quite possible, for example, to give a good deal more authority and responsibility to corporations ... I am looking for a legal order to enclose and to make coherent what is being done in this country by the corporations.

And he stresses several times that his vision means "a new and different type of state," "something new, a qualitatively different way of looking at the economy ."

Father Murray, the Jesuit member of the panel of consultants, who took a prominent part in the discussions, thereupon spoke the following, not at all antagonistically:

> I know that you have expressly disclaimed that what you wish is socialism, and quite rightly, especially in the classic definition. It doesn't seem to me that that is what you wish. However, the tendency of your paper is to install intervention of a sort that is referred to technically as the corporative state. I don't mean the corporative state of the fascist sort, which was frankly totalitarian ... [Murray explains he means the corporative state as invented by "some German economists and political thinkers" as an alternative to both capitalism and socialism.] You seem to be aiming at something of the same sort. You seem to want an integration of the economic processes and political processes, if you will, or a constitutionalization of it. The net effect would be radically new.*

5

This observation by Father Murray, which was not a criticism, ties up with the views of another Jesuit social thinker who had recently published on the question. This is Father Harbrecht, whose brochure *Toward the Paraproprietal Society* (1960) had appeared with a laudatory

---

* It should be remembered that the Catholic Church officially has its own program for a sort of corporatism (also called "industry council plan," etc.), a very elastic one: it has been interpreted into anything from Mussolini's fascist corporations to mere labor-management committees. Father Murray can therefore raise the question of corporatism more objectively than most.

introduction by none other than Berle.

Harbrecht's thesis is that our social system is turning into a system of property tenure which is neither socialism nor really capitalism. His analysis starts at the same place as Berle's discussion of the fiduciary institutions and the new stage of divorcement between property and power. In this new order "beyond property," inevitably "the economic power that is growing in the institutions is being drawn, or shunted away, from the generality of the people ." The result has "striking parallels" with feudal institutions, which also "began with a separation of control from the ownership of productive property." Today corporations correspond to the Great Domains of the baronial principalities. "A man's place in medieval society was determined by his place in the domain. Today men are bound to their corporations ... the present-day corporate managers are like the vassals of the great domains. They have control, but not ownership of great wealth, yet their tenure in power is in fact limited by their continuing ability to perform a service ."

Thus Father Harbrecht in his own book. It is easy to see why it delighted Berle. For Harbrecht, this process of "feudalization" of the corporate-political structure is his own version of the Wave of the Future.

Now we learn from Father Murray (in the Center discussion) that Harbrecht made a criticism of Ferry's paper. He found that Ferry wants to go too far with "the *politization* of the economic process" — that is, the imposition of outside political (state) controls *over* the corporations (the baronial powers), whereas Harbrecht sees the increased power as going *to* the corporations.

Faced with the explicit posing of this question, Ferry denied that Harbrecht's criticism applied to his position: "I do not accept the criticism. *I will accept Father Harbrecht's own proposal for imposing larger responsibilities on corporations* ." (Emphasis added.)

The distinction is very important for our purposes. What is being worked out here is not simply more of the familiar liberal-collectivist trend toward increased statification, a line running from Croly through the New Deal and on to Schlesinger and others today. This, as Berle likes to stress, is an attempt at a "non-statist" alternative: the

Neither Socialism nor Capitalsm

assignment of political power not *over* the corporate bodies of the economy but *to* them.

6

The Center consultant who has developed a more clearly thought-out program of corporatism, perhaps thereby inspiring Ferry, is Scott Buchanan. Buchanan was a leader of the Wallace Progressive Party in 1948; I do not know what his politics became after that, but when he published his *Essay in Politics* in 1953, the preface explained that it was based on conversations in 1947 which led most of the participants to join the Wallace movement the following year. The 1953 book presents essentially the same views he has now.

In a 1959 discussion at the Center, Buchanan criticized Ferry along the same lines as Harbrecht: for wanting to give too much power to the government instead of giving more powers to the corporations. But the government, he argued, "is obviously incapable of dealing with the big economic, military, and other problems that arise ... When you turn this all over to the government as is done in Sweden, you get a very dull, not necessarily stupid, kind of society," So—

> What I am thinking of, as some of you are guessing, is that you don't hand such a function over to the government - the national government. You hand over this function to a new kind of corporation which is chartered to determine its own function and legalize its own operation - a self-governing body. This might be some federal scheme. You would not have one national economic corporation. You would have 200 or 500 corporations, or whatever they are, and some kind of congress of corporations that would deal with political-economic matters through legal means.

The corporation, said Buchanan, should "think about itself in terms of the rule of the law":

> This would mean that the corporation think of itself literally as a government, as Berle has put it often enough, and try to constitutionalize itself in some way. This doesn't necessarily mean that we should impose a democratic dogma on it. It means that the corporation, if it isn't going to be democratic, should say it is not going to be and find a mode of operation that will discharge its responsibilities and be efficient in its own operation.

This is laudably clear: not democracy but efficiency. In another brochure issued by the Center in 1958, Buchanan ties up a number of things in the olio:

> The Marxist used to speak vividly, if not too accurately, about the concentration of capital and the expropriation of the worker. If the dialectic is still working, he ought now to point out the next stage or moment when the labor union applies for corporate membership in the big corporation whose directors grant annual tenure and salaries, pensions, and the power of veto on the policy of the corporation instead of the right to strike. As a result, the corporation is a government by and with the consent of the workers as well as the stockholders. As Adolf Berle puts it in "The 20th Century Capitalist Revolution," creeping socialism has become galloping capitalism, and, we might add, corporate communism, free-world variety.

It is not surprising to find him adding that Russia has gone ahead to entrust its economy to "three separate but coordinated giant corporations" and "The other socialist countries have invented other forms to meet their needs. It is not to be supposed that we are lacking in inventive imagination ."

Neither Socialism nor Capitalsm

The final chapter of his 1953 book even presents some modest details of a New order in which the corporations have taken on certain sovereign powers making the corporate structure autonomous and coordinate with the government. (Example: the N.A.M. becomes the "sponsor" of the Federal Trade Commission.) There is a separate House "representing managers, engineers, and workmen ." The same corporations which "moderate socialists mark for nationalization" are in this scheme to be given wide self-governing "powers and privileges ." The "chronic civil war between labor and the corporation" will be eliminated. The "three giant corporations" of the Soviet system (which are the Trade Unions, Soviet, and Consumers Cooperatives!) "should be intelligible to us as a kind of preview of ourselves if we continue to increase our corporate development in the same way in the future as we have in the past .. ." The vision is global: "incorporated trading companies, making cartel treaties in the twentieth century, could become the United States of the World .. ."

7

Buchanan is the most unreserved of our neo-corporatists, but Berle is recognized as their leading theoretician. Berle, as far as I know, has not put it as bluntly as some others, and I am not certain how far he would go. He is, to be sure, entirely uninhibited in describing the present system as corporate collectivism. He militantly insists on labeling it collectivism as often as possible - "true collectivism," etc. - and since he also quite calmly describes the corporate system as "an automatic self-perpetuating oligarchy," we need not suppose he has any illusion that we are living under a *democratic* collectivism. Nor does he think there is an unbridgeable gulf between this system and the bureaucratic-collectivist system on the other side of the Iron Curtain:

> The private property system in production ... has almost vanished in the vast area of American economy dominated by this system. Instead we have something which differs from the Russian or socialist system mainly in its philosophical content.

Beyond the Third Camp

Nor, for this matter, is he even exercised about democratic controls over this spreading collectivism. One of the troubles with liberals, he writes, is that

> ... they thought of ownership by "the people" as something real, whereas a moment's thinking would make it clear that "the people" was an abstraction. Its reality meant some sort of bureaucratic management.

And if bureaucratic management is inevitable, it should be efficient bureaucratic management. The oligarchic methods of the corporation "work remarkably well" and "Conventional stereotypes of 'democratic procedure' are not particularly useful in dealing with this problem."

"Public consensus" is counterposed to "public opinion." The important difference, of course, is that "public opinion" can finally be ascertained only by the conventional stereotypes of democratic procedure. But public consensus? This is the body of "unstated premises" lying behind the superficialities of public opinion. It does not emanate from the people, that abstraction; nor merely from the business community. Where then? Here is the answer: from "the conclusions of careful university professors, the reasoned opinions of specialists, the statements of responsible journalists, and at times the solid pronouncements of respected politicians." These constitute "the real tribunal to which the American system is finally accountable," and it is their consensus which confers legitimacy upon the system.

So the bureaucratic nature of this corporate collectivism - which by Orwellian rules he sometimes calls "the reality of economic democracy in the United States" - does not give him pause. It would indeed take a riotous imagination to equip the new corporate order with the aforesaid "conventional stereotypes" of democracy. In his good society, "organizations in each industry and inter-industry" - like the Iron and Steel Institute, which is properly "not Statist" - can be encouraged to "synchronize or harmonize" their planning, with the assistance of "relief from some of the rigidities of the antitrust laws."

Neither Socialism nor Capitalsm

Like Buchanan, he sees that "in any long view the American and Soviet systems would seem to be converging rather than diverging ..." For here too "power centralizes itself around a politico-economic instead of a governmental institution," the politico-economic institution on this side being the corporation. He is as enthusiastically in favor of cartels as Buchanan, with a similar vision of a corporate world government:

> In point of surprising fact, the large American corporations in certain fields have more nearly achieved a stable and working world government than has yet been achieved by any other institution. The outstanding illustration is the case of the oil industry.

For Berle, corporatism is the American surrogate for socialism. Socialism, he writes, was the instrument of the 20th century revolution in many countries, but "In the United States, the chief instrument has proved to be the modern giant corporation." If the corporations "do not assume community responsibilities, government must step in and American life will become increasingly statist ." The corporation's powers are in fact "held in trust for the entire community ."

> The choice of corporate managements [he writes in the chapter "Corporate Capitalism and 'The City of God,'" in The Twentieth Century Capitalist Revolution] is not whether so great a power shall cease to exist; they can merely determine whether they will serve as the nuclei of its organization or pass it over to someone else, probably the modern state ... It seems that, in diverse ways, we are nibbling at the edges of a vast, dangerous and fascinating piece of thinking.

Vast, dangerous and fascinating it is, and Berle is nibbling.

Beyond the Third Camp

8

In discussions of corporatism, the word corporation is more often than not used in more than one sense. The broader and earlier sense is any body (of people) corporate, whose association for some purpose is recognized; the narrower sense is the business corporation. The "corporations" of Italian Fascist theory were, however, not business corporations nor joint-stock companies, but associations of labor and capital assigned a given role in society. Corporatist ideologies have not necessarily begun with the business corporation; but as we have seen, our own neo-corporatists do begin this way. While beginning this way, however, do they go on to a broader conception of corporatism?

The bridge from the narrower to the broader sense is constituted by the question of who are the "members" of a corporation.

Once you entertain the idea of turning the corporation into a sovereign power, of turning autonomous political powers over to it in some fashion, you must bethink yourself that it will not do to confer this boon simply on the Board of Directors. The base must be widened to receive the weight. The corporation must be more inclusive, if it is to be turned into a political community or the base for one. We do not want to strengthen management at the expense of labor - no, we are all liberals and believe that labor must be treated equally. The solution is plainly to integrate labor *into* the corporation ... on an equal basis, naturally ... In a number of steps presented as expanding the "membership" of the corporation, the business corporation of today becomes the politically autonomous body of corporatist theory. Basic is the unity of all classes inside the confining forms of the corporate structure.

Buchanan has it all laid out: he wants "a highly structured corporation in which the union would be a part of the structure ." Not only investors and managers but "creditors, workers and buyers" should all get "explicit status as members or citizens of these governments [corporations] ." Hutchins opines it is labor itself, not the union as such, which should be included in the structure of the corporation, since the idea "does not necessarily involve the maintenance of a national union of any kind ." We have seen that in

257

Neither Socialism nor Capitalsm

Father Harbrecht's wave of the future, "men are bound to their corporations ."

In the Mason tome, Prof. Abram Chayes of Harvard elaborates a "more spacious" conception of "membership" of the corporation: "Among the groups now conceived as outside the charmed circle of corporate membership, but which ought to be brought within it, the most important and readily identifiable is its work-force ." Does this mean worker representation in its managing board? Apparently not, however. Still, something has to be done about the present sad state of affairs in which labor and management "are made to appear as hostile antagonists in a kind of legalized class-warfare ." (The reference is to ordinary collective bargaining.) By bringing the labor force *into* the corporation, negotiations become merely an act of adjusting common relations. Chayes is arguing that class collaboration, as against class struggle, entails the corporatist principle as the method of tying up two now-warring constituencies into a single constituency.

For Frank Tannenbaum in *A Philosophy of Labor*, the unions must save the corporation by endowing it with "a moral role in the world, not merely an economic one ." "In some way the corporation and its labor force must become one corporate group and cease to be a house divided and seemingly at war ."*

In that one of his many, and not always consistent, books in which he comes closest to a kind of corporatism, Peter Drucker also naturally turns up with the notion that the trade union must be made an institutional part of the corporate structure. This is in his *The New Society* (1949), written under the impress of the British Labor

---

* In 1921 (*The Labor Movement*, N.Y.). Tannenbaum was for the revolutionary mission of the working class and socialism, and friendly to something he called the "dictatorship of the proletariat," but it is interesting to see how, even then, this revolutionism was based on as reactionary and anti-humanistic a version of the organicist theory of society as I have ever seen and was combined with insistence on the outlawry of strikes and the excommunication from society of strikers.

Beyond the Third Camp

government. A man who thinks in managerial terms from first to last, Drucker views the trade-union leader as just another type of manager, who, like the corporation executive, has a responsibility not to his organization's members but to the Organization as such. Integration of the union will also help to make the government of the corporation "legitimate," he argues.

Interesting is the context of Drucker's approach to corporatism in this book. Generally speaking Drucker is a militant conservative, and in his other books he is usually a fervent apologist for the corporation and its managers as a going concern. Here, however, Drucker has a remarkable section on "Democratic Socialism," plainly meaning mainly the ongoing British Labor regime, in which he *defends* it against American misunderstanding - in his own way. His own way is the corporatist way.

He announces that capitalism has failed at least outside our own charmed country, that the New Society will be (naturally) "beyond capitalism and socialism," and insofar as he concretizes this vision, it is in terms echoing what we have already considered. The modern industrial enterprise is already "collective," it is a "governmental institution"; it is, however, "independent of the State in its origin as well as in its function. It is an organ of Society rather than one of the state ... There is not one prime mover in our society but at least two: State and enterprise ." The investor (shareholder) deserves no special rights in the corporation; the thing to do is to put the de-facto situation on a legalized basis, so that the sovereign control of the corporation by its managers is institutionalized.

From here Drucker naturally goes over to the question of how to broaden the corporate structure in line with its broader role: we get an echo of Ruml's trustee-tribunes. We get the theory of the convergence of the capitalist corporation with the Russian system, a characteristic accompaniment.* And we also get the already

---

* This theory of convergence and its popularity deserves an article by itself. One of the most amazing examples is *Industrialism and Industrial* (continued...)

Neither Socialism nor Capitalsm

mentioned integration of the trade unions into the "membership" of the broadened corporation, which is now ready to fulfill its bigger tasks.

9

Our neo-corporatist school consists of liberals, not conservatives or reactionaries.

The people of the Santa Barbara Center are in general conscious liberals, as evidenced by their output on other questions like war and nuclear disarmament, civil liberties and civil rights, etc. Berle is a certified liberal, being a leader of the New York Liberal Party. Buchanan was what I am accustomed to call a Stalinoid-liberal, and probably still is. Drucker, the conservative proved the rule, as explained, in the book in which he approached corporatism. Tannenbaum is an ex-socialist; and so on.

The trend is cropping out of the bureaucratic-collectivist side of today's liberalism. It is not the only outcropping; the dominant one is still what Berle would call "statist." But it is an especially interesting outcropping.

These are not the first liberals to discover corporatism. The famous German liberal capitalist Walter Rathenau embodied it in the new social order outlined in his book *In Days to Come*, written during the First World War. In 1947 John Fisher in *Harper's* (he was then one of its editors and is now editor-in-chief) offered a well developed program of corporatism as platform for the revival of liberalism, very similar to Buchanan's finished product. In return for this dispensation, "In a few peculiarly vital industries, however, labor

---

* (...continued)
Man, by Clark Kerr and three colleagues (Harvard, 1960), which paints the coming New Order as an authoritarian society ("a new slavery") extrapolated almost entirely from the convergence of a bureaucratized capitalism with a somewhat mellowed Stalinism. The authors insist this is the wave of the future to be accepted without vain "moral indignation."

might have to forego its right to strike: and in return it would have to receive a special standing and special privileges comparable to those of the civil service." Rightists, he admitted, "might try to convert it into a corporative state."

Probably more significant are the views of the liberal whose economics is the bridge between liberalism and Laborism, J.M. Keynes. In *The End of Laissez Faire* (1926) Keynes advocated a status for corporations as "semi-autonomous bodies within the State":

> I propose a return, it may be said, towards medieval conceptions of separate autonomies. But, in England at any rate, corporations are a mode of government which has never ceased to be important...
>
> But more interesting than these is the trend of Joint Stock Institutions, when they have reached a certain age and size, to approximate to the status of public corporations rather than that of individualistic private enterprise. One of the most interesting and unnoticed developments of recent decades has been the tendency of big enterprise to socialize itself...
>
> ...The battle of Socialism against unlimited private profit is being won in detail hour by hour ... It is true that many big undertakings ... still need to be semi-socialized ... We must take full advantage of the natural tendencies of the day, and we must probably prefer semi-autonomous corporations to organs of the Central Government ...

Note that views similar to those which are American school *counterposes* to socialism are here offered as socialistic. To confound the picture further, the reader has no doubt been aware that corporatism is most notorious as a fascist ideology. Well, then, is corporatism liberal, socialist, or fascist? Or are there three distinct

Neither Socialism nor Capitalsm

kinds of corporatism? When a liberal adopts corporatism, is he falling for a fascist theory or is he rescuing this theory from the fascists? Where, in short, does this neo-corporatism fit in?

10

The difficulty arises because corporatism is thought of as being a fascist theory. It became so, of course; we shall see how. But historically it arises as a *socialist* idea, and as such it has a far from negligible past. Its liberal incarnation, which we have been observing, is only an extension of this phenomenon.

Its main appeal to socialist thought, as to Berle, was as a framework for the radical reform-from-above of capitalist society through what were thought of as "non-statist" or non-political channels. It looked to a transformation of society not through a struggle for political power but through the assignment of social powers to autonomous economic bodies. (This in fact is the basic definition of corporatism in whatever form it presents itself.)

Some elements usually associated with corporatism go back very far in pre-Marxist socialist thought, particularly a beehive-view of society as an organic whole of which the human individual is only a cell (organicism) and a related "communitarian" outlook. But these are by no means peculiar to corporatism, being common in all forms of socialism-from-above. Fourier's phalanx, Cabet's Icaria and Robert Owen's model factory can also be taken as ancestors, but these utopian socialisms, of course, saw their autonomous economic bodies as infiltrators on the margin of society rather than commanders in the center.

The first prophet of a full-fledged corporatism was Saint-Simon — not a utopian and not really a socialist — who was fertile in schemes for the radical reform-from-above of society through autonomous economic and social bodies which would dispense with "politics" and rule by direct administration, under the benevolent control of financiers, businessmen, scientists, and technicians. In Saint-Simon labor and capital were institutionally amalgamated not only in theory but in terminology: the very term "workers" meant primarily the capitalists who carried on productive work as distinct from the

Beyond the Third Camp

"idlers" of the old ruling class. (Derivative trends in bourgeois thought stem from Saint-Simon's disciple, Comte, and the schools of sociology basically inspired by him; *vide* Durkheim.)

The conception of a new order built along the lines of a corporate society was one element in Edward Bellamy's version of socialism. Bellamy's system, though mainly modeled after military organization, explained the great change in terms of pushing the corporate development to its final conclusion, "the one great corporation in which all other corporations were absorbed ."

Perhaps the classic statement of "socialist" corporatism was expounded by Charles P. Steinmetz, prominent socialist in his day as well as eminent scientist. In his *America and the New Epoch* (1916) "socialism" is a society where the giant corporations, like his employer General Electric, literally rule directly, having eschewed profit and embraced the goal of sheer efficiency.

But the most massive corporatist element in the development of socialist thought was injected by syndicalism. The basic conception of the re-organization of society through (presumably) non-political but autonomous economic bodies was here the distinctive content of the movement.

Here corporatism diverged in two quite different directions. Saint-Simon, Bellamy's *Looking Backward*, and Steinmetz were almost purely authoritarian, not to say totalitarian. But syndicalism, like socialism as a whole, was a movement with two souls.

One was a socialism-from-below which looked toward the organization of democratic control of governmental authority through workers' control; the other was a thoroughly anti-democratic, elitist and "administered" view of the new order which was associated with the anarchist element in anarcho-syndicalism.* The former strain later dissolved itself into the general socialist movement and early

---

* I am aware that this passing remark flies in the face of the myth of anarchist "libertarianism" and "anti-authoritarianism ." I have dealt with this legend in Vol. 4 of *Karl Marx's Theory of Revolution*, published by Monthly Review Press.

Neither Socialism nor Capitalsm

revolutionary Communist movement, where its positive outcome was represented in such tendencies as guild-socialism and acceptance of a workers-council basis for a new type of democratic state. (These can still be termed "corporative," if one absolutely insists, insofar as they look to the assignment of power in society to "occupationally" determined bodies, although these bodies were not "economic" but thoroughly political.)

The latter strain flowed into the later bureaucratic-collectivist ideologies of corporatism, the ones to which that term actually became attached. In the heartland of the syndicalist movement, pre-1914 France, this current in syndicalism was documented in the book which most bluntly concretized the syndicalist new order: Pataud and Pouget's *Comment Nous Ferons la Revolution* (1909). When syndicalism traveled north to England, its anarchist element tended to dissolve out, leaving guild-socialism as a deposit; but when it traveled south to Italy, it was anarcho-syndicalism and Georges Sorel's protofascist reading of syndicalism which expanded.

Now it was this latter wing or current of syndicalism which transformed itself organically into the "black socialist" wing of Italian Fascism, and which thereby created what we know as the corporatism of the fascist ideology. Its architects were Enrico Corradini, Edmondo Rossoni, and other syndicalists-turned-fascist, plus D'Annunzio-type nationalists-turned-syndicalist like Alfredo Rocco and Dino Grandi. Corporatism was the *serious* ideology only of this "socialist" face of fascism. As is well known, though Mussolini later adopted it officially it remained an empty facade for purely social-demagogic purposes.*

In German fascism too, within the Nazi movement, it was the assigned manipulators of the "Labor Front" who played with it and it

---

* For the benefit of Berle, it should be emphasized that even if the corporative structure had ever been realized, it would not and could not have been "non-statist" in any meaningful sense. The state power would still have been omnipotent, however dressed up. The "non-statist" illusion about corporatism is analogous to the "non-political" illusion of its ancestor syndicalism, which was thoroughly political.

was the *serious* ideology only of the "black socialist" wing. Strasser developed it into a view of a new corporate order called "state feudalism," with a chamber of corporations, etc. Here it was not even officially adopted for demagogic purposes; the Hitler regime rejected it.

We see, then, that corporatism enters the fascist world not *as* a fascist ideology but as a socialistic idea, indeed as *the* program to transform fascism into socialism. In this role corporatism is a direct and organic outgrowth of that one of the "two souls of socialism" which I have called socialism-from-above.

Once having arisen in this way, fascist corporatism had a powerful reactive impact on the socialist movement itself. It attracted - sucked out toward itself, so to speak - precisely those socialist currents which felt their kinship to it. In the case of the Marquet group in the French Socialist Party and the Mosley group in the British Labor Party, wings of the socialist movement split off to become fascist themselves. But more significant were the currents which were attracted specifically by corporatism *without* going over to fascism.

A hand of ideological sympathy to the Strasser wing of Nazism was stretched out by the not-insignificant tendency in the Social-Democracy led by the German-Czech social-democrat Wenzel Jaksch. Bernard Shaw, the no. 2 architect of Fabianism, was enthusiastically pro-Mussolini before he became even more enthusiastically pro-Stalinist; in a sober lecture before the Fabian Society in 1933 he described the Italian corporate-state plan and added, addressing Il Duce in the name of Fabianism:

> I say "Hear, hear! More power to your elbow ." That is precisely what the Fabian Society wants to have done ... Although we are all in favor of the corporative state, nevertheless it will not really be a corporative state until the corporations own the land in which they are working ...

In Belgium, the socialist party leader Henri de Man, who had made a great if now forgotten reputation as a "revisionist" offering a

Neither Socialism nor Capitalsm

theoretical alternative to Marxism within the socialist movement, wrote *Corporatisme et Socialisme* in 1935 and later became virtually a Nazi collaborator. Lincoln Steffens—I list him here rather than as a liberal; the distinction becomes terminological—glowed with ardor for both Mussolini and the application of the corporative idea to the U.S. Without throwing him into the very same bag, I would also suggest a look at Leon Blum's introduction to the French edition of Burnham's *Managerial Revolution*.

Corporatism was also an element in the ideological jumble of the New Deal, but my impression is that it was more prominent in non-socialistic New Dealers like Hugh Johnson than in the radical wing, who tended to be overweeningly "statist."

11

This identification of corporatism as a *socialist* current - as one of the strains in the history of socialism-from-above - rather than as an idea necessarily connoting fascism, is the first key to understanding the burgeoning of new corporatist ideologies today. But now widen the focus on this picture:

"Socialism-from-above" did not arise from socialism. It was and is merely the form taken within the framework of socialism - the intrusion *into* socialism - of what is in fact all-pervasive in the entire history of man's aspirations for the good society and a better life. This is true everywhere, in all times, and in all ideological guises. It is the expectation of emancipation or reform from some powers-that-be who will hand down the new world to a grateful people, rather than the liberating struggle of the people themselves, associated from below, to win and control the good society for themselves. It is the octroyal principle, which is still dominant as always, versus the revolutionary-democratic principle, which during most of man's history could be nothing but a phantasm and which could become a realistic aspiration *only* within the framework of socialism. What is distinctive about socialism is not its dominant "socialism-from-above" wing, for this is dominant everywhere, but the fact that it and it alone could generate the ever-arising and so-far-defeated movements for emancipation-from-below.

Beyond the Third Camp

Reform-from-above, under the economic and political impulsions of a period when the dominant social system is decaying, characteristically takes the form of a bureaucratic-collectivist ideology. Corporatism is one of the bureaucratic-collectivist ideologies which arises. It arises quite inescapably both inside and outside the socialist movement. What we have examined in the case of the American school, in a country with a tiny socialist movement, is its rise in circles outside the socialist movement. But in most countries of the world, ideologists like Berle, Buchanan, Ferry, *et al.* would not be outside the broad socialist movement; they are social-democratic types. Their ideology would arise within the framework of socialism and take on a socialistic coloration and vocabulary, instead of taking care to couch itself in non-socialist or even anti-socialist terms. This American development is an anomaly in that it produces a corporatism stripped of any socialist dress.

But this means that if we look abroad, we should expect to see its analogues *with* a socialist dress. And we do plainly enough; in fact, the picture is gratifyingly simplified when we find that both sides recognize their affinity.

The British co-thinker of our American school is C.A.R. Crosland, the leading theoretician of the right (Gaitsekll) wing of the British Labor Party. He, in turn, is the apostle of a new "revisionism" (his term) for which he claims most of the European social-democracies.

Prof. Mason appeals to Crosland's book *The Future of Socialism* for British evidence that "the form of ownership of large enterprise is irrelevant" and that the large corporation is fundamentally the same whether private in the U.S. (where it is called capitalism) or public as in Britain (where it is called an installment of socialism). If this is so, then the transplantation of Crosland revisionism to the private "corporate collectivism" of the U.S. produces a resultant ideology similar to the neo-corporatism we have been discussing.

Prof. Rostow states his understanding of Crosland-Gaitskellism in terms of the American problem as follows: "In England, socialists say that the managers have already socialized capitalism, so that it is no longer necessary to invoke the cumbersome formality of public ownership of the means of production ." By the same token - this is

Neither Socialism nor Capitalsm

Rostow's point - the managers may also be said to have already socialized capitalism in the U.S. Thus Crosland equals Berle plus a difference in latitude and longitude.

The chapter in Mason's book on the British corporation was, in fact, assigned to Crosland himself, as collaborator with the American authors. Crosland winds up this essay by quoting the 1957 thesis of the Labor Party, *Industry and Society*, in which the anti-nationalization view was established: "The Labor party recognizes that, under increasingly professional managements, large firms are as a whole serving the nation well ." This is why nationalization is unnecessary, according to Crosland. It follows that the big corporations, under even more professional managements, are serving the U.S. at least as well if not better.

Industry and Society was the official theoretical exposition of this revisionism; and especially because it was a formal "resolution" and not simply an article, it is interesting to see, in "motto" form at the head of a chapter, not a quotation from Marx but one from Berle's *20th Century Capitalist Revolution*. Quoted also is the Drucker of *The New Society*. This is symbolic of a fact. The line of analysis in *Industry and Society* is essentially Berlean.

If W.H. Ferry proposes a corporatist program for the U.S., he himself at any rate sees no great difference between this and the views of the Swedish social-democrat Gunnar Myrdal, or with the British and New Zealand welfare-states. Scott Buchanan says he wants to see his ideas worked out by a Fabian Society.

12

It is this relationship, mutually recognized, between American neo-corporatism and the new post-war trend of European social-democratic reformism which helps to explain both. I refer to the trend toward the repudiation of public or social ownership (*not* merely nationalization) as an important part of the socialist program. Crosland (*Encounter*, March, 1960) chortles that "nearly all the European socialist parties" have gone this way.

Beyond the Third Camp

But this is not traditional or historical social-democratic reformism in economic program, any more than Molletism in France has been traditional reformism in politics. The qualitative transformation that has taken place was pointed up when Crosland denounced "the extremist phraseology of the Party's formal aims" in its constitution regarding nationalization, and demanded that it be rewritten. This phraseology, now "extremist," was written in by Sidney Webb and Arthur Henderson.

Why is this neo-reformism engaged in a precipitous flight away from public ownership? First it should be seen as analogue to Berle's evolution from New Deal "statism" to his new enthusiasm for "non-Statist collectivism," which we have discussed. The line of thought goes like this

Public ownership is no longer necessary for the gradual reform of capitalism into socialism because capitalism is socializing itself in other forms. The transference of power in the corporations to socially responsible managers means that the forms of private property are no longer incompatible with our ends. Socialization will now go forward with the inevitability of gradualism in these new corporate forms. Public ownership can now be stored away in the cellar of our program because the development of the new corporate collectivism is adequately doing the job which the socialist movement once thought it was called on to perform .

"What is accepted as the road to "socialism" is the ongoing process of bureaucratic- collectivization of the capitalist world. This neo-reformism of the European social-democrats and the neo-corporatism of our American liberal school are analogous forms of one type of bureaucratic-collectivist ideology.

New Politics 1962

NOTES

1 The role of the corporation in dissolving the property relations of capitalism was already explained in some detail by Marx in *Capital*, III, 516-22 (Kerr, ed.); cf. 450-59; see also Marx-Engels, *Selected Correspondence* (N.Y. ed.), p. 105, and the passage which stands at the head of this article.

Neither Socialism nor Capitalsm

2. For an acadamese version of the comparison, see Richard Eells, *The Meaning of Modern Business* (N.Y., 1960), which invents the term "metrocorporate feudalism ."

3 See W.H. Ferry, *The Economy Under Law* (1960), published by the Center; also his *The Corporation and the Economy* (1959). The Center also published Scott Buchanan, *The War Corporation and the Republic* (1958) and Berle, *Economic Power and the Free Society* (1957).

The New Social-Democratic Reformism

The thesis of this article is that the ideology of the dominant wing of the European social-democracy has, since the end of World War II, visibly become something different from the traditional reformism of the Second International; it has entered a new stage and demands a new analysis, a tentative sketch of which is offered here.

"New" is always relative, of course; there is no doubt that the new ideology is an organic outgrowth of the old, as it claims to be; but it continues so far along the lines implicit in the old that a qualitative change must be registered.

By traditional reformism I mean the political ideology which assumed clearest self-consciousness in the form of Fabianism in England and Bernstein's "revisionism" in Germany. It looked to the gradual transformation, or metamorphosis, of capitalism into socialism by an inherent process working out through patchwork changes, however minute but cumulative in effect, which would eventually mean that capitalism itself grows into socialism, without any visible break in the continuum of change. Capitalism would not be "abolished," let alone "overthrown"; it would *become* socialism. The movement toward socialism was simply the sum of collectivist tendencies immanent in the present system. Reformism's perspective was the inevitable collectivization of capitalism itself, its self-socialization from above, rather than its change by action from below.

Hence the reformists' equation was: *collectivized capitalism equals socialism*. To the extent that statification was one important form of such collectivization, though not the only one, they had a second equation: *statification equals socialism*. (There is a generation of socialists today who associate this formula only with the Stalinist ideology: this deprives the old reformists of their proper historical credit.) The reformists, both Fabian and Bernstein varieties, left little room for the idea that workers' democracy, in the sense of some type of democratic control of production from below, was a *sine qua non* of socialism.

Before 1914 the lively conflict in the Second International between the revisionists and the "orthodox Marxists" was in large part fought out over ideology; in practice, it is notorious that there was considerable agreement on what to do from day to day (except in crises). Ignoring what this

Neither Capitalism nor Socialism

reflected about the "orthodox," I point out only that today, on the contrary, what has been conspicuously new about the new reformists has in many cases been their *practice*, above all.

The most spectacular case has been the practice of the Socialist Party of France under Guy Mollet, undoubtedly one of the blackest chapters in the history of the international socialist movement. On August 4, 1914 the German Social-Democrats made history by voting for the Kaiser's war credits; and the Second International collapsed. That was traditional reformism. But let us imagine that instead of simply going along with the patriotic current, a Social-Democratic government had been in charge of the famous "rape of Belgium," and moreover had modernized it with concentration camps, torture of prisoners, organized massacres. ... This gets nearer the difference between Philip Scheidemann, who was an old-fashioned type, and the modern Guy Mollet, who as Premier of France and leader of the French Socialists, stubbornly carried on the "dirty war" against Algerian liberation, by a regime and by methods which revolted even half-decent French liberals, not to speak of Senator John F. Kennedy.

The Molletist regime organized - not tolerated; it *organized* - a brutal fascist-like repression in Algeria, not under the personal direction of some reactionary assigned to do the dirty job while the government held its nose and pretended not to look, but under the personal direction of a close "socialist comrade" of Mollet's acting as his political right hand man and obdurately defended by him. This social-democratic regime organized McCarthy-like crackdowns on dissidents within France; the leading McCarthyite was Mollet himself. Naturally it also brought about a whole series of expulsions from the SP itself. The most noted expulsion was not of a left-winger but of an old-line reformist, André Philip; and the most vicious expulsions and persecutions were directed against the young socialists and student socialists.

This led to a rather unusual type of split in the Party, precipitated not only by the Algerian policy but more immediately by Mollet's role in bringing de Gaulle into power.

The break was not a left-right split, though of course all leftist elements went along with the new Party formed (Parti Socialiste

Beyond the Third Camp

Autonome, now merged into the present Parti Socialiste Unifié). What characterized the leaders of the minority that split, such as Depreux and Mayer, was that they were largely *traditional* reformists, who could not live with Molletism.

Finally, the Mollet party produced another startling phenomenon: a proto-fascist wing, around the figures of Lacoste and Lejeune—a wing so seen not simply by Mollet's opponents in the party but even by *Le Monde*.

Nothing like the Mollet phenomenon can be ascribed to the practice of the reborn German Social-Democracy; here we point first to an ideological development. After the death of Kurt Schumacher and with growing Cold War prosperity in Germany, the German party moved simply to dump *socialism* from its program. Now I do not want to get this statement involved in a terminological dispute over the word, for of course the new reformists maintain stoutly that what they propose is still "socialism." What is important for present purposes is the safe statement that what was dumped from the new reformist program was that which the *traditional* reformists would have accepted as elementary socialism. They eliminate all connection between socialism and *any* conception of advance toward the social ownership of the means of production; they make protection of private enterprise one of the key features of the new reformism's economic policy on the same grounds as they make allowance for any state interference with private enterprise.[1]

Since the formalization of its new politics in the Bad Godesberg program of 1959, the German party under the practical leadership of Willy Brandt, has deliberately set out to become as indistinguishable in political program as possible from Adenauer's Christian Democrats, on the model of the American two-party bi-partisan system. Only incidental to this has been its throttling of elements in the party aspiring to anti-war action or its suppression of the socialist student organization.

The change in Germany has been the most noteworthy but not the only one, nor the first, among the Western European social-democracies. The Austrian Socialist Party disembarrassed itself of socialism in its new program in 1958. This party has been in a permanent government-sharing coalition with the Catholic party (People's party) since 1945: a whole

Neither Capitalism nor Socialism

generation has never seen a wholly independent action by its socialist party. Here, in a sense which the old social-democracy never knew, the social-democrats have integrated their whole party existence with the state structure. It probably also has, incidentally, the most bureaucratized and monolithic party structure in the International.[2]

Here and there, another question about these parties forces itself on the attention: unusual social composition. The traditional social-democracy was not only indisputably a workers' party, but also (what is not always the same thing) *the* party of the working class in the country. It still is in West Germany, Austria, and other countries as far as mass membership is concerned. But in the two countries where the Communist Party has mass workers' support and membership, France and Italy, where therefore the social-democratic leadership is relatively freed of the social weight of the working class, and where those workers who do stay with it in spite of all tend to be a self-selected kind, visible internal social changes have taken place.

It has been reported that one quarter of the membership of Mollet's SP are state employees (petty functionaries in nationalized industry, government bureaus, municipal offices, etc.)[3] Shortly before he died Marceau Pivert described to me how the Mollet party leadership had finally succeeded in winning a majority in the traditionally left-wing Paris region of the party: he detailed it in terms of the mobilization of the functionaries concentrated in Paris, who were or became members of the SP, as against the traditional working-class population of the party region who were predominantly "Pivertists." In Italy, Saragat's Social-Democratic party is notoriously lacking in working-class support. Virtually the entire working class of the country is divided between the Communist Party and the Socialist Party led by Nenni (the latter also containing the *traditional*-reformist wing of the movement) with a more conservative labor wing adhering to the Christian Democrats.1

---

1 Although the Saragat party is in my opinion one of the most extreme examples of reformism, I have not discussed it here because, frankly, (continued...)

Beyond the Third Camp

This aspect of Mollet's French party, combined with its extreme political record, has more than once caused a big question mark to be placed over its basic character. It was put perhaps most directly by Maurice Dufour in Pivert's *Correspondence Socialiste International* (March 1958 — i.e., at the lowest depth of Molletism):

> Certain passages of Djilas's book [*The New Class*] give food for thought. Let us put the question brutally: has not the French Socialist Party become the nursery of this new class? The French nationalizations supply a valuable example: the heads of the nationalized enterprises, many of whom hold a party card, behave like the old bosses: same attitudes, the same reactions. Perhaps there is this difference: the new bosses claim to be of the proletariat! So, the French SP has not colonized the bourgeois state; the other way round is nearer the truth.

Along with the other statifications desired by the reformists, the reformist party itself gets statified. ...

All of this is intended to raise the same question about the new European social-democratic reformism which I have already raised in *New Politics* about certain currents in American liberalism: viz., relationship to the burgeoning of various types of *bureaucratic-collectivist ideologies*. To repeat briefly: "By 'bureaucratic-collectivist' I mean in this connection the ideological reflection or anticipation of a new social order ... which is based on the control of both economy and government by an elite bureaucracy - forming a new exploitive ruling class - which runs the fused economic-political structure not for the private-profit gains of any individual or groups, but for its own collective aggrandizement in power, prestige, and

---

1 (...continued)
I do not know how it can be documented. My own view was formed in the course of considerable discussion in Italy in 1957-58 with both Saragatists and others.

Neither Capitalism nor Socialism

revenue, by administrative planning-from-above ." This entails the view that the particular type of totalitarian statified economy developed under Stalinism in Russia, and now elsewhere, is only *one* form of bureaucratic collectivism. We are concerned with others.

I have reviewed some phenomena of the post-war social-democracy only in order to indicate, inconclusively at this point, how the question of the *bureaucratic-collectivization of social-democratic reformism* is posed not only by the writings of certain reformist theoreticians, but also in life, in the political arena. The rest of this article will be devoted to analyzing, from this standpoint, the theoretical formulations of the new reformism by its leading ideologue, who otherwise might too easily be written off.

C.A.R. Crosland, the British Labor Party M.P. has systematically set out to formulate the ideology of the new reformism (which he calls "revisionism"); in doing it, he has set himself forth as the theoretical champion of the continental social-democracies, which he counterposes to the "extremist" British; and the continental social-democrats, insofar as they are interested in theoretics, perforce look upon him in this light. It is interesting that when an International Socialist Conference of reformist theoreticians, mainly from the Low Countries, met in Holland in early 1960 to discuss the new social-democratic programs, Crosland was the only Briton present; and, in his introduction to its published papers, J.M. den Uyl (of the Netherlands) cold think of only two books which "might be regarded as a renewing of socialist theory" - Crosland's *Future of Socialism* and Jules Moch's *Confrontations*.1

---

1 Moch's book is pretty much a standard rehearsal of reformist tunes with Gallic bravura; it has about as much relation to Moch's actual hatchet-wielding operations as Mollet's Minister of Interior as the Declaration of Independence has to the activities of the D.A.R. The papers presented in this conference, including Crosland's on "Economic Backgrounds," were published in a little pamphlet entitled *Orientation--Socialism Today and Tomorrow*, Part 1, (Amsterdam, 1959); and a report of the conference, including two interventions by Crosland, was published under the same title, Part 2 (Amsterdam, (continued...)

Crosland has this further distinction, as compared with his "revisionist" friends and co-thinkers like (say) Douglas Jay or Roy Jenkins: he has gone farthest in putting the new politics bluntly, frankly and uninhibitedly. For all these reasons, it is from him that we can best learn what is happening.

Nothing in the following discussion is intended to refute Crosland's views; the sole aim is to exhibit their internal logic.

The first distinctive feature of Crosland's "revisionism" is its enthusiastic satisfaction with the social system which others call Western capitalism. He was of course delighted with the Labor Party's Gaitskellite statement in 1958 that "under increasingly professional managements, large firms are as a whole serving the nation well ." In the essay which he contributed to *The Corporation in Modern Society* (ed. E.S. Mason) he used this for all it was worth as his peroration. But this is mild. For as lyrical and uncritical an account of the operation of the present economic system as one can find anywhere left of Nelson Rockefeller, one must read Crosland's paper at the Dutch conference, keeping in mind that he is presumably not writing only about Britain:

> There is no shadow over permanent full employment; "even Right-Wing governments" will maintain it without question; there is "a general feeling of contentment;" standard of living has risen gratifyingly especially for the poorer; the benefits of the system are distributed "more equally and more justly"; there is no "suffering from oppression or capitalist exploitation"; the employers have in good part assumed "the social responsibilities of industry"; "feelings of social justice" are now a big problem only among "socialist idealists," not the people. And:
>
>> Aggressive individualism gives way to a suave and sophisticated sociability; and the traditional capitalist ruthlessness is replaced by a belief in modern, enlight-

---

1 (...continued)
1960).

ened methods of personnel management. Large-scale industry has become humanized...

Much more of this, and *that's all; there is no other side; there are no other aspects to the economic picture.*

A comparison with the Bernsteinians, such as Crosland insists on, would be entirely beside the point. The traditional "revisionists" were mild, pinkish, tepid *critics* of the system; Crosland is one of the most eulogistic defenders of the system known to economic science today. It gives pause.

One of the more unusual aspects of Crosland's lack of inhibition about justifying virtually everything about the economic status quo is his insistence on fiercely defending even the advertising industry, as it exists not only in Britain but also in the U.S., against the kind of far-from-basic strictures made by (say) Vance Packard's books. He counterposes the hoary myth of "consumer sovereignty." The present set-up permits the consumer "libertarian judgments" because the individual decides for himself what he wants and registers his opinion by buying it..."[4]

I am trying to underline that there is something new here. All previous differences among socialists have been over differing degrees and forms of *hostility* to the economic system. Crosland is the first socialist theoretician in history, as far as I know, to take his stand on *complete identification with the going system.* Insofar as this is accepted as socialism at all, there could scarcely be any more finished exemplar of a socialism-from-above.

It should not be supposed that Crosland's contentment with the economic system is simply founded on the character of the British situation, where the Labor movement and Labor governments have had a special impact. Another one of Crosland's sides that brings one up sharp is his insistence on specifically extending his eulogies to the U.S. He sometimes verges on representing the United States as being the country nearest the socialist ideal, with the possible exception of Sweden. "In the U.S.A. the Trade Unions have invaded the prerogatives of management in such a way that we might almost speak of industrial democracy there," he said in Holland. After claiming that in Britain the trade unions "remain effective masters of the industrial scene" even under the Tories, he has the amazing fortitude to add the note: "This is increasingly true in the U.S. also." The leaders of the AFL-CIO will be glad to learn about their master over "the citadels of capitalist power."[5] But then they will be happy to know, also, that Crosland considers the American labor movement a model in another respect:

> Workers who take managerial posts are not condemned as traitors to their class. Trade Union leaders are not thought to be in danger of contamination if they have large cars, and smoke cigars, and draw huge salaries. The Unions are not thought guilty of treachery if they cooperate with management to boost sales or raise productivity, or even accept a wage-cut to save a firm from bankruptcy ...[6]

Lucky American workers to have such modern type leaders! Crosland should explain why these American paragons, shored up by their huge salaries and rejoicing in mastery over the citadels of capitalist power, have not been able to get even a feeble medicare program, let alone socialized medicine.

It is inevitable that Crosland should enthuse also over the "convergence of political attitudes" of the contending parties both in the U.S. and England; i.e., in the U.S., the absence of political differences between the Democrats and Republicans. He specifically complements the "mature, educated voter" in the U.S. for making his choice in the 1960 election "on the basis of such issues as ... simply the complacency of the existing [Eisenhower] regime."

We, not the Tories, have the right to claim American society for our own, says Crosland:

> It is in fact a complete illusion that British Conservatives really want a mobile equal-opportunity society on the

Neither Capitalism nor Socialism

> American pattern... Their true ideology is poles apart from the restless, egalitarian ideology of contemporary America. This indeed comes much closer, though this is not always understood in England, to the egalitarian ideas of the Left than to the more static, conservative instincts of the Right.[7]

Crosland, of course, would be a heartfelt charter-member of the club which is now raising a banner with a strange device paraphrased from Earl Browder's old slogan: "Americanism Is Twentieth-Century Socialism!" In the United States, he finds, "there is little trace of a elite psychology," a claim which can be understood - not accepted but just understood - if we assume that Crosland is thinking only of the peculiar British forms of institutionalized status symbols such as the "public" schools and accent-snobbery.

Crosland not only identifies himself with the going economic system, but also strives heroically to identify himself as completely as possible with all of American bourgeois society - viz., the only society left on earth where capitalism is still entirely self-confident and feels the bloom of health. There are, of course, far more numerous elements in British society with which one *can* identify, and in that country various positive features can be ascribed to the impact of the socialist movement; but in the United States this interpretation is impossible. Crosland draws the inevitable conclusion: he would *not* be a socialist in the United States; or, in other words, there is no need for a socialist movement in this blessed land - not even a "revisionist" one. This seems to be the plain sense of his rather tortuous statement that in the U.S.

> ... a Leftist, who was a socialist in Britain, would be much less concerned to promote more social equality of material welfare, of which plenty exists already, than with reforms lying outside the field of socialist-capitalist controversy...[8]

Beyond the Third Camp

At this point we get a peculiar inversion of the Bernsteinian "revisionism" of which Crosland thinks he is merely the continuator. Bernstein became notorious for saying, "The movement is everything, the goal nothing." Crosland now envisions the full transformation of the U.S. into a socialist society, apparently, without any socialists at work, without any socialist *movement* at all. As far as I know, he is (another record) the first socialist theoretician in history to have stared this thought in the face. What it sets down without any equivocation is, for one thing, the perspective of socialization-from-above in fullblown form. The system is going to have to socialize itself, for sure.

For another thing, this makes it *very* difficult for Crosland to have American disciples, since their first duty on agreeing with him fully is to commit hari-kari (politically speaking). As a matter of fact, this is more or less what has happened periodically in the later history of American socialism: there has been little or no room for reformist socialism to take root, and rightwing developments have tended to propel themselves, in the course of finding self-awareness, outside the socialist movement.

However, the system with which Crosland identifies himself is no longer to be called "capitalism," naturally; it is a new and better one. At his most definite, he dates this after the Second World War; when - he is a little more vague, it is something that is in process of happening, or is "almost" true. It would be unprofitable to make anything of his varying formulations, for the underlying thought is both clear enough and inevitable for him: capitalism effectively no longer exists.

Now it is very important to understand that he is not and cannot be merely talking about "Socialist Britain." He must apply this just as much not only to the U.S., as we have seen, but also to Western Europe, since it is the theoretical basis of his prescriptions for the new "revisionism," and since it is the continental social-democracies that have taken up this new "revisionism" most favorably. Croslandism, therefore, must literally claim that Adenauer's Germany and de Gaulle's France have also left capitalism behind in their ascent to the new progressive order, but I am not aware that Crosland has ever specifically faced this picture.

The theoretical dilemma is deepgoing: the German Social-Demo-

Neither Capitalism nor Socialism

cratic Party is perhaps his favorite party and there is no question about his admiration for its "post capitalist" politics; but if post-war Germany abolished capitalism, this happy event actually took place *under the aegis of a right-wing government, which was being roundly denounced by the Social-Democracy all the time the "revolution" was going on.* If, in the U.S., he looks forward to the full blossoming of a "socialism" without any socialist movement, in Germany he implicitly sees the abolition of capitalism by a right-wing government with the socialists in opposition.1

It is no part of this article's restricted task to discuss the way in which he "abolishes" capitalism from today's world. It has to do with a demonstration that there is no special connection between capitalism and profit (production for profit, profit system, or what-have-you), nor anything to do with the ownership of the means of production. His simplest approach was in his contribution to *New Fabian Essays*,[9] where it was done by *defining* capitalism as laissez-faire, right through the '30s.[10] I do not comprehend how he could do this without being hooted out of at least the Fabian Society; but at any rate it is clear that if capitalism means laissez-faire, then it certainly was abolished, if it ever existed at all. But then this happened long before Attlee and Gaitskell's administrations, and so even in England we find Crosland's theory (but not Crosland) detaching the demise of capitalism from the device of socialism.[11]

---

1 In passing I want to point out the close analogy between Crosland's theoretical dilemma and that of the "orthodox Trotskyists" after the war. If Russia is a "workers' state" because its economy is nationalized (statified), then the new East European states must have also become workers' states as statification became complete. Now this "social revolution" must have taken place, at the time, behind the backs of the Trotskyists, who registered the fact of the "revolution" only some time later, after a good deal of puzzlement. They thus invented the category of a social revolution which creates a workers' state not only without a visible revolution but without a revolutionary party and without the support or even the participation of the working class. In fact, the current theory of neo-Trotskyism is entirely based on this theory of the bureaucratic revolution-from-above, which is no easier to swallow than Adenauer's revolution-from-above.

Beyond the Third Camp

Even in the same book, his latest, in which he has most thoroughly "abolished" capitalism, statements like this keep creeping in "Post-war full employment appeared to demonstrate that capitalism had solved its inner contradictions."[12] Now it is very difficult for a system which has been abolished to solve contradictions; but Crosland does not mind admitting the existence of capitalism if he can say something nice about it. His way of being nice to the system involves being very contemptuous of the men whom the old-fashioned leftists, in their deplorable dogmatism, consider to be the business rulers. Referring to the very summits of business power in both the U.S. and Britain, Crosland scorns them as *"impotent"* where yesterday's Morgans and Rockefellers used to have overweening power. Directly referring to the "organization men of Shell and I.C.I. [the British chemical trust]" Crosland informs us that they are only "jelly-fish where their predecessors were masterful ... slaves to their public relations departments, constantly nervous ... Suburban ... Apologetic .. ."[13]

At any rate this system, which seems to superficial people to be run on the economic side by the impotent jellyfish slaves, is not the old capitalism; and Crosland does not label it socialism as yet. It is merely a new, progressive social order in which all our economic problems have been essentially solved. Crosland once played with the problem of giving it a name: shall it be "the Welfare State, the Mixed Economy, the Managerial State, Progressive Capitalism, Fair Dealism, State Capitalism, the First Stage of Socialism," he asked? "Differences of opinion about the right nomenclature will partly reflect merely ideological differences," he mused. To show how true this is, he chose a name which reflected uninhibitedly the nature of his ideological inclination: *Statism*.[14]

He was not unaware of the tactical embarrassment:

> The name is ugly, and has too unfavorable a ring. But the most fundamental change from capitalism is the change from laissez-faire to state control, and it is well to have a name which spotlights this crucial change.

Given the triumph of the new progressive social order Statism (if we

Neither Capitalism nor Socialism

may continue to use the label properly understood), what is left of the socialist program, and why is something to be called "socialism" still to be pursued at all?

Crosland admits that Statism already puts into effect "a very large part of [socialism's] traditional programme" and himself asks "what (if anything) there is of socialism which statism does not already give ." Of the 1951 Frankfurt programmatic declaration of the re-established Socialist International, he says, "Now what is significant about this declaration is that socialism, as here defined, already largely obtains under statism "[15]. In five different writings from this date (1952) on, Crosland has listed what is left of socialism in his view. The five different formulations pretty much add up to the same thing,1 though there is difference in detail. For convenience only, I take up this briefest version, from an article in *Confluence* (Summer 1958). It has four items:

(1) ..". altering, not the structure of society in our own country, but the balance of wealth and privilege between advanced and backward countries ." - There is no indication why this is so specifically socialistic, in his opinion, that Statism cannot do it handily, particularly the U.S. variety. In any case the crux is the negative clause.

(2) More welfare, to take care of "residual social distress," by which means (he explains) "the misfortunes of small or exceptional groups" like backward children rather than "large categories," no problems existing about the latter. There is no indication why the wonderfully progressive society of Statism would not be sufficient to clean up these corners. (Besides, in his 1960 pamphlet *Can Labor Win?* Crosland rendered the judgment that "full employment and the Welfare State" are

---

1 The main exception is the point in his earliest version[16] emphasizing the need "to give the worker a sense of participation" to change "the general tone and atmosphere in industry ." True, this came to things like "joint consultation schemes" even then, but the question itself ceased to have any importance in his later versions. Completely lacking in all versions is any recognition of peace and an anti-war foreign policy as a socialist issue at all. This points to a whole sector of the new reformists' ideology which this article does not discuss.

now obsolete as issues.)

(3) Getting rid of the special British "obvious social stratifications," especially the elite educational system peculiar to the island. - This is so far from being a distinctively socialist issue that, as Crosland often stresses quite rightly, it does not even exist in other countries.

(4) "A number of socio-cultural reforms" such as an amelioration of divorce laws, abortion laws, sex-perversion laws, urban sprawl, censorship, amount of art patronage, and the like.

"It is therefore an illusion to suppose, so far as Great Britain is concerned, that the advent of the full-employment Welfare State has denuded the Left of causes to fight for," concludes Crosland. No doubt: after Crosland's list is exhausted, there will also be the struggle for Mental Health, an international language, anti-smog laws, more bird sanctuaries, and other worthy causes the value of which I would not derogate. But the puzzling question is this: why would Crosland insist on bringing about another "social revolution" and transforming society all over again, from its present gratifying progressive and advancing New Social Order, to still another one which he calls socialism?

Or to put it another way: if Crosland were not already saddled for purely historical reasons with a party and movement whose members insist on calling it "socialist" and advocating a society called "socialism," would it ever occur to him that the amiable objectives he now sets forth need still another new social system, and have to be advocated by a sectarianly separate party which arouses antagonism by calling itself "Labor" or "socialist," and has the unpleasant habit of singing *The Red Flag?* If he could get rid of the old rubbish any other way, he would not have to bother to write long rationalizations, directed to these historically pointless nuisances, designed to prove that they ought to act as if it were all a mistake to begin with. In this case, why should he ever dream of *creating* a socialist movement in Britain any more than he sees any need for a socialist movement in America?

There is another aspect to this, which Crosland brought out quite unawares in his first book, *Britain's Economic Problem* (1953). He has a chapter of "Conclusions" presenting economic policies to be pursued by

Neither Capitalism nor Socialism

a Labor government to solve Britain's trade difficulties. As always, he starts by averring that the issue of "public or private ownership" of economic wealth is irrelevant. Why then is a *Labor* government needed? Not for any socialist aims, he answers categorically.

> But the social reform and egalitarian aspects of Labor's programme are directly relevant to the plan. It is vital to its success that the confidence and cooperation of the workers should be won; they are asked to surrender many deeply-ingrained attitudes and practices, which they will naturally decline to do, and so frustrate the redeployment of resources, if they feel that the privileged classes are strengthening their position in the period of national strain. It is therefore of the first importance, quite apart from any considerations of socialist principle, that the economic programme should be accompanied by a programme of radical reform...

"It is for these reasons that the leadership must come from the Left," he continues. No substantial increase in standard of living can be expected for five years. "There can thus be no loosening of belts," since "total consumption ... must be rigidly restrained if the necessary home and foreign investment is to be secured ."

The whole program of the new reformism would, then, follow for Crosland even if there were no question of socialism - even if he were not a socialist - since only such a policy could persuade the workers to accept the rigid restraints contemplated. It should be stressed that Crosland wants to *persuade* them; he is an English democrat, not a totalitarian. If this were not true, we would be dealing with a different variety of bureaucratic-statist mentality; but with this not unimportant difference, we have above another member of that family of ideologies in which a kind of anti-capitalism is assigned the role of reconciling a working class to a regime of rigid restraint.

The program left for socialism, which we have already discussed, will not (he concedes) "arouse the same emotions, or evoke the same degree of devoted and militant mass support" as before; this is inevitable. "Some people view this decline in political passion [note the word!] with concern ." But Crosland makes clear he is not one of these; he is unperturbed by the prospect that the people should be even more uninvolved than before in their own destinies, that fewer should participate in politics as subjects rather than mere objects. The main danger which he does see in this development underlines the point: this danger is simply that the situation may lead to lack of "a sufficient cadre of active recruits of high quality to man all the necessary full-time and part-time positions in national and local government and the party organizations ." That is, *the* danger is lack of competent functionaries.

"Nor is there any sign of a dangerous degree of apathy amongst the electorate as a whole," he claims. All that has happened has "merely diminished the degree of mass emotional excitement [note the words!] attaching to the political struggle and reduced the numbers, though not necessarily the quality, of the minority of political activists and intellectuals ." The first is a healthy sign, he asserts. And he now has worked himself to the following:

> The second also, in my view, is not an unhealthy development, though many politically-minded intellectuals find it so. Looking back on the nineteen-thirties, the extent to which the intelligentsia then concentrated on and was obsessed by political as opposed to artistic or cultural goals, although entirely natural and proper in the context of the time, was greater that would normally be desirable. *We do not necessarily want a busy, bustling society in which everyone is politically active* and suspends his evenings in group discussion and feels responsible for all the burdens of the world. [Emphasis added.]

No, the cadre of high functionaries will take care of these things for us ... *Back to apathy!*

Some other remarks in Crosland become less odd. He goes distinctly out of his way to deny that socialists should be concerned as such with the problem of *bureaucratism:*

Neither Capitalism nor Socialism

> ...the issue of managerial and bureaucratic power ... has little to do either with socialism, which historically has been concerned only with the economic power of private business, or with capitalism.[17]

Now it is true that historically socialism did not use to be concerned with the issue by and large; *hinc illae lacrimae*. One would imagine, however, that more recent history has made it impossible for the question to be fobbed off. Three pages later comes this after discussing the Webbs:

> Permeation has more than done its job. Today we are all incipient bureaucrats and practical administrators. We have all, so to speak, been trained at the L.S.E., are familiar with Blue Books and White Papers, and know our way around Whitehall.

He has a program for the cadre of functionaries and incipient bureaucrats - some modest proposals for the further bureaucratization of the Labor Party apparatus:

(1) Direct representation on the party National Committee for the parliamentary party - the MPs, who already have too much autonomous power. (It is this group, for example, that now elects the Party Leader, not the party.)

(2) "More staff at much higher salaries" at party headquarters.

(3) This point requires attention: Crosland has been complaining that the Labor Party's image is *too* working-class; it should reflect an all-class People's Party. The MPs too should be even more representative of "all social classes" than now. Hence, to implement this, "we need first more young Trade Union MPs, drawn partly from the newer industries and occupations and *representing the emergent social groups discussed above* .. ." At first blush there appears to be a contradiction when he complains of an overly working-class composition and then proposes "young Trade Union MPs" to remedy the imbalance. We must understand that he does *not*

Beyond the Third Camp

mean working-class candidates. By "young Trade Union MPs" he means new rising union functionaries, aspiring bureaucrats, the professional manager types for which he frequently calls in other places; and he looks on these as representing a New Class, or New Class elements.

Then there is a point calling for public-relations experts to be hired by the party; and more attention to youth, since youth give "a more classless air ." (He does not mention that the party leadership regularly expels young socialist leaders and whole organizations, even periodically dissolving the youth affiliate, since the youth tend to be too left.)

The demand for putting the movement into the hands of professional managers - the accent is on "professional" - is one of the most frequent notes in Crosland's proposals. He denounces "the snobbish anti-professionalism which permeates so much of our national life ." His remedy for the ills of the Co-operative Movement is: higher salaries for the managers; more university personnel; less "interference with management by elected lay boards," and a stronger, more professional national leadership - a platform which has the indubitable characteristic of being single-minded - and he attacks the Movement's "supposed interests" of "equality and democracy" which stand in the way of these changes.

Although he tends to lean heavily on "equality" when putting together definitions of socialism that will exclude social ownership, he cannot be accused of being passionate on the subject of equality of reward. He is in fact a loud advocate of bigger and better rewards for managers, in the interest of "efficiency ." He attacks the New Left because they want to bear hard on "those [inequalities] which derive from personal effort," referring to the managers who really run the corporations, whereas he wants to bear hard on "those which derive from inheritance ." His approach is first to minimize the size of top management rewards in private industry. Then he argues that outsize rewards for managers are inevitable in any economic system.

The proof to which he appeals is the "very high bureaucratic and managerial rewards even in the closed societies of the Communist bloc ." He is not attacking this, you understand; he is accepting it as natural and proper. "The process," he explains, "began with Stalin's famous speech in

Neither Capitalism nor Socialism

1931 in which he denounced 'equity-mongering' and called for a new attitude of 'solicitude' towards the intelligentsia. ... ." Even though the trend has been "partially reversed" under Khrushchev, "the goal is by no means egalitarian ."

Did this perhaps develop under Stalin because of the fact of dictatorship? This is not adequate explanation, he argues: Lenin was wrong and Stalin was right—

> For the original impetus towards inequality came not from political motives of tyranny or self-aggrandizement, but from the harsh *economic* necessities of the First Five-Year Plan. Lenin thought that with large-scale production the functions of management "have become so simplified and can be reduced to such simple operations ... that they can be easily performed by every literate person, can quite easily be performed for ordinary 'workmen's wages,' and can (and must) be stripped of every shadow of privilege, of every semblance of 'official grandeur.'" Stalin found otherwise; and *the extreme inequalities of the Stalin era represented a hardheaded economic policy designed to remedy the desperate scarcity of managerial and technical personnel* ... [Emphasis is added but the history is Crosland's.]

There has been a change under Khrushchev, true—

> But the Soviet rulers continue to believe that substantial differentials are a necessary condition of rapid growth; and in particular they attach a central importance to the creative role of management in fostering growth. *In view of their actual growth-rate, it is hard to say they are wrong.* [Emphasis added.][18]

Beyond the Third Camp

One rubs one's eyes: so Stalin was right after all. If it was right for him to institute these policies under Harsh Economic Necessities, then is it easy to say he was wrong in also instituting the only political policies which could make the Russian people accept these harsh necessities — i.e., the Stalinist terror? Don't misunderstand: Crosland himself is a democrat and a humane Englishman; it is a good thing he did not personally face Stalin's harsh necessity.

We have seen that, to Crosland, bureaucratism is not a socialist concern. We can now add that there is little room left in his scheme for workers' control or workers' democracy in industry. Crosland does not reject the idea *in toto*; after all there are always the joint consultation schemes. An article by him on this subject comes out unusually pointless (he does usually *say* something), with a conclusion about leaving the question to sociologists for research.

However, the major relationship between Crosland's program and this question does not appear in his explicit discussions. It emerges from the nature of his proposals for the extension of public ownership, in those instances where he is willing to consider such steps. He is for government share-buying:

> ...the object is not to acquire *particular* capital assets with a view to their control; it is *generally* to increase the area of public ownership. There is therefore no need for the compulsory purchase of entire firms or industries; it is sufficient to extend public investment in any direction... Indeed, it would be a positive nuisance to be saddled with control...[19]

What stands out about this method of extending "public ownership" is that it is the one which guarantees completely leaving all management rights and relations undisturbed. It is designed to leave the same bosses in control no matter what level of "public ownership" is thereby reached. Crosland is utilizing the well-known split between share-ownership and management control to *introduce the same schism between public ownership*

Neither Capitalism nor Socialism

and public control. His program for "extension of public ownership" is at the same time a program for maintenance of managers' control.

If we find heavily bureaucratic-collectivized notions informing the new social-democracy of Crosland, we need not be surprised to find that he is willing to go along with the increasingly popular theory of the *convergence* of Western society with the bureaucratic collectivism of the East. This has not played a big role in Crosland's writing up to now, but it is interesting that it makes its appearance in the last chapter of his last book. Douglas Jay plays it bigger[20].

Now the perspective of convergence of the two societies does not make any sense within the framework of Crosland's *rhetoric*. If we in the West are already in a new, progressive, advancing social order, with *more* democracy and equality than ever, and more coming, then even if Crosland swallows the tales about the coming liberalization and democratization of Russia, the picture that results is not of convergence but of a slow catching-up at the best. The real theorists of "convergence" mean, as they must, that a collectivized capitalism gets bureaucratized while a Stalinist-type bureaucratic collectivism gets "liberalized"; the two systems move in each other's direction.

Now this is what is actually happening not only with Crosland's "Statism" but also with the social-democratic theory *about what is happening*. Hence Crosland as well as Jay can in fact accept the reality of "convergence" perspective which makes no sense at all in terms of their theory.

It is the historical function of the new social-democratic reformism to act as the ideological formulation of one of the main processes in the bureaucratic collectivization of capitalism and its society. This is the reality behind what Crosland calls the "new progressive social order" — just as, analogously, a finished form of totalitarian bureaucratic collectivism is the reality behind the vaunted "victory of socialism in one-fifth of the globe ."

New Politics 1963

Beyond the Third Camp

NOTES

1 For an explanation of why the new reformists have become so tender about private enterprise, see the end of the previous chapter, where C.A.R. Crosland is briefly touched on.

2 For a rollcall on the new programs of other social-democracies in Western Europe, see Crosland's article in *Encounter*, March, 1960.

3 *Socialist Call*, Nov.-Dec., 1958, article by Leila Seigel.

4 *The Conservative Enemy* (London, 1962), p. 67. Hereafter abbreviated CE.

5 *The Future of Socialism* (London, 1956), p. 94. Hereafter abbreviated FS.

6 FS, p. 250.

7 FS, p. 219.

8 FS, p. 521.

9 Edited by R.H.S. Crossman (London, 1952). Hereafter abbreviated NFE.

10 NFE, pp. 33, 36, 41, 55.

11 Douglas Jay's bid for recognition as a revisionist theoretician, *Socialism and the New Society* (London, 1962), also, in passing, defines capitalism as laissez-faire at one point, p. 58. (Hereafter abbreviated SNS.)

12 CE, p. 114.

13 CE, p. 55.

14 NFE, p. 43.

15 NFE, p. 57-60.

16 NFE, pp. 65-66

17 FS, p. 521.

Neither Capitalism nor Socialism

18 References are to CE, pp. 29-33.

19 CE, p. 47-48.

20 SNS, p. 102.

HOW THE MILITARY ECONOMY WORKS: THE SYSTEM –
Seymour Melman

STATE CAPITALISM is a business economy whose top directorate is located in government. The state-capitalist part dominates the entire economy even though private business may still operate within it.* With respect to decision-making on production, the enterprises and the top management of state capitalism retain the essential characteristics of private-business capitalism. These features include separation of decision-making from producing; income linked to decision-making role; organization of decision-making on a hierarchical basis; a professional-occupational imperative among the decision-makers to extend their decision power individually and in competition with other management groups. These features continue under state capitalism even as the forms of control are different from private-business capitalism.[1] In the classic business economy, the chiefs of the larger industrial and financial units usually had substantial political influence. In state capitalism the chiefs of the economy are also the political chiefs of government. Hence, state capitalism joins peak political and economic decision power. This is visible in the mainly civilian-oriented state capitalism of Western Europe and Japan. In the United States and in the U.S.S.R., with their permanent war economies, military power is added to this concentration.

At the enterprise level, state capitalism involves substantial changes for the management of individual firms. Typically, the management of an enterprise cannot be autonomous as under private capitalism, where a business may be small but still independent, controlled by its managers or manager-owners. Owing to the location of the chiefs of state capitalism in government, political considerations are introduced into the relationships among local-enterprise managers. In dealing with higher authority they do not confront senior managers,

---

*. Various writers refer to "mixed economy" as one that is only partly state capitalist, by various criteria--like percent of GNP coming from the "public sector." Rather than using taxonomic categories of "private" and "public sector" to differentiate economies, I prefer to focus on functional features of which mode of decision-making on production is central.

Neither Capitalism nor Socialism

as in private capitalism, but top managers who also wield political power.

Since the top management of state capitalism spans the whole economy in its sphere of control, its enterprise planning takes the effective form of national planning, even affecting enterprises that may be privately owned and controlled. At once this opens up opportunities for stability for the individual state-capitalist enterprise insofar as it is relieved of at least a part of the uncertainties stemming from dependence on unpredictable market behaviors. Thus a state-capitalist top management can, if it so wishes, guarantee the market for its subordinate firms. This is notably the case under the military form of state capitalism, where the government is the only legal purchaser of the product.

However, instability (as in unresolved class and race antagonisms, prices, production levels and relative value of national currency) remains a feature of state capitalism. The sustained competition for extension of managerial control among the sub-managers, competition among the state managers of nations with state-capitalist economies, and the effects of the parasitic qualities of military economy all contribute to instability.

Under both private and state capitalism, access to capital is a crucial consideration. The state-capitalist enterprise manager (civilian-oriented) must compete for his share of capital by political-economic methods. The position is changed for the state-capitalist enterprise manager in military economy. He is assured of priority in capital allocation, since the military economy is given first place in the attention of government decision-makers.

In place of the self-correcting mechanisms of private capitalism, state-capitalist economy, especially in its military form, is more typically regulated by a system of subsidies. Such payments from government appear under private capitalism when government moves in to regulate parts of the economy. But subsidy systems flourish to their fullest under state capitalism, where the chiefs of the economy use their political decision power to enforce their economic priorities. Subsidies appear in civilian-oriented state capitalism, but they take on special characteristics where military economy is the priority state activity. In the latter case the subsidy is rendered on behalf of economically parasitic activity, thereby yielding no economic return to the society for the subsidy grant.

In the Marxist school of economics in particular, attention has been focused on inequality of income under capitalism, associated with occupational (class) position. From this standpoint, military economy introduces a new factor: relatively higher pay, job for job, in the military economy encourages loyalty to that system, thus blurring class and other interest-group conflicts. Thereby, state capitalism, in its military form, cuts through conflict of class versus class and introduces income inequality based upon type of industry and even geographical location, rather than upon occupation. Classic conditions of exploitation are thus revised in accordance with the military priorities of the state-capitalist rulers.

The military economy is more than a collection of enterprises and assorted research organizations that maximize costs and subsidies. On a macroeconomic or system level it is the core of a specifically American form of state capitalism.

The idea of the military economy as an economic subsystem within the larger economy is no theoretical abstraction, for that economy has been made into a deliberately managed industrial system. In *Pentagon Capitalism* (1970) I showed that there is a formal managerial organization, with detailed procedures for decision-making and for controlling the military-industrial and allied system. Further evidence on the system level of economic planning by the Pentagon comes from studies of the pattern of contract allocations, their location and their timing. For more than a decade military contracts have been awarded among major firms so that levels of activity could be sustained. As the work on one project was phasing out, a fresh contract was allocated to start a phasing-in process.[2] No pattern of this sort could endure over an extended period simply by chance or as the outcome of free-wheeling competition for the new money grants. The whole mode of operation has the characteristics of a production control system, unusual only for the large scale of operations.

Neither Capitalism nor Socialism

As an entity the military economy has unique characteristics which affect the surrounding economy and society. A set of key characteristics is summarized here, without pretending completeness, in order to portray the range of consequences from the system as a whole. These are in four parts: first, aspects of the parasitic quality of military economy and its extension-of-control dynamic; second, the expansionist propensity of the managers of military economy; third, major impact on the civilian economy; fourth, the dominance of the military over the civilian economy in America's state capitalism.

The Parasitic Nature of Military Economy

The gross national product is composed of productive and parasitic growth. As usually measured and presented, GNP includes all of the money-valued output of goods and services — without differentiation in terms of major functional effect. To appreciate the nature and effects of a permanent war economy, a functional differentiation is essential. Productive growth means goods and services that either are part of the level of living or can be used for further production of whatever kind. Hence, they are by these tests *economically* useful.*
Parasitic growth includes goods and services that are not economically useful either for the level of living or for further production.

Military goods and services are economically parasitic. This differentiation is fundamental. When it is applied it is possible to perceive and diagnose a series of consequences that flow from military economy. In the absence of the differentiation between productive and parasitic growth, the activity of military economy appears as simply an extension or a part of the ordinary civilian economy. All money income, regardless of source, is then treated as contribution to wealth.

For most Americans, effects attributable to parasitic economic growth are not apparent. Such differentiations are virtually nonexistent in textbooks of economics. Accordingly, the generations of Ameri-

---

*. There are, of course, other kinds of usefulness: political, esthetic, military, religious. Here we are interested primarily in economic usefulness. Thus, the absence of economic usefulness does not preclude other effects.

cans who have been instructed via the usual economics texts and courses are not equipped to see a part of the economy as parasitic. Instead, their appreciation of economy is dominated by theories about competitive market relations, the allocation of incomes, and the role of government as a regulator of economy.

In a permanent war economy whole industries and regions that specialize in military economy are placed in a parasitic economic relationship to the civilian economy, from which they take their sustenance and to which they contribute (economically) little or nothing. This results in the operation of a system of "internal imperialism" among the states of the Union. This phenomenon shows up in the relation of federal tax payments by the individuals and businesses of a particular state to federal expenditures in particular states.

For example, in New York State from 1965 to 1967, $7.458 billion was paid out in taxes to the federal government in excess of the federal expenditures in New York State. Similar relationships, though in lesser amounts, showed up for New Jersey, Pennsylvania, Illinois and Michigan. On the other hand, certain states enjoyed large net gains. During the same period, California received more than $2 billion yearly in expenditures from the federal government in excess of the total tax payments made from that state. Texas received $1 billion annually in excess of taxes paid out, and Virginia received $1.3 billion each year more than its tax payments.[3] Similar exploitative relations contribute to the industrial and general community deterioration in, for example, older New England and Midwestern civilian-industry areas as against the locales of military-industry concentration with their abundant evidence of good living and flashy "high-technology" work places.

The economic significance of parasitic economic growth is often rendered obscure by the apparently small magnitude of some of the spending involved. Money spent on military research and development reflects economically parasitic activity, but research and development costs are rarely a major item of expense in manufacturing industry. On the average, U.S. manufacturing firms spend about 3 or 4 percent of their net sales dollars for these purposes. In the nation's gross national product about one and a half percent has been spent on military research. But the significance of this activity cannot be measured by its proportionately small cost. Thus, when research and development is not properly done on behalf of civilian industry, results like poor product design or poor production methods can have disastrous effects on the economic position of the industry. When as little as one and a half percent of U.S. national product is diverted to military research it seems little enough, but that accounts for more than half of the national research and development effort and has left many U.S. civilian-products industries at a competitive disadvantage due to faltering product designs and insufficient improvement in industrial-production efficiency.

The Propensity to Expand

A second basic feature of state capitalism is the relentless thrust for enlargement of decision power that is normal to management. Under state capitalism this conventional occupational imperative is given unprecedented capability in terms of the resources that can be applied to these goals. In turn, the state managers have enlarged their goals in keeping with their ability to draw larger resources from the national income for their purposes. By 1965 the state management of the Pentagon actually advertised for advice on how to "maintain world hegemony."

The Army Research Office announced a public request for bids for a wide-ranging study on methods of achieving a Pax Americana. Here is the exact announcement as it appeared in the U.S. Department of Commerce *Daily Bulletin* asking for bids for government work:

Service and materials to perform a research study entitled "PAX AMERICANA" consisting of a phased study of the following: (a) elements of National Power; (b) ability of selected nations to apply the elements of National Power; (c) a variety of world power configurations to be used as a basis for the U.S. to maintain world hegemony in the future. Quotations and applicable specifications will be available upon request at the Army Research Office, 3845 Columbia Pike, Arlington, Va., until 1 May 1965.[4]

Beyond the Third Camp

With goals of such dimensions, we may begin to understand why there has been a sustained growth of the budgets of the Department of Defense throughout the 1960s and even the further planned growth from 1973 through 1980.

The military-industry system operates under the assumption that indefinitely large capital funds are available for the military and related plans of the state management. In this understanding the state management is strongly supported by key members of Congress, as, for example, by Congressman F. Edward Hebert. (Democrat, Louisiana), chairman of the House Armed Services Committee. Said Congressman Hebert in 1972, "I intend to build the strongest military we can get. Money's no question."[5]

As the military economy endured, its enterprises looked like reasonable investment opportunities. With the enlargement of assets, private and government-provided, these, in turn, became part of the scope of decision-making to be conserved by the Pentagon's top managers.*

In 1964, Senator George McGovern and thirty other members of the Senate, paralleled by similar efforts in the House, offered legislation for setting up a National Economic Conversion Commission. The bills were killed by decisive pressure from the White House and senior officers of the Pentagon.[6] Thereby, these men saw to it that there was no ordered capability in the United States for moving from a military economy to a civilian economy. Job dependence on the Pentagon was maintained. The Council of Economic Advisers in 1969 defined an agenda of productive economic replacements for military spending (which I will discuss in Chapter Eight). Its work was ignored

---

*. At the same time the employees and communities involved in the military economy became, for obvious self-interest, protagonists of the larger policies that sustained a permanent war economy. When Ernest Fitzgerald appeared at the gate of an aerospace firm in California for a meeting on the war in Vietnam, supporters of the war policy distributed lapel stickers with the motto "Don't Knock the War that Feeds You."

Neither Capitalism nor Socialism

and never followed up. The military-industry firms and the state management that directs them have avoided or opposed steps to prepare for a peace economy, apparently on the assumption that to do that would remove a major justification for the continued high level of military budgets.

The Impact on Civilian Economy

The economic consequences of a permanent war economy for the host society are a compound of civilian goods and services forgone and major damage inflicted on the economically productive economy. The full cost to a society of parasitic economic growth exceeds the money value of the materials, man-hours and machinery used up for military products. Equivalent inputs turned to economically productive uses yield their direct output many times over. Beyond that, the outputs include improvements in the quality of labor and capital.

The operation of a permanent war economy entails a large cost for American society, measured in terms of what has been forgone in order to build and operate an immense military system. From 1946 to 1975 the combined budgets of the Department of Defense were more than $1,500 billion. This exceeds the value of all commercial and residential structures in the United States.[7] Thus by putting this much effort into the military system what was forgone was an opportunity to reconstruct physically whatever has gone into disrepair in America's towns and cities. Here is another view of opportunity forgone: I once estimated that $22 billion a year would spur economic development—worldwide; about a third of America's military economy bill for 1946-75 would have funded such a worldwide effort for twenty years.[8]

Calculating the cost of the Vietnam War to the U.S. economy will doubtless engage the attention of economists and others for many years. For a start, Tom Riddell estimates the cost at $676 billion, including not only the direct military outlays but also the military assistance to client governments, interest on national debt and payments for veterans which will endure for a long time.[9]

How have the U.S. military outlays actually affected other kinds of spending within the American economy? After all, the same dollar can't be spent on different things at the same time. What exactly have we not purchased by buying a permanent war economy?

Professor Bruce Russett at Yale has researched this problem by means of statistical analyses of the main parts of the U.S. national-income accounts. These data, appropriately diagnosed, can answer the question: For each dollar spent on the military, what did we buy less of? Russett has shown that, on the average, over the period 1939-68 each U.S. dollar spent for military purposes was associated with $.163 less expenditure for durable consumer goods, $.110 less for producers' durable goods, and $.114 less for homes—among other decreases.[10] "Guns" take away from "butter" even in the United States, with a gross national product valued annually at over $1,000 billion.

Actual U.S. investments in machinery and nonresidential buildings was $1,481 billion from 1946 to 1973. At the same time, because of heavy military spending, the U.S. economy missed out on major new capital investment. The value of the production equipment and buildings that were forgone in U.S. economy from 1946 to 1973 because of military spending was at least $660 billion, or 45 percent as much as was actually invested. If one includes a further allowance for a compounding effect in such calculations—i.e., machines producing other machines in addition to final products—then the total capital outlays forgone in the United States from 1946 to 1973 because of the preemption of capital for the military exceeds $1,900 billion, or 135 percent of actual investment. However conservative the mode of estimation, one result is clear: the relatively poor condition of plant and equipment in many U.S. industries is no mystery. U.S. policy traded off renewal of the main productive assets of the economy for the operation of the military system.[11]

Ordinarily a civilian economy can look forward to making substantial advances in its total productivity because of the gains that can be made in the efficiency of machinery and in the efficiency of labor. Thus as new machinery is designed and used in production there is

Neither Capitalism nor Socialism

more output per unit of labor time, and very often even more output per unit of capital invested. The increments of additional output per unit of capital continue as long as the new machinery is used. However, if new machinery, however efficient, is installed for producing military materiel, then what emerges is military materiel which no factory can use for any further production. The result is that the normally available addition to production capability which stems from installing new production equipment is forgone for the whole society. That is also the reason why investment in military industry, while adding to the flow of money, does not serve as a competent offset to declining investment in new productive machinery.

Similar reasoning applies to the productivity of labor. Economists have been giving increasing attention to improvement in the quality of "human capital," meaning especially the better work capability that is the consequence of good physical and intellectual upbringing. For individuals, that capability leads to improvement in real income. The same is true for societies. The cost of education to the individual or to the community can be viewed as an "investment" that yields a net return to the individual and the community in the form of increases in actual earnings, due to a greater work capability. Such an annual increase can be calculated as a percent of the "investment" to show an estimated "rate of return." Thus high-school education has been associated with yearly improvements in earnings that amount to 28 percent of the cost of the education. For college graduates the average gain in earnings has been at the rate of 15 percent yearly on their educational "investment."[12]

When the investment in fresh educational competence, at whatever level, is subsequently applied to nonproductive economic activity, then the community loses the potential economic gain from human competence that ordinarily accrues to it when that capability is applied to productive work.

A second major form of impact of the military on the civilian economy is a process of industrial deterioration that generates uninvestable capital and unemployable labor. An unprecedented phenomenon has appeared in the United States: the formation of a large network of depleted industries and a flight of capital from the country. (Chapter Four will give details on "depleted" industries: those that have lost capability for serving all or part of their domestic markets and have been replaced by foreign producers because of a combination of technical, managerial and economic deterioration.)

Many theorists of capitalist economy, especially those in the Marxist tradition, have sought to explain recurring problems of capitalism as a result of the tendency of a business-based economy to generate surpluses of capital and surpluses of labor. Uninvestable capital and unemployable labor were certainly fundamental features of what happened in the United States during the Great Depression, 1929-39. The World War II economy soaked up surpluses of capital and of labor. In the chapters that follow, I will provide evidence to demonstrate that the U.S. permanent war economy, through depletion of industry and the flight of capital, has been a prime generator of uninvestable capital and a prime generator of unemployable labor.

The sustained normal operation of a large cost- and subsidy-maximizing economic system produces a major unintended effect in the transfer of inefficiency into the civilian economy. Insofar as the cost-maximizing style of operation is carried with them by managers, engineers or workers as they move individually from military to civilian employment, the civilian economy becomes infected with the standards and practices that these men and women learned in the military sphere. For civilian industry, the introduction of such practices is definitely counterproductive. To be sure, this need not apply to all individuals in the same degree. But to the extent that professional-occupational patterns are transferred, the transfer of inefficiency is "impersonal" — i.e., it operates independently of particular features of individual personality.

The U.S. civilian economy has also suffered from domestic inflation and a decline in the value of the dollar — both effects strongly impelled by the permanent war economy, and accelerated by the disastrous war in Vietnam.

In 1950 the Treasury of the United States had $24 billion in gold reserve.[13] This declined to $9-10 billion by 1973. This dissipation of the

Neither Capitalism nor Socialism

U.S. gold reserve has been due substantially to a massive net accumulation of dollars in the hands of foreigners as a consequence of foreign military spending by the U.S. government. With large military forces overseas since the end of World War II, U.S. bases in thirty countries, and fighting the Korean and Vietnam Wars, U.S, armed forces have spent dollars heavily abroad. Dollars were accepted in payment for goods and services rendered and the relative value of the dollar was maintained until 1971, when the dollar holdings abroad exceeded three times the U.S. Treasury's gold reserve. Around the world doubts arose about the Treasury's ability to redeem these dollars in gold. The unreadiness of foreigners to buy American goods at existing market prices combined with the glut of dollars to generate a crisis in the value of the U.S. currency, culminating in the financial debacle of August 15, 1971. The U.S. government suspended redemption of dollars held abroad for gold, and the relative value of the dollar dropped. The full financial and political consequences of this process have yet to be seen. Economically parasitic output contributes to price inflation. While price inflation has diverse causes, there is no escaping the fact that war-making in the United States since 1945 has occasioned sharp price increases. This was especially true for the period 1965-73. Having the ideological consensus faith that the U.S. economy is indefinitely productive and able to turn out guns *and* butter as desired, the Johnson administration proceeded to heat up the war in Indochina. But there was no "reserve army" of unemployed and underemployed skilled workers around as in 1939, so the swift pile-up of war-serving economic demands from 1965 on fueled a fast price inflation.

After all, parasitic economic growth involves payment for work whose product immediately leaves the marketplace. The materials, power and equipment that are used up for making military products, and the goods consumed by the military-industry labor force must be supplied by the civilian labor force, which receives nothing that is economically productive from the military economy. This is not to say that harsh political control measures might not restrain such a process; but that would imply a rather more controlled society than has been acceptable to Americans. Significantly, the military economy suffers little or no hardship from inflation or decline in the relative value of the dollar. For the military top management receives a fresh levy of capital each year as a proportion of the national income. Rising prices at home or abroad have not deterred maintenance or enlargement of the military economy.

The Dominance of the Military Economy over the Civilian
How important is the state-capitalist controlled military economy in relation to the traditional civilian economy? Which economy in the United States is the more powerful one? I propose three tests of importance: (1) control over capital; (2) control over research and development; and (3) control over means of production of new technical personnel.

The name of the economy is capitalism, and control of capital is a decisive feature of the system. Capital, in conventional usage, means the accumulated funds of a size that makes them useful for investing purposes. Thereby a million dollars is not only a million times greater than one dollar; for the latter can be used primarily to get consumer goods, while the former can be used to buy machinery and buildings and to engage workers to do the bidding of a management. It is therefore vital to know what is the relative position of the managers of the state-capitalist military economy as controllers of capital, as against the private economy. Profits retained by corporations and the sums set aside for capital consumption (machinery and buildings "used up") are a measure of the fresh capital available to private U.S. management for investment. In 1939, for every dollar of this private corporate capital, the War and Navy Departments received thirty-five cents from the federal government. By 1971, for every dollar of this private corporate capital the budget of the Department of Defense alone received $1.06. That means that by 1971 the government-based managers of the U.S. military system had superseded the private firms of the American economy in control over capital.[14]

The main military department of the federal government could deploy for its purposes more than the maximum capital fund that remained (after tax levies) for the managers of all U.S. industrial and

Neither Capitalism nor Socialism

commercial corporations. That the federal government as a whole, not to say one section of it, should have such economic power reflects a substantial change in the institutional location of economic decision power, from the private corporation to the federal government's state management.

Americans who have been critical of concentration of economic power have focused on the corporate giants of U.S. industry. The new state-capitalist power, however, dwarfing the big firms in physical assets and scale of operations, was erected and sustained in the name of defense, and has been bolstered by an ideological consensus that strongly justifies its operation as a fine pillar of the economy. However, no Presidential budget message — from Truman to Nixon — ever declared the desirability of making the federal government into the top management of a state-capitalist economy. People would be dismayed at the very idea.

The second criterion is control over research and development. Its importance is indicated by the fact that this function determines control over new technology for products, materials and production methods. This is a key element in the operation of any technology-dependent society. In this respect the dominance of the federal government and of its military agencies has been over whelming. More than half of the research and development brains of the United States has been applied to military and related research activities during the decades 1950-70. The military and related agencies of the federal government have accounted for 80 percent of the federally sponsored research money, which has dominated the field.[15]

The third criterion is control over means of production of new technical talent. During the 1950s and 1960s the federal government and its military-serving agencies in particular played a dominant part in enlarging funds for research and for graduate-student support and in opening up new job opportunities for young engineers and scientists. One of the main effects of these initiatives was to induce the deans and faculties of American engineering schools to revise their curricula and research orientations to emphasize knowledge and training best capable of servicing the expanding requirement of the new military economy. Owing to the new emphasis on where the action was (money, jobs), there was a relative deemphasis of manpower, attention and money in the universities and technical schools from training men and women for civilian-industry technologies. "Sophisticated technology," the code word for military-sponsored work, became the obvious center of attention for bright young people who were set on "making it" in the universities and the "nonprofit" think tanks that were speedily established in response to the money proferred from the Pentagon. In the engineering schools of the country the period 1950-70 saw the flowering of "engineering science," with highest prestige accorded to no-application, pure research, flashy new facilities and lots of support for graduate students, especially in fields like electronics — with direct or indirect military or space-agency interest. At the same time, curricula and technical research in classic fields of civilian-engineering responsibility, like power engineering, were accorded lesser priorities.* By these tests of decision power the new state-capitalist economy has become the dominant one as against the private-capitalist economy in the United States. I do not imply that the corporate managements of private capitalism have withdrawn from the scene or have ceased to utilize their position to affect government policies that are favorable to their interests. However, the new condition of economy and society means that the chiefs of the state-capitalist economy dominate the scene and utilize their peak

---

*. In universities, commitments to programs and to faculty, once made, can be long-enduring. I therefore remember the comment of a senior electronics engineer, saying that during the 1950s and 1960s those who went into power engineering were "the dregs" of the profession. With this "I'm all right, Jack" outlook, this man's main concern was to justify the priority accorded his brand of work, and never mind these awkward problems about energy supply and utilization. By implication such problems can be left to "the dregs." In a similar vein a bright undergraduate in a leading engineering school assured me that there was little point in his school's curriculum being cluttered up with instruction bearing on how things are made, since the school was not really interested in training engineers so much as in training "leaders."

authority over economy, politics and the military to direct domestic and foreign policy to their purposes. This has introduced new ca[12]-pability for systemwide policy flexibility, made visible by the moves toward detente with the U.S.S.R. and China, coupled with impressive budget increases for the military core of the state-capitalist economy at home. This ability to maneuver at will nevertheless does not denote indefinite policy rationality and control. For the successes of state capitalism, in its own terms, bring about a range of effects, mainly unintended, that are crisis-producing in the wider economy and society.

The Permanent War Economy 1974

NOTES

1. Many theorists of capitalism have characterized it as consisting essentially of a system of markets, of exchange relations. This is the recurring theme of the main-line literature of economics, from textbooks to scholarly journals. But wherever there is division of labor there must be exchanges of products for life to continue. It is scientifically useless to imply that capitalism corresponds to any economy that includes division of labor and necessarily associated exchange relations. For there is division of labor and exchange in feudalism and in the economics of primitive societies, and in nonmanagerial democratically controlled economy. See M. Herskovits, *Economic Life of Primitive Peoples*, New York, 1940.

2. J. R. Kurth, "The Political Economy of Weapons Procurement: The Follow-on Imperative," *American Economic Review*, May 1972.

3. J. R. Anderson, "The Balance of Military Payments among States and Regions," in S. Melman, ed., *The War Economy of the United States*, St. Martin's Press, 1971, Chapter 17.

4. Cited in *I. F. Stone's Weekly*, May 10, 1965.

5 .Article by jack McWethy, *Washington Post,* March 26, 1972.

6 .*National Economic Conversion Commission,* hearings before the Senate Committee on Commerce, 88th Congress, 2nd Session, on S. 2274, May 25, June 22, 1964.

7 .U.S. Bureau of the Census, *Statistical Abstract of the United States,* 1973, p. 337.

8 .S. Melman, *The Peace Race,* Ballantine Books, Braziller, 1962, Chapter 8.man, *Our Depleted Society,* Holt, Rinehart & Winston and Dell Books, 1965, Chapter 7.

9 .T. Riddell, "The $676 Billion Quagmire," *The Progressive,* October 1973.

10 .B. M. Russett, *What Price Vigilance?,* Yale, 1970, Chapter 5.
"In this volume I do not attempt a full assessment of the direct cost of military operations to the American economy. It would probably require a reckoning of at least three elements as a first approximation: the direct budgets; the economic use values forgone; and the capital prcductivity forgone. The first is the sum of Department of Defense budgets 1946-75, about $1,500 billion. The second is the money worth of the economic use-values that were forgone because the $1,500 billion was used for non-economic purposes. (Note that this is not the same as the opportunity cost concept, since the tradeoff here is not between the use of a set of inputs for one or another *economic* output. In the case of the military application of a set of inputs there is no economic use value that emerges at all. There are military or political use values. But that is not the same thing. Hence there is a social cost in the absence of the ordinarily present economic use values. This is an issue in value theory that deserves further attention.) Third, there is the estimated capital productivity gain forgone. Altogether, these would add up to more than $3,600 billion, an immense social cost, exceeding in magnitude the national wealth of the United States. (See U.S. Department of Commerce, *Statistical Abstract of the U.S.,* 1973, p. 337. "

11 .The regression coefficients of the effects of U.S. military spending on civilian activities are given in B. Russett, *op. cit.,* p. 140. These factors for producers' durable equipment and nonresidential structures, .178, plus an allowance of 25 percent as marginal productivity of capital in the U.S.

Neither Capitalism nor Socialism

(Russett, p. 144) were applied to actual U.S. military expenditures, 1946-73 *(The Budget of the U.S. Government, 1974,* and other years). The estimated total capital-goods output forgone as a result of the military spending of a given year was, therefore, military outlay x .178 x .25 x number of years to 1973. The sum of effects for each year from 1946 to 1973 is $661.19 billion. When allowance is further made for a compounding effect, reinvesting of 25 percent of new capital outputs, then the estimated sum of these effects from 1946 to 1973 is $1,992.7 billion. These estimates are compared with actual producers' fixed investment in the U.S. (U.S. Department of Commerce, *Survey of* Current *Business,* March 1973; *Business Statistics, 1971)* 1946-73, which totaled $532.6 billions of nonresidential structures, $948.6 billion of producers' durable equipment.

12 .See discussion and bibliography in U.S. National Commission on Productivity, *Education and Productivity,* by T. W. Schultz, Washington, D.C., June 1971.

13 .For early discussion of these developments see T. McCarthy, "The Garrison Economy," *Columbia Forum,* September 1967; also S. Melman, *Our Depleted Society,* Holt, Rinehart & Winston and Dell Books, 1965, Chapter 7.

14 . "Undistributed profits (after inventory valuation adjustment) and capital consumption allowances" define the internal sources of funds for U.S. "nonfarm, nonfinancial corporate business" for 1971 (Board of Governors of the Federal Reserve System, in *Economic Report of the President,* 1973, Washington, D.C., 1973, p. 282). Equivalent 1939 data from U.S. Bureau of the Census, *Statistical Abstract of the United States, 1942,* Washington, D.C., 1942, pp. 224 ff. U.S. military spending, 1939 and 1971, from *Economic Report of the President,* 1973, p. 193. Since the data for capital available to private corporate management includes the funds of nominally private military-industry firms, the 1971 ratio of military funds to private capital is understated.

15 . See William M. Magruder, "Technology and the Professional Societies," *Mechanical Engineering,* September 1972.

APPENDIX A
THE MYTH OF BRUNO RIZZI

Whenever the theory of bureaucratic collectivism or, indeed, any theory that holds that the bureaucracy is a new, exploiting class is mentioned, the name of Bruno Rizzi is inevitably raised.[1] Like many another author, his reputation is in inverse proportion to the number of people who have read his work. His best known book, *La Bureaucratisation du Monde*, was published in Paris in September of 1939 and most copies were destroyed by the Nazis.[2] The French popular front government had earlier impounded it because of its virulent antisemitism.[3]

It is clear that most who refer to it have not read it.[4] None of those who refer to it seem to be aware of the pamphlets written in Italian by Rizzi in the forties, in which he emphasized the profascist conclusions he drew from his theory.

Because the most widely known theory of bureaucratic collectivism is the one discussed in this book and because *this* theory of bureaucratic collectivism was developed as a consistent defense of a third camp political opposition to both Stalinism and capitalism, it is generally assumed that Rizzi's theory was also an attack on this new class. Trotsky's characterization of Rizzi in his article *The USSR in War* as a former adherent of the Fourth International and his implication that Rizzi developed his ideas in that milieu[5] lends credence to this interpretation. But it is false.

Rizzi was *never* associated with the Trotskyist movement and the Italian Trotskyists would have nothing to do with him.[6] He was a Socialist before World War I and was for a short time, prior to the fascists' seizure of power, a member of the Communist Party. After the fascists came to power, Rizzi dropped out of active participation in politics. He developed his theory as an explicit justification, one should rather say glorification, of fascism. Mussolini and Hitler, although they had not yet gone as far as Stalin in destroying capitalism, were moving in the same direction. Like Burnham, his profascism was theoretically based on the then almost universal conviction that planned statified property was the answer to the capitalist catastrophe of the Great Depression. Unlike Burnham he did not, initially, have to deal with a public hostile to fascism or with the Trotskyists' continued commitment to workers' power and workers' democracy.

In order to deal with the myths surrounding Rizzi and his place in the development of the theory of bureaucratic collectivism and of new class theories in general it is necessary to give a brief summary of his position as it is found in *La Bureaucratization du Monde*.

Rizzi begins by referring to all the reports from the Soviet Union on the condition of the working class in that country. The one thing on which all agree, except of course the Stalinists, is that the position of the working class is that of an exploited class with even less rights than those that are permitted in capitalist countries. The Communist party is, in Rizzi's phrase, nothing but a dog which the shepherd, Stalin, uses to keep the sheep in order.

He has no illusions, however, that this class has anything in common with the capitalist class. It comes to power because capitalism has failed:

> The possession of the State gives the bureaucracy possession of all goods, moveable and immoveable, which, in being socialized, do not any the less, belong 'in toto' to the new ruling class...
>
> This new form of society resolves, from the social point of view, the unsustainable antagonism which renders capitalist society incapable of any progress. In capitalist society, the form of production has been collective for a long time, because the whole world takes part, directly or indirectly, in the production of every kind of good. But the appropriation of goods is individual, that in consequence precisely of private property. In socializing property and in submitting it effectively to the direction of a class, acting as a complex harmony, the antagonism that exists in the capitalist system is made to disappear, replaced by a new system.[7]

While rejecting Trotsky's arguments and those of his followers who maintained that the Soviet Union was still a workers' state, Rizzi had no quarrel with the idea that nationalized property was progressive:

The Myth of Bruno Rizzi

Socialism is, in the final analysis, an economy of distribution and division of products. It is not possible until production is so vast that any increase in consumption, even an increase in the requirements of the state, is met.

Over production at present is nothing but the saturation of the capitalist market. To provide what is required for the inhabitants of the earth, the maximum production of 1929 has to be multiplied. A task of that kind cannot be met by capitalism and its supporters who, after having murdered 10 millions of men from 1914 to 1918, are of a mind to recommence what their 'immortal principles' demand. Such a task is assumed by the state and by the class which has the courage to make itself master of the state. Only the productivity of the state — not the speculation of individuals — rationalized, perfected, electrified can give a new impulse to production and achieve greater wealth for humanity ...[8]

The published sections of Rizzi's work are sections one and three. These sections contain Rizzi's speculations on the development of Russia and New Deal America. The third section, entitled *Quo Vadis America ?* argued that the New Deal was also the first installment of socialism. A proposition which many New Dealers — and their right wing opponents — agreed with. The second section, according to Pierre Naville the French Trotskyist who had seen it, was an apologia for Mussolini's Italy. It did not appear in the published book. Apparently, Rizzi felt it might be too strong for a French public. He had already been repulsed by the French Trotskyists in emigration because of his profascism.

Nevertheless, the published sections, especially an appendix *Where is the World Going ?*, are full of examples of Rizzi's indiscriminant dictator worship.

The political program that followed was spelled out again and again. Internationally, the progressive dictatorships had to partition the earth into reasonably sized autarchies which would provide the nationalized economies proper scope for rational planning:

At this historical conjuncture, in order to provide space and raw materials for fascism and national socialism (Rizzi here refers to Russia — EH), that is to say, to divide the world in a rational manner and then exploit it rationally, Hitler, Stalin, Mussolini and the world proletariat must ally themselves to ward off the last blow of the old sorcerer of capitalism.[9]

This rational division of the world was especially necessary because the monstrous forms which the 'autarchies' have taken are the result of capitalist encirclement:

> The political forms which you see today in Italy, Germany and Russia are not those which the new society chooses to begin its task. You see a militarized, police state which is the product of historical necessity. In Russia, the bureaucracy has to finally finish the job of establishing itself on the throne which historically was left to it and which it had, of necessity, to snatch from the proletariat. In the midst of economic and political tempests it has performed miracles, and the Russian proletariat has performed them too in supporting it all. The bureaucracy finds itself once more in a crisis of under production and the preparation for world war is a deadly threat to it, as it is for everyone. After the hostility we have shown this bureaucracy we must guard against any grudge.[10]

Characteristically, Rizzi assumes the posture of a man who has risen above the partisan battle and can view the victory of his former enemies with equanimity.[11] They are, after all, only the products of historical necessity. At one point, Rizzi looks down with pity on the great dictators. They are only "prisoners, even if prisoners in a golden cage." The philosophical detachment is only the other side of political impotence and defeat. It masks a grudging admiration for the strength of the victors.

This division of the world into "seven or eight great autarchies" left no room for the rights of small nations. The principle of the right of small nations to self-determination, which had played such a role in the antiwar left wing in 1914-1918 and had become a point of honor in the early communist movement, was one of the principles which Trotsky had accused the Stalin regime of abandoning. Rizzi had no use for it. Having dissolved the connection between socialism and a mass movement from below, democratic principles of any sort became so many obstacles:

> Far from us is the desire or wish to be brutal with respect to those little peoples who are highly civilized and live tranquilly and inoffensively. We believe it will not be necessary to sacrifice them completely and that they will of their own accord attach themselves to the autarchy that offers them the most favorable conditions of economic integration. But, if one wishes peace in the world and the growth of production, it is necessary to find a peaceful means to provide space and the raw materials necessary for the construction of the German and Italian autarchies. The sacrifice of the independence of some small state or other is a necessity long since proved for the development of the economy. Since the autarchy has as its aim economic organization and not political hegemony it will not even be wise to deal harshly in the matter of the customs, languages, culture and liberty of the populations.[12]

This was written between the Nazi rape of Czechoslovakia and the partition of Poland by Hitler and Stalin. Both actions, as is well known, were taken in the interests of peace.

What remains for the working class? Rizzi time and again returns to the proposition that it has forfeited any claim to lead society. That is the job of the bureaucracy. What is more, the transition to socialism was purely a matter of economic rationalization, democracy had nothing to do with it. The progressive economy was all to use Burnham's 1937 phrase. Nevertheless, the working class had a role to play as an auxiliary force. It was to act as a political and economic fifth column pressuring the French, British and American bourgeoisie to

Neither Capitalism nor Socialism

concede to the autarchies the space and peace they needed to develop towards socialism. The antiwar slogans of 1914-1918 are used over and over — against the French, British and American plutocrats not against the progressive dictators who have begun to build a new order alongside their proletarians.

> The proletariat must convince itself, and soon, that the fascist movements are a kind of anticapitalist movement; they must demand an alliance with them ... the proletariat (must) push for the creation of an anticapitalist bloc to which it will adhere all the national anticapitalist forces, that is to say the fascist forces which have detached themselves from capitalism and the petit bourgeoisie who will provide the largest number of technicians for the new ruling class.[13]

Part of the ideology of this bloc, as might be expected, was to be antisemitism. Rizzi carefully distinguished his antisemitism from that of the Nazis. It was not racial. Rather, it was based on two 'sociological' premises. The first was that the Jews have culturally adapted themselves to capitalism as an economic system to such an extent that they could not be assimilated into the new society as a whole. There was, of course, nothing personal about this. Rizzi pointed out that two of the most well known anticapitalist writers — Marx and Trotsky — were Jews. Rizzi made it a point to emphasize how much he owed to them.

> We respect and honor Marx and Trotsky and a few others of our obscure friends of the Jewish race. Certain isolated and very beautiful flowers can grow in dung heaps, but as a whole the Jewish people have become a capitalist dung heap.[14]

Some of his best friends ... .

The second problem with the Jews, connected with the first, was their internationalism, what Stalinists in the forties were to call 'cosmopolitanism'. Since Stalinism and fascism were both heavily dependent on nationalism and the glorification of the nation state, antisemitism and xenophobia were inevitably elements in their ideology.

It is hard to see, after all this, what there was to Rizzi's theory other than pure and simple adaptation to the fascist regime. Even the relative 'moderation' of his antisemitic views as compared to the Nazis was not unusual for an *Italian* fascist.

After all, Italian fascism had never been that much concerned with racial ideology. It was always more 'sociological' even 'marxistical' in its glorification of the state.

Nevertheless, even if Rizzi's theory was, in the final analysis, only a grand rationale for adaptation to fascism by a man who had always been on the periphery of the working class movement, it still had to be taken seriously. In the first place, Rizzi could have found other ways of adapting to fascism personally. He could have just dropped out. Instead, he felt a need to work his way through old convictions to a new position. He generalized his personal despair with a theory that 'proved' that the working class could never lead society out of its impasse.

In the second place, the ideological bridge to his profascism was the progressive statified economy which was the central plank in the socialism of so many on the left. The Webbs, George Bernard Shaw and Lincoln Stephens among many other, less well known, 'progressives', also saw Mussolini as well as Stalin as a model anticapitalist dictator. In their case it was not the pressure of local authorities but the attraction of authoritarian state planning itself that led them to identify the regimes of Stalin and Mussolini.

But what about the Trotskyist movement? There was no profascist tendency there and Trotsky's opponents in 1939-40, for whom 'Bruno R' was apparently a kind of stalking horse, were at the opposite pole from him on the issue that was tearing the Trotskyist movement apart. The dispute, beginning in 1937, had been provoked by Trotsky's insistence on the slogan 'unconditional defense of the USSR' and the differences on this point had become irreconcilable with the Hitler-Stalin pact. But Rizzi had been in favor of collaboration between, if not the unity of, the fascist and working class movements *before* the pact. The imperialist division of Poland could have made no difference to him given his views on the rights of small nations and he clearly had overcome any revulsion he might have had towards Nazism. What connection he had with Trotsky's internal opponents is a mystery.

Here are three possible suggestions why Trotsky dragged the unfortunate Rizzi into the debate:

(1) Clearly, Trotsky intended to frighten his polemical opponents, and, perhaps even more, his wavering supporters with the possible consequences of their opposition to the idea that Russia was still a workers' state. "If you admit that a new class has arisen capable of defending historically progressive collectivist property then you must admit that socialism is nothing but a utopia. You must admit as Rizzi does that the working class cannot hold power. You must reconcile yourself to the grim task of defending the slaves of this new class and give up all thought of remaking society." It is doubtful that Trotsky took this position of extreme fatalism seriously.

(2) Throughout this debate, Trotsky tried to shift the ground of the argument from the defense of the Russian state in the period of the Hitler-Stalin pact, where he was floundering, to the 'higher ground' of the class nature of the Russian bureaucracy, where he knew his opponents were divided and only beginning to think through their position. This would account for his silence with respect to Rizzi's voluminous comments on just this matter of the war. Rizzi's position here was embarrassingly close to the one Trotsky was defending. If Rizzi argued that Hitler as well as Stalin was fighting a progressive war, he also based it on the progressive character of nationalized property.

(3) Finally, there was this underlying question of progressive collectivist property itself. If the pessimism of Trotsky's prognosis was partly sham, polemical demagogy, everything he had

The Myth of Bruno Rizzi

written since 1923 on the matter of collectivist versus private property indicated that on this point his confusion was genuine. He had no answer to those, like Rizzi, who argued that it was Stalin and Hitler and Mussolini who were taking this next step forward for the human race. Instinctively, Trotsky rebelled against this conclusion. He would be on the side of the oppressed slaves of the new order, but he was unable to counter the argument that totalitarianism, if it could abolish private ownership of the means of production, was really the wave of the future. He projected this position onto his opponents inside the Trotskyist movement, with what justification we have seen, but it was also his position.

Rizzi himself has claimed some responsibility for the development of the theory of bureaucratic collectivism within the Trotskyist movement.[15] If anything the remarks by Trotsky, which until 1948 were all that American Trotskyists had seen of Rizzi's ideas, inhibited thought along these lines. If Rizzi's real, profascist, views had been known they would likely have had an even more discouraging effect. In any case, Rizzi himself states that it was the arguments of "B and C", presumably Burnham and Craipeau that started him thinking about these questions. As it turned out, when, in 1948, a copy of his book was obtained by American Trotskyists, it was easily dismissed. Adherents of Carter's theory of bureaucratic collectivism could counter that it was Trotsky, not they, who was close to Rizzi.[16]

NOTES

1. Daniel Bell,"The Strange Tale of Bruno Rizzi", *The New Leader*, September 28, 1959, p. 20.

2. The book was not that difficult to obtain, however. It was catalogued and microfilmed by the Hoover institution and was listed in the National Union Catalogue. It was listed under B for Bruno R which is how Rizzi signed his books and how Trotsky referred to him.

Neither Capitalism nor Socialism

3. Bruno Rizzi, *The Bureaucratization of the World*, translated with an introduction by Adam Westoby (The Free Press, New York 1985).

4. Leon Trotsky does seem to have had access to copy directly or indirectly. See his references in *In Defense of Marxism*.

5. "The USSR in War" in *Defense of Marxism*, Pathfinder, 1973 p.10)

6. Pierre Naville *Le contrat social* 1958.

7. Bruno Rizzi, *La Bureaucratisation du Monde*, (Paris 1939) p.25,26. In Westoby's translation this passage can be found on page 50.

8. *Ibid.* p.240.

9. Ibid. p. 314.

10. Ibid..

11. The pose here is similar to that taken by a far more serious political writer, Isaac Deutscher.

12. *La Bureaucratisation* p.250.

13. Ibid., p. 324,325.

14. Ibid., p. 300.

15. In 1958, Hal Draper, one of the two principal American proponents of the thesis that the bureaucracy was a new ruling class visited Rizzi at his home in Italy. Rizzi claimed he had "proof" that James Burnham had pirated his book in *The Managerial Revolution*. Rizzi spent some time frantically searching for this "proof". When he was unable to find it Draper asked him what the "proof" was. Rizzi claimed that he had an invoice indicating that one (1) book had been sold in New York. When asked how he knew the recipient was Burnham Rizzi replied "Who else could it have been?" For a more detailed treatment of Rizzi and his claims see my article in *Telos* No.66 and the other articles on this question in that issue.
Rizzi's exchange with Isaac Deutscher and the Italian leftist Alfonso Leonetti reprinted in this issue of *Telos* is especially interesting. Hal and Anne Draper were both struck by the evidence of Rizzi's mental instability when they met him in 1958 and Adam Westoby mentions in the introduction to his translation that Rizzi had been institutionalized at one point. In his letter to Deutscher reprinted in *Telos* Rizzi claims to have had a political conversation with Mussolini at the request of the SS

The Myth of Bruno Rizzi

officer who held Mussolini in protective custody. Both Deutscher and Leonetti clearly regarded this as a fantasy and evidence of Rizzi's instability.

16. James M. Fenwick "The Mysterious Bruno R. *The New International* September 1948, p.216.

APPENDIX B
THE MYTH OF MAX SHACHTMAN

In 1962, a collection of articles by Max Shachtman entitled *The Bureaucratic Revolution*, appeared. In his introduction, Shachtman claimed the theory of bureaucratic collectivism as his own. We have seen what historical justification there is for this claim. Even in a collection of his own articles, Shachtman might have made some mention of the contributions of those whom he had once denounced as objective supporters of capitalist restoration for advancing the thesis he now expropriated. But there were more serious consequences of this misrepresentation. The most obvious was that opponents of the theory of bureaucratic collectivism were able to use Shachtman's continued slide to the right, which was already well under way by 1962, as an example of what would happen to people who entertained such dangerous ideas. This argument would be shameless demagogy even if it were based on fact.

The main difficulty, however, with this book as a statement of the theory of bureaucratic collectivism, which is how both its title and its introduction present it, is that Shachtman did not write the principle articles or resolutions in which this theory was developed. When he was not polemicising against them he was passively endorsing them. The resulting distortions take three forms in the 1962 book. The first is simple bowdlerization by Shachtman of his own articles. The most obvious example is the second article of the collection which purports to be a reprint of an article called "Is Russia a Workers' State" which appeared in the December 1940 issue of the *New International*. A whole section in which Shachtman argues for the historical significance, that is the historically progressive character, of collectivist property forms and the consequent necessity of defending them against capitalist attack, is deleted. The October 1941 resolution, which openly attacked the defenders of the Carter resolution and reemphasized the traditional Trotskyist warnings against the imaginary capitalist restorationist tendencies against which an alliance with Stalin was necessary was, of course, not reprinted.

Neither Capitalism nor Socialism

Secondly, some of the most important questions were ignored in this collection. The bureaucratizing tendencies outside Russia — in the Communist parties which refused to tie their fortunes to the Russian regime, the Yugoslav, Chinese and European parties; in the Social Democracies; and in ostensibly procapitalist theoreticians, parties and strata — were left out of consideration simply because Shachtman had written almost nothing on these questions and had opposed much of what was written. He clung as long as he could to the Trotskyist tradition that considered the overturn of capitalist property relations by an antiworking class party impossible.

Thirdly, one of the two articles which Shachtman did write from the perspective of the theory of bureaucratic collectivism was left out of the collection. This is the article "Aspects of the Labor Government" included as the first selection in chapter five of this collection.

The only article in the 1962 collection which does, unreservedly, adopt the point of view Shachtman had originally rejected is "Reflections on a Decade Past" which was written in 1951. It is the first selection and the most theoretical. But it is only one of two articles he wrote in 1951 on this theme. The second, which was also adopted as a party resolution, was a treatment of the first postwar labor government in Britain. We quote here once more the key paragraph:

> Five years of the new Labor government have brought the country and its working class to a fork in the road. *If* the present basic economic and political trend were to continue *uninterrupted* in Britain, the means of production and exchange would all end up in the hands of the state and the state in the hands of an all powerful bureaucracy. Beginning in a different way, with different origins, along different roads, at a different pace, but in response to the same basic social causes, Britain would then develop toward the type of totalitarian collectivism which is the distinguishing mark of Stalinist society, Mr. Attlee's denunciations of Russia as a "bureaucratic collectivist state" notwithstanding.

The Myth of Max Shachtman

There are several reasons why this article might have been left out. For one thing it obviously overstates the anticapitalist tendencies of the Attlee government. Why not, however, include it with appropriate footnotes and warnings. After all, even Marx and Engels often overestimated the strength of social trends and still felt their comments were worth republishing for the theoretical value contained in them. If Shachtman still held, in 1962, to the view that bureaucratic collectivism represented a third alternative to socialism and collectivism on a world scale, and not just a purely Russian phenomenon, why not reprint the one article in which he discussed the idea?

Part of the reason surely lies in Shachtman's politics of 1962. For someone who had come to see the Social Democratic parties of western Europe as the major independent force opposing Russian Communism, a view expressed in his introduction to the work under review, it would have been indiscreet to mention the bureaucratic tendencies within this movement.

But Shachtman's politics had changed at a more fundamental level. Consider the following passage from his introduction:

> There are three main reasons why I have not found it possible to subscribe to all the views of those who, like myself, have held that a new class society and a new ruling class exist in the Stalinist countries.
> One is that most of them regard "bureaucratic collectivism" or the "totalitarian state economy" or the "managerial society" as the social order common to Stalinist Russia, Hitlerite Germany and even (at least in incipient form) New Deal United states. To me, this contention is an absurdity. It is theoretically false; it ignores what is essential in Stalinism; it is refuted repeatedly by big events and conflicts; it precludes intelligent participation in political life. I hold the difference between capitalism — be it Fascist or democratic — and Stalinism to be fundamental and irreconcilable...

Neither Capitalism nor Socialism

We are back to 1940. Once more the secondary question — are the capitalist states exhibiting tendencies towards bureaucratic-collectivization of the economy similar to that which prevails in Stalinist Russia is confused with the fundamental question — are such tendencies, however strong they may be in a given country, a step towards socialism and progress or not. The fact that all the tendencies lumped together in the first of the two paragraphs quoted also considered this new society based on a planned, statified economy to be progressive is not mentioned. In fact, nowhere in this collection does Shachtman emphasize, as the adherents of the Carter position did, the central importance of this question.

That is because nowhere did Shachtman explicitly repudiate this notion which he originally shared with Trotsky and the variegated tendencies amalgamated in this paragraph. He could not find an article to include and he could not mention the fact in his introduction without giving up his claim to have originated the theory of bureaucratic collectivism.

For this purpose it was necessary to conceal the fact that there had been *two* theories of bureaucratic collectivism. One, espoused by Shachtman, held that collectivist property forms were *per se* progressive, a conquest of the Russian Revolution that had to be defended no matter what class was the immediate beneficiary (or victim) of the social relations based on these forms. The other, originally proposed by Carter, insisted on the primacy of class relations. Carter insisted against Shachtman that the bureaucracy's control of collectivist property condemned the working class to a new form of exploitation and represented a step backwards for modern civilization.

The total effect of this collection of essays is to reinforce the picture of Stalinism as a purely Russian phenomenon. This is not just because Shachtman, by 1962, was already far gone in his drift towards a the defense of "the West" against "totalitarianism". It is also an accurate reflection of Shachtman's political history. He never assimilated the concept of the bureaucracy as a new, third social class competing with capitalism and the working class for power but remained most comfortable with Trotsky's view of the Russian bureaucracy as a 'sport' a

The Myth of Max Shachtman

mutation that could not survive outside its peculiar Russian environment.

Behind this emphasis on Russia lay an even more fundamental confusion in Shachtman's thinking.

From the beginning, from 1934, Trotsky insisted that socialists had to choose between two alternatives:

1) Russia was a sport, a mutation, which would disappear either in a workers' revolution or a capitalist counterrevolution.

2) Russia was, indeed, the "wave of the future" and socialism was a utopia, a dream. The rule of the bureaucracy was the next, predetermined, stage in the history of mankind, historically progressive if undesirable. Decent people would, of course, be on the side of those defending "the interests of the slaves of the totalitarian bureaucratic society."

Again, whether Trotsky believed this stuff himself or was simply trying to frighten his supporters away from dangerous thoughts is difficult to say. Shachtman's political trajectory, however, does seem to indicate that he, at least, took this Hobson's choice seriously. For as long as was decently possible for an opponent of totalitarianism he clung to the notion that the bureaucracy was only defending the historically progressive property forms created by the Russian Revolution.

When, in 1948, that became impossible, he was literally struck dumb. For several years he wrote nothing on the subject. Then, briefly, he supported the bureaucratic collectivist position he had originally denounced as a capitulation to capitalist reaction. But this was only a point on a trajectory. Trotsky's dichotomy still dominated his thinking and he soon moved towards a position of defending "democracy versus totalitarianism" which was his version of defending "the interests of the slaves of the totalitarian bureaucratic society".

Of course, there were other forces, nonideological forces, acting on Shachtman — and others. The relative weakness of the working class

Neither Capitalism nor Socialism

movement in both capitalist and bureaucratic collectivist societies has conditioned everyone's political evolution since the end of World War II. Socialists, Communists, Trotskyists, and liberals all felt the pressure to hide behind whatever the lesser evil seemed to be at a given time. Nevertheless, all of them were political people and they all required some theoretical defense for the choices they made. Trotsky's dichotomy seems to have provided Shachtman with his bridge from defense of the bureaucracy as the lesser evil to that of defense of "democracy" as represented by American imperialism as the lesser evil.

The weaknesses of Shachtman's 1962 collection are easily overlooked because it contains several brilliant essays defending the heritage of the Russian revolution and debunking the claims of several apologists for Stalinism such as Isaac Deutscher.

But Trotsky's *The Revolution Betrayed* also defended the Russian Revolution while flaying the apologists for the bureaucracy. A major step beyond Trotsky had been taken by the advocates of the theory of bureaucratic collectivism. The portrait of that position in Shachtman's 1962 collection is badly distorted.

INDEX

20th Century Capitalist Revolution 268
A Philosophy of Labor 258
Abern, Martin 3, 10
   and "Workers' State" 4
   unconditional support to USSR 6
Academic Philistines
   and ignorance of Marx . . . vi
Action Committees
   as ersatz soviets 178
   in Czech coup 178
Adam Smith Institute xvii
Adamic, Louis
   and Tito-Stalin split 188
Adenauer, Konrad 273, 281, 282
Adle, Mortimer J. 245
AFL-CIO 278
aid on a silver platter 199
Albania 202
   and Tito-Stalin split 202
   Tito's economic policy towards 203
Algerian War 271, 272
All-China Labor Congress . . 218
Allied Labor News 223
Amerasia
   Anna Louise Strong in . . 224
American Committee for a Democratic Far Eastern Policy . 223
American imperialism
   at Archangel 124
   in China 131
American Revolution i
   and Louis XIV 131
America's Sixty Families . . . 244
Anarchism 263, 264
Anglo-American imperialism
   and Chiang Kai-shek . . . 131
   and China 132

   and Stalin 130, 132
   conflict with Japan 126
   in China 153
   in Ethiopia 153
Anglo-French imperialism
   and Belgian independence 130
Anglo-French imperialism
   and Czech nationalism . . 130
Anticommunism viii
antisemitism
   and B runo Rizzi 318
   and Nazis 318
Archbishop of Canterbury . . 179
Armenia 165
Attlee, Clement
   and bureaucratic collectivism 326
Austro-Hungarian Empire
   and British imperialism . 130
   and Serbia 130
Authoritarian vs.
   Totalitarian regimes viii
Azerbaidjan 165
Bad Godesberg 273
Balkan Federation 200, 201
   and economic drive behind Tito 200
   as anti-Russian slogan . . . 201
   economic necessity of . . . 200
Balkan nationalism
   and Tito-Stalin split 196
Barbarism xix
Beard, Charles A.
   on Yugoslavia 190
Belgium
   and Anglo-French imperialism 130
Belgrade 202
Bell, Daniel
   on Bruno Rizzi 313

Neither Capitalism nor Socialism

Bellamy, Edward 262, 263
Belloc, Hillaire xviii
Beneš, Eduard 173, 184
    and Czech coup 173
    pro-Russian politics of 180, 181
    view of Stalinist parties . 173
Berle, A.A. Jr. ... 243, 245, 246, 248-254, 256, 260, 262, 264, 267-269
Berle, Adolph xvi
Bernstein, Eduard 270, 271, 277, 280
big bourgeoisie
    elimination of 65
Bismarc, Otto von
    as "socialist" vii
Blomberg, Field Marshal Werner von 70
Blum, Leon 35, 266
Bogomolov, Oleg xvii
Bolshevik Central Committee
    in October Revolution .. 177
Bolshevik Party
    destruction of 137
    elimination of 141
Bolshevik revolution .. 87, 97, 99
Bolshevism 51
    of Russian working class 178
Bonapartism
    and Stalinism 139
    as form of bourgeois rule 139
Borba
    defends Anna Lousie Strong 227
    response to Albanian CP 202
bourgeois counterrevolution . 16
bourgeois governments
    planning 194

bourgeoisie
    and Czech coup 175
    view of Stalinist parties . 175
Brad, Jack 207
Brandt, Willy 273
Brauchitsch, Field Marshal Walther von 70
Brinkmann, Rudolf 81
Britain
    role in war 123
Britain's Economic Problem . 285
British imperialism
    and Ethiopia 131
    and Serbia 130
    in Ethiopia 124
British imperialism
    and Arab revolt 130
    and Turkish Empire 130
Brittan, Samuel xviii
Browder, Earl
    on "exceptionalism" 224
    on "The Thoughts of Mao Tse-tung" 224
    purge of 224
Bruning, Heinrich 66
Buchanan, Scott 248, 252-255, 257, 260, 267, 268
Bukharin, N. 74, 85, 100
    and "Right Opposition" .. iii
    Imperialism and World Economy 73
    on "Imperialism and World Economy" 83
Bulgaria
    and Balkan Federation .. 201
    comparison with Yugoslavia 190

bureaucratic collectivism 60, 72,
    241, 242, 254, 260, 264, 266,
    269, 275, 291, 292
  and Labor government . . 326
  and pre-Tito bourgeois governments 193
  in China 215, 219
  in Nazi Germany 72
  in Yugoslavia 193, 202
Bureaucratic Collecvtivism . . 135
  and German invasion of Russia 135
  and theory of "socialism in one country" 142
  economically reactionary character of 143, 144
  socially reactionary character of 143
bureaucratic dictatorship . . . 15
bureaucratic regime in USSR . 4
bureaucratic state capitalism 113
  in China 208
bureaucratic state socialism . 112
Burnham, James . . vi, 3, 41, 42,
    206, 266
  and Fascism 318
  antisemitism of 318
  on "plutocrats" 318
  on role of working class 317, 318
  unconditional support to USSR 6
Bush, George H. W.
  and Gorbachev ix
Cabet, Etienne 262
Can Labor Win? 284
Cannon, James P. 3, 10
  and "three factions" theory 5
  and "Workers' State" . . 4, 6
Canton commune 215

Capital 243
Capitalism
  "bureaucratic collectivization" of xi
  "really existing" i
  end of 60
  failure of 45
  permanence of ii
capitalist class
  and state power 140
Capitalist Manifesto 245
Carter, Joseph 22, 135, 328
Catholic Church 250, 273
Center for the Study of Democratic Institutions . . . 242, 248
Central Powers
  and Polish nationalists . . 130
Chayes, Abram 257
Chiang Kai-shek 128
  as agent of Anglo-American imperialism . 131
child labor xii
China . . . . xii, xvi, xvii, xix
  and Gorbachev ix
  and slave labor ii
  as imperialist power 118
  Mao's conquest of 171
  purge of oppositionists in 211
  role in war 123
Chinese capitalism
  failure of 209, 210
Chinese Stalinism viii
  and Yugoslav CP 211
  as Bonapartist model 214
  as new ruling class 218
  desertion of organized working class 216
  independent of Russia . . 210
  problems of 221
  role of army in 213, 214

social base of 212
Chinese working class
   under Japanese 217
   under Stalinism 217, 218
Cho En-lai 211
Christian Democrats . . . 273, 274
Chu The
   replaced by Lin Piao 226
Churchill, Winston
   and Atlantic bloc . . . 188, 201
   compared to Tito 188
clergy of the Middle Ages . . . 27
Co-operative Movement . . . 289
Cohen, Stephen
   on collectivization v
Cold War 272
collectivist forms of property 111
collectivist property
   historical significance of . 118
collectivization . . . 242-244, 251,
   254, 255, 267, 269-271, 292
collectivized property
   and imperialism 124
colonial revolution 207
Cominform 195
   and socialism in
      one country 196, 197
   and Tito-Stalin split 188, 195
Comment Nous Ferons la Revolution 264
Committee for a Democratic
   Far Eastern Policy 227
Commune xiii
Communist Party . . xv, 273, 274
   and Czech coup 171
   as instrument of
      proletarian rule 98
   in Czech coup 183

Communist Youth 98
Comte, Auguste 262
Confluence 284
Constituent Assembly 166
Constitutionalizing the Corporation 248
Coolidge, David 133
Copernican Circles 10, 11
Corey, Louis 42
Corporate Capitalism
   and 'The City of God 256
Corradini, Enrico 264
Correspondence Socialiste International 274
Council of Nicea 23
Craipeau, Yvan 2, 25
Croatia
   and feudal property
      relations 188
   backwardness of 190
Croix de Feu
   as partisans of USSR 25
Crosland, C.A.R. 267-269,
   273, 275-292
Cultural Revolution xii
Czech bourgeoisie
   pro-Russian politics of . . 180
Czech Communist Party
   influence among workers 176
Czech coup
   compared to occupation of
      Poland 186
Czechoslovakia
   Communist Party
      coup in 171, 172
   comparison with Spain . 185
   general strike in 175

De Gaulle, Charles
   and Bonapartism 173
de Man, Henri 265
defeatism 17
   and German invasion
      of France 133
   and German invasion
      of Russia 133
   in China 131
   in Soviet-Finnish war ... 132
defense of the conquests of
   October 33
defense of the Soviet Union . 122
   and Hitler-Stalin Pact ... 127
   and Nazi invasion 127
defensism 17
DeGasperi, Alcide 184
degenerate workers' state ... 15
degenerated workers'
   state 141, 165
Dej, Georghiu
   and socialism in
      one country 196
Democracy
   as "plebiscitarian show" . xiv
Democratic capitalism
   not viable in postwar
      Europe 173
Democratic Centralists iii
Democratic League
   and Marshall 209
   social base of 209
Democratic League
   (Chinese party) fate of ... 208
Depreux, Édouard 272
Deutscher, Isaac iii
   and East German revolt .. vi
   and New Class vi
   on collectivization v
dictatorship of the proletariat 25

Dimitrov, Georgy 202
   and Balkan Federation .. 201
Djilas, Milovan 274
   on socialism in one
      country ... 197
Doncea, Constantin
   purge of 205
Draper, Hal .... xx, 172, 187
   on Bruno Rizzi 321
   on Czech Coup 172
Drucker, Peter 258-260, 268
Dufour, Maurice 274
Durkheim, Emile 262
Dutt, Palme 66
D'Annunzio, Gabrielle 264
East Germany
   and ex-Communists ii
Eastman, Max 42
economic counter-revolution . 28
economic drive behind Tito . 200
   and Balkan Federation .. 200
Economic General Staff
   and economic planning .. 72
Economic planning 41
Eden, Anthony 35
Engels, Frederick 94, 97, 100, 101
Erber, Ernest 122, 153
Essay in Politics 252
Ethiopia 153
   and British imperialism . 131
   and Italian imperialism .. 131
European revolution
   and Stalin 130
Evil Empire .... xii, xiii
Fabian gradualist reforms 99
Fabians .. 265, 268, 270, 271, 282
FAI 37
fascism ... xiv, xv, xviii, 14, 41,
   172, 184, 242, 250, 256, 261,
   264-266, 271, 272

and "March on Rome" .. 172
and big bourgeoisie 108
and economic planning .. 66
and foreign policy 86
and new class 108
and state socialism 109
as form of bourgeois rule 139
Fascist bureaucracy
and nationalized property 41
as new ruling class 72, 89, 110
compared to Stalinist ... 110
favored nation status ix
Fenwick, James M.
on Bruno Rizzi 321
Ferry, W.H. . 242, 248, 249, 251, 252, 267, 268
feudal society 13
Finland 122, 127
Finnish "civil war"
invention of 133
Fisher, John 260
Five Year Plan 16
in Yugoslavia 195, 200
Five-Year-Plan xv
Four Year Plan 65, 69
Fourier, Charles 241, 262
Fourth International 25, 87, 181, 187
and fundamental concepts of Marxism 135
in possible civil war 165
on "political revolution" 113
view of Stalinist parties . 173
Fox, Victor 7
and "three factions" theory 5
Franco, Francisco 4, 184
Free Enterprise .... xii, xiii

Free Market
in Nazi Germany 62
Free Market .... vii, x, xiii
and socialists ii
disastrous effects of ii
Free World ix
Freedom of press
as revolutionary demand 134
French imperialism
in the Black Sea 124
French Revolution i
Friedman, Milton xviii
Fritsch, Colonel-General Werner Freiherr von 70
Gaitskell, Hugh ... 267, 276, 282
GATT xi
Gaulle, Charles de 281
General Dynamics 247
General Electric 246, 263
General Motors xviii
Georgia 165
German imperialism
in Finland 124
in the Ukraine 124
German invasion of Russia . 121
and independent Ukraine 134
and self-determination .. 134
German Social Democracy
and Treaty of Rappollo . 125
Germany
and Irish revolutionary movement 130
economic crisis in 63
role in war 123
Glos Ludu
and socialism in
one country 197

Goering, Hermann 65
    and economic planning 69, 72
Gomulka, Wladislaw
    as "Titoist" 205
Gorbachev, Mikhail i
Gottwald, Clement 175, 178
    as "lesser evil" 183
GPU 7, 25
Grandi, Dino 264
Gronlund, Laurence 287
Guerin, Daniel 13, 25, 66
Haile Selassie 128
Harbrecht, Paul P. . . 250-252, 257
Hayek, von xviii
Henderson, Arthur 269
Hilferding, Rudolf 71
    on "state capitalism" . . 77, 79
Hindu caste of Brahmins . . . 100
Hitler, Adolf . 35, 41, 62, 67, 264
    and Soviet Union 125
    as economic conservative 66
    Bruno Rizzi on 316
    timidity of 109
Hitler, Adolph
    as "socialist" vii
Hitler-Stalin Pact . 41, 45, 55, 56,
                        126, 172
    defended by Anna Louise
        Strong 223
Hook, Sidney 42
Howe, Irving
    on Czech Coup 176
Hoxha, Enver
    on Tito-Stalin split 203
human rights v. property rights 51
Hume, David 18
Hutchins, Robert 249, 257
In Days to Come 260
Independent Socialist
    Mimeogrphia xx

individualism 277
Industrial Feudalism . . . 241, 242
Industrialism and
    Industrial Man 259
Industrialization
    and national sovereignty 192
Industry and Society 268
International Socialist
    Conference 275
Invisible Hand 243
Irish revolutionary movement
    and Germany 130
    and Marxists 131
Iron and Steel Institute 255
Iron Curtain 254
Italian imperialism
    in Ethiopia 124
Jacobin xiii
Jaksch, Wenzel 265
Japan
    conquests in China 208
    role in war 123
Japanese imperialism
    at Vladivostok 124
Jay, Douglas 276, 282, 292
Jenkins, Roy 276
Johnson, Hugh 266
joint-stock companies 241
Junkers
    elimination of 65
Kardelj, Edvard 192
Kautsky, Karl
    as red herring 167
Keitel, Field Marshal Wilhelm 70
Kelso, Louis O. 245
Kennedy, John F. 271
Kepler, Johannes 11
Kerensky, Alexander . . . 175, 177
Keynes, J. M. 260
KGB ix

Khrushchev, Nikita 289, 290
Kidric, Boris 198
Kirov 204
Kohl, Helmut
   and Gorbachev ix
Kolko, Gabriel 130
Kravchenko, Victor
   on contradictions of totalitarian planning 206
Kremlin
   and Balkan Federation .. 201
kulaks 136
Kuomintang 171
   and bureaucratic state capitalism 208
   social base of 208
   U.S. support for 208
Labor Action xx
   on Tito-Stalin split 188
Labor Front 264
Labor party . 258, 259, 265, 267, 268, 275, 276, 278, 284, 285, 288
Labour Monthly 66
Le Monde 272
Leadership in Administration 247
Lenin, V. I. xiii
Lenin, Vladimir Ilych .. 289, 290
Lenin, Vladimir Ilyich .. 74, 75, 85, 87, 97, 102, 104
   and new class 105
   and slogan "Oust the capitalist ministers!" 174
   in Czech coup 175
   on non-capitalist imperialism 116
   on October Revolution .. 177
   on proletarian state 32
   on state socialism 109

Leon Trotsky
   and "defense of the Soviet Union" 122
   and class character of the Soviet Union 135
Leonetti, Alfonso
   on Bruno Rizzi 321
Ley, Robert 62
Li Li-san
   as part of "Russian group" 226
Liberal Party (New York) ... 260
liberalism 251, 254, 257, 260, 261, 265, 269, 271, 275
Libertarianism 277
Lin Piao
   as part of "Russian group"226
   replaces Chu The 226
Lindberg, Anne Morrow 41
Liu Hsiao-chi 212
Looking Backward 263
Lovestone, Jay 8
Luxemburg, Rosa 75
MacDonald, Dwight 41, 60
MacDonald, Ramsay 175
Magidoff, Richard
   accused of spying against Soviet Union 222
Majority (of SWP National Committee)
   and "proletarian economy"12
Managerial Revolution 41, 49, 266
   and "super-states" 59
   and abolition of the market 49
   and class relations 49
   and destruction of British Empire 56
   and new class 49
   and New Deal 57

and state ownership 50
and totalitarianism 53
curbing of the masses by 54
elimnation of unemployment
by 50
end of economic crisis ... 50
in Germany 55
in Russia 55
labor camps in 50
managers
as ruling class 103
managers and bureaucrats .. 52
Manchuria 228
Russians in 225
Mao Tse-Tung
interviewed by Anna Louise
Strong 223
victory of 171
Marshall Plan 173
analogous to Soviet
treatment of satellites . 198
Marshall, George C. 208
and China policy 208
Marx, Karl ...... xi, 46, 60, 61,
97, 102, 172
and new class 105
quoted by Trotsky 105
Marxism
and self-emancipation ... 181
crisis of 135
Marxists
view of Stalinist parties .. 172
Masaryk, Jan 173
and Czech coup 173
pro-Russian politics of .. 181
view of Stalinist parties .. 173
Mason, E.S. 243, 247, 257,
267, 268, 276
McCarthy, Joseph 272
Means, Gardiner xvi

Means, Gardiner C. 245
Militant (official organ of Socialist
Workers Party)
on Czech Coup 173
military economy
capital flight as result of . 305
cause of inflation 306
competition among states 299
control of capital 307
control of research 308
control over education .. 308
decline of the dollar under 305
effect on "human capital" 304
effect on civilian economy 305
making the bad worse ... 305
McGovern's failed
attempt .. 301
money no question 301
parasitic nature of .. 298, 302
Pax Americana 300
rlentless enlargement of . 300
small cost of ? 300
Millis, Walter 249
Mixed Economy .... xii, xiv
Moch, Jules Salvador 276
modernization xii
Mollet, Guy .. 268, 271-274, 276
monopoly capitalism 76
Montenegro
backwardness of 190
Morrison, Herbert xviii
Morrow, Felix 5
Moscow Daily News
founded by
Anna Louise Strong . 222
Moscow Trials 55, 67
Mosley, Oswald 265
multinational corporations .. xiv
Mumford, Lewis 83

339

Neither Capitalism nor Socialism

Munich Pact
    and Russia 126
Munich Peace 126
Murray, J.C. 249-251
Mussolini xv
Mussolini, Benito 35, 172, 264, 265
Myrdal, Gunnar 268
NAFTA xi
Nanking government
    negotiates with Russia (over Mao's head) 225
Napoleon I i
National Economic Chamber
    stripped of its powers . . . 71
National-Socialist Party (Czech party not Nazi party) . . . 173
nationalization
    equals socialism 181
nationalized economy 15-17, 24
    and counterrevolution . . . 16
    destruction of 16
nationalized property 92
    equals socialism 90
Naville, Pierre
    on Bruno Rizzi 315
Nazi Germany
    and industrialization . . . 193
Nazi radicals
    compete with bourgeoisie 65
    purged 65
Nazism . 42, 44, 51, 53, 264, 265
    and bureaucratic collectivism   41
    and foreign policy 80, 81, 83, 84
    and Second Four Year Plan 67
    as economically progressive . 64
    as new form of capitalism 44
    as savior of capitalism . . . 56
Nearing, Scott vii
Negrin, Juan 128
Nenni, Pietro 274
neo-corporatists 243, 245, 246, 248, 254, 257, 260, 261, 267-269
Nepmen 136
Neurath, Baron von 70
New Class iv
    and Tito 194
    in Yugoslavia 194
new class struggle xiv
New class theories 274, 288
New Constitution (of 1936) . . . 7
New Deal 42, 51, 63, 242, 251, 266, 269
    and economic planning . . 67
    and managerial revolution 57
    anticapitalism of 65
    as new form of capitalism 44
new democracy
    in China 213, 219
New Directions in the New World 246
New European Order 85
New Left 289
New Order . . . . vii, 241, 251, 253, 262-264
new ruling class 72, 104, 241-244, 249, 250, 255, 260, 274, 275, 288
    in Nazi Germany 72
New Society 259
New Statesman and Nation
    on Polish Three Year Plan 195
    on Yugoslav industrialization 195

New York Tribune 241
Niebuh, Reinhold 249
night watchman state xiv
no party state xv
nomenklatura x
Nove, Alec
   on collectivization v
October Revolution 18
octroyal principle 266
Officer Corps
   elimination of 65
OGPU 7, 25
   and German invasion of
      Russia 134
one party state 15
   as collective owner 32
one-party dictatorship 98
   as instrument of
      proletarian rule 98
Orwellian 255
Owen, Robert 262
Papen, Franz von 66
parliamentarism 288
parliamentary forms
   in Czech coup 179
Parti Socialiste Autonome .. 272
Parti Socialiste Unifié 272
Pataud, Emile 264
Pauker, Anna 202
People's Liberation Army ... 218
People's Party 173
   in Czech coup 173
People's Capitalism 243
Philip, André 272
Pivert, Marceau 274
Planned economy 30
   as progressive 34
Planned Society .. 242, 255, 265,
      275, 285, 290
Poland .... x, 41, 122, 127

and ex-Communists ii
attack on Soviet Union .. 125
Popular Front v
Pouget, Emile 264
POUM 37
Power Without Property ... 243
progressive or reactionary war 122
Progressive Party 252
Proletarian Economy 12, 89
Proletarian Outlook 77
Proletarian property rights .. 13,
      14, 95
   and Dictatorship of Proletariat
    14
   under capitalism 14
proletarian state
   with bureaucratic deforma-
      tions 32
proletariat
   and state power 140
   as ruling class 96, 98
property rights
   and bourgeois state 14
Rabi, I.I. 249
Rakosi 202
Rakovsky, Christian 32
   and collectivization v
Rathenau, Walter ...... xvi, 260
Rauschning, Hermann 83
Reagan, Ronald i
Red Army
   as reactionary force 6
   in Spanish Civil War 6
Reichswehr
   and Treaty of Rappollo . 125
Reimann, Gunter 71
Republicans
   and "military industrial com-
      plex" xi

revisionism 265, 267, 268, 270, 271, 275-277, 280-282
Revolutionary Defeatism ... 121
   and Soviet Union 121
Revolutionary socialists
   and defensism 144
   and Hitler's attack on Russia 144
   and popular revolts against Stalinism 144
Ribbentrop, Joachim von 70
right to strike 253, 258, 260
Right Wing of the Bolshevik Party
   as threat from the left ... 138
Rizzi, Bruno 293
   and "The Managerial Revolution" 321
   and Communist Party .. 313
   and Fascism 313, 319
   and Fourth International 313
   and Hitler-Stalin pact ... 320
   and Stalinism .. 313, 314, 319
   and theory of "bureaucratic collectivism" 313, 314
   and Trotsky 313
   and Trotskyists 319
   compared with Burnham 313
   in "The USSR in War" .. 313
   on failure of capitalism .. 315
   on Hitler 316, 320
   on Marx 318
   on Mussolini 315, 321
   on nationalized property 314
   on New Deal 315
   on new ruling class 314
   on rights of small nations 317
   on role of working class . 317
   on Trotsky 318
Rocco, Alfredo 264

Rockefeller, John D. 282
Rockefeller, Nelson 276
Roman Empire 174
Roosevelt, Franklin D. 131
   and China 131
Rossoni, Edmondo 264
Rostow, Eugene V. 248, 267
ruling oligarchy 33
Rumania
   Russian economic policy towards 202
Ruml, Beardsley 245, 259
Russell, Maud 223
Russia 123
   as capitalist state 123
Russian Imperialism
   compared with German . 126
   contrasted with finance imperialism 127
   in Bessarabia 127
   in Finland 127
   in Poland 126
   in the Baltic states 126
Russian proletariat 25
Russian Question 87
Russian Question, The v
Russian Revolution . 53, 118, 123
   as economic blow to capitalism .. 123
   as political blow to capitalism . 123
   failure of i
Russification of Yugoslav economy 199
Sachs, Jeffrey x
Sacred Union 36
Saint-Simon, Claude Henri de Rouvroi 262, 263

Saragat, Giuseppe 274
Schact, Hjalmar 56, 65, 66, 72, 81
    and New Plan 67
    as economic conservative 75
    economic dictatorship of 65
    failure of 66, 69
Scheidemann, Philp 271
Schleicher, Kurt von 66
Schmidt, Conrad
    Engels' letter to 21
Schumacher, Kurt 272
Schuman, Franz 184
Second Four Year Plan 65
Second International 270, 271, 273
Second World War 270, 281
Selznick, Philip 247
Serbia 184
    as imperialist power 118
    backwardness of 190
Serge, Victor 177
    on October Revolution . . 177
servile state xviii
Shachtman, Max 4, 5, 9, 41, 87, 325
    agrees with Trotsky . 150, 151
    "Defense of
        Soviet Union" . . 152,153
    and "historical significance
        of collectivist property" 152
    and "three factions" theory 5
    and "Workers' State" 5
    and bureaucratic
        collectivism 327
    and class character of the
        Soviet Union . 146-148
    and Red Army 6
    and Social Democracy . . . 327
    as "Trotskyist" 328, 329
    defends nationalized
        property 150
    agreement with Trotsky . 149

    Stalinist Russia economically
        progressive 149
    on "bureaucratic
        collectivism" 158
    on "revolutionary party" 159
    on "Russian Question" . . 155
    on "theory of bureaucratic
        collectivism" . . 325, 326
    on Bonapartism v.
        Stalinism . 158
    on bureaucratic class . . . 159,
        161, 162
    on capitalism as
        "main enemy" 163
    on class character of
        Stalinist Russia . . . 155
    on Fascism and Stalinism 327
    on possibility that
    proletariat would "fight in
        Stalin's army" 163
    on Russian society 146
    on Soviet Union in war . . 123
    on Soviets 159
    on superiority of
        bureaucratic class . . . 162
    on superiority of
        bureaucratic collectivism 163
    on superiority of Stalinism 158
    self-bowdlerization of . . . 325
Shaw, George Bernard . 265, 319
    profascism of 319
slavery 259
Slovenia
    backwardness of 190
Smedley, Agnes 224
Smith, Adam xi
Snow, Edgar 224
Social Democratic Politicians
    and ignorance of Marx . . . vi
social v. political revolution . . 32

social-democracy   265, 267-270,
    272, 273, 275, 281, 291, 292
Socialism i
    "really existing" ii
    and anticapitalism 187
    death of i
    equals state ownership .. vii
    failure of ...... xviii, 47, 48
    impossibility of ii
    in one country 12
    Nazi Germany and vii
socialism in one country
    and Cominform ... 196, 197
    and Tito-Stalin split 196
    Djilas on 197
socialist economy xiii
Socialist Workers Party
    and Czech coup 173
    on Czech coup 172, 185
Sorel, Geaorges 264
Sotsialistichesky Vestnik 77
sovereignty of parliaments ... 51
Soviet bureaucrats 27
    as ruling class 27
Soviet State
    and "defeatism" 18
    as instrument of privileged
        strata 22
Soviet Union 17
    "political revolution" in .. 7
    and "defeatism" 18
    and "Workers' State" 11
    and bourgeois morals 25
    and divorce 25, 33
    and imperialist attack ... 125
    and militarism 33
    and nationalism 33
    and new class 88

and new class of exploiters 26
and religion 25
and social differentiation . 26
and the family 25, 33
as classless society 25
as fascist state 166
as workers' state 24
class nature of 135
defense of .. 18, 33, 114, 118
economic policy towards satel-
    lites 198
neither a bourgeois nor a
    workers' state 21
new aristocracy in 26
policy in China 19
policy in Spain 19
revolutionary defense of . 19
unconditional defense of . 19
use of internal passport in 25
Soviets 7, 15, 96, 98
    and German invasion of Russia 134
    as deceptive label 33
    as instrument of proletarian
        rule 98, 106
    compared to Czech
        Action Committees ... 178
    in Czech coup 175
    Soviets 134
Spanish Anarchists
    and Tito-Stalin split 188
Spanish Civil War 6
    comparison with Czech coup 185
Spanish revolution
    and Stalin 130
Spencer, Herbert xviii
Spotlight 223
Stakhanovists 25

344

Stalin, Josef 128, 188
   and Anglo-American Imperi-
      alism 130, 132
   and bourgeois restoration 136
   and collectivization 1
   and counterrevolution . . . 1
   and European revolution 130
   and theory of "socialism
          in one country" 136
   as "better choice" 25
   as "bureaucratic centrist" 136
   break with Tito 171
   defense of October
          Revolution . . . 171
   executes function of Hitler 8
   interests coincide with
      those of proletariat . . 128
Stalin, Joseph xv
   ad restoration of capitalism iii
   as "centrist" iv
   as "ideologue" iv
Stalin-Hitler Pact v
Stalin-Laval Pact 125
Stalinism . . . . xv, xviii, 41,
      42, 121, 172, 181, 242, 246,
      259, 260, 265, 271, 275, 290, 292
   and "new democracy" . . 182
   and "proletarian economy"12
   and "the dictatorship of the
      proletariat 9
   and "Workers' State" 4
   and counterrevolution 87, 99
   and counterrevolution . . . 9
   and defense of
      collectivized property . 121
   and monopoly of
      foreign trade 8
   and national pride viii
   and nationalized property 8
   and restoration of
      private property 6
   and theory of "socialism
      in one country" . . . 141
   as "lesser evil" 180, 183
   as defender of bourgeoisie 9
   as new exploiting society . 91
   corrupting influence of . . 181
   foreign policy of 4
   in Asia 207
   in China 209
   in Spanish Civil War 8, 9
   internal role vs. external role8
   liberalization of 181
   potentialities outside
      Russia 172
Stalinist bureaucracy
   and industrialization 193
   and nationalized property 41
   as "historic accident" . . . 102
   as new ruling class 90, 99, 100
   as ruling class 142
   as trade union 31
   as trade union
      bureaucracy 117
   compared to Fascist . 107, 110
   defends nationalized
      property . . . 138
   imperialist drives of 115
   internal role vs. external role8
   progressive role of 41
Stalinist Counterrevolution . . 27
   by the dry route 28
Stalinist imperialism 115
   in Baltic countries 116
   in Bessarabia 116
   in China 116
   in Finland 116
   in India 116
   in Iran 116
   in Poland 116

in Turkey 116
Leon Trotsky on 117
Stalinist parties
   character of 175
Stalinist Russia
   as ally of imperialism . . . 126
   as economic threat to capitalism 124
   destroys political threat to capitalism 123
State and Revolution xiii
state capitalism 72, 73
   and permanent war economy . . 295
   and military economy . . 295
   bypasses class conflict . . 297
   dependence on state subsi 296
   independence from market 296
state feudalism 264
state ownership 49
Statesmen-Managers 247
statification 242, 251, 271, 275, 281
Steele, Jonathan xvii
Stein, Gunther 224
Steinmetz, Charels P. 263
Stephens, Lincoln 319
   profascism of 319
Stolper, Gustav
   on "German Economy" . . 76
Strasser, Otto 264
Strong, Anna Louise . . . 212, 221
   accused of spying against Soviet Union 221, 222, 226
   arrest of as warning to Chinese 226
   as Chinese "agent" 225

as propagandist for Chinese Stalinism . 224, 227
defends Hitler-Stalin pact 223
founds Moscow Daily News . . 222
in "Amerasia" 224
interviews Mao 223
on "The Thoughts of Mao Tse-tung" 224
Tannenbaum, Frank 258
Tass
   on Anna Louise Strong 223
Tawney, R.H.
   on China 212
Telos
   exchange o n Bruno Rizzi 321
Thatcher, Margaret . . . . i, x
   and "privatization" x
   and Gorbachev ix
The 20th Century Capitalist Revolution 245, 246
The bureaucracy
   as collective owner 29
The Bureaucratic Revolution 325
The Corporation in Modern Society 243, 276
The Dream We Lost 50
The End of Laissez Faire . . . 260
The New International xx
   on Bruno Rizzi 321
The New Leader
   on Bruno Rizzi 313
The New Society 258, 268
The Partisan Review 41
The Red Flag 285
The Revolution Betrayed . iii, 1, 21, 26, 90, 93
   and new class 26, 105

theory of the state 13
Thermidor
    in Russian Revolution 136, 137
Third Camp 171, 187
    and Hitler's
        attack on Russia . . 146
Third Camp slogan 133
Thorez, Maurice 175
Thyssen, Fritz 56
Tito, Josip 171, 202
    and new class 194
    and peasantry 204
    break with Stalin 171
Tito-Stalin split 187
    and Albania 202
    and Balkan nationalism . 196
    and China 224
    and industrialization 189
    and socialism in
        one country 196
    compared to colonial
        revolt . . . 189
    economic drive behind . . 189
Tory Party 246
totalitarian State
    as economically
        progressive . . . 65
Totalitarian state planning . . vii
Toward the Paraproprietal
        Society . . . 250
trade unions xiii
    in Yugoslavia 191
trade-unionism 253,
    254, 257-259, 278, 288
Treaty of Rappollo 125
Triangle of forces 187
Trotsky, Leon 1, 4, 8,
    15, 16, 41, 50, 60, 62, 64, 87, 88,
    96, 102, 114, 184
    abandons Marxist view . . 138

    accepts possibility of a new
        ruling class 90
    and Bruno Rizzi 313
    and "defense of USSR" . . 319
    and "slaves of the totalitarian
        bureaucratic society" 329
    and "three factions" theory iii
    and 1936 constitution 2
    and class character of
        the Soviet Union . 147
    and First Five Year Plan . 137
    and Hitler-Stalin pact . . . 319
    and new "minimum"
        program 91
    and New Class . . . . . . iii, 104
    and new revolution v
    and Soviet Union ii
    and the new class 2
    and theory of "bureaucratic
        collectivism" 320
    and theory of "socialism in
        one country" 136
    and theory of permanent
        revolution 210
    and war economy 64
    and workers' state 98
    and "Bolshevik-Leninist" . iii
    and "new Trotskyism" . . . 1
    defense of October
        Revolution 171
    denies existence of new class 26
    in Czech coup 175
    on "political revolution" . 113
    on "symmetry" between
        Fascist and Stalinist
            bureaucracies . 107
    on class character of
        Stalinist Russia 156
    on collectivized property 321
    on Finnish "civil war" . . . 133

on new ruling class 329
on October Revolution .. 177
on Poland 133
on socialist character of
  state industry 138
on Stalinist imperialism . 117
on superiority of Stalinism 151
on threat of "Nepmen" ... iv
proved wrong by events 137
Trotskyists 25
and slogan "Communist Party
  to power!" 174
and slogan "Labor Party to
  Power!" 174
Turkish Empire
  and Arab revolt 130
  and British imperialism . 130
Ukraine 165
united fronts
  with Communist Party . 166
United States
  backwardness of 59
  bacwardness of 59
  domination of world market 84
  isolationism in 59
United States of the World . . 254
Utley, Frieda 42, 50
utopia xviii
Utopians, the 262
Uyl, J. M. den 276
Versailles Treaty 58, 87
Vodka Cola ix
Wagner, Josef
  and Four Year Plan 69
Wall Street
  and New Deal 63
  and Tito-Stalin split 187

Wallace, Henry 179, 252
  and Tito-Stalin split 188
Wang Ching-wei 208
War Communism 98
war economy 64
Warriner, Doreen
  on Polish Three Year Plan 195
  on Yugoslav industrialization 195
wave of the future 41
Webb, Sidney 269, 288
Webb, Sidney and Beatrice .. 319
  pro fascism of 319
Welfare State 283, 284
West, Rebecca
  and Tito-Stalin split 188
Westoby, Adam
  on Bruno Rizzi 313
Whampao clique 208
White Russia 165
Wilkie, Wendell
  and New Deal 63
Wizard of Oz xiv
Wolfe, Bertram 8
Word of God 10
Worekers' state 44
workers' movement
  in Czech coup 183
  role in Chinese revolution 219
Workers' Opposition iii
Workers' Party 88
Workers' State .. 7, 8, 10, 15, 17,
    18, 31, 87, 108, 123
  and nationalized property 9, 11
  and transition to socialism 10
  as economic blow to imperial-
    ism 123
  defense of 18
workers-council 263

working class
    and Czech coup 174
    and Kuomintang 215
    as ruling class 7-9
    failure of 48
    role in Chinese revolution 215
    under Stalinism 218
Xenophobia xi
Yalta
    and Russian influence in
        Manchuria 226
Yenan 223
Yugoslav Five Year Plan 200, 203

Yugoslavia 171
    agrarian overpopulation in 192
    and industrialization 191, 192
    bureaucratic collectivism in 171
    compared to pre-1917 Russia 190
    comparison with Bulgaria 190
    resistance to Nazis 191
    resistance to Stalin 191
    trade unions in 191
Zagreb
    as financial center 191
Zimmerwald Left 109
    on state socialism 109

Made in the USA
Lexington, KY
29 December 2011